WITHDRAWN
UTSA Libraries

The Politics of Mourning

The POLITICS of MOURNING

Death and Honor in Arlington National Cemetery

MICKI McELYA

Harvard University Press

Cambridge, Massachusetts
London, England
2016

Copyright © 2016 by the President and Fellows of Harvard College
All rights reserved
Printed in the United States of America

First Printing

Library of Congress Cataloging-in-Publication Data

Names: McElya, Micki, 1972- author.
Title: The politics of mourning : death and honor in Arlington National
Cemetery / Micki McElya.
Description: Cambridge, Massachusetts : Harvard University Press, 2016. |
Includes bibliographical references and index.
Identifiers: LCCN 2016008043 | ISBN 9780674737242 (cloth)
Subjects: LCSH: Arlington National Cemetery (Arlington, Va.)—History. |
National cemeteries—Virginia—Arlington—History. | Nationalism—United States—History.
Classification: LCC F234.A7 M35 2016 | DDC 975.5/295—dc23 LC record
available at http://lccn.loc.gov/2016008043

Library
University of Texas
at San Antonio

For Alexis

CONTENTS

The Politics of Mourning

INTRODUCTION

A Nation's Heart

It has been said that Arlington is the heart of the republic.

—*Arlington: In Eternal Vigil* (2006)

As you read this, a member of the U.S. Army's storied Third Infantry Regiment is guarding the Tomb of the Unknown Soldier in Arlington National Cemetery. No matter the day, time, or season, in every condition, a sentry watches. He, or perhaps she, wears a uniform that is impeccable: Army Dress Blues if the cemetery is open to the public; Battle Dress or combat fatigues if it is night. Shoes gleam, the weapon is spotless. During the day, the soldier "walks the mat" before the tomb, eyes forward, rifle shouldered, twenty-one steps across and then twenty-one steps back; pause at each end to make a quarter turn toward the tomb, wait for twenty-one seconds, make another quarter turn, and pause for twenty-one seconds before starting a new round, the loud click of the heels at every turn the guard's only sound. Tomb Guards walk and watch, guided by a creed that reads in part, "It is he who commands the respect I protect, his bravery that made us so proud. Surrounded by well-meaning crowds by day, alone in the thoughtful peace of night, this soldier will in honored glory rest under my eternal vigilance."[1]

The central aspect of the Tomb Guard's ritual, and the most iconic practice of Arlington National Cemetery today, is the ceremonial changing of the guard. This occurs every half hour during the cemetery's summer hours of operation, in deference to greater numbers of tourists, and every hour during the winter schedule. The ceremony involves three soldiers, moving and interacting in precise choreography, as one guard leaves and another begins the walk. A third inspects the guard and provides the only moment of direct address to those who watch from the steps. After saluting the tomb, the guard turns to face the crowd, introduces himself, and says, "The ceremony you are about to witness is the changing of the guard. In keeping with the dignity of this ceremony, it is requested that everyone remain silent and standing." A moment reinforcing both military authority and the solemnity of the site, the guard's admonition is also a reminder of the constant safeguarding of a nation's traditions in the face of potentially unruly publics. Personnel and ceremony have changed over time, but this is the Guard's most enduring mission, which dates to 1926, when the first sentries were placed there to discourage boisterousness and keep visitors from sitting on or picnicking at the tomb.[2]

Such cues for appropriate behavior greet everyone who enters the cemetery through the main entrance and visitors' center, where a large sign reads,

> Welcome to Arlington National Cemetery
> Our Nation's Most Sacred Shrine
> Please Conduct Yourself with Dignity and Respect at All Times
> *Please Remember These Are Hallowed Grounds*

The sign encourages pause among the millions who visit each year. It compels visitors to hush, to revere, or to feel profoundly American. An average of thirty interments and inurnments occur at the cemetery every weekday, and the sign attempts to mediate the tensions among the cemetery's roles as a site for individual grief, collective mourning, and tourism, while serving as a tacit recognition of their fundamental inseparability. It implores visitors to conduct themselves in a manner respecting the nation's hallowed ground, while its entreaty to "remember" that fact takes the site's sanctification as a given.

In a long address at the burial of the World War I Unknown in 1921, President Warren G. Harding encouraged an understanding of Arlington National Cemetery as the central organ or affective embodiment of the United States. "Sleeping in these hallowed grounds are thousands of

Americans who have given their blood for the baptism of freedom and its maintenance," he explained. "Burial here is rather more than a sign of the Government's favor, it is a suggestion of a tomb in the heart of the Nation sorrowing for its noble dead."[3] Harding's metaphor conveys two powerful and connected meanings, making the "heart of the nation" spatial and tactile within Arlington's memorial landscape, while also imagining a vast population made into one body—sharing a heart—through the act of mourning.[4]

While much has changed in the cemetery and the nation since 1921, Harding's description of Arlington's unique meaning and emotional resonance remains just as apt today. That meaning is what draws so many people to visit, to crowd with others at well-known memorials, to witness the changing of the guard, or to stand in a quiet corner and gaze on seemingly endless rows of identical headstones. The vast majority of those who journey to the cemetery do not go to mourn a friend or family member but to experience patriotism's more intangible connections and to feel "Our Nation's" history by honoring its military dead.[5] Arlington is the only cemetery in the United States that holds remains from all of its wars beginning with the American Revolution. Millions go there every year because they want to be in the presence of heroes.

A place among this valiant congregation and the promise of perpetuation is what makes burial in Arlington National Cemetery so desirable. It is a signal honor that is now available to only a limited number of Americans who have served their country on active military duty or in extraordinary nonmilitary capacities, along with certain immediate family members. As hallowed ground, it has transformational qualities that are without parallel, distinguishing it from other cemeteries in the national system and from the overseas military cemeteries of the First and Second World Wars. Burial in Arlington is meant to recognize an individual's honorable life and heroic death and grant him or her an eternal place among the country's "noble dead."

As Harding reminded his audience in 1921, the national cemetery also represents the obligations of the nation to those who wear its uniform. It is an indication of the "Government's favor" in the granting of a benefit promised and earned through service. In the aftermath of World War I, in April 1920, this benefit was expanded to include all veterans who had "served, or hereafter shall have served during any war in which the United States has been, or may hereafter be, engaged."[6] While the law reiterated extant policy that made national cemetery burials a lifetime benefit available not only to those killed in war but to any honorably discharged veteran, it now made clear that this was a permanent expectation and that the federal obligation reached forward to all veterans of any war into the "hereafter." In declaring a permanent benefit, the law also acknowledges an eternally valuable part of the citizenry who merit such care. It defines some Americans as officially honorable and worth the cost in taxes and treasure because they do and risk so much, because they incur far greater costs for the nation.

Today's perpetual guard and precise ceremony at the Tomb of the Unknown Soldier is a spectacular manifestation of these costs and the nation's obligations to honor them. Or, as Arlington's current visitors' brochure explains, it is part of a place and tradition that "remind us of service, sacrifice and valor—and are examples of the dignified way we take care of those who have defended and protected our freedoms."[7] The history of Arlington National Cemetery, its creation and many transformations over time, reflects the development of this obligation to account for, take care of, and honor the military dead. More than this, it is the story of the nation itself, of the ideas of American freedom, democracy, and promise and the fierce struggles to define and realize them. As a landscape of death, Arlington is an assertion of who among the living are honorable, are deserving of care, and best represent the character and values of the country. It is an expression of who belongs and why and a projection of that vision of the nation outward, beyond the cemetery's gates. Arlington's past is the history of "hereafter." It is a story unfinished. But it is also a story that has yet to be fully told.

The creation of the American national cemetery system dates to the early years of the Civil War. At least 620,000 Union and Confederate soldiers died between 1861 and 1865. The immensity of this figure is often highlighted by comparing it with the death tolls of other wars in which Americans fought: it is roughly equal to the number of military dead from the Revolution, the War of 1812, the Mexican War, the Spanish-American

War, World War I, World War II, and the Korean War combined.[8] At the closer level of waging war, however, this was an incremental horror and escalating logistical problem that necessitated a governmental response never before seen or expected. Dead bodies from both sides were strewn across battlefields, hastily buried in shallow graves or together in trenches, and interred around hospitals and encampments where soldiers succumbed to their injuries and illness. Growing numbers of civilian dead presented additional complications. As much as dealing with pensions for surviving veterans and their families later, the federal government's assumption first of the necessity and then the obligation to locate, identify, and rebury individual Union remains facilitated the growth of the bureaucratic state. It also signaled new and lasting attachments between citizens and the government forged through war.

Like many policies of the Civil War, most practices for dealing with the dead were improvised and first enacted in the field. Unprepared for the number of casualties at First Bull Run in July 1861, the Army issued orders making commanding officers responsible for the burials of their men and for reporting their deaths to the Adjutant General's Office. Subsequent orders refined procedural directives for burying and marking the dead and recording and reporting their passing. At the same time, in 1862, Congress authorized the president's authority to purchase land for burying those "who shall die in service of the country." The first national cemeteries were soon established near hospitals in Washington, Alexandria, and Annapolis, among other cities, and at the battlefield of Antietam. A visitor to Alexandria's new Soldiers' Burying Ground described "the sound of muffled drums [that] told us there was a soldier's funeral coming." She watched as the man from New Hampshire was interred in an area where a number of open graves awaited, "ready for occupants," and another body arrived before his funeral ended. The military cemetery was a location "as busy" and active as the capital city itself, she concluded. "I had never seen anything like this before. Sad sights here. All this desolation & mourning caused by Slavery."[9]

It was not until the dedication of the cemetery at Gettysburg on November 19, 1863, that the broader meanings of a national cemetery, of all that "desolation & mourning," were more fully articulated by Abraham Lincoln. Notably, the Pennsylvania cemetery had been created through local initiative and was not yet part of the new federal system. "We are met on a great battle-field," Lincoln intoned in his now famous address, "to dedicate a portion of that field, as a final resting place for those who here gave their lives that that nation might live." The president went on to argue, "We can not consecrate—we can not hallow—this ground. The brave men, living and dead, who struggled here, have consecrated it, far above our poor power to add or detract. The world will little note, nor long remember what we say here, but it can never forget what they did here."[10] Lincoln's conception of hallowed ground resonates deeply across American history, including Arlington National Cemetery's popular designation as the country's most hallowed place.

Yet this conception does not easily fit the story of the cemetery's creation or early uses. When a federal cemetery was hastily established on the Arlington Heights in 1864, nothing about it seemed hallowed. Rather, it was something much closer to expedience. Washington was overflowing with the sick, wounded, and dying, and running out of places to put them. The first soldiers interred at Arlington had died in one of the city's military hospitals. Their bodies were taken across the river and buried on land that had yet to be officially designated for such use and would not be for another month.

The story of how this site was available to military officials for an improvised cemetery begins well before the war, when it was a showcase Virginia plantation and place of slavery. Built in the early nineteenth century by enslaved laborers for George Washington Parke Custis, the adopted grandson of George Washington, the Arlington plantation and mansion were designed to honor the first president and to broadcast the Custis family's status in the new nation to the capital city just across the river. In 1831, Robert E. Lee married Custis's daughter, Mary Anna Randolph Custis, in Arlington's parlor, and it became his home, too. Lee wrote his resignation from the U.S. Army on the eve of the Civil War there. As strategic high ground just above Washington, the plantation was occupied by federal forces a month after Lee's departure and remained so throughout the war.

Visually punctuated by the enormously columned plantation house on the heights, Arlington was—and remains today—a monument to slavery. Enslaved people molded the land there, buried their dead, and made claims to the place and their own histories within it. Their sweat, blood, and tears had already sanctified that ground long before 1864. In the Lees' absence, some remained or found their way back to the plantation, where they began life anew. Many more joined them when the War Department made it the site of a model community and "contraband" camp for the formerly enslaved, called Freedman's Village. The community would become a home or stopover to thousands seeking freedom and confronting new struggles in their quests for self-possession, fulfillment, and citizenship. Along with vast Quartermaster stables and bivouacked troops for the capital's defense, Freedman's Village was the first significant federal use of the confiscated plantation. When parts of Arlington were then designated a federal military cemetery in 1864, many contemporaries understood both uses of the land to be fitting and just.

Over time, the interconnection of these uses and the histories of the enslaved and their descendants were overshadowed by powerful narratives of white reconciliation and reunification after Reconstruction. Arlington's development as a national cemetery in the later nineteenth century reflects the popular reframing of the Civil War as a struggle to save the Union rather than for black freedom. More than this, it became a primary location for promoting these claims, particularly with the creation of a Confederate Section in 1901. The processes of making that ground hallowed were simultaneously acts of exclusion and erasure, of drawing sharp limits around the parameters of who was to be remembered as an honorable American.

The veneration of the citizen-soldier had already narrowed those definitions considerably. Describing the wartime volunteer or conscript, rather than the professional soldier or sailor, the concept dated to the Revolutionary War but was enshrined in the mass mobilizations of the Civil War. Military service and sacrifice—of time, comforts, physical abilities, or lives—came to represent not only citizenship's purest expression but also the inseparability of its rights from its obligations.[11] The fulfillment of those obligations meant that one had earned the benefits of citizenship signaled by the material compensations of pensions, soldiers' homes, and burials. The line between earned and unearned benefits quickly shaded into distinctions between the deserving and undeserving and between those with the capacity for honor and those without.

These associations were shaped by gender, race, and, for a time, region. The common equation of citizenship with military service excluded all women and, until the Emancipation Proclamation made black soldiering for the Union possible, most nonwhite men. Black military service became the most visible arena for demonstrating the heroics of self-liberation, rights earned, and civic fitness through manly honor. As Frederick Douglass argued in a July 1863 address urging black enlistment, "Once let the black man get upon his person the brass letters U.S., let him get an eagle on his button, and a musket on his shoulder, and bullets in his pocket, and there is no power on earth or under the earth which can deny that he has earned the right of citizenship in the United States."[12] This made it much harder to see the heroism, freedom struggles, and citizenship claims of the significant majority of black men, women, and children who did not wear the uniform during the war, like many who were once enslaved at Arlington or lived in Freedman's Village.

The history of Arlington National Cemetery is necessarily the history of the legal, political, cultural, and affective relationships between American citizenship, belonging, and military service. Over time, many others have sought recognition of their full citizenship rights or a path to naturalization through the U.S. Armed Forces, from a diversity of women to Native Americans and immigrants from every corner of the world. Others have fought for the right to serve and perhaps die in the military openly as lesbian and gay, religiously diverse or nonbelieving, and as vocal critics of particular wars, military decisions, or foreign policies. Many who did not wear the uniform, because they could not or would not, have pursued recognition of their own patriotism, national contributions, and activism—of *their* honor. All have sought representation and inclusion in Arlington over time; many have been thwarted in these aims.

In the process of making hallowed ground, the military and federal government imbued the land with the ability to affirm the honor and national significance of the dead within its borders. This ability was braided with the power and identifications already defined by the land's former status as a plantation and contraband camp. Designated from the start as ground for the relocation of war dead from far-flung places, Arlington was in some ways seen as truly national only when those places were overseas and repatriation was proffered as a definitive policy of the modern American state. With the creation of the Tomb of the Unknown Soldier in 1921, claims to the cemetery's status as the country's most sacred ground would be secure. Where once the bodies had defined the land, from this point on, inclusion within those grounds would establish the value and meanings of the bodies.

As a place for honoring certain deaths, individuals, and events, Arlington defines "the people," what constitutes honor, and how that honor is best demonstrated. It produces a tangible representation of the national citizenry, one that can be visited, walked through, and felt, by marking graves and facilitating certain forms of mourning.[13] The cemetery's paper brochure and map, which remains the primary guide and souvenir for visitors, augmented by a new downloadable smartphone app called ANC Explorer, reiterates the common claim that Arlington "encapsulates America's history—a living tribute to our Nation's past and how it continues to thrive through the service and sacrifice of those willing to dedicate their life to its ideals."[14] In the national cemetery, this history is invariably military, the marking of graves also denoting the nation's wars and armed conflicts. The equation of the nation's history—and future—with its military history necessarily excludes vast proportions of its past and populations in the process of narrowly defining honorable sacrifice, citizenship, and love of country.

Yet Arlington, sometimes in spite of itself, carries reminders of all its historical uses and inhabitants, of those long revered and remembered as well as the forgotten, misremembered, or unidentified. It is a saturated landscape, where individual and collective memories, history, and commemoration overlap and intrude on one another. The organization of the cemetery often defies easy periodization in ways that mimic the function of memory itself. The dead of disparate times and wars and monuments to past events are nestled together, framed by loose chronologies made spatial through layers of cemetery expansion, new land acquisition, and spikes in the numbers of burials that come with war and the passing of generations.

Although Arlington National Cemetery has more than tripled in size since 1864, it remains a small physical portion of land—less than 700 acres—that is meant to represent the whole of the country and its history. It is intensely managed and constantly changing but is designed to seem inevitable, uniform, and eternal, producing a version of an enduring America ennobled by sorrow and sacrifice, made strong and heroic through vulnerability, and always triumphant in the face of loss. There is no other place in the United States invested with this particular kind of symbolic weight. But there was nothing inevitable or obvious in this development. And because of this, there is no other terrain so deeply political in its transformations and role in the wider culture.[15] Since before its inception as a cemetery during the Civil War, Arlington has been the scene of pitched struggles over the use and shape of the place, struggles that have always been about the larger meanings of freedom, sacrifice, citizenship, honor, state authority, and the nation itself and about which bodies, alive and dead, are most representative, most capable and valuable, and most difficult to lose.

In tracing the broad national themes and larger histories made evident at Arlington National Cemetery, I am mindful of the fact that every grave there represents an individual with a past, connections, and stories, that each marks a person lost and missed. Many were and are far from their homes and loved ones, which has long been the nature of the place and the potential cost of burial there for surviving family and friends. Susan Zerbe's son, Daniel, was killed in Afghanistan with twenty-nine other U.S. service personnel and eight Afghans when his Chinook helicopter was shot down in 2011. Sgt. Daniel Lee Zerbe had been in the Air Force since enlisting after graduating from high school in York, Pennsylvania, in 2001. His mother describes the difficult burdens that come with Arlington National Cemetery's unique comforts. For her, it rests in the intersection of all the cemetery's uses, in its mix of tourism, mourning, and nationalism. "I knew Dan wanted to be buried" in Arlington, she says. "At first it was very hard that he would be so far away from home, but then I started reflecting on that and realized that he would never be without visitors, and not only today, but all year long. So it makes me feel good that there is always someone passing through, to pay their respects to him."[16]

Ultimately, this book argues that the cemetery's official claim to "encapsulate" all of U.S. history is, in fact, true, if not in the ways that it was intended. Approaching Arlington National Cemetery as a site that is inclusive of all of the nation's stories, the wonderful, the messy, and the terrible, the awe-inspiring and shameful, the achingly beautiful and the devastatingly sad, is an opportunity to expand the contours of the honorable and brave, not diminish them. It is an opportunity to forge a vision of national belonging and identification that is dedicated to remembering through reckoning, rather than forgetting.

Chapter 1

KEEPER OF THE KEYS

I fear that this will be the scene of conflict & my beautiful home
endeared by a thousand associations may become a field of carnage.

—Mary Custis Lee (1861)

A FAMILY OF FOUR POSES in front of Arlington House in what appears as a simple record of a visit to the cemetery and the sights.
Perhaps it was one stop among many on a tour of Washington, DC, one
moment of a long-ago family vacation. Closer inspection of the photographs prompts questions, however. The family is a bit formal and more
properly dressed than usual tourists, even in the context of a historical
past less populated by the casual clothes so common among tourists in
the nation's capital today. The family is African American, a fact that necessarily shifts the register of their poses before the famous Virginia plantation house. A label provides identities: "Henry Gray Gillem & Family Visit
the Birthplace of Grandfather Harry W. Gray at Custis-Lee Estate."[1]

The photograph says a great deal about Arlington's long and inter-
twined black and white family histories. Referring to the house by its
official name at the time, the moniker "Custis-Lee Estate" identifies both
its first owner, George Washington Parke Custis, adopted grandson of
George and Martha Washington, and its most famous resident, Custis's
son-in-law, Robert E. Lee. The Gray family, enslaved and then free, had
a long history at the place and in the wider community of Arlington,
Virginia. Harry Gray, Henry's grandfather, was born into slavery there
around 1852 to Selina and Thornton Gray. The family, including Harry

and five of his brothers and sisters, lived in a single room at the west end of one of two slave quarters behind Arlington House, identified today as the "South Dependency" by the National Park Service. As a free man, Harry went on to build for his own family the first red-brick, Italianate-style house in the city of Arlington, modeled after the homes he saw near his work at the U.S. Patent Office in Washington, DC. Like the slave quarters of Gray's birth, his brick house is now also on the National Register of Historic Places.[2]

Although Harry Gray's story anchors many accounts of the family's passage from slavery to freedom, it is his mother, Selina Gray, who holds the more significant place in histories of the Arlington Estate. Herself born into slavery there around 1826, Selina became one of its primary housekeepers and a personal maid to Custis's daughter and Lee's wife, Mary. While mentioned with some frequency in the many letters written by members of the Custis and Lee families, Selina Gray assumed a central role in the history of the plantation and the mythology surrounding General Lee when she was left with the keys to the house as Mary fled south just before federal troops occupied Arlington in the early days of the Civil War.

The fame of both Selina's owners and the place where she was enslaved has rendered her history both more and less knowable to us today. The archives of the Custis and Lee families have been carefully saved and tended over the years, making it possible to find evidence of the people they owned, particularly those who worked in and around the big house and had closest contacts with individual family members. At the same time, those impressions come through the eyes, ears, and pens of slave owners, committed to their own needs and beliefs in their superior humanity compared to those they held in bondage. More often, the enslaved appear throughout the documents of plantation management, slave owning, and generational wealth—inventories, insurance applications, invoices, wills—documents that list people as things and that can only hint at the humanity of those enumerated within them.

By the time Selina Gray's descendants posed before the big house, Arlington had assumed its current status as the preeminent national cemetery in the United States. But this photo, like the columned mansion its subjects pose before, reminds us that it was first a plantation built by enslaved people. The landscape and all its uses was—and continues to be—defined by this fact. Officially, the "Custis-Lee Estate" was a monument to the Grays' former owners and a national memorial to Robert E. Lee. Yet Selina and her descendants represent an alternative narrative of ownership, legacy, and national heritage.[3]

The land along the Potomac that became the Arlington Estate had once been home to several Algonquian-speaking Indian communities. Like much of the area, it became known to the English in 1608 through John Smith's surveys of the Chesapeake Bay region for the Virginia Company. Starting with a 6,000-acre land grant to Captain Robert Howsing from the Royal Governor in 1669, which the seafarer promptly sold less than a month later for 6,000 pounds of tobacco, the wooded higher ground and alluvial bottomland was broken into smaller portions. It went in time from being part of a colony to the commonwealth of Virginia and from English to American ownership, while it was passed along the generations by inheritance or sale and worked by tenants and enslaved laborers.[4]

In 1778, John Parke Custis bought 1,100 acres of this land to build a family estate close to his stepfather George Washington's Mount Vernon and his wife's family. He moved her and their young children into a house already on the property. Another son, George Washington Parke Custis, was born three years later. Shortly after, John was called to Williamsburg to serve as an aide to Washington. There he contracted "camp fever" and died before the conclusion of the Revolutionary War. Washington promised to provide for his stepson's two youngest children, including George, not yet a year old, eventually moving them to Mount Vernon. George Washington was the only father G. W. P. Custis ever knew.[5]

With the deaths of the first president in 1799 and his wife, Martha, in 1802, Custis came into his inheritance, including three plantations once belonging to his biological father and a significant number of enslaved people. George Washington's will freed all of the people he owned outright, 123 of the 316 souls in bondage at Mount Vernon, effective upon the death of his wife. Expressing fear for her safety, given that her demise was all that stood between the group and their freedom, Martha Washington freed them a year later. The remaining people, numbering almost 200, the "dower slaves," had come into the marriage with Martha from her first husband or were descended from them. When Martha died, her will divided them, like other properties of the estate, among her four grandchildren, including G. W. P. Custis.[6]

Custis chose to live on the land that he eventually called Arlington and moved into a rustic, four-room former tenant's house near the river. He inherited several household goods and decorative items from his grandmother and purchased more at the sale of her estate, all of which he added to the number of George Washington's belongings that he had already acquired. Accounts hold that it was the fate of these Washington relics, including flags and tents from the Revolutionary War menaced by rodents and mold, that prompted Custis to set to work on a new, more secure house on the heights above the Potomac. It would rise above and look across to the new national capital, which had been moved from Philadelphia in 1800.[7]

It was G. W. P. Custis who first imagined Arlington as a commemorative landscape in relation to the emergent federal capital across the river. Custis's new house on the heights of what he initially called "Mount Washington" was a small, brick structure. Not grand, it was still nicer than his first house down the hill, which was soon to become the residence of the plantation's overseer. Custis wanted his home and the plantation it anchored to stand as a shrine to George Washington, to broadcast his family's lasting significance to the nation and its leaders in the capital, and perhaps most importantly, to cement in the minds of others his own ties to the first president's legacy. Some historians have seen in Custis's collecting and display a preservationist sensibility that predated formal national efforts in the United States by several decades. His mission at Mount Washington seemed to aspire to more than a modest brick building on the heights.[8]

To design the new house-cum-exhibition-space that would be the plantation's central feature—a house Robert E. Lee later claimed could be seen from afar with even "half an eye"—Custis hired the architect George Hadfield, a former superintendent of construction at the unfinished U.S. Capitol.[9] Constructed in stages by enslaved people between 1802 and 1818, the house that Hadfield planned for Custis is one of the earliest examples of Greek Revival residential architecture in the United States. Its temple-and-wing design is composed of a two-story central structure flanked on either side by smaller, single-story spaces, all visually dominated by a large front portico supported by eight enormous Doric columns. Far more temple-like than the iconic white-columned Southern Colonial Revival architecture of the late nineteenth century and Old South imagination with which it is most associated today, at the time of its construction, the house echoed the form, classical lines, and aspirations of the nation's new capital city. By 1804, Custis had dropped the name "Mount Washington" for his plantation in favor of "Arlington," in apparent homage to an original Custis family property in Virginia of the same name. In July of that year, he was joined there by his new bride, Mary Lee Fitzhugh Custis. Together, they had four children at Arlington, only one of whom, Mary Anna Randolph Custis, lived to adulthood.[10]

The house was an imposing statement of power, wealth, and refinement, built as it was on the highest, most visible point of the estate. The effect was enhanced by the use of stucco and paint to transform its brick construction into the approximation of marble and stone, including veins painted on the columns. Concerned mostly with perceptions of the house from the front—looking across from the federal city or as one approached the house from the river—Custis never had the posterior stuccoed in his lifetime.[11] One might find deeper meaning and dark truths in the spaces between appearance and actualities at Arlington. If dazzling from a distance, the house was less enchanting upon closer inspection. Writing in 1832 of a visit to the American capital, an English traveler noted of the Custis mansion, "It is visible for many miles, and in the distance has the appearance of a superior English country residence beyond any place I had seen in the states, but as I came close to it, I was woefully disappointed."[12] He was not the last to suggest that the home's grandeur and impact lay in viewing it from afar.

The plantation at Arlington was designed as a show place, as an assertion of life well and genteelly lived, and of ancestry and nation honored. A portion of the estate was put to agriculture and animal husbandry, including Custis's attempts to breed a sheep native to the United States. This kind of work occurred closer to the river and alongside the other five slave quarters and overseer's house. In 1811, Custis had a covered reception area constructed just off the river near the main entrance to his plantation, where he could exhibit his livestock and entertain day-trippers from DC. This eventually became an eight-acre recreation area, called Arlington Spring, for visitors who arrived by ferry to picnic, purchase light refreshments, and listen to Custis spin stories of George Washington and his own youth. By the 1850s, 50 to 200 people were visiting every day but Sunday during the spring and summer, drawn "by that generous hospitality which is everywhere prevalent in the South," explained Benson Lossing, a popular historian of the day and guest at Arlington House.[13] This famed hospitality was inseparable from the enslaved people who worked and lived in close proximity at the lower slave quarters. The farm and market gardens nearby yielded enough for the plantation's needs with some left for sale in Washington. Arlington was never intended to be lucrative or even to break even; rather, it relied on the profitability of Custis's other holdings in land, beasts, and people—holdings such as the Romancock (later Romancoke) and White House plantations located within ten miles of each other on the Pamunkey River. Custis was largely an absentee owner of those properties, leaving their day-to-day operations to overseers and farm managers.

Most of Custis's vast enslaved property labored at these nearby plantations in conditions far different from those at Arlington or were hired out, isolated from family and friends on year-long contracts. Over time, his slave ownership was marked by neighborhood gossip and more official complaints of neglect, slave unruliness, and lax supervision, indicating poor conditions on those plantations and resistance from the enslaved. While limited management could mean greater freedom for enslaved people, violence and degradation at the Pamunkey plantations reached such levels as to be shocking to other owners and resulted in more than one investigation over the years, with charges ranging from starving enslaved people and providing inadequate housing to drowning or whipping individuals to death. The year Custis died, he wrote to his new manager at White House that he was "greatly pained, disappointed and mortified to hear" how terrible the state of the enslaved was there and their "deprivations," noting, "it ought not be so, my negroes have been heavier worked than many slaves in Virginia, so much so, that neighbors of my estates have addressed to me anonymous letters complaining of the subject."[14]

In spite of this evidence, Custis has come down to us as a "good slave owner," proffering a mutually affectionate, paternalistic quality of slavery at Arlington, particularly in histories and guides produced for tourists. Old southern grace and hospitality are made visible in the presence of the enslaved and their faithful servitude and affections for Arlington and their white masters. In *Historic Arlington* (1892), Karl Decker and Angus Mc-Sween contend, "In his treatment of his negroes, Mr. Custis was as considerate as he was regarding any other class of human beings, and the glaring evils of slavery were never apparent upon his property."[15] The compassionate quality of slavery at Arlington is argued in Custis's supposed tendency to spoil his human property and in his easy manner, the latter usually described in contrast to his son-in-law Robert E. Lee's famed self-possession and discipline. A century after the publication of *Historic Arlington,* the Lee biographer Emory M. Thomas argued that among the very few good qualities he could find in the dilettantish and feckless Custis is that "to the extent that any slaveholder could, [he] indulged his slaves and gave them freedom in his will."[16] This is echoed in a popular history and guide book, recently published in its third edition, that claims Custis treated his slaves "with great affection, and demanded little of them," continuing that he "indulged" and "coddled" the men, women, and children he held in bondage.[17] Testament to the toxic durability of nineteenth-century proslavery ideology, the notion of "indulgence" casts all enslaved people as childlike while suggesting that the hardest work of slavery was in owners' responsibility for the enslaved.

While G. W. P. Custis is a central figure in these narratives, there is marked focus on the more tender aims and work of the white women in his life, his wife, daughter, and extended family members. Mary Custis created a school at Arlington for the enslaved and made available Sunday school and Bible study as promoted by the American Colonization Society (ACS), founded in 1816. Aiming to remove slavery and black people from the United States, the ACS urged education and moral training as critical preliminaries to manumission and emigration to Liberia, West Africa.[18] Mary Lee, writing in her diary after her mother's death, expressed her wish to keep this work going: "In looking over my dear mother's papers the great desire of her soul was that all our slaves should be enabled to emigrate to Africa . . . not only for their own benefit but that they might aid in the mighty work of carrying Christianity to that dark heathen country." In the event of her own death, she expressed hope that her husband and children would continue in this "great work" and facilitate the education, gradual emancipation, and emigration of their slaves. Intimating that her family would not share these desires, she urged them to understand her diary as a will and sought to persuade, "What is life worth if you cannot accomplish something for the benefit of others especially of those so entirely dependent upon our will & pleasure?" Although the Custises were very active in the ACS, its aim of emigration was not popular among their slaves. Only one enslaved family at Arlington, called "pioneers" by Mary, gained their freedom by moving to Liberia.[19]

Despite the common view of slave ownership that casts white women of the planter class as potential mediators and fellow dependents, the plantation household was one in which white women wielded various forms of power over the enslaved and were integral to its day-to-day maintenance.[20] Mary Custis, described by her daughter as consumed "for years" in her "hopes & prayers" for the Custis slaves' emancipation and colonization, celebrated for her efforts at slave education and religious training, was herself well acquainted with the violence of domestic slavery. In a letter to her grandson William Henry Fitzhugh "Rooney" Lee, Mary Custis recounted coming upon an enslaved man, Perry Parks, beating a dog in the yard. When asked why, he replied that he did so in order to make the dog mind, about which she drolly wrote to Rooney, "the absence of that salutary Discipline is what prevents *his* minding."[21]

The Arlington Estate could not be distanced from the harshest aspects of plantation slavery, however obscured by faithful slave narratives and benevolent paternalism. Like Custis's house itself, appearances are deceiving. Even if the most brutal day-to-day aspects of chattel slavery were kept more remote from the Custises, their extended family, and guests, the fact remains that their lifestyles, self-understandings, and public personas depended on its maintenance. And all were tied to the ownership and profit of one man, George Washington Parke Custis.

Arlington's reliance on these wider networks and economies was never clearer than when they were no longer there. When Custis died in 1857, his will separated his properties. He left Arlington to the use of his daughter, Mary, for her lifetime, and to then be turned over to her oldest son, George Washington Custis Lee, called "Custis," while Romancoke and White House were to pass immediately to his two younger grandsons. Each of his four granddaughters was to receive a $10,000 cash inheritance. The will named son-in-law Robert E. Lee the executor of the estate, charging him with managing Arlington and making it self-sufficient, as well as seeing to the outlined distribution of property. This was no easy task given the enormous debts and general disarray Custis left behind. To the very end, his devotion to appearances had reigned. His will reflected far more significant wealth than he actually possessed and left Lee with a heavy burden, one that fell, as it always had, on the enslaved.[22]

Although today Arlington House is officially the national Robert E. Lee Memorial, it was never actually owned by the Confederate general. Nonetheless, the place felt like home to Lee long before he actually lived there. He later recalled happy visits to the plantation in his youth and his close attachment to the Custises. In time, those ties were bound up with his affections for his third cousin Mary. They married on June 30, 1831, an anniversary still celebrated at Arlington House every year as part of wider fund-raising events to support education and ongoing renovations at the site. After the marriage, Mary Lee and the children, who eventually numbered seven, often maintained residence in her father's house, while her husband, Robert, was stationed at various far-flung posts. All but their first son were born at Arlington. Near the time of Mary's mother's death in 1853, the family was joined by a beloved cousin, Martha "Markie" Custis Williams. All considered Arlington their home, including Lee, even though he was rarely there for very long. Writing to Markie in 1854 from West Point, Lee pined for "dear" Arlington and called it the spot where his "affection & attachments are more strongly placed than at any other place in the world."[23] Lee was stationed in Texas when he got word of his father-in-law's death in 1857 and was summoned to Arlington as the executor of the will. While in Virginia, he was called on to lead the detachment of U.S. Marines who put down John Brown's raid on the federal arsenal at Harpers Ferry in 1859.

G. W. P. Custis's estate at his death included 196 enslaved people, all of whom he stipulated were to be freed within five years of his passing.

Whether he did this to mimic George Washington's will or to satisfy his deceased wife, it led to his son-in-law Robert's attempt to use that five-year window to make as much money from the slaves' labors as possible. This meant driving them harder and renting a significant number out to others around the region. No enslaved family at Arlington was spared a temporary or permanent separation. Lee feared that the slaves could still never labor enough in five years to offset the debt and fulfill the will's stipulated cash payments to his daughters, so he went to court seeking an amendment to its conditions that would tie the slaves' freedom to the full payment of both.[24]

Rage and resistance were quick among those who understood themselves to have been freed by Custis's will and expected their manumission to be immediate. The unruly were punished and the runaways hunted and returned, only to be sent to different plantations or on to Richmond to be hired out or sold. Mary Lee recounted in a letter that "scarcely had [her] father been laid in his tomb" when two men appeared at the plantation "tampering" with the enslaved and "telling them they had a right to their freedom *immediately* & that if they would unite & *demand* it they would obtain it." She concluded that only "the merciful hand of kind providence & their own inertness . . . prevented an outbreak."[25] Despite Mary's belief that the Lees had been saved by God's sanction and their slaves' unwillingness to revolt, all around her resistance grew. A few months later, Robert Lee wrote to his son, Rooney, about some recent "trouble" he had had with "some of the people." Lee explained, "[Three enslaved men] rebelled against my authority—refused to obey my orders, & said they were as free as I was [et]c. [et]c." Rooney would have known the men his father identified as Parks, Edward, and Reuben, the last of whom Lee had called a "great rogue & rascal" in an earlier letter to a different son. Soon after posting this letter, Lee sent the three enslaved men to Richmond to be rented or sold.[26]

Mary in her diary expressed anger and hurt tinged with some surprise at the behavior of the enslaved at Arlington after her father's passing. A few weeks before Lee vented his frustrations about managing "the people," Mary recorded, "The ingratitude & bad conduct of these slaves here for whom my dear mother all her life toiled & prayed for whom I have ever since my earliest recollection done all I could & denied myself many things to give to them has wounded me sorely, some of them now whom I least expected such conduct have done worst of all yet I pray the most merciful Father to pardon their ignorance [illegible] & bring them to a sincere repentance." Mary went on to bemoan what she saw as the indiscriminate manumissions ordered by her father's will, saying it made "no distinction between the good and the bad," which added to her husband's already "difficult" task as executor. Her next entry started, "Constant trouble in our domestic affairs." The summer ended as it began in Mary's diary, as she noted in August, "Have been made very unhappy by the misconduct of our servants, may God forgive them."[27]

A year later, resistance persisted. The flight and subsequent capture of siblings Wesley and Sally Norris and their cousin George Parks in that time prompted one of the most notorious events in Robert E. Lee's slave ownership and management. It was a great scandal in its day in the context of abolitionism and the pitched politics of slavery just before the secession crisis and war.[28] In the summer of 1859, the three slaves— believing, as Wesley Norris put it, that G. W. P. Custis's death meant "they should be forever free," because their owner had promised them as much in life and had ordered it so in his will—ran away from Arlington headed for the North. They were captured near Westminster, Maryland, not far from the border with Pennsylvania, and imprisoned there for fifteen days while Lee was notified. They were then returned under guard to Arlington.[29]

Describing the events that followed for the *National Anti-Slavery Standard* in 1866, Wesley Norris detailed a horrific scene of violent punishment inflicted on all three upon their return to Arlington:

> We were immediately taken before Gen. Lee, who demanded the reason why we ran away; we frankly told him that we considered ourselves free; he then told us he would teach us a lesson we never would forget; he then ordered us to the barn, where, in his presence, we were tied firmly to posts by a Mr. Gwin, our overseer, who was ordered by Gen. Lee to strip us to the waist and give us fifty lashes each, excepting my sister, who received but twenty; we were accordingly stripped to the skin by the overseer, who, however, had sufficient humanity to decline whipping us; accordingly Dick Williams, a county constable, was called in, who gave us the number of

lashes ordered; Gen. Lee, in the meantime, stood by, and frequently enjoined Williams to "lay it on well," an injunction which he did not fail to heed.

But "not satisfied with simply lacerating our naked flesh," Norris continued, Lee "ordered the overseer to thoroughly wash our backs with brine, which was done."[30]

Within weeks of the incident, two outraged and anonymous letters appeared in Horace Greeley's antislavery *New York Tribune* providing similar, if at times contradictory, detail. Both included their accounts in the context of wider arguments about the abuse of slaves at Arlington and the illegality and immorality of their continued bondage by Robert E. Lee as executor of Custis's estate. In a letter dated June 19, 1859, "A Citizen," who identified him- or herself as living a mile away from Arlington, reported, "Last week three of the slaves ran away; an officer was sent after them, overtook them nine miles this side of Pennsylvania, and brought them back. Col. Lee ordered them whipped. They were two men and one woman. The officer whipped the two men, and said he would not whip the woman, and Col. Lee stripped her and whipped her himself." Dated two days later but published in the same issue of the *Tribune,* an author, identified only as "A.," described a similar scene: "They were transported back, taken into a barn, stripped, and the men received thirty and nine lashes each, from the hands of the slave-whipper, when he refused to whip the girl, and Mr. Lee himself administered the thirty and nine lashes to her." The writer concluded with an appeal to the memory of George Washington and the assertion that Lee's actions were an affront to his memory and the American freedoms he embodied, calling G. W. P. Custis Washington's "body guard." "Next to Mount Vernon, we associate the Custis place with the 'Father of this free country,'" the writer averred. "Shall 'Washington's body guard' be thus tampered with, and never a voice raised for such utter helplessness?"[31] Of course, a number of those who remained enslaved at Arlington were themselves "dower slaves" from Washington's Mount Vernon. While the letter writer is disturbed by the violence she or he describes, the writer's central concern and understanding of freedom is the contractual sanctity of the will and that Custis's right to decide the fate of his own property be maintained. The incident was reported, including a reprint of both letters to the *Tribune,* in Frederick Douglass's *Monthly.* The paper urged its readers to see the wider implications of Lee's brutality: "The first impulse of the reader is to declaim against the injustice; and cruelty of Lee. But . . . the injustice and cruelty are in the state of society which slavery necessarily produces, and which Lee only typifies before the world."[32]

The idea that Lee might have brutalized a half-naked Sally Norris himself, rather than watching and directing her whipping from the edges of the barn, has prompted some people to reject the story of the punishment altogether as abolitionist propaganda.[33] With deep archival support and careful analysis, the recent Lee biographer Elizabeth Brown Pryor convincingly dispels the denials of those among her cohort, past and present, and concludes that the events happened as Norris described them. She suggests that it is unlikely that Lee whipped Sally himself, since her brother, who was also whipped and had his wounds brined that day, did not describe it that way and seems unlikely to have left out such a detail in the near aftermath of Lee's surrender.[34] Robert Lee did not deny the story at the time, writing to his son, Custis, "The New York Tribune has attacked me for my treatment of your grandfather's slaves, but I shall not reply." In an 1866 letter to a friend, the same year Wesley Norris gave his testimony, Lee said of the accusation, "There is not a word of truth in it."[35] Like previous captured runaways from Arlington, the Norris siblings and their cousin were separated and sent South for hiring out, Sally to Richmond and Wesley and George Parks to Nelson County to work on the Orange and Alexandria Railroad and then further south to Alabama to work a different line.[36]

This period in Lee's long history as a beneficiary of enslaved labor and slave owner himself has proved vexing to those who insist that the general was opposed to slavery. Such sentiments wind their way through a number of histories of Arlington House and Arlington National Cemetery, just as their tendrils creep along shelves groaning under the weight of copious Lee biographies and Civil War histories. One popular history of the cemetery, often still available in its gift shops, frames Lee's actions over these five years as his alone, dropping Custis and his will from the equation altogether to argue that Lee "planned for the legal freeing of the slaves and also arranged that they be trained for freedom, rather than turned loose to fend for themselves."[37] More commonly, this period from October 1857 to December 29, 1862, when the Confederate general lost his case to amend Custis's will and was required by Virginia courts to pause his work of war to file the papers freeing all of the Custis slaves, is framed as a terrible ordeal for Lee. Little is said of the trials endured by the enslaved.[38]

As Lee sought to increase the productivity of the people and land at Arlington, one seventeen-acre parcel remained out of his reach, as did the free black people who lived on it. The land belonged to Maria Carter Syphax, who lived there with her enslaved husband, Charles Syphax, and their free children. Despite past denials and a continued parsing of words in some accounts, it is now widely held that Maria Carter Syphax was the daughter of George Washington Parke Custis with an enslaved woman from Mount Vernon, Airy or Arianna Carter. They may have been among the people "A Citizen" referred to in his or her letter to the *New York Tribune,* claiming, "Custis had fifteen children by his slave women. I see his grandchildren every day; they are of a dark yellow."[39] Several enslaved women and their children were given their freedom at Arlington in potentially similar circumstances, although Maria Carter Syphax was the only child of such a relationship to be given land.[40] Born a slave at Arlington in 1803, Maria remained so until she was in her twenties. In 1826, she married Charles Syphax, twelve years her senior and a Mount Vernon "dower slave" who worked in Arlington's dining room. After the birth of the couple's second child, Custis freed Maria and the children and gave her the triangular, seventeen-acre plot carved from the southwest corner of his plantation, a notch now followed by Hobson Drive and still marking the jagged edge of the cemetery near the Argonne Cross.

Like Wesley and Sally Norris, Charles Syphax remained legally enslaved until Robert E. Lee filed his manumission papers in 1862. Reasons are unclear as to why Custis never freed Charles. Some sources say that Charles "refused his freedom," while others simply note that he remained enslaved while living on the Syphax claim and call him the "head" of the dining room, most "trusted," most "respected," or a "leader" among the enslaved at Arlington in the estimation of those who owned him. This intimates faithfulness in Charles and potential familial affection among the Syphaxes, Custises, and Lees, representing what one National Park

Service publication calls the "complicated and sometimes conflicting relationships between the Lee and Custis families and their slaves."[41] It is just as likely that Charles Syphax remained enslaved because G. W. P. Custis simply refused to let him go, wanting to keep Maria close or finding more value in the display of an enslaved person from Mount Vernon in his own household or both.

Arlington House may today be a memorial to Robert E. Lee and his strong geographical and emotional attachments, but it was his wife for whom the plantation was the central concern of her entire life. Mary shared her father's commitment to place and heritage, understood in essential ways as George Washington's legacy and her mother's investments in paternalistic slave ownership. Arlington's loss in the war was for her a waking nightmare that only worsened after her husband surrendered at Appomattox Court House. Much to his alarm, it was a loss she attempted to forestall by refusing to leave Arlington House even when it was clear that federal occupation was inevitable and imminent. Lee had departed for Richmond and his new post in the Confederate military on April 22, five days after Virginia voted to secede from the Union and four days after he resigned his commission as colonel in the United States Cavalry. Perry Parks, once the butt of Mary Custis's "joke" about beating slaves and dogs, carried the letter to General Winfield Scott. Parks was soon carried to war by Lee as his enslaved body man.[42]

　　Within days of Lee's departure for Richmond, a rumor spread through northern newspapers that he had amassed 5,000 Virginia troops on the Arlington Heights ready to attack the capital, just "two miles, as the bird flies, from the White House and Treasury Building," noted the *New York Herald*, "so that cannon of long range might from there destroy the city."[43] Quickly diffused as false, the rumors nonetheless made clear the obvious strategic advantage of Arlington's high ground. Lee wrote increasingly anxious letters to Mary encouraging her to ready the house and remaining family for quick departure and to leave for some family member's plantation deeper in Virginia, suggesting at one point that she let their son Custis decide where that should be.[44] Mary continued to delay what to all was inevitable. Writing of those days later in 1865, she explained, "I was anxious to remain not fearing personal insult & believing I could protect a place dearer to me than my life, the scene of every memory of that life whether for joy or sorrow, the birth place of my children, where I was wedded, & where I hoped to die & be laid under those noble oaks by the side of my parents." When informed by a cousin still in the Union army that occupation was imminent, Mary sent her daughters to her aunt's Ravensworth plantation and hurriedly packed. Some of the Washington china, papers, and letters, along with "small gems, family relics, and momentoes" of the Lees, she had sent to Alexandria, bound for Richmond.[45]

When Mary learned that the invasion had been postponed, she felt the small delay was "like a reprieve from execution" and went about directing a more methodical packing "to set my House in order." Enslaved people removed paintings from their frames, packed bedding belonging to the Washingtons, and boxed the wine and some food stores to go to Ravensworth. They took carpets and curtains to the attic, locked as many books as would fit into two closets, and filled another in the stairwell with "engravings, ornamental books & treasures." Finally, Mary noted that "the Cincinnati and State China from Mt. Vernon was carefully put away & *nailed* up in boxes in the cellar."[46] The Order of the Cincinnati was organized in 1783 by Continental officers who fought in the Revolutionary War and was composed of men from all of the new nation's thirteen states and several of their allies from France. George Washington was the society's first president general, a position he held until his death. Robert E. Lee's father, Henry "Light Horse Harry" Lee, was a member, as was Pierre L'Enfant, whose plans for the federal capital define the geography and memorial terrains of the city we know today. Long steeped in the cultures of refinement that fueled desires for luxury goods and porcelains from Asia, the society of Revolutionary elites turned their national aspirations to direct American trade with China, one product of which in 1785 was the commissioning of the Cincinnati ware. A full complement contained 302 pieces for dinner, tea, and breakfast service in white porcelain ringed in cobalt-blue decorative borders with gold details; a trumpet-blowing, winged female figure of Fame carrying the badge of the society floats in the center.[47]

Mary came to regret leaving these and other pieces in the cellar. She lingered for as long as she could, for to her, "the idea of leaving this home could scarcely be endured."[48] She wrote to Robert that the land, eerily quiet, was "more beautiful" and "perfectly radiant" than ever and rich with the scent of jasmine.[49] Mary Lee finally left Arlington around May 18, 1861. She never set foot inside the house again.

A few days later, thousands of Union soldiers, including the Seventh Regiment of New York, poured across the Potomac under a full moon and occupied much of Fairfax County, including the Arlington Estate. A correspondent for the *New York Times* reported, "Last night . . . the 'sacred soil' of Virginia received the imprint of thirteen thousand feet on the march to the vindication of the Union."[50] The Seventh set up camp near Arlington Spring, close to the plantation's overseer, who remained along with his wife, and the slave cabins, which were also still inhabited. The soldiers removed trees, cleared sight lines, and dug earthen fortifications for the protection of the capital. They were soon joined by the New York Eighth, which set up camp to the immediate south of Arlington House, amid the shade trees and the rose garden. The New Yorkers complained of the heat, "sultry" and "almost unbearable," as the days advanced toward nights without much relief. None referred to the thick air as jasmine scented.[51] All were under the command of Major General Charles W.

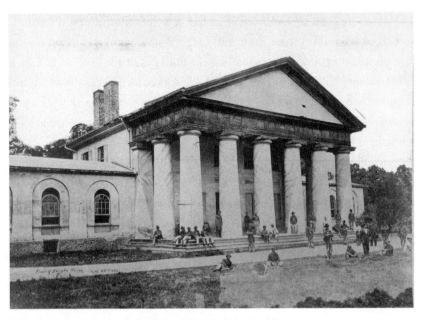

Union troops pose in front of Arlington House, June 28, 1864.

Sandford, who lived in his own tent in front of Arlington House, his new headquarters. Within days, Sandford was replaced by Brigadier General Irvin McDowell, commander of the U.S. Army of Northeastern Virginia. A longtime friend of Robert E. Lee, McDowell similarly eschewed living in the house-turned-headquarters but stayed in the tent on the lawn.

Like the officers, the soldiers occupying the Heights were acutely aware of the plantation's owners, connections, and legacies. They noted with pride and some pleasure their use of the rebel Lee's land, while claiming to be generally unimpressed with his house. That they consistently understood Arlington to be Lee's plantation and home, not Custis's, is notable and marks an important transformation in the site's history.[52] Within a week of federal occupation, a member of the New York Eighth described their environs for readers of the *Times* back home: "Our field and staff officers occupy the residence of Gen. Lee, of the rebel army, formerly Colonel in the United States Army. This Col. Lee's the grandson of Gen. Lee of the Army of the Revolution. He (Col. Lee) married a granddaughter, or great-granddaughter of Martha Washington."[53] The soldier joked that Virginia was crawling with characters claiming the thinnest connections to Revolutionary heroes. Others reported the state of the mansion, finding it wanting: "The Arlington Estate—the property of Gen. Lee—is the head-quarters of Gen. McDowell. The New York Eighth, with their splendid battery of eight guns, are guard to the General commanding. The house—a noted but dilapidated one—is occupied. All the pictures have been taken from the frames and carried away by Mrs. Lee, but the frames remain against the wall."[54]

Arlington's dilapidation was a common note struck among Union observers and occupiers. Arriving with the New York Seventh, Theodore Winthrop, a young officer descended from the Puritan Winthrops of the Massachusetts Bay and Connecticut colonies, dwelled on its decay as indicative of a kind of romantic regional corrosion, elements of which appeared in later authors' appeals to the doom of the Lost Cause and Virginia plantation mythologies. Winthrop was killed in battle in 1861, and his observations were serialized in the *Atlantic Monthly* and published posthumously in *Life in the Open Air, and Other Papers* (1863). Of Arlington, he exclaimed, "Grand name! and the domain is really quite grand, but ill-kept." Likening the yellow mansion to gingerbread, Winthrop said it was "disposed to crumble [and] . . . has a pompous propylon of enormous stuccoed columns. . . . The interior has a certain careless, romantic, decayed-gentleman effect, wholly Virginian."[55]

John G. Nicolay, secretary to Abraham Lincoln during his first administration, was more direct in his association of Arlington's state with the decline of Virginia's morals and degradation of its Revolutionary principles. In his diaries, he recounted visiting the plantation shortly after its occupation on a ride with John Hay, fellow secretary and future coauthor with him of several works on Lincoln. They rode across the river that day with the president's son Robert. "The house looks quite old," writes Nicolay. "I do not know when it was built, but it was evidently in its day a grand affair; and its arrangement, furniture, pictures, &c. at once carry one back to the good old 'first family' days of Virginia before her social decay . . . had bred political and moral corruption. In those days plantation grandeur atoned somewhat for their assumptions of family pride."[56]

More than the house itself, Nicolay and company seemed most enchanted by—and saw the strongest connection to George Washington in—their conversation with an enslaved man, one of the many who remained after the Lees' evacuation. "In the garden we found an old negro at work who was born at Mt. Vernon before General Washington's death. We asked him many questions—delighted him by introducing 'Bob,' the President's son, in whom the old darkey expressed a lively interest—and further pleased him with a gift of small change," reported Nicolay.[57] Nicolay's daughter, Helen, writing her own history of Washington, DC, several years later, said that her father and Hay "came to regard this old negro as their special find, a bit of concrete history, to be enjoyed as one enjoys a first edition and to be exhibited" to friends and Union allies.[58] They were not the last to see those who were formerly enslaved at Arlington as objects of history, as chattel turned relics with deep associations to and special knowledge of their illustrious former owners.

While Nicolay, Hay, and the younger Lincoln were visiting Arlington, Mary Lee was at Ravensworth fuming. She had been anxious to express her outrage and to exercise from afar her control over the plantation and the people who still labored there. On May 30, 1861, the day before the president's secretaries and son took their ride, Mary had written to the commanding officer of the troops now bivouacked around her home. "It never occurred to me, General Sandford, that I would be forced to sue for permission to enter my own house and that such an outrage as its military occupation to the exclusion of me and my children could ever have been perpetrated by any one in the whole extent of this country." Her greatest concern, she claimed, was her need to "make some further arrangements for the comfort of [her] servants many of them old and infirm," although her epistle moved quickly to her own condition: "so I am homeless." She appealed to Sandford's military and manly honor: "I implore you by the courtesy due to any woman and which no brave soldier could deny, to allow my old coachman by whom I send this letter to get his clothes." She also asked that Sandford give enclosed letters to the plantation manager with directives "relative to the farm" and to provide passes for several of the enslaved men to see their wives in the District or "the neighborhood," as they were accustomed. Finally, she implored, "allow the servants to go on with their usual occupations unmolested by the soldiers and protected by your authority" and permit an enslaved woman, Marcellina, to send some small things that Lee had left behind. "She and the woman in the yard, Selina, can get what I want out of the house. I will not trouble you with any further requests—only pray that God may ever spare you and yours from the agony and inconvenience I am now enduring."[59]

Reflecting Mary Lee's desire to continue managing Arlington and "her people," as well as exhibiting the care and feminine refinement that came with her authority, her angry letter also suggests her unerring belief that the enslaved would continue on just as they had, remaining loyal and at work. While some people have read this letter as an indication of the responsibility and sincere concern she felt for the slaves still at Arlington, it must be understood primarily as an expression of mastery and ownership, which in the common proslavery ethos of the day required assertions of paternal care.[60] In a letter full of appeals to Sandford's sense of honor, Mary Lee makes clear her own honor in her profession of paternalism. Lee's letter never reached its intended, as Sandford was already gone and replaced by McDowell. She found a sympathetic ear in an old friend, and McDowell was quick to assure Mary that her directives would be followed and the house and its contents protected to the best of his abilities.[61]

Others also feared for the fate of their belongings at Arlington. Just before the First Battle of Bull Run, Markie Williams returned to the plantation to retrieve some of her letters and other items that Mary Lee had not thought important enough to take. Having gained permission from General Winfield Scott, Markie traveled from Philadelphia to find occupied Arlington a scene "once so familiar. Now, so strangely distorted." She stopped at "Selina's house" to get the enslaved woman to help her retrieve her things, she wrote to Mary later, and described Selina as "delirious," which we might take to mean she was exhausted, at her wits' end, or both as she and her family confronted occupying Union troops.[62]

Selina Norris was born a slave at Arlington around 1826 to Leonard "Len" Norris and Sally Norris, who had themselves been enslaved at Arlington for most of their lives.[63] The oldest surviving child, Selina eventually had three siblings: Wesley, Mary, and Sally—the same Wesley and Sally Norris who fled Arlington with their cousin in 1859 only to be captured, returned, brutally punished, and sent away again for hiring out. Selina worked for Mary Lee from a young age, becoming a personal maid to her and housekeeper by the time Mary assumed the role of Arlington's mistress. Selina was around six years old when Mary and Robert E. Lee married in the mansion's parlor. Some years later, Mary orchestrated Selina's own marriage to Thornton in the very same room, with an Episcopalian minister to perform the nuptials, just like the one who had married her and Robert. Of course, by the laws of Virginia, the Grays' marriage was not legally binding or recognized, yet Mary's actions served to bind the enslaved woman ever more intimately to herself and her own story.

By the time of G. W. P. Custis's death, Selina and Thornton were married and had six children: Emma, Sarah, Harry, Annie, Ada, and little Selina. They all appear right after Selina's parents and siblings in a new family group in the inventory of Custis's estate. Two more children, John and Florence, were born during and just after the war. In fact, it is possible that Selina was pregnant with John on the eve of Arlington's occupation.[64] The entire Gray family lived in what is today called the South Dependency, just behind the main house.

Union troops in the rear yard of Arlington House near the Gray family quarters, June 28, 1864.

The structure is divided into three parts, and the Grays lived in the western third of the building, farthest from the mansion's back door. The middle segment served as a smoke house, while the eastern third was locked food storage for dry goods and slave rations, the keys kept by Mary Custis and then her daughter Mary Lee, who controlled distribution. This part of the building was nearly square, and eight people—two adults and six children ranging in ages from about seventeen years to a toddler—lived in a room of eighteen by sixteen feet. The children all slept in a loft space, which two of them later described as not tall enough for a teenager to stand upright. Selina and Thornton slept in a bed on the main level next to the interior wall that their living space shared with the smokehouse room, their own hearth on the opposite wall.[65]

The Grays were among a large number of enslaved people who stayed at Arlington throughout and after the war, including some who returned after having been dispersed. Their ties to the place and to one another, their shared pasts and uncertain futures, and their complex relationships with the people who enslaved them all shaped these decisions. So, too, did federal seizure of the plantation and the opportunities afforded by the two primary uses to which it was put after serving initially as an Army headquarters—first as a "contraband" camp called Freedman's Village and then as a national cemetery. That was later, however. In the earliest days of the war and federal occupation, the situation at Arlington was confusing, volatile, and frightening. With the flight of the owners, the status of the enslaved was unclear. Freedman's Village was one outcome of strategic military responses to this uncertainty, with a declaration that those who escaped to Union lines or were left behind were "contraband" of war. The enslaved, for their part, assessed their situations and their now-broader but still-constrained options, which is what the Grays were doing along with the others at Arlington. This included negotiating the presence of troops and officers around the big house and across the plantation and the continued presence of the overseer and his wife down near the spring among the majority of the slave quarters and farm buildings. One Union soldier provides a window onto these negotiations in a letter detailing, "Lee's 'niggers,' about fifty in number, still occupy their quarters and make themselves useful by washing for the soldiers, etc."[66] Markie wrote to Mary Lee describing her July visit to retrieve her things, "The carriage was directed by the Sentinel to halt at Selina's house or by the side of it. . . . I think I bowed, but passed on as quickly as I could with Selina who with the carpet bag I had brought, led the way to the house, through the tents and soldiers."[67] The Grays' house was surrounded by encampments and the workings of war.

By that time, McDowell's troops at Arlington and around Alexandria were 35,000 strong, and he was preparing for the strike against the Confederates that would be the First Battle of Bull Run. It was the first significant battle of the Civil War, and its outcome spelled the end of McDowell's command over the Army of Northeastern Virginia, although not of his stay at Arlington. On the afternoon of July 21, Union troops were repulsed near Manassas Junction and fell into a disorderly retreat back toward Washington. Congressmen, their wives, and others from the capital who had followed McDowell's troops with picnics to witness a battle they were sure would be swift and decisive were caught in the panicked flow along the turnpike. Although the Confederates were unable to capitalize on their victory and Union disorganization to follow the retreat to DC, fleeing soldiers and civilians were convinced that this was happening and that "Beauregard might at any moment commence firing bombs at the Capital from Arlington Heights."[68] Among those who were terrified and waiting were Thornton and Selina Gray and their children, who listened to the roar of cannons and stayed awake all night, for fear they would need to flee before dawn.[69]

The Confederates did not come, and the Grays stayed. While Union forces continued to occupy Arlington, Selina and Thornton decided that their family should occupy the entire South Dependency. Thornton cut two matching doors in each interior wall, turning the structure into a long, shotgun-style house. The couple's next two children were born in more spacious quarters.[70] Thornton's renovations stand in contrast to Mary Lee's assumption that the enslaved who remained at Arlington would faithfully go on exactly as they had, if sadder for her absence, awaiting the family's return and continuing their usual labors. The Grays took the opportunity of the Lees' departure to better their situation and to make a claim on the spaces of their bondage. Thornton's doorways were filled in and plastered over in 1929 during the renovations of the building following Arlington's designation as a national monument, the Gray family's clear hope in 1861 that the Lees would not be home anytime soon sealed away beneath white plaster.[71]

Although McDowell had been replaced by Major General George B. McClellan, commander of the newly named Army of the Potomac, he stayed in his quarters among the thousands of troops who remained at Arlington constructing more forts and greater defenses for the capital. McClellan maintained his home and base of operations in Washington. On October 16, 1861, William Howard Russell, a war correspondent for the *Times of London* who had witnessed McDowell's preparations and reported on Bull Run, now saw a humbled general whom he believed to have been unfairly demoted. McDowell rested "in front of his tent at Arlington, for he prefers the canvas to the mansion," Russell explained.[72] This was a view shared by another Englishman, the novelist Anthony Trollope, who stopped at Arlington during his wartime North American travels in 1862. Describing the big house as "picturesque" but "neither large nor good" and totally overwhelmed by its colonnaded portico,

Trollope explained that "the whole place was . . . one camp," the gardens "trodden into mud," and home to the headquarters of McDowell, recently "most wrongfully" charged with losing First Bull Run.[73]

Mary Custis Lee remained determined to regain Arlington, its furnishings, and the "Washington Treasury" until the day she died, long after her husband's defeat and the war's end, but it seems as if Robert was already accepting its loss in December 1861. On Christmas Day, he wrote to his daughter Mary, "Your old home if not destroyed by our enemies has been so desecrated that I cannot bear to think of it. I should have preferred it to have been wiped from the earth, its beautiful hill sunk, and its sacred trees buried, rather than to have been degraded by the presence of those who revel in the ill they do for their own selfish purposes."[74] To his wife, Lee wrote on that same day, "Even if the enemy had wished to preserve it, it would almost have been impossible. With the number of troops encamped around it, the change of officers, etc. the want of fuel, shelter, etc., & the dire necessities of war, it is vain to think of it being in a habitable condition. I fear too books, furniture, & the relics of Mount Vernon will be gone. It is better to make up our minds to a general loss."[75]

Mary read this letter at Rooney's White House plantation, to which she and the girls had moved from Ravensworth. She spent the holiday there with many of her children, her daughter-in-law, and a new grandchild. The Lees' son Robert Jr., for his part, described having "a delightful Christmas" with everyone there. Writing to his sister Mildred, who was not with them for the holiday, young Rob noted that she had never been to the White House plantation and described its terrain and activity under their brother's mastery: "The house is small but very comfortable & very nicely furnished; the grounds around the house are being improved daily. But the most delightful thing about the place is the set of negroes. They are the real old Virginny kind, as polite as possible, devoted to their master & mistress, who are devoted to them & do every thing for them."[76] At war, with his mother and younger siblings in flight from Arlington and his father in Richmond making battle plans, warm domesticity and family connection meant to Rob the presence of enslaved people, their devotions, and perhaps most importantly, Rooney's and his wife's assumption of paternalistic responsibility. In such unsettled days, he took comfort in what he believed to be the timeless loyalty of slaves and the endurance of these relationships. Rob's description of the shared fidelity of owner and owned was a statement of these values and a kind of assurance to his sister that they would persist despite the war. Just a few months after writing his holiday letter to Mildred, Rob left the University of Virginia to join his brothers and father in the Confederate army, and the White House plantation lay in ruins.[77]

Some time before Christmas, Selina Gray went to McDowell to report that someone had broken into locked areas of storage in the house and that some of the Lees' things belonging originally to George Washington had been pilfered or damaged. By the end of the year, McDowell sent a number of the Washington items to the U.S. Patent Office for safekeeping, including some pieces of the Cincinnati china, Washington's field tents from the Revolutionary War, furnishings, and a blanket under which the first president was said to have died. Making no mention of Selina, northern papers celebrated McDowell's respect for property and heritage and credited him and the "antiquarian" Caleb Lyon with protecting the "most valuable momentoes" of the first president, carelessly left behind by Mary Lee. The relics were put on display in January 1862 in an exhibit titled *Captured from Arlington,* where they remained until they were deposited in the Smithsonian.[78]

While many people showed interest in the objects spirited from Arlington, there was similar excitement for stories of the return of the formerly enslaved to the plantation scene of their bondage. With Lee compelled to honor the terms of his father-in-law's will, everyone enslaved at Arlington, Romancoke, and White House was legally free on December 29, 1862, two days before Lincoln's Emancipation Proclamation freed all those enslaved in unoccupied states "in rebellion." Of course, many thousands of those people had already freed themselves or, like the Grays and others at Arlington, were living with an autonomy approaching freedom. As Lee settled contracts for those he had hired out and had manumission papers prepared, he noted in a letter to his wife, "They are already free & when I can get to them I will give them their papers."[79] Passage of compensated emancipation in Washington, DC, in April 1862, had only increased the numbers of runaways pouring into the city and its surrounding environs. A desire to move these populations out of the District, where temporary encampments overflowed, was partly the motivation for establishing Freedman's Village on the Arlington Heights in May 1863. With the contraband camp laid out near the old slave quarters, those who remained at Arlington were now joined by several thousand refugees from all over the region.

Later that summer of 1863, Wesley Norris returned to Arlington to live with his parents after three years away. His work as a hired-out slave on Confederate railroads had brought him back to Virginia during that time and eventually to Richmond. Wesley left the Confederate capital with what he presented as a pass from General Custis Lee identifying him as free and headed back to Arlington, back to his family. When he got to Union lines near Culpepper, Wesley promptly reported Confederate troop movements and numbers to the officers there, noting that "if any troops had been moving from or to Charlottesville he would have known it" and that they were not. Norris's intelligence was sent along to the headquarters of the Army of the Potomac.[80] At some point in the next year, his sister Sally similarly joined her siblings and parents back at Arlington. A story in the *New York Independent* titled "Arlington Slaves Returned" reminded readers of the 1859 incidents, saying that all involved had "returned to Arlington, free." The paper made special note of Sally: "the young woman who was so badly treated by Lee, and whose case was the subject of some controversy in the papers about the time of the rebellion, is among them, and is living near her aged and worthy parents."[81] Wesley recounted his experiences in 1866, referencing his "escape through rebel lines to freedom," and concluded, "I have nothing further to say; what I have stated is true in every particular, and I can at any time bring at least a dozen witnesses, both white and black, to substantiate my statements: I am at present employed by the Government; and am at work in the National Cemetery on Arlington Heights, where I can be found by those who desire further particulars; my sister referred to is at present employed by the French Minister at Washington, and will confirm my statement."[82]

While Wesley and Sally returned to their family and home place and Freedman's Villagers began to build new lives on the plantation, Mary Lee ached for Arlington and longed to return. But she could not, even when failure to do so meant losing it altogether. In September 1863, Arlington was assessed a tax bill of $92.70, to be paid in person by the legal owner of the property, under an 1862 law authorizing "the collection of direct taxes in the insurrectionary districts within the United States." Failure to pay meant the property could be sold at public auction or, after an 1863 amendment to the law, purchased by the federal government if deemed critical to the war effort. Mary Lee, physically debilitated by her chronic arthritis and unlikely to have appeared even if able, sent her cousin Philip Fendall to pay the taxes. He was refused, and Arlington was slated for auction on January 11, 1864. Lincoln ordered the plantation to be purchased for the government on January 6. With a clear, if still contested, title, the national cemetery joined Freedman's Village as a federal use of the land in summer 1864.[83] In 1866, William Syphax, son of Maria and Charles, successfully petitioned on his mother's behalf for recognition of her title to the seventeen-acre portion, which was approved by Congress and signed into law by President Andrew Johnson. "We have a claim on this Estate," he wrote, that unlike Mary and Robert E. Lee's was ultimately considered legitimate and legal.[84]

Mary Lee's quest for the return of her plantation and belongings dominated her thoughts and her days until her death in 1873, fueled by grief after Robert died in Lexington in 1870. She grew increasingly obsessed, hounding acquaintances, friends, relatives, and at least one former slave for information about the whereabouts of and assistance in retrieving her possessions. Surely wearying for all involved, Mary's determination also produced a most remarkable historical document in a four-page letter written by Selina Gray to her former owner in November 1872. Responding to yet another request from Mary for information about furnishings left behind in 1861, Selina's letter is testament to the intricacies, intimacies, and horrors of relationships produced in slavery and their persistence in freedom. In Selina's reporting of the news of her family and other former slaves, in her description of the plantation's postwar uses, in her kind words for the Lee children, and in the inclusion of a pressed rosebud and greenery from the grave of Mary Lee's mother, we can read both care and resistance. There is an emotional depth to those connections between the women, born of closeness, coercion, and violence.[85] The letter is Selina Gray's declaration of emancipation and self-possession. It tells of a relationship between the former owner and the formerly owned forever changed. It is the quiet revolution of a self and family claimed and free.

The letter opens simply, "Mrs. Lee," with no salutation. The script is careful and precisely rendered on lined stationery but may not be in Selina's own hand. The 1870 census indicates that she was unable to write and that her husband, Thornton, could neither write nor read.[86] Selina begins, her sentences unbroken by punctuation or capitalization, "I received your letter and was happy to hear from you and I was hoping to see you once more at Arlington it is a most lovely place now everywhere around it look beautiful there is not a tree to be seen except in the cemetery the whole of it is rented to the freemen they have little huts all over that beautiful place and besides that they have a large military school of signal co and the place is changed so you wold hardly know it." It is hard not to read some satisfaction in Selina's report that Arlington is so beautiful and so changed and that it is populated by the dead, continued federal military presence, and former slaves. All are there where Mary so longs to be. Selina's letter then moves on to responding to Mary's query, the prompt for her to write at all: "your things at the time of the war was taken away by every body so the officers would have them in their tents and all over the ground and when they moved a way they would give them to the persons that waited on them the quartermasters and officers would take first what they wanted every time they moved away the book case that you speak of I cannot tell you any thing of it I don't remember of seeing it since you left I suppose it was carried off like every thing else."[87] Mary's request is odd. By 1872, she knew full well the fates of most of her belongings and had already involved Selina in helping her daughters make inventories of the missing items. It seems that Mary continually searched her mind and ran over lists of furnishings, relics, and decorative items, asking for information that she had already been provided time and time again. Mary's letter might represent a different sort of attempt at reclamation, seeking contact with or to grasp at another former possession—Selina.

By 1872, Selina and Thornton Gray and their younger children no longer lived at Arlington, having recently moved. "I underwent a great deal to stay at Arlington as long as I did having so many inferior persons to contend with but I am very happy that I have got a comfortable home of my own now down by the factory a bout half way to Alexandria we have ten acres of land it is very poor but we hope in time to improve it."[88] Selina's reference to "inferior persons" could mean any combination of troops, Freedman's Villagers, and civilian laborers at Arlington. In the 1870 census, the Grays had still been in their self-renovated quarters behind the big house, listed in the enumeration between some white immigrant laborers from Germany and Ireland, on one side, and a barracks of white soldiers at Fort Whipple, on the other.

Selina continues, describing the full lives and employment of her husband and children, no longer possessions of Mary Lee.

> Harry has grown to be quite a larg man he is just 21 and as big and tall as father he is very steady and quite a working young man and is a great help to his father his father and him has been working up at Arlington all the summer each getting 45 dollars a month Emma and is a fine looking girl and very much like her father she gets 10 dollars a month in washington as a chambermaid Sarah and Anice is hired out too Sarah as a chambermaid and Anisce as a nurse she has been washing for 3 years now and all the ladies give her the praise of being a good nurse she is very fond of children Ada Selena Johnny and Florence I have at home with me Florence is my baby she is seven years.[89]

Selina is proud of her hardworking, good-looking, praiseworthy children and proud to report their wages, perhaps taking special relish in describing her husband's and son's work at Arlington earning forty-five dollars a month on the very plantation where they once labored for the Custises and Lees as slaves.

Selina moves in her letter from reporting news of her immediate family to updates about her parents and siblings and other formerly enslaved people she was close to or with whom she had shared close quarters: "my dear old mother and father both are gorn I trust to a better world they were both afflicted for years before they died mother was blind and helpless for 4 years father was afflicted so that he did not lie down any for 1 year with shortness of breath and he longed for death he died perfectly happy all Austin Gramham and Louisa bingham are the only ones of the old servants that are still living mary is working for Dr Garnett in Washington and she is in very bad health Sally and Wesley are still at Arlington in mothers old house g."⁹⁰ This part of the letter is not only set off by a floating "g," but when it gets to the fourth and last page, the hand becomes heavier, the ink more consistently dark in places, and it no longer carefully follows the lines of the stationery. The writer visibly wobbles. Perhaps it was written at a different time, the "g" suggesting a word or thought unfinished and not picked up again when Selina returned to the letter. Or it could have been later in the day, and by night lighting, she could no longer see the faint blue lines well enough to follow them. Or perhaps writing of her recently deceased parents, of her ailing sister Mary, and of her brother and sister Wesley and Sally, specially linked at least since 1859 when they ran from Arlington with their cousin and now quickly mentioned together to their former owner, wife to the man who had whipped and brined their wounds before renting them away again, was all more than Selina could easily handle. If dictating her letter, she simply stopped.

While Selina's letter brims with claims to self-possession, if not overt anger or rejection, it closes with concern and sympathy for the woman and her family to whom Selina and hers had been bound so intimately and violently. For readers seeking evidence of faithfulness and love, looking for Scarlett's "Mammy" in Selina, they might believe they had found it here. Selina asks that Mary remember her kindly to the Lee children, whose news their mother had clearly shared in her own letter. "To Mr Robert," she said, "I am sorry to hear of his trouble I have seen him once since the war and he remind me so much of his father," his "trouble" a reference to the fact that Rob's wife of less than a year had just passed away in September. "I trust I may see the day yet when you all will have Arlington I hope that I may yet be able to see you as I am very anxious to." And then, incorporating the formal valediction common to nineteenth-century letters, "I remain your faithful and obedient" or "humble servant," Selina closes her letter, "no more from your humble servant Selina Gray." But there is more, in a postscript written in the same hand but different ink, crossing the bottom of the letter at an angle in larger, sloppier script: "PS this piece of green and this rosebud I send you is some that you planted at your mother grave." Below it are two gummy stains, traces of the memorial botanicals once glued there.⁹¹

Selina must have been thinking of her own mother, who had died at some point earlier that year, as she clipped the rosebud and greenery from

Mary Custis's grave to include with her letter. Perhaps she imagined what might be a comfort to herself in different circumstances. In 1870, both of Selina's parents had still been alive, recorded in the census with a full, multigenerational household. Wesley and Sally were both living with them, along with Sally's two children, Edward, four, and Aurelia, five months—Sally, called Sarah, possibly revealing a nickname and her place as the namesake to one of Selina's daughters, is listed by her married name, Hoffman.[92] Her husband drops out of the record, and by 1880 she and Wesley were living together again in Arlington with her children, who now numbered three, with the addition of young Rensellar Hoffman, age two. Twenty years later, the siblings still lived together. They continued to, it seems, until Wesley's death sometime before 1910. In 1920, Sally was in her eighties, living with her oldest son, Edward C. Hoffman, a school principal, and his wife and several grandchildren. She was still close to the cemetery, the Syphax claim, and her nephew Harry's house in today's Arlington View neighborhood, as well as the school her son led. It was the only public school for black children in the county, and was named in his and another educator's honor in 1932, the Hoffman-Boston School.[93] These are the bare facts of Sally's and Wesley's lives after the war, drawn from the slim bits of official documentation collected on the lives of average people: census records and birth, marriage, and death notices. But like their decision to run away together in 1859 and their similar return to Arlington during the war, the fact that Wesley and Sally lived together on or near that place for most of their adult lives speaks of an uncommon bond, one perhaps forged by their all-too-common experiences of violence, family separation, and dispersal via markets in slaves.

Selina Gray was simply "the woman in the yard" to Mary Lee in 1861 and does not appear at all in her 1865 reminiscence of her flight from the plantation, unless she was among the collection of nameless "weeping servants" whom Mary described as witness to her departure. Selina over time became one of the most storied and celebrated enslaved people at Arlington, however. In histories, biographies, public exhibits, and tourists' guides, she emerges as the "keeper of the keys," faithful slave and trusted confidante to Mary Lee, protector of the Washington treasures, and organic historical preservationist. In each instance, Selina Gray is defined by her proximity to the big house and the people and things within it, from her relationship with Mary to her recognition of the value of the Washington relics and her willingness to challenge the Union troops who threatened them. Her own day-to-day existence, her needs, hopes, and family ties, are made secondary or ignored altogether.

In later popular and scholarly accounts of the removal of the Washington relics to the Patent Office in the capital—including those that prevail today—it is Selina Gray who was responsible for protecting the objects and ensuring that McDowell got them out of the house. A version of this account has been in the record since at least 1929, when Selina's daughters provided information to the Army's architects working on Arlington's restoration as some of the last people still alive who had been at the house before the Civil War. It is only in the past thirty years, however, that a version of the story of Selina Gray as protector of the Washington treasury and "keeper of the keys" in Mary Lee's absence has come to dominate the history of the site and interpretations for the touring public.

In the midst of transforming Arlington House into a national monument in 1929, architects for the Quartermaster General Corps of the United States Army, which managed the house and the national cemetery that surrounded it, looked to a small number of still-living, formerly enslaved people for eyewitness accounts of the organization of the house and its outbuildings and for clues as to how best to restore the site to its antebellum condition. Four Gray daughters made up most of this group. In December, they joined the architects at Arlington and walked them through the spaces in pairs. Their testimony is recorded at frustrating remove in two documents composed by the architects, who summarized, gave few direct quotes, and dwelled mostly on structural notes and remembered decoration. Reading them today, one aches with the knowledge that so much must have been said during those visits, so much forgotten, vaguely recalled, or deemed simply unimportant to the Army's task at hand. And much was probably not said or was shared among the sisters out of the architects' earshot. The man in charge of the restoration, Luther Leisenring, recorded his conversation with Emma Gray Syphax and Sarah Gray Wilson, who explained that they were about seventeen and fifteen years old, respectively, when the war began. He noted, "When Mrs. Lee left Arlington, she gave the keys to their mother, who turned them over to General McDowell. They said the Union troops came up the back road and their mother went out with the keys. They stated that people later went in the house and took things out of it, women as well as men, but their mother (Salina Gray) told them 'never to touch any of the things, that they were Miss Mary's things.'"[94] This gave a fuller picture to the depiction of these events in Enoch Aquila Chase's semiofficial history of Arlington published earlier that year, which contained a breathless account of Mary's evacuation and attempts to hide the Washington treasury, noting ultimately that "the Washington relics in the attic and cellar of the house were soon discovered by the soldiers. Under orders of Secretary of the War Stanton they were sent to Washington and the Patent Office for safe keeping."[95]

Chase said nothing of the role of enslaved people in his version and seemed unaware of or uninterested in the Gray descendants' information. In later publications on the restoration, Chase did include information from a different formerly enslaved informant.[96] Gray's story is not included in either book written by the former Arlington House historian Murray Nelligan, whose vast research files form the heart of the Arlington House archive today. In his 1955 and 1962 guides to the property, Nelligan wrote of the evacuation, "All was excitement as the family portraits were taken from their frames and, with the plate and the most valuable Washington relics, sent off for safekeeping. Curtains and carpets were packed away in the attic, books and engravings put in closets, and the china stored in boxes in the cellar. Most of the furniture had to be left behind, but this Mrs. Lee trusted she could recover later. When every thing was in order, it was time to say farewell to the weeping servants, and to leave her home for what was to be the last time."[97] The NPS site brochure from 1978 is similarly silent on Selina Gray, noting only that "remaining family possessions were moved to the Patent Office for safekeeping" after some, including "Mount Vernon heirlooms, had already been looted and scattered." Slavery gets little mention in this pamphlet other than to identify the room in the house where Mary Custis and then Mary Lee provided education to "prepare Arlington's slaves for a useful life as free men." The South Dependency is "servant's quarters."[98]

While pieces of the Gray sisters' story circulated among site historians and were manifest in restoration efforts from the 1930s on, it was not until the 1990s that Selina Gray's role in preserving the Washington relics assumed prominence in the story of Arlington during the war. Part of wider efforts to account publicly for the histories of slavery, emancipation, and their legacies at Arlington, this particular story about Selina took on enormous proportions as an example of black heroics and shared patriotism across racial lines. Driven by individual historians and rangers at Arlington House, this new focus drew energy from invigorated work by the National Park Service to better interpret and make public the role of slavery and contributions of enslaved people at all of its Civil War sites, with particular emphasis on battlefield parks.[99] This newly integrated history found easy purchase with the wider narratives of reconciliation and reunion that have dominated Arlington National Cemetery since the turn of the twentieth century.

Two articles published in very different venues and separated by almost a decade have had significant influence on the shape of this story and its contemporary iterations in popular, public, and academic histories: Edward C. Smith's "The Keeper of the Keys" (1989) and Karen Byrne's "The Remarkable Legacy of Selina Gray" (1998). Writing in different veins of revisionism, both aim to recover and celebrate Selina Gray's contributions to the preservation of a national heritage that is necessarily biracial and mutually affectionate. They look to dispel racism and forge reconciliation by claiming an integrated past grounded in notions of loyalty and faithful slavery. Neither includes citations, and both purport access to the interior lives and motivations of both Selina Gray and Mary Lee that are impossible to verify and verge on the fantastic.

Edward C. Smith, a retired professor of anthropology and the founder of the Civil War Institute at American University, has long been a lightning rod for controversy, most recently in his promotion of black Confederate military history and celebration of Robert E. Lee as an antiracist hero. He is highly regarded among Neo-Confederates as an African American scholar who authenticates many of their historical claims and diversifies their meetings with his presence.[100] Appearing in the popular periodical *Civil War,* Smith's article is a celebration of loyalty, black contributions to the American story, and legacies of reconciliation that he seeks to effect in the present through venerations of a "moonlight and magnolias" southern slave past.

> Mrs. Lee summoned Mrs. Selina Gray, her long-time head housekeeper, who had been born on the estate and had lived there with her family since 1833. Selina Gray was much more than a servant to Mrs. Lee—she was a trusted and valued friend. Their relationship, which was replicated in numerous households throughout the South, was one nurtured upon mutual respect and admiration for each other's capacity for the manifold duties they shared. They were veteran partners in promoting the well-being of the Lee household. Mrs. Lee explained to Selina that the family would be relocating to safer areas further south and that during her absence from the estate she was awarding to Selina the responsibility of becoming the "Keeper of the Keys" of Arlington House. In Southern culture this was a most coveted honor and an expression of total respect and trust. In her new role, Selina Gray was to be responsible for the preservation of the prized personal possessions of the Lee family.

Smith goes on to imagine Selina's decision to stay at Arlington as bound to her sense of this responsibility: "Mrs. Gray attended to her duties with impeccable care and loyalty. She remained at Arlington House in her curatorial capacity for the duration of the Civil War."[101]

Karen Byrne writes with a very different kind of authority as then–National Park Service historian at Arlington House. Her history of Selina Gray appears in the NPS's *CRM: The Journal of Heritage Stewardship,* aimed at public history and resource-management professionals. "The Remarkable Legacy of Selina Gray" promotes the narrative of Selina as protopreservationist and beloved confidante to Mary Lee that prevails today. Building from Selina's and Thorntons' daughters' 1929 accounts, Byrne notes that their marriage ceremony was orchestrated by Mary Lee and officiated by an Episcopal clergy member in the parlor where she had wed Robert. Byrne then departs from the slender information included in the architect's report to argue that the wedding itself was a clear sign of the "mutual respect and genuine affection" that the enslaved woman and plantation mistress held for each other. It was one among their many shared experiences at Arlington, Byrne argues. "Both women presided over large families: Mary Lee gave birth to seven children and Selina bore eight," she writes, searching for shared womanhood and emotional attachment, and "the joys and frustrations of motherhood served as another common bond between the two women."[102] In the complex attachments that these two women shared, the only "bond" that surely linked them was slavery. One woman's maternity was potentially negated and kinship ties dissolved at the whims and economic fortunes of the other. One woman's children were born into Virginia's slaveholding elite; the other's were born their property. Like Smith, Byrne argues for a usable past of common womanhood and reconciliation and celebrates a shared commitment to national heritage:

> Once she had secured her treasured family heirlooms and prepared to leave, Mrs. Lee summoned Selina Gray. As she entrusted the household keys to her slave, Mrs. Lee explained to Selina that henceforth she would serve as the head of the household. Thus the responsibility for the house and all its venerable contents passed from owner to slave. The enormity of this event cannot be overemphasized. Mary Lee's decision to place Selina in charge testified to her supreme confidence and trust in the woman's abilities. Well aware of the national significance of the vast collection that had been left in her care, Selina understood the importance of her new role. Not only did she assume the stewardship of the Lees' revered possessions, she also became the guardian of their heritage, and, in a broader sense, the heritage of the entire nation.[103]

The article ends by framing these commitments as generational and enduring in the work of Selina's daughters in 1929. While trafficking in so many of the same tropes, Byrne nonetheless argues that common representations of Gray as a faithful slave have hidden her preservation work. "For her crucial role in the preservation of the nation's past, Selina Gray deserves a place in history."[104]

Selina Gray's role as the "keeper of the keys" and trusted servant forms the central narrative of slavery at Arlington House, as well as the primary depiction of the Lees' slave ownership. It is repeated in NPS brochures and site maps, on permanent interpretive panels, and in temporary special-event signage and publications. In 2001, the NPS opened an exhibit on slavery and freedom at Arlington, titled *We Have a Claim on This Estate*. Located in the eastern third of the South Dependency, in what was once locked storage for slave rations, the exhibit is composed of large wall panels of narrative text and captioned images moving clockwise around the square room from slavery through the war and creation of Freedman's Village to emancipation and the lives and legacies of former slaves and their descendants at the cemetery, Arlington House, and in the wider surrounding community. This narrative is populated primarily with members of the Syphax, Norris, Gray, Burke, and Parks families. At the center of the room is a large, encased model of Freedman's Village commissioned by members of the Black Heritage Museum of Arlington (BMHA), including a Syphax descendant and Dr. William Talmadge, the late founding president of the museum, and constructed by students from the School of Architecture and Design at Howard University with the support of the Virginia Foundation for the Humanities. Recently, the room next door, once used for smoking meats, housed the bookstore and gift shop usually located in the North Dependency. One can purchase images of Arlington House and Robert E. Lee on objects ranging from magnets to Christmas ornaments and home décor. While there are books available on or by George Washington, G. W. P. Custis, and Robert E. Lee and his family, as well as the Civil War and the cemetery, there is often little concerning slavery, emancipation, Reconstruction, or African American history in general. The final third of the South Dependency is the Grays' reconstituted one-room slave quarters. It is not open to the public but can be seen by peering through a darkened pane of glass in the door. There is nothing to indicate that the Grays once cut throughways between all of these rooms to turn the entire south structure into their home.

For most of the twentieth century, the original Gray quarters were interpreted as "Selina's Room," suggesting that Selina alone and then only in her roles as housekeeper and "keeper of the keys" was truly important to the history of Arlington House and isolating her from her own family to tie her more closely to the Lees. The moniker also made it easy to miss the fact that eight people lived in the small space. Even more absent than Thornton and the children in South Dependency exhibits and interpretations are Selina's brother and sisters, Wesley, Sally, and Mary. They go completely unmentioned, unless one looks carefully at the reproduction of the Custis inventory from 1858 on one of the wall panels. Contemporary public history affects family estrangements that mirror those of slavery, bringing to mind Frederick Douglass's description of his own past in *My Bondage and My Freedom* (1855): "Brothers and sisters we were by blood, but slavery had made us strangers."[105] Enslaved people enter the story in terms of their relationships to their owners and the place on which they labor. In Selina's case, her parents form a link to Washington's Mount Vernon, while her siblings, so clear in the documentation but never referenced, form a link to the Lees' brutality and abuses of the enslaved.

This lifting of Selina from her complex connections to family and community among the enslaved at Arlington to focus on her immediate ties and supposed affection for and from the Lees is reiterated and reinforced in the interpretive signage outside the South Dependency. A single plaque describing aspects of Selina Gray's history at Arlington House is the only interpretive text external to the building. By its location and solitary status, it necessarily introduces visitors to the history of slavery and Freedman's Village and to the very process of historical preservation—all through the prism of what is essentially a faithful slave story. Until 2013, the left third of the plaque depicted a single picture of Selina above her name in a large font. The central portion included descriptive text, while the right third had small photos of Thornton and two of their daughters, who provided information to the Army in 1929, along with a picture of the South Dependency. The central text read,

> Selina Gray, the daughter of Leonard and Sallie Norris, was a second generation Arlington slave. For a number of years, Selina was the personal maid of Mrs. Robert E. Lee. By 1861, Selina had become the head housekeeper at Arlington. When Mrs. Lee abandoned her home in mid-May 1861, she left the household keys, symbolizing authority, responsibility, and her trust in Selina Gray. Locked away inside Arlington were many of the "Washington Treasures." These pieces were cherished family heirlooms that had once belonged to Mrs. Lee's great-grandmother, Martha Custis Washington, and President George Washington.
>
> The U.S. Army assumed control of Arlington on May 24, 1861. Later, U.S. Army officers occupied the house and looting began. When Selina discovered that some of the treasures had been stolen

she confronted the soldiers and ordered them "never to touch any of
Miss Mary's things." Selina alerted General Irvin McDowell, commander of the Union troops, to the importance of the Washington
heirlooms. The remaining pieces were sent to the U.S. Patent office
for safekeeping. Through Selina's efforts, many of the Washington
pieces were saved for posterity.

Eliding the family's own actions in claiming their freedom after the Lees'
departures, the text continues, "The Grays received their freedom in 1862
as specified in the 1857 will of George Washington Parke Custis, Mrs. Lee's
father. Eventually the Gray family left Arlington to live in nearby 'Green
Valley.' Gray descendants still live in Arlington County, Virginia."[106]

The last decade has witnessed significant archaeological, research, and
interpretive work on slavery at Arlington, along with major renovations
to the main house, supported by a Save America's Treasures grant in 2000
and subsequent, ongoing private fund-raising. In 2009, the NPS introduced a new tour brochure for the site that exhibits greater attention to
slavery at Arlington, in conjunction with extensive webpages providing
information and analysis, historical documents, and web-based exhibits,
as well as touring information and directions.[107] A comparison of the old
and new brochures reflects significant changes in design and focus. The
older brochure targets Robert E. Lee's biography, a house tour and history, and includes images only of Lee, his wife, two Arlington House in-
teriors, and the South Dependency. It guides visitors through the house
room by room, providing anecdotal information about events that transpired there, and, in the last lines, identifies the slave quarters, bookstore,
and public bathrooms to be found at the back. This is next to a picture
that shows two people visiting the slave quarters, the caption to which
references Selina Gray by name and notes the presence of an exhibit on
slavery and the Freedman's Village inside.

In an obvious attempt to broaden the historical frame to include the
lives and experience of all of the people, enslaved and free, who lived and
worked at Arlington, the new, much-larger brochure is visually defined
on one side by artist renderings of scenes at and around the house and in
Freedman's Village. Produced by the artist and Caldecott Medal–winning
illustrator Jerry Pinkney, these images form part of the black artist's large
body of commissioned and private work on African American history.[108]

The cover image depicts Lee in his U.S. Army uniform on horseback riding up to the house. A multigenerational, biracial group stands on the portico in welcome, while young Rob and a family dog run to greet him. The caption explains, "Rob Lee runs to meet his father, returning in 1848 from the war with Mexico. Waiting are Lee's wife Mary, holding their daughter Mildred; her parents Mary and George Washington Parke Custis; and head housekeeper Selina Gray and her daughter Sarah." When the brochure is opened, this scene abuts another diverse group shown around the dining-room table. G. W. P. Custis and the Lees are seated, while Charles Syphax and an unidentified young woman and boy serve them. The caption includes a reference to the Syphax plot: "Charles Syphax, serving at left, oversaw the dining room. In 1826 Custis freed Syphax's wife Maria and her children and gave the family use of a 17-acre section of Arlington." While being careful to mark the relationship of black figures to the Custises, Lees, and the property as one of labor—Selina's daughter holds a broom, and neither she nor her mother looks at Robert E. Lee, and the three black figures in the dining scene are all working, the boy looking at Syphax, not the gesticulating Custis—they still suggest a white and black family in slavery, eliding the fact that the Syphaxes were biological family or, as one journalist said, "tied by blood and bond" to Custis and George Washington's Mount Vernon.[109]

After years of archaeological digs, new landscaping, restoration and renovation work on the main house and both slave quarters, and closures of different parts of the site, 2013 brought the return of the furnishings to Arlington House, the opening of a newly restored and interpreted North Dependency, and new explanatory signage. Now clearly designated the "Gray Family Quarters," a new plaque exterior to the South Dependency is vastly improved in its representation of Selina Gray's history but continues to appeal to the faithful slave, preservationist narrative. Titled across the top "Guardian of a Nation's Heritage," the bulk of the text sits beside the same photograph of Selina, now with a ring of keys superimposed over the lower corner. The description reads,

> Selina Gray, her husband, and their eight children lived in the room to your right. She was Mrs. Lee's personal maid and later the head

housekeeper. Her parents had been Mt. Vernon slaves, so she grew up steeped in the lore of George Washington.

In May of 1861 on the eve of the Civil War, Mrs. Lee abandoned her home, she left the household keys with Mrs. Gray, entrusting her with the "Washington Treasury," cherished heirlooms that once belonged to George and Martha Washington (Mrs. Lee's great-grandmother). By assuming stewardship of these revered artifacts, Mrs. Gray became, in a broad sense, the guardian of the heritage of the young nation.

Removing the dialect, condensing the narrative, and foregrounding her immediate family, the plaque moves into the dubious and impossible-to-substantiate claim that as the child of "Mt. Vernon slaves," she must have held special regard for George Washington, making her an excellent steward of the abandoned treasury. In addition to a picture of occupying Union troops on Arlington's portico, the plaque carries images of one of Washington's field tents, a dinner plate from the Cincinnati china, and a small end table that had come to Arlington from Mount Vernon. In the lower center is a much larger picture of a blue-and-white Wedgewood jasperware cream pitcher returned during the Arlington House restoration in the 1930s by Selina's daughters. They described it as having been a gift from Mary Lee upon her departure that was subsequently passed down in the Gray family. On the sign, it is proffered as evidence of a special relationship between Selina and Mary and a legacy of preservation and care for the objects of Arlington in the next generation of women.

While such gifting of a fine decorative piece is not impossible to imagine, it is exceptional. It may, in fact, have been a token of Mary Lee's trust and affection. There is a large chip along the inside lip of the pitcher that is visible in the image on the plaque; perhaps it was deemed no longer fit for the big house. It is also possible that the pitcher came into the Gray family during the war by other means. Perhaps it was liberated in the Lees' absence or gifted by a departing Union soldier or officer, as Selina described in her 1872 letter. These possibilities are aggressively foreclosed in NPS histories and interpretations, however—hidden or glossed over like Thornton's renovations of the South Dependency and Selina's siblings. If entertained, they could threaten the popular narrative of Selina's faithful slavery, veneration for George Washington, and preservation work. They would make it harder to think of her as the trusted "keeper of the keys" or uncontested "Guardian of a Nation's Heritage."

This picture is further complicated by the 2003 discovery of three large shards of Cincinnati ware in excavations of the slave quarters behind Arlington House. Someone "behind the big house" was probably using or displaying some of the china. It is hard to believe that Mary, so proud and protective of the Washington relics before and after her wartime flight from the plantation, would have gifted such pieces to an enslaved person, even if they were damaged. Again, the possibilities are unexplored.[110] Suggesting the suspicions that the shards necessarily raise, without actually engaging them, one NPS resource-management source lumps the china pieces with other objects found at the site, including a broken china doll hand, a ceramic marble, a toy cup from a tea set, and what appears to be an iron hook or door latch. It explains, "It was not uncommon for slaves who worked in the master's house to receive cast off items from the master's family."[111] There is no suggestion that these items might have been acquired through other means, including by the enslaved people's own resources. It is an opportunity missed. The introduction of complicating interpretations in exhibits for the touring public that highlight the variable motivations of enslaved people, as well as the analytical work of historians, and that ask visitors to use their own critical imaginations could only strengthen the presentation of black histories in slavery and freedom at Arlington.

Today, visitors collect in a serpentine line along the front portico, where they are handed a brochure with the Pinkney illustrations and given introductory information by a ranger before being allowed into the house for a semiguided tour in small groups. Rangers upstairs and down give information about the family, rooms, and furnishings and answer questions. Visitors are moved through the house's two stories via a clearly designated path and then out a back door, past a donations collection box, and into the yard near the South Dependency. While the brochure noted the existence of an exhibit on "Arlington's enslaved workers and on Freedman's Village" in the summer of 2013, as in years before, there was no signage along the house tour directing people to it or to the slave quarters in general.

✳ ✳ ✳

In September 2014, a volunteer for the National Park Service made a startling discovery while perusing auctions on eBay: a stereo-view photograph of Selina Gray and two of her daughters, one a teenager and the other a toddler. He recognized Selina right away from the only other known image of her, an oft-reproduced photo on Arlington House signage and publications. Inked onto the back of the stereograph is a short label reading, "Gen Lees Slaves Arlington Va." Originally purchased as part of a box of "unwanted" pictures at a flea market in Kent, England, the online seller listed the photo for a starting price of $20. It sold for $700, purchased by Save Historic Arlington House, a not-for-profit organization partnered with the NPS, which promptly donated the photo to the Park Service. The image and its unlikely journey "home" to Arlington were widely reported as it was put on exhibit at the mansion in October.[112]

The photograph depicts Selina and her older daughter seated on a bench or two chairs in close proximity, with the younger child perched between them on their laps. All three stare directly into the camera and are carefully posed; the teenager's left hand, pointer finger raised along her cheek, frames her face; the toddler's hands are clasped and the skirt of her dress carefully arrayed. The back of the furniture is just visible

Noncommercial stereograph card showing Selina Gray with two unidentified figures, most likely her daughters, posed outside their quarters, ca. 1861–1865. Viewed through a stereoscope, the paired images produce the illusion of a three-dimensional image.

under Selina's propped elbow, while the rest is completely obscured by the elder pair's large hoop skirts. Their clothes are fine, are carefully presented, and seem visually coordinated for effect. The group is outside in a dirt yard in front of a brick structure that fills the background. No sky or edges to the building, other than its foundation, are visible. To those who are familiar with Arlington, however, it is clearly the end of the South Dependency facing the main house—Selina and her daughters are posed beside their slave quarters.

There is much we do not yet know—and may never know—about the circumstances of this photograph and the stereograph it was made into. This includes the photographer, the client, and the date of its creation, which some people presume to be near the end of the war, as well as the details of its journey to England. Nor do we know for whom or when it was composed for stereoscope, with its side-by-side pair of identical images, and labeled by hand. At the same time, Park Service employees and journalists assume a great deal about the adult woman in the picture and the people who owned or once owned her. In popular reports and NPS texts, the image was quickly enfolded in the narratives that have dominated the site and the story. The image is proffered as further evidence of those stories' veracity, historical significance, and emotional impact. The image has quickly become a vehicle for reiterating claims of Selina's faithfulness, the Lees' benevolence, and the true American heroism shared by Selina Gray and Robert E. Lee.

The story of the found photo was reported widely in the United States and England, fueled by the fame of Robert E. Lee and heightened hungers for Civil War stories in the closing months of the sesquicentennial. An evening news story from a DC-area ABC affiliate, WJLA, and the *Washington Post* provided the baseline information for most of the news stories to follow. All dwelled on Selina Gray's close relationship with the Lees and her role as "keeper of the keys" and protopreservationist. The WJLA news team reported, "Today, historians credit her with saving the home and the treasures inside from being destroyed or stolen as Union troops swarmed the estate." In the same report, an NPS ranger says, "Selina was an incredibly courageous woman. . . . She stood up to Union generals to save this place, save these priceless heirlooms from President George Washington that were here in the home of a Confederate general."[113] A more deeply researched article in the popular magazine *Civil War Times* reiterates this narrative in its title, "Arlington's Enslaved Savior." The article that follows tells the same story of trust, mutual affection, and heroism, noting that Selina's "faithfulness in a time of war had certainly been well proven. Today the Gray family story is a key part of the history of Arlington House, and the continued existence of some of America's most treasured artifacts."[114]

The depiction of ownership produced by this image and its caption is so different from that of the photograph of Selina's great-grandson and his family that was taken a century later in front of Arlington House rather than behind it. Together, they speak to a long history of black and white family legacies claimed, carefully preserved, often twisted, and utterly constrained at Arlington. By the time Selina and her daughters posed for the picture during the war, it is likely that they had already been joined on the plantation by hundreds of former slaves seeking to create their own new stories and relocated by the War Department to Freedman's Village.

Chapter 2

FREEDMAN'S VILLAGE

Don't feel as if I was free, 'pears like there's nobody free here.

—anonymous Freedman's Village resident (1864)

A WEEK INTO THE FEDERAL occupation of Arlington, readers of the *New York Times* devoured dispatches about multiple Virginia fronts of the new war. Amid the news of troop movements and political machinations emerged key questions about what to do with Confederate combatants and civilians, prisoners, and property, including enslaved people. The news reflected the contradictions and confusion in federal policy during the war's early days, often initiated by military actors on the ground, some of whom saw only their own environs and immediate concerns, while others had larger ambitions for themselves and national transformation.

The fate of the Arlington plantation and its inhabitants—those remaining and in flight, enslaved and free—was central to these questions and fresh on the minds of correspondents just as the land itself was freshly dotted with new Union encampments. Noting that Arlington belonged to the Lees and calling it perhaps "the most valuable property in Virginia"— an erroneous claim economically, if, perhaps, not symbolically—the *Times* suggested that confiscating and selling the property might do more to bring the rebellion to heel than "any one act that could be done." At least it would swell federal coffers by upward of $250,000, the correspondent speculated, and that was value "apart from the negroes." This led to further consideration of what should be done with the enslaved: "It was alleged that the negroes of the South would follow their masters to the death. Our experience thus far does not justify this declaration. There was one negro deserted by his master at Alexandria, and there were twelve left on the Arlington Estate. None of them evinced the slightest desire to run after their masters. They are, therefore, in a measure, the charge of the Government." The estimate of twelve remaining at Arlington was quite low, probably reflecting only those in the quarters behind the main house, including the Gray family. Current numbers notwithstanding, the writer argued, many more were sure to fall to the government's responsibility. "We are likely to have more chattels than it will be possible for us to take care of, if we still profess to hold them in bondage. The Government has no desire to interfere with private property, and will not, but it cannot be expected that the Government will take the place of owners when the owners abandon their property."[1] Raising the thorny issues of property rights, responsibilities, and black dependency, and presuming little agency among those who had been "deserted," the *Times* writer wondered to whom it fell to provide for them.

Just as pressing was the issue of runaways on Union lines, who were claiming their freedom and seeking protection. A story printed just alongside the description of Arlington detailed "The Landing at Newport News." It included reports of General Benjamin Butler at Fortress Monroe and suggested a different picture of who truly needed whom. "About a hundred fugitives came in this morning," the report explained. "They were provided with rations and set to work, their services being greatly needed. They represent that they were to be either sent South or put to work on the rebel batteries."[2] Still understood as *chattel* and *fugitives*, the term and concept of *contraband* had yet to assume the central place it would in news, policy, and northern popular imaginations.

Matters were quite different in the western part of Virginia, readers discovered as they continued to scan that day's front page. Many of these white Virginians, some of them slave owners, maintained Unionist sympathies that eventually led to separate statehood for West Virginia in 1863. General George McClellan crossed into the state with his troops from Ohio and issued a statement that the *Times* now reprinted. The Union army came, he assured western Virginians, as "friends and brothers," only to safeguard their interests. "Your homes, your families, and your property are safe under our protection. All your rights shall be religiously respected. Notwithstanding all that has been said by the traitors to induce you to believe our advent among you will be signalized by an interference with your slaves, understand one thing clearly; not only will we abstain from all such interference, but we will on the contrary, with an iron hand, crush any attempt at insurrection on their part."[3] Although West Virginia statehood carried gradual emancipation for those who were enslaved within its borders, McClellan's assurance that property rights in human beings would be respected forecast federal policies concerning slavery in the border states of Kentucky, Missouri, Delaware, and Maryland.

Throughout the Civil War, movement from, to, and across Arlington was a common reference point as the plantation yielded to Union troops, then to thousands of "contrabands," and eventually, to even more dead bodies. All, perhaps, ultimately made up the collection that Selina Gray referred to as "inferior peoples," her letter a reminder of those who staked an earlier claim to the place. The Lees were gone, never to reside at Arlington again, but many whom they had enslaved remained at war's end. While the Gray family eventually moved on, others never left, including Wesley Norris, who had made his way back to the estate and his parents, traveling across Confederate territory and battlefields to get home, to the place he would live for the rest of his years with his sister Sally, who had also returned.

Over time, as Radical Republican calls for abolition and the enlistment of black men increased, and Lincoln continued to insist that slavery was not near its total destruction, many thousands negotiated their options and freed themselves by running or, like those at Arlington, grasped their emancipation in their owners' flight. The latter has been obscured by the more popular figure of the runaway presenting himself at Union encampments, locating action and agency only in geographic movement out of the South on the way to seeing it only in the marches of United States Colored Troops (USCT). W. E. B. Du Bois's oft-cited argument for the role of the enslaved in transforming the war into one for liberation relies on this metaphor, for instance: "with perplexed and laggard steps, the United States Government followed the footsteps of the Black slave."[4] The enslaved person fleeing to Union lines holds enormous emotional and po-litical power, but often the lines found them.

From the war's start, Arlington was a microcosm for wider issues re-lating to the Union's "problem" of what to do with abandoned plantation lands and the once and currently enslaved. Where one stood held great importance in these developing wartime geographies of battle, occupation, slavery, freedom, and nation. In the midst of it all, as a single location not overly large in acreage but enormous symbolically, was Arlington. In four years, the plantation originally built to honor George Washington and to broadcast slave-power patriotism went from being on American soil to becoming part of the Confederate States of America and then Union-occupied territory before being officially confiscated and put to perma-nent federal use. In 1863, the former Lee slaves, Union encampments, and Quartermaster's corrals were joined on the heights by a sprawling con-traband camp. Desperate to remove thousands of formerly enslaved refugees from Washington and effect a policy for quickly relocating new arrivals, military officials proffered the occupied plantation as an ideal solution. They promoted Freedman's Village as both an answer to local problems and a new kind of contraband camp, regularly exhibited to public officials and foreign dignitaries visiting the District. Freedman's Village would become home to thousands of relocated former slaves who had fled to Washington and Alexandria and a smaller number who had left the country altogether only to be returned after the failure of Lincoln's last colonization attempt to Haiti. More than this, it made Arlington a kind of nearby laboratory for the federal management of black freedom and the policies that would guide Reconstruction.

On May 5, 1863, Lieutenant Colonel Elias M. Greene from the Quar-termaster Department of Washington had proposed to his commander that the land south of the Potomac—Arlington—"abandoned by rebel owners" and "now lying idle," could be put to better use. "The force of contrabands, males and females, now idle in the City, and a dead weight on the Government, can be employed to very great advantage" in culti-vating the land and could be provided for there at far less expense than in the city. Greene offered a solution to the problem of "idle" lands and people, merged in his vision as a great, sucking drain on Union resources that, with proper management, could become quite the opposite. "Besides this, there is a decided advantage to them of the salutary effects of good pure country air, and a return to their former healthy avocations as 'field hands,'" he claimed, suggesting that younger and older contrabands, as well as the disabled, could be put to lighter gardening work, producing vegetables for the "old women" to sell in Washington or perhaps to feed troops. He saw in this not only relief from the cost of provisioning contrabands with military rations but an opportunity to profit from them. It may be "simply stated as a scheme to give employment to all of the contrabands in this Department, and make such employment profitable both to them and to the Government." Greene's plan was sent with endorsements up the chain of command to Quartermaster General Montgomery C. Meigs and then to Secretary of War Edwin Stanton, who approved the scheme.[5] Less than a week later, on May 22, 1863, Freedman's Village was established at Arlington.

Managed through the joint efforts of the military, civilian officials, and the American Missionary Association (AMA), the camp was intended to provide free people, some of whom had been enslaved at Arlington, with the structure, surveillance, and opportunities for industrial education and agricultural labor that officials and the AMA believed necessary to engender the industry, responsibility, and self-sufficiency needed to move quickly into the "free labor" market. Freedman's Village was never intended as a permanent settlement or redistribution of confiscated lands; rather, it was seen as a way station for learning the obligations of the condition of freedom.

Those who managed Freedman's Village did not believe that responsible freedom came naturally to black people but were sure that dependency and indolence did. Largely unknown outside the chain of military command and civilian officials was the fact that the construction and maintenance of the camp was supported by a racially targeted tax on all black male military laborers, no matter their former status as free or enslaved, called the Contraband Tax. Monthly fees collected from camp residents, often referred to by similar nomenclature, would later supplement that fund. Yet Freedman's Village, like other camps and federal supports after the war, was largely understood by the War Department, by government officials, and in wider popular white opinion as only federal largesse. The Contraband Tax itself kept African Americans' contributions to the Union effort at a remove, signaling their dependence on the government, rather than representing their literal investments in it.

Once again, Arlington became a show place, privileged in its proximity to the capital and thus more impactful in its argument for a particular kind of managed black freedom. This was especially true in the midst of pitched congressional struggles over the future shape of the agency that became the Freedmen's Bureau, which assumed responsibility for Freedman's Village after the war. Touring and evaluating this place allowed reformers, military officers, federal officials, and the simply curious to imagine what the postwar nation might be like and how to effect changes in labor relations, manage the absorption of the formerly enslaved, and settle on the limits of both. In the ensuing contexts of Reconstruction and reunion, Freedman's Village came to be seen as a public nuisance and barrier to cemetery operations and expansion. Attempts to disband the community began as early as 1866, but it endured for another twenty-five years.

As the war generated new identities and movement, fungibility and mobility took on meanings that surpassed the logistics of provisioning troops, tending the injured and ill, burying the dead, and dealing with civilian populations. The terms described conceptual and subjective movements from citizen to soldier, from vital to debilitated or dead, from presence to memory. They also denoted the transmutation from slave to contraband or soldier on the way to becoming a free person and potential citizen—a path persistently bedraggled by official fears of stasis and dependency.

From the outset, enslaved men, women, and children took opportunities presented by the uncertainties of war and the presence of Union forces not only to claim their own freedom but to make clear that for them this was always a war for liberation, despite official policies stating otherwise. Military in the field negotiated a confusing environment in which the Union was not working to end slavery or challenge claims to human property where it already existed—both in the states in rebellion and the border states—but to stop the spread of slavery to the West. Lincoln had made this clear in his first inaugural address in March 1861, just weeks before the first shots at Fort Sumter. Attempting to halt the march to war,

Lincoln urged, "I have no purpose, directly or indirectly, to interfere with the institution of slavery in the States where it exists. I believe I have no lawful right to do so, and I have no inclination to do so."[6] This was federal policy, but the experiences and demands of enslaved people, abolitionists, Union and Confederate troops and officers, public officials, slave owners, and civilians were all far more complicated, and in those early days, the contours of the war itself were still terribly unclear.

Among the thousands of people on the move, the actions of three enslaved men helped to force the Union's hand and sparked the creation of one of the most enduring and vexing conceptions of the Civil War—the human "contraband." In May 1861, the men appeared at Fortress Monroe, a federal military installation along the Virginia coastline that remained in Union control throughout the war, claiming their freedom and seeking protection. They fled as their owner was attempting to move them further south to keep them in his possession. When his representative arrived at the fort to collect them, General Benjamin F. Butler refused to turn the men over, invoking the legal justification that they amounted to "contrabands of war." Had the three men not been enslaved in Virginia, their fates would surely have been different. Just a month earlier, Butler had offered his Massachusetts volunteers to put down a rumored slave revolt in Maryland. In states that remained loyal to the Union, slavery was to be protected and slaves on the run from those places returned to their owners under the provisions of the Fugitive Slave Act, which remained the law of the land.[7] As the "contraband" scenario was unfolding at Fortress Monroe, another struggle over the status and fate of Confederate properties, including enslaved people, was beginning closer to Washington when Union forces crossed the Potomac and occupied the Arlington Heights without resistance on the night of May 23.

Butler's designation of the men as "contrabands" and his decision to put them to work for the Quartermaster division at the fort was affirmed by the secretary of war, Simon Cameron, who noted, "The question of their final disposition will be reserved for future determination."[8] Word of Butler's actions spread quickly, and while his improvisation was never made official policy, it was subsumed within top-down directives and the First Confiscation Act passed at the end of the summer. The name *contraband* for those who were fleeing enslavement—freeing themselves—

held on throughout the war and persists to this day. The term stuck because it condensed an enormous amount of cultural and political work. The persistence of the figure of the "contraband" helped to soothe fundamental concerns about the national inclusion of four million once-enslaved black southerners. While it continued to frame them as objects and property, not wholly distinct from chattel, the term *contraband* served as a category between slavery and freedom, suggesting a space of transition and potential for transformation.[9] The contraband camp, of which Freedman's Village became a model, made that conceptual space both literal and geographic.

Word of Butler's actions spread most quickly among those for whom freedom and recognition of their full humanity was on the line. By late July, more than 900 formerly enslaved men, women, and children were living and working at the fort. Many more flowed into Washington, DC, and its surrounding areas. Following Butler's lead, General Joseph K. F. Mansfield, commander of the Department of Washington, had designated all refugees from Virginia slavery in the District to be "contraband," while those from Maryland were to be returned to their owners and their enslavement.[10] A portion of the newly established Old Capitol Prison was designated to house and feed homeless former slaves with the aim of finding them employment, oftentimes with the prison itself or the military. The contrabands joined Confederate prisoners of war, political prisoners, insubordinate Union officers, spies, and prostitutes in the red-brick structure to the east and within clear sight of the unfinished Capitol dome. Acquiring its name when it had been the temporary site of Congress after the British destroyed the original building in the War of 1812, it had since been a private school and boardinghouse. The states'-rights and nullification champion Senator John C. Calhoun of South Carolina had died in his apartment there in 1850. Before closing as a prison, it housed several accused conspirators in Lincoln's assassination, and its yard and gallows became the scene of execution for the director of the notorious Andersonville prison. The building was eventually razed to make way for the new U.S. Supreme Court building in the 1930s.[11]

Housing fugitive slaves in a prison was largely a decision of expediency, but it added or sustained suggestions of deviance and criminality of formerly enslaved people, now contrabands. It also suggested continuity;

captured runaway slaves were often imprisoned before they were returned to their owners or taken to auction. In the end, it was perceptions of contrabands as contagions and potential carriers of disease, either to the places they worked or to the white prisoners they lived with, that got them removed to the adjacent tenements of Duff Green's Row—today the site of the Folger Shakespeare Library—when the new District military governor, General James Wadsworth, ordered their relocation.[12]

It was left largely to the military to respond on the ground, directing policy locally and then claiming national authority over the fate of the newly free. These early initiatives took on grander proportions in November 1861 when the Union navy quickly dispatched Confederate defenses at Port Royal Sound in South Carolina, sending troops and white civilians fleeing and leaving the majority black population behind on vast Sea Island plantations, with cotton still in the fields ready to be harvested. What was to be done with the abandoned lands, the cotton, and more than 10,000 new contrabands? Thus began what the historian Willie Lee Rose called a "rehearsal for Reconstruction," as Union officers, Treasury Department agents, Congress, abolitionists, missionaries, teachers, and capitalists sought to profit from and prove the superiority of free labor and the capacities of the formerly enslaved to become, with training and protection, self-reliant free workers. Often at odds, this collection of people seeking to shape the transition from a slave economy confronted the wills, resistance, and dreams of the formerly enslaved themselves, who had their own visions for the future and their places within it. In collective acts of protest, rage, and vengeance, some destroyed plantation big houses and cotton gins, neglected the cotton in the fields, and planted food crops for themselves.[13]

As if asking anew the *New York Times*' questions from the first weeks of the war, another New York newspaper, the black-owned *Anglo African*, reported on the occupied coastal areas of South Carolina and queried in a front-page headline, "What Shall Be Done with the Slaves?" The paper urged a wide policy of confiscation and redistribution of plantation lands to those who were once enslaved on them at the war's end. "What course can be clearer, what course more politic, what course will so immediately restore the equilibrium of commerce, what course will be so just, so humane, so thoroughly conducive to the public weal and the national advancement, as that the government should immediately bestow these lands upon the freedmen who know best how to cultivate them, and will joyfully bring their brawny arms, their willing hearts, and their skilled hands to the glorious labor of cultivating their OWN, the lands which they have bought and paid for by their sweat and blood."[14] The paper argued the former slaves' moral and labor value in the land. Resistant to early attempts to impose free-labor ideologies and enforce waged work, the *Anglo African* urged that the former slaves had already "purchased" their land and freedom, that they could not and should not be classed as dependents on land that was rightfully theirs.

Free people's desires for independence through land ownership were mostly frustrated as military and government agents and reformers compelled them to pick cotton for wages and as land was distributed in large portions for commercial purposes. This area was the scene of hope and heartbreak again when General Sherman's Field Order No. 15 of January 1865 designated the Sea Islands and some coastal land from South Carolina to Florida for the exclusive settlement of former slaves, to be distributed in forty-acre allotments and worked with the use of Army mules. Rather than effecting the confiscation and redistribution of land that so many formerly enslaved people hoped for, however, the plan and land claims were abandoned by President Andrew Johnson, labeled war measures that were never intended to be permanent.[15] Federal officials sought to follow a similar path at Freedman's Village, first attempting to disband the community in 1868. The villagers' ability to stay on the land for two more decades and ultimately get small reparations from the federal government when finally evicted and dispersed made the camp the longest-lived wartime redistribution scheme, in spite of, rather than at the largesse of, the government.

For much of the war, Abraham Lincoln seemed convinced that the best way to deal with former slaves was to facilitate their removal from the country altogether. Whether this derived from his pragmatism or from his inability to conceive of true social equality for black and white people is hard to say. In his December 3, 1861, message to Congress, Lincoln addressed "what to do with contrabands," arguing that many already existed due to actions in the field and the Confiscation Act and that many more were sure to come. He encouraged Congress to assume responsibility for the undertaking, adding that free black people already in the United States might be encouraged to emigrate, as well, depending on their wishes, and could "be included in such colonization."[16] Lincoln had already encouraged private colonization schemes to Haiti, Honduras, and Nicaragua and continued to work on various plans through 1864. Most fell through, in part because they were hard sells to generally unenthusiastic recently enslaved and free people and met with significant resistance from many abolitionists and activists, including Frederick Douglass.[17]

In the early days of the war, colonization was the constant companion to various plans circulating for dealing with contrabands, confiscation, and emancipation. All enslaved people in Washington were freed when Congress passed and Lincoln signed a compensated emancipation act in April 1862. The law called for the creation of a commission to assess the value of and then pay owners for their human property and appropriated funds for colonization to "the Republics of Hayti or Liberia, or such other country beyond the limits of the United States as the President may determine."[18] Even after the Emancipation Proclamation, colonization schemes remained on Lincoln's agenda. On the eve of its signing, Lincoln made a contract with the New Yorker Bernard Kock, committing the federal government to paying fifty dollars a person for 500 free people to be transported to a small island off the southern coast of Haiti called Île à Vache. There they were to work cultivating cotton, sugar, and coffee and cutting timber, with some of the profits going to Haiti and the rest to Kock, who referred to himself as the island's governor. The contract was canceled after Kock was revealed to be less than reliable but signed again with two other men from New York, who promptly hired Kock as their manager. In May 1863, Kock and 453 black emigrants left for Haiti.[19]

Since the founding of the American Colonization Society (ACS), the notion of an orderly mass exodus of black people out of the United States in the aftermath of emancipation was far more limited in its execution and appeal than its outsized place in the political culture might suggest. To be sure, the idea was by no means restricted to white advocates. Many

black people saw great potential in leaving. Everybody on that ship to Île
à Vache had their own reasons for wanting to go. Perhaps they imagined
black futures free from surveillance, racism, and painful pasts in the
United States and saw potential for a different kind of freedom in leaving,
one not tied to American citizenship and political liberalism. They held
tight to what the historian Robin D. G. Kelley has termed their "freedom
dreams."[20]

Many others believed that their dreams were best fulfilled in the United
States and in recognition of their national belonging, however. They were
aghast at the notion of leaving or being compelled to leave. Arlington had
been a scene of these tensions in 1853 when William and Rosabella Burke
and their four children—the family Mary Lee had called "pioneers" in
her diary—left the plantation to go to Liberia with the ACS.[21] In letters
to the Lees, the Burkes detailed their hardships and successes in their new
African home, which they named "Mount Rest." They remained stead-
fast in their hopes that more who had been enslaved at Arlington would
join them.[22] In a letter to the ACS secretary, thanking him for "looking
up" the Burkes' "relations at Arlington and elsewhere, and causing them
to write" to the family during the war, William said, "[My sister] writes
me that the place abounds with contrabands. I wonder if they could not
be persuaded to seek a home in this land among their fathers; it seems
they must ere long find a home somewhere."[23]

For the immigrants to Île à Vache, their dreams of freedom and a "home
somewhere" became waking nightmares. Provided no adequate shelter
or provisions and victims of brutal discipline and sporadic payment of
wages, which by the end ceased altogether, a number fled to the Haitian
mainland while many others fell ill or died from diseases made worse by
malnutrition and exposure. After survivors were brought back to the
United States by the Navy at Lincoln's orders in March 1864 and reset-
tled at Freedman's Village, Congress enacted a law to prohibit expendi-
ture of public funds for any such colonization schemes in the future.[24] The
celebrated runaway, author, and abolitionist Harriet Jacobs was among
those "to welcome the emigrants returned from Hayti" at the water's edge
in Alexandria. "It was a bitter cold day," she wrote to Lydia Maria Child
in a letter published later in the *National Anti-Slavery Standard*, "the
snow was falling, and they were barefooted and bareheaded, with scarcely

rags enough to cover them." Jacobs described the group loaded into wagons and taken to Freedman's Village, which she called "Green Heights." She worried for their suffering and upon visiting Arlington the next day learned that three had died overnight. "I comforted myself with the idea that this would put an end to colonization projects."[25] This meant the end to Lincoln's own freedom dreams that slavery's destruction might be finite because the once enslaved would no longer be in the Union. Yet from the very start of the war, the ever-increasing number of contrabands had belied that dream.

Harriet Jacobs, whose *Incidents in the Life of a Slave Girl, Written by Herself* (1861) had been published under a pseudonym the year before, spent the summer of 1862 reporting on conditions at Duff Green's Row, which she called "Government headquarters for the contraband." Reporting for the *Liberator*, she described the camp as overwhelmed by the numbers of needy who suffered greatly in their confinement in tight quarters, including many children who "pine like prison birds" for the open air of the fields. Referring to the Gray family and others who remained at Arlington and possibly a small collection of runaways who had located themselves near the mansion, Jacobs described better conditions and happier people working and living among the troops encamped there, calling it "a delightful place for both soldiers and the contraband."[26] While Jacobs understood the former Custis-Lee slaves who remained to be contrabands and freedom seekers just like those crowding Duff Green's Row, their official status was always understood as distinctly tied to the plantation. In January, the secretary of war had ordered the commanding officer of the Union encampment to provide for the "old and infirm negroes of the Arlington Estate," given that it was "now in possession of the Government" and had been "charged by its former owner . . . with the care of these old people." Nearly two years later, after Freedman's Village had opened on the heights, the camp's superintendent was ordered to provide the same clothing given to contrabands to "people belonging to the Arlington Estate." This notion that the former Custis-Lee slaves "belonged" to and were defined by the plantation held throughout the war. It marked the flip side to the Grays', Norrises', and Parkses' claims that Arlington belonged in lasting ways to them and facilitated ideas of their faithful servitude.[27]

Jacobs worried about the ways a life in slavery could degrade a person and was concerned that others, particularly white people, understand that this was not inherent to black people but to the institution of slavery. Addressing readers of the *Liberator*, she implored, "Have patience with them. You have helped to make them what they are; teach them civilization. You owe it to them and you will find them as apt to learn as any other people that come to you stupid from oppression." Jacobs continued her work for the New England Freedman's Aid Society in Alexandria alongside Julia Wilbur from the Rochester Ladies' Anti-Slavery Society and was eventually joined by her daughter, Louisa Jacobs, a teacher.[28] All three would find themselves at odds with the civilian superintendent of contrabands for Alexandria, the Reverend Albert Gladwin, who they believed was brutal, corrupt, and wholly unsuited to the position. Jacobs came to see running interference for newly arrived contrabands against Gladwin as a major facet of her work, including trying to get them settled before he could record them in the contraband rolls and make them known to military authorities and thus subject to their discipline.[29]

Private relief organizations, black and white, formed complex alliances with the military, which relied on them for religious, educational, and moral instruction and ministering to the formerly enslaved.[30] Jacobs was not alone in her frustrations with the Army and the civilian men it appointed to leadership positions, such as Danforth B. Nichols, a Methodist minister and longtime reformer active with the American Missionary Association, who served as superintendent of contraband in Washington and oversaw Freedman's Village. Many observers noted the marked increase in formerly enslaved people seeking refuge in the District after the enactment of compensated emancipation there. In an appeal for relief funds, the Reverend Henry M. Turner of the Israel Bethel AME Church marveled that the numbers of formerly enslaved people had gone "from hundreds to thousands, and still they come."[31] The conditions at Duff Green's Row were terrible and crowded. After a deadly outbreak of smallpox, the military governor of Washington authorized Nichols to take a block of empty military barracks on North Twelfth Street to house the healthy, in hopes of stopping the spread of illness and dealing with overcrowding.[32] His orders stated that the new camp should be "for the use of the families of Contrabands employed by the Government," although this limitation was never put in practice.[33] The relief provided by this contraband community, called Camp Barker, was short-lived. For many observers Camp Barker became synonymous with sickness and degradation, infamously foul and overcrowded. Its reported horrors helped fuel interest in a different kind of camp across the river on the Arlington Heights.

During the summer and fall of 1862, concerns about racial difference, the individual consequences of enslavement, and potential for contrabands' dependency intersected with debates about how to fund the war and who should fight it. In July, Lincoln signed into law the Revenue Act, the Second Confiscation Act, and the Militia Act. Joining the year's earlier Legal Tender Act, which had established a paper currency (the "greenback") used to pay Union soldiers and military laborers, the Revenue Act responded to the rapidly escalating costs of war and added to the era's significant transformations in the place of the federal government in American daily life. Along with new excise taxes on various consumer goods, it created the country's first progressive income tax and a Bureau of Internal Revenue, a forerunner to today's Internal Revenue Service.[34] This law was followed midmonth by the Second Confiscation Act, which affirmed the freedom of all formerly enslaved people in Union-held territories, including women and children explicitly for the first time. The Militia Act established additional quotas for soldiers from each state through enlistment or conscription and specified a minimum payment for black laborers working with the Army and Navy of ten dollars per month, three dollars of which could be in equivalent clothing, including uniforms. This was much less than the average white laborer could expect and was later the source of differential payments for U.S. Colored Troops in 1863.

These new policies were enacted in the context of increasing popular discontent with the costs of war. In addition to protests of new state drafts, white violence erupted across midwestern and northern cities and border areas in response to real and perceived threats of depressed wages and competition from imported contraband labor.[35] This fury was fueled by popular racism and contradictory assumptions of contrabands' idleness and happy dependence on government relief. For instance, five months after General Butler began receiving and employing former slaves at Fortress Monroe, a Mankato, Minnesota, newspaper railed at readers, "$62,000 of your money taken [there] . . . to keep in idleness a lot of vagrant negroes."[36] Schemes to relocate and put to work formerly enslaved people outside Union-held territories had emerged almost as soon as the contraband rationale did. A Newport, Rhode Island, man who had been an active proponent of gradual emancipation in the South in the 1850s now offered a plan in July 1861 to have contrabands "distributed among the Free States" as domestic laborers to be "billeted" for the war's duration in singles or pairs with individual families, depending on the size and needs of the household, which would assume responsibility for their support in return for labor.[37] The following month, the New York abolitionist Lewis Tappan suggested to Butler that former slaves collecting at Fortress Monroe be moved to New York City, where they could enter domestic service.[38] With contrabands always understood as both sources of labor and potential drains on government resources, plans for what to do with them, including camps, fieldwork on occupied plantations, and eventually enlistment, all demonstrated a persistent lack of interest in black self-determination, kinship, and community ties. The plans presumed a kind of interchangeability of formerly enslaved people, made easier through the objectifying term *contraband,* which carried undeniable similarities to the logic of the slave trade.

A week after the carnage at the Battle of Antietam, with more than 23,000 men killed, wounded, or missing, Lincoln issued a preliminary emancipation proclamation forecasting his plans but making them contingent on whether the Confederacy continued its rebellion. It was a plea for a restored Union that could include some limited slavery or compensated emancipation.[39] The following day, Brigadier General James S. Wadsworth, the military governor of the District of Columbia who had been quick to implement Butler's earlier contraband order, wrote to the secretary of war noting that "several hundred coloured men" were employed by the District Quartermaster Department earning twenty to twenty-five dollars per month and rations. He qualified that "most of these men are fugitives from slavery" and that while they "are receiving these very high wages, which many of them are incompetent to take care of, and waste in dissipation, the Government is supporting six or eight hundred women & children of the same class, who are unable to find employment." Wadsworth recommended that five dollars per month be subtracted from the pay of "all the coloured laborers" working for the Quartermaster Department in Washington and Alexandria, to be expended by the War Department "in providing for the women & children referred to" and to fund a contraband hospital.[40] This was so ordered on September 27, 1862.

Wadsworth's letter makes clear that the Contraband Tax as policy was designed to assuage a number of racial and gendered concerns about dependency and personal, familial, and collective responsibility. Claiming black men's inability to steward their own resources in appropriate ways and thus rationalizing the military's authority to do so, the tax framed contrabands as familial dependents—"women & children"—neglected by incapable or irresponsible patriarchs. With these dependents fallen to the mercy and care of the government in this scenario, the military sought to offset its own costs and enforce this responsibility by taxing black men. The gendered racialization of dependency implied in the Contraband Tax was twofold, associating all black people and suggesting that contrabands' needs were thus the fundamental responsibility of African Americans rather than of the government or citizenry at large. Later attempts to get rations and housing in contraband camps for the wives and children of black soldiers showed that this notion of collective responsibility did not flow both ways in the eyes of many officials. Resisting such provisioning, the superintendent of Freedman's Village argued, "I have no authority to provide quarter rations for the wives of colored soldiers. I should be warranted in taking care of the children, I think, but not the women who can support themselves."[41] This was despite the fact that black recruits in Virginia had been promised rations and housing for their wives and children.[42] Everyone in this conversation presumed that black women should be working for wages, that their freedom did not entail the kinds of domesticity, motherhood, and wifery promoted for white women. They were not entitled to the "privileges" of their husbands' patriarchal independence.[43]

Resistance to the tax was swift and came in overt and subtle forms, including refusal by many black men to work for the Army when they could find jobs as laborers and teamsters in civilian industries at full wages. The military was uneven in applying the tax, at first only drawing it from black employees of the Quartermaster division. This prompted an officer at the depot in Alexandria to complain about the practical effects of the tax, given that other black workers at the same depot employed by the Commissary were not subject to it. His letter was sent along to Quartermaster General Meigs with a note that the difference "places the Quartermaster at a great disadvantage and renders it extremely difficult for him to procure laborers." Meigs agreed and consulted Secretary of War Stanton, who solved the problem by ordering a tax on the workers of the Commissary Department as well.[44]

Some black workers protested the tax directly, petitioning the Army to cease collection. Often arguments in support of these requests depended on the idea that as free black people before the war, the petitioners held no common condition with contrabands, claiming the invalidity of lumping together all black people. In August 1863, a group of black employees in the Alexandria Depot Commissary, now included in the tax by Stanton's orders, petitioned their boss, Colonel George Bell, for relief from payment, noting their depressed wages and the rising expenses of a wartime economy. Careful to identify themselves as "free born men" who since their youth had been "working hard" for themselves, they claimed to have "no friends on this Contraband list." This was especially galling, they argued, because by their estimation, "contrabands has all the attention from evey private source," along with government provisions for housing, food, and fuel. They noted with not a little pride, "We always as well as now, had to depend up on our own labor for the support, of our selves and families." Bell sent the petition to Secretary Stanton, who promptly rejected it. Undeterred, the men petitioned Stanton directly a few days later, this time seeking a raise to offset the tax. "It is true that the government, has great expence, it is nomore then wright, that the contrabands employed in the government, service should be curtailed in wages for the surport of they fellow men, but we free people I dont think sir has any rite to pay a tax for the benefit of the contrabands any more than white labours of our class."[45] The tax was a double insult, they concluded, making it difficult for them to care for their own families, who had no access to military relief efforts, while, just as damning, suggesting they held anything in common with those who were on relief. Contrasted with contrabands' dependency, they offered their own independence and responsible patriarchy, hindered by an unfair tax. No raise was forthcoming.

This presumption that black men employed by the Army—no matter their own status as formerly enslaved or free, married or single, and whether or not they were fathers—should be taxed to help support contraband women, children, and the aged stemmed from a clear and growing two-tiered distinction between self-possessed and able-bodied free persons, soon to be understood primarily as black soldiers, on the one hand, and dependent contrabands, on the other. This distinction was reinforced as a gendered dichotomy, despite the prevalence of formerly enslaved women as laborers for individual soldiers and the military (primarily as cooks, nurses, and launderers) and the tens of thousands of men counted among the contrabands.[46] True manhood relied on independence, a category that had come to embrace the "free soil, free labor, free men" ethos of the Republicans and helped to lift waged labor out of the realm of potential dependence via professions of the freedom of contract. In this context, the Contraband Tax became yet another lesson for free people in racial difference and the fettered individualism of "free" labor. By the same logic, the Commissary employees in Alexandria resisted the elision of all black people by claiming their long-standing independence and free-labor commitments, by staking their claim to free manhood, which included shared revulsion at contrabands' dependency and desperation.[47] With the creation of the U.S. Colored Troops after Lincoln's Emancipation Proclamation cleared the way for black men's enlistment as soldiers, the sometimes fraught distinction between free black people of longer standing and the recently enslaved was displaced in popular consciousness and policy by the new dominant dichotomy of the blue-uniformed black soldier as an agent of freedom and the contraband as a destitute and desperate dependent.

Prompted by the Emancipation Proclamation, the War Department looked to devise plans for managing formerly enslaved people and their new freedoms. To facilitate this process, the secretary of war established the American Freedmen's Inquiry Commission in March 1863. Tasked with assessing past and current conditions of free people and making recommendations for future policy, the commission collected reams of testimony through lines of questioning that reflected overriding concerns about black people's abilities, the effects of slavery, and the potential for dependency. The commission's final 1864 report called for the creation of a short-term Bureau of Emancipation and urged Congress to "offer the freedmen temporary aid and counsel until they become a little accustomed to their new sphere of life" and to, "above all, guard them against the virtual restoration of slavery in any form, and let them take care of themselves," a clear statement of the commission's animating tensions between calls for intervention and fears of its permanence.[48] In March 1865, after more than a year of pitched debates in the House and Senate, Congress established the Bureau of Refugees, Freedmen, and Abandoned Lands, or the "Freedmen's Bureau."

DC Superintendent of Contrabands Nichols testified twice, first in April shortly after the commission's creation and again in September 1863. Responding to questions about the work habits of contrabands employed by the military, Nichols said that there had been no complaints, that officers had found them to be "very industrious faithful and obedient" and "preferred them to whites." This struck a common theme across the commission's investigation and questionnaires, which sought comparisons between black and poor white laborers, the latter often identified as Irish, as well as between black and "mulatto" people. In this instance, Nichols turned the inquiry to focus on concerns about the Contraband Tax, which he argued kept many able-bodied black men from seeking employment with the military and was unfair in its applications, given, he said, that it was collected "no matter wither the workman were originally free people or not" and without consideration for whether their own families were in a position to "receive the benefits of the fund," foreshadowing the complaints of the Alexandria Depot Commissary workers a few months later. Furthermore, Nichols noted that collection of the full tax occurred even when men could not work enough hours to earn their full wages.[49]

Nichols addressed the state of contraband camps in the capital, dwelling on overcrowding and the especially poor conditions he saw at Camp

Barker, where it was not uncommon, he said, to have twenty-six people living in a ten-by-twelve-foot cabin. When asked, "Do you consider camp life, such as they are obliged to lead, to be demoralizing?" Nichols responded, "most decidedly, the longer they stay here the worse they become; the more vicious their habits, and the less inclined to work." This was not a natural disinclination, he assured the commissioners, but a product of their circumstances in the camps, which seemed as bad to him as, if not worse in their effects than, the contrabands' past enslavement. Nichols concluded that it would be far better to get contrabands out of the city, as they "would be delighted if they could go out and work on a farm under employment."[50]

By the time Nichols responded to questions again in September, he was discouraged. Contrabands were proving unruly and resistant, wasting their money, for instance, on "gaudy dress and good things to eat" rather than finding houses of their own. While they lacked discipline and the willingness or ability to assume the responsibilities of freedom, he averred, the contrabands "have very strong wills many of them, and are hard sometimes to control where food, clothing or wages are concerned." What the formerly enslaved needed, Nichols explained to the commissioners, was systematic "preparatory training" for freedom. "Let these people for example remain on a plantation like one of these Govt. farms under proper training, two or three years and then permit them to go and do for themselves. This is provided they can be placed under good wholesome instruction and proper facilities are afforded for learning the arts of life."[51] This sounds very much like the stated aims for Freedman's Village, which had just been established that summer and which Nichols now oversaw as its civilian superintendent.

Lt. Colonel Greene urged swiftness in his proposal to locate a contraband camp at Arlington, as little time was left to get crops into the ground, and he asked for resources and "control" of all of the healthy people at Camp Barker. He proposed to retain Nichols, "well qualified for the position he holds," as superintendent of contrabands and to add to his responsibilities supervision of a camp and farm on the heights. With final approval from Secretary Stanton, it took Greene only a week to get started. All contrabands in Washington and Alexandria who were not already employed by the Quartermaster division were to report to Nichols, and Greene was authorized to "take possession of all rebel lands, farm houses and tenements thereon, at present abandoned by their owners," south of river and within the lines of "this command"—the Arlington plantation—and "to cultivate said lands by such Contrabands, and in such a manner as may be most beneficial to the Government."[52] From this point, Freedman's Village and its fields would share space, not always easily, with former slaves like the Grays already living and working on the abandoned plantation, encamped troops, a massive Army corral complex, and grazing lands. Julia Wilbur described the scene on an overcast afternoon in June. After visiting the USCT regiment on Mason's Island nearby in the Potomac, designated today the presidential monument Theodore Roosevelt Island, she went "to Arlington House, garden, graves of Custis & wife. Talked with Lee's former Slaves, gathered flowers . . . then to Contraband Camp on flats & had an interesting visit." By nightfall, her thoughts turned to Lee's troop movements: "City very quiet. Rebs in Pa."[53] The battle at Gettysburg began a week later.

Under the authority of the Quartermaster Department and paid for with funds generated by the Contraband Tax, the camp's day-to-day operations were supervised by Nichols and relied on the work and resources of the American Missionary Association and the American Tract Society (ATS).[54] With the camp established for a month and a half and composed of military-issue tents in clusters named after local officials and dignitaries (Springdale, Wadsworth, and Todd among them), the village authorities held a celebration on July 4, punctuated by an address from "trusty servants of Rebel General Lee." An agent for the American Missionary Association, the Reverend J. R. Johnson, writing of his work that summer in Arlington, described his own preaching and that of the contrabands, noting that he liked to attend the meetings conducted by the recently enslaved "in their own earnest way" so that he might "know the better how to talk to them." He described a sermon that he gave in the late morning of July 12, less than two months after the camp's opening and already being home to more than a thousand people. He based the sermon on the Book of Job and encouraged the former slaves to see the war as part of God's plan for their emancipation. "Manifest your gratitude for what God has done for you in delivering you from *slavery,* by the war," he preached, "by using all your powers for improvement. Be industrious, saving, cleanly, &c. Depend not on others to elevate you, elevate yourselves by energetic and well directed action."[55]

With the completion of permanent housing suitable for winter and a new school and hospital, courtesy of the American Tract Society, a formal dedication of Freedman's Village was held in early December.[56] Julia Wilbur was in attendance, along with several high-ranking military officials, "notables," and "elegantly dressed ladies." They were serenaded by a group of formerly enslaved children and addressed by several speakers, whom Wilbur described as "all very good & exactly the thing." Surveying the scene, Wilbur was thrilled by the implications, writing excitedly in her diary, "It was a gay sight within & without. The sight affected my heart, on Va. Soil! On the Chief rebel's estate! Twas glorious!"[57]

In these early days, Freedman's Village seemed "exactly the thing" to many people, including military authorities, federal officials, reformers, and residents, if not always for the same reasons. Some observers looked hopefully to the success of the camp in stimulating among the contrabands the gratitude and self-reliance that Johnson promoted in his sermons, summed up in another witness's description of the dedication in the *New York Observer and Chronicle:* "One of the most interesting events that has recently transpired in this centre of excitement and in this day of momentous events, was the dedication, yesterday, of Freedman's Village. . . . Here on the estate of Gen. Lee, the leader of the rebel armies, the experiment is to be tried, on an extensive scale, whether those who were recently slaves, but by the progress of the war have been brought into the condition of freedmen, are able to care for themselves and their families."[58] Obscuring the former slaves' flights, journeys, and acts of self-liberation that brought them to Freedman's Village in a tangle of passive-voice verb constructions and presumptions of dependency, this observer echoed others who saw the free people as objects to be moved about, trained, and transformed, rather than agents in their own right. Definitions of "care," self-sufficiency, and moral family life quickly came to focus on readiness for wage labor and rejection of government support—the "arts of life," in Nichols's terms.

This image was reproduced as an engraving in *Harper's Weekly*, May 7, 1864, making it one of the most common images of Freedman's Village in circulation, then and now.

Freedman's Village was always meant to be a temporary way station on a path to learning the values of free labor and the obligations attending the condition of freedom. This was outlined in a widely reprinted article that celebrated the first seven months of Freedman's Village by describing what visitors would find: "There will be seen a kind and firm administration of government and industry. They who will not work must go beyond our lines. The village and the farms being designed only for the training of fugitive slaves into skilled and self-supporting laborers, but ten dollars a month are paid to them in addition to their rations and quarters. The inducement of self-interest stimulates to the speedy qualification for outside employment. So room is constantly made for new-comers on the farm and the new ignorant in the school." The article's author goes on to explain that the village taught new ways of understanding not only one's labor and self-interest but also one's very humanity, defined by dominant norms of gender and domesticity: "There will be seen the New England Sabbath, neat homes favorable to the development of the family and the cultivation of the household virtues, the joyous sense of being in a secure refuge from slavery, and the divine stimulus of a realized manhood and womanhood."[59] While this was to be achieved through marriage and patriarchal domesticity, "realized womanhood" for the formerly enslaved always incorporated wage work outside the home. This necessitated alternative definitions of being a good wife, from reformers, military authorities, and eventually, Freedmen's Bureau agents. In *Plain Counsels for Freedmen,* published by the American Tract Society, Clinton Fisk explained, "Eve was made for a 'help meet.' This is the word. A wife must do her very best to help her husband make a living.

She can earn as much money sometimes as he can, and she can save money. . . . Much of the good and happiness of home depends on the good sense, economy, and industry of the wife."[60]

Once out of military-issue tents, Freedman's Villagers lived in identical structures designed to house nuclear family units. Yet while officials spoke of and imagined villagers in these terms, the demographics of Freedman's Village increasingly came to resemble other contraband camps spreading across the occupied South, with its predominantly female, very young, very old, and sick or disabled population. Able-bodied adult men, who had always been valuable to the military as laborers, were now also potential soldiers.[61] Regardless of the actual composition of camps, the patriarchal family remained central to federal policy and popular understandings of freedom and self-possession.

Shortly after the village's official dedication, all of the inhabitants at Camp Barker were ordered to report to Nichols on the Arlington Heights for resettlement on December 21, 1863. This was met with protests from Camp Barker residents. Later reports detailed a disorderly transfer to Freedman's Village and inadequate winter accommodations awaiting the relocated. An agent with the AMA described the newly arrived at Freedman's Village as "truly pitiable," with no one properly clothed, all "filthy," and not enough bedding in the middle of winter, while the captain at the government farm just east of the village described them as being in a "*shamefully wretched* and destitute condition." Another recounted the response of villagers to the newcomers: "inhabitants of the village were unwilling to admit them into their houses or associate with them until they had been furnished with new clothing and placed in the proper condition," a claim that seems intended to signal how bad off Camp Barker residents were but could suggest horrified action on the part of Freedman's Villagers to secure adequate clothing and resources for their comrades.[62] Nichols and Greene both defended the process, adding that the speedy absorption of 132 people necessitated housing them in military-issue tents until more permanent structures could be constructed.[63] Of course, they thought they were going to be moving several hundred more.

The vast majority of those who were living at Camp Barker refused to go to Arlington, their reasons reflected in their own complaints or the testimony of missionaries and teachers in a subsequent Army investigation.

An alternative version of life in the urban camp emerged here, one that was not easy but not as degraded and unhealthy as officials claimed, suggesting that the Quartermaster's real goal had been simply to get contrabands out of Washington. Residents wished to stay in order to maintain old and new family and community ties in the city, while others resisted the idea of moving into a Confederate state and back onto a plantation. Lucy Smith, seventy-six years old and a resident of Camp Barker for two years, testified that she did not want to leave the city where her children were and noted that her brother had discouraged her from moving as well. The assistant to Camp Barker's superintendent explained, "A report or word in some way got into Camp among them that they were going over to be under slave owners or those who had been slave drivers and others were afraid to go where they said they had heard the guerillas came."[64] For some of the Camp Barker residents, the prospect of living once again under the authority of Danforth Nichols was enough to keep them away. Nichols was the subject of numerous complaints and more than one official investigation, and free people described harsh punishments, cruelty, and violence at his hand, purportedly fueled by drunkenness. Lucy Smith said that she never saw Nichols drunk but that he did become enraged and abusive. A former slave from Maryland and longtime Camp Barker resident, thirty-one-year-old Lewis Johnson testified to Nichols's constant inebriation, brutality, and persistent withholding of full rations. "My owner was better than many masters," he explained, "but I speak from my heart before the Lord when I say that the conduct of Mr. Nichols was worse than the general treatment of the slave owners."[65] One New Jersey woman who had come to DC to work with free people in the camps and as a teacher described a stable population of about 700 residents in Camp Barker in November and December before the move. She noted that while an outbreak of smallpox had occurred in November, it was mostly contained by the next month and that housing and bedding were sufficient for the winter, although they struggled to get enough warm clothing from donations. "The large portion of people remained in Washington," she said, despite her and others' encouragement that they go to Freedman's Village: "Most of them refused to go to Arlington because they would be under Nichols. . . . Some replied that they would rather starve in Washington than go to Arlington to be under Nichols who was remembered as the former Superintendent of Camp Barker—They seemed reluctant to give their reasons and appeared to have an instinctive dread of the place."[66]

In fact, most contrabands in the DC and Alexandria areas avoided living in the camps for long or at all. More than 15,000 people moved through or had lived at Camp Barker since it opened in the summer of 1862, but fewer than 700 remained in December 1863. Arlington had just recently been the scene of another coerced relocation to Freedman's Village when an organic community of former slaves was removed from their encampment outside Fort Albany along the backside of the official contraband camp. This was the group's second relocation, as they had originally been living in front of Arlington House, about sixteen families strong at the time. A lieutenant with the First Massachusetts Heavy Artillery had been responsible for finding their new location after his superior officer said their camp "injured the look of the estate."[67] Civilian reformers seemed generally pleased with their self-sufficiency and pluck. Nichols described giving advice on the design of their new shelters and said they were making a "commendable effort to support themselves."[68] The commander at Fort Albany wished them removed and placed under the direct authority of Freedman's Village, however, and the new commander for the Department of Washington, General Christopher C. Augur, agreed. In November 1863, the community, having grown to more than 150 people, was surrounded by troops in the late afternoon and forcibly evicted. Most of the able-bodied men were still away at work, many with the Quartermaster Corral or Engineer Corps. The wife of the First Massachusetts Heavy Artillery chaplain, who had been in the process of securing funds for a school for the community, described to her horror, "the men who were absent at work, came home at night to find empty houses, and their families gone, they knew not where!" She continued, "In tears and indignation they protested against tyranny worse than their past experiences of slavery."[69]

The charge that this arbitrary movement and disrespect for family, community, and individual self-determination was equivalent to or worse than enslavement was a common theme to the protests. Nichols testified that the dispersed residents "said they were as much slaves now & they ever had been; they said they would rather be independent; did not want to be of any expense to the government and desired to live on the produce of their own labor & did not want any superintendent or overseer." This was echoed by Luisa Jane Barker, the chaplain's wife, who said the men of the community "expressed great reluctance to enter the contraband camp, because they felt more independent in supporting themselves, and families, after the manner of white laborers."[70] Framed through the free-labor concerns and vocabularies of Nichols and Barker, the men argued that the military was thwarting both their own aspirations to patriarchal independence and their desires to claim land and build a home free from white authority and surveillance.

Ongoing protests to the Contraband Tax made similar assertions of the military's contradictory limitation of black men's ability to support their families. "I was employed by the United States as a blacksmith about eleven months," explained George W. Simms from Alexandria. "They reduced my wages five dollars or retained it and said they had a right to do it, to every colored man. . . . I left because I could not support myself and family." In November 1863, three black employees of the Quartermaster Department wrote to Secretary of War Stanton protesting the tax, saying that they spoke for one hundred black men working at the Kendall Green and Railroad Parks in Washington, DC. Robert Stanley, James Waters, and John Slocum described working for the department for two years, during which time they had "never yet received wages averaging more than twenty (20) dollars per month from which have been deducted a tax of five (5) dollars per month for the assistance of the numerous contrabands or (freed men women and children) that have been and are now stationed within the limits of the District of Columbia." With the additional reduction of a 1 percent hospital fee, they took home on average the "paltry sum" of $14.85 per month. "In view of the fact that we are a portion of that class of colored men (termed free) and pretending as we do to have some faint conceptions of the value of our labor, regard this as being unequal to the services we render and the demands of the times." Echoing other protests to the collapsing together of all black men, they asked for reprieve from the Contraband Tax. Workers in Alexandria filed a similar petition the following day.[71]

This Kendall Green and Railroad Parks petition prompted questions from Stanton, who did, in fact, approve a raise in the wages of "mechanics, teamsters, and laborers" and sought from Greene his opinion of the tax in general, wondering whether it should be continued at all. Greene's response was not only in support of the tax but became an argument for the demonstrable successes of Freedman's Village, concluding that the two were inseparable. "So much has already been accomplished by the 'Contraband fund,'" he argued. "Our enterprize may be so far considered a decided success, and has attracted considerable attention." Greene elaborated on the types of work and training available to contrabands along with moral instruction in the village, including at the school and church that were run "without expense to the Government or the 'Contraband fund.'" The proof of the tax's wisdom, he urged, was "the praise which all parties accord, to the results accomplished on the Arlington Estate, by the fund thus raised"—praises stemming, he continued, from the fact that neither friend nor enemy could deny the beneficial effects: "The best friends of the black race, are satisfied to find, the physical, & mental, Condition of the Colored people so well cared for; while their antagonists, who have blamed the Government, for supporting the contrabands in idleness; no longer have it in their power, to censure the authorities, for their humanity; as the paupers among the colored people, are supported by a not burdensome tax, upon that portion of them able to labor." Failure to continue collecting the tax and neglecting opportunities to open more camps like Freedman's Village would result, Greene finished, in contrabands once again scattered about the city, "living idly in crowded barracks in the close air," where smallpox and close association with "the worst class of citizens" was common and where they would live "a life of idleness at the public expence."[72]

As a model free-labor experiment close to the capital, Freedman's Village was often visited during the war by congressmen, members of the Lincoln administration, and foreign dignitaries and diplomats, occurrences to which Greene had alluded in his letter. Put on display by policy makers and military officials, the village was designed to make a case for the federal management of black freedom in the transition from slavery. Its successes, measured in educational facilities, moral instruction, and free people's speedy employment and self-sufficiency, were celebrated as those of men like Greene, while unruliness, "idleness," and failures to

Adults and children pose with books in Freedman's Village, ca. 1864–1865.

conform to free-labor expectations were placed squarely at the feet of contrabands and racial predisposition.

Visits to Freedman's Village also quenched the curious thirst that so many people had for looking at, assessing, and being close to former slaves in a controlled environment. For instance, in March 1864, Greene informed Nichols that Speaker of the House Schuyler Colfax, Republican of Indiana and later to become Ulysses S. Grant's vice president, would be arriving any day with "family and friends" to inspect the village. With a tone reflecting Greene's increasing exasperation with Nichols, he ordered, "You will therefore meet him and treat him with courtesy and attention, and give him all the information he desires in regard to the enterprise, its history, prospects, etc." Two months later, a Quartermaster officer escorted the chairman of the House Committee on Freedmen's Affairs to the site. Greene ordered Nichols to "have the school kept in session, and also the women kept at work in the Tailor Shop until after their visit, so that they may see everything in full operation."[73] By the end of the year, the African American newspaper the *Christian Recorder* was celebrating the village's ability to persuade. "Visitors, especially our legislators, have been furnished with indisputable evidence of the intellectual capacity of the colored race. In this respect, it [Freedman's Village] has been, during the respective years of its existence, a living-witness, and thus the means of great good to the whole of this wronged and oppressed people." Elizabeth Keckley effected a kind of literary or imaginative tour of the place and its people in her 1868 slave narrative and account of her relationship with Mary Lincoln, *Behind the Scenes; or, Thirty Years a Slave, and Four Years in the White House*, noting that "whoever visits the Freedmen's Village now in the vicinity of Washington will discover . . . evidence of prosperity and happiness."[74]

While Freedman's Village gained increasing stability in 1864, military authorities expected those who lived there to be mobile and brief in their residency. Central to their project of transforming the formerly enslaved into free laborers was making employment opportunities readily available. For Freedman's Villagers and those on nearby Mason's Island, this could be in DC or as far away as Vermont, with a private family, industry, or local government. Camp officials, the military, and those who looked to hire new workers all understood border-area contraband camps to be essentially state-run labor agencies, which in turn produced a far-flung geography of contraband labor.[75]

With placement coordinated through Greene and the Quartermaster division, Freedman's Village records team with requests, contracts, and travel papers for domestic servants and laborers, locally and throughout the Northeast. The wording of these documents suggests the presumption of possibility and variety on the part of those who were making requests, not unlike slave auctions. For instance, one March 1864 request to Nichols reads, "Mr. Collins wishes to obtain a bright mulatto boy about twelve years old, will you please send one in tomorrow if possible. Mr. Bright also wishes to get a woman about twenty years old to take care of his child, she must be neat and smart," while another from a month later shows that the procurer wished to decide for himself: "The bearer Mr. M. Sallad is desirous of procuring from Freedmens Village a girl from 12 to 13 years of age (black colored preferred) to act as household servant. You will please give him every attention to further his object."[76] Other orders were even more open-ended: "You will allow Mr. Simabaugh to take such a woman as he may select."[77] Freedman's Villagers were also a source for official state and federal requests. In April, Greene sought "two respectable and trustworthy colored servants for the Hon. H. Hall, Gov. of Vermont," and then during the summer sought to put every man over the age of sixteen who was not absolutely necessary to village or farm operations to work cleaning the streets of Washington and surrounding areas.[78] The orders left unclear what, if any, space was available for a free person to refuse his or her selection, employment, and movement.

Not long after the would-be emigrants' harrowing experience on Île à Vache and just a week after their relocation to Freedman's Village, they were offered employment with the Union Pacific Railroad and the state of Massachusetts. In identically worded orders, Mr. Clark Bell and "representatives" for the Union Pacific Railway Company and Massachusetts were given "authority to take from Freedman's Village, Greene Heights, VA as many families of the colored colonists lately secured from the Isle of Vache as may be willing to accompany him to labor . . . [so as] to guarantee that said families will never hereafter be a burden upon the United States Government."[79] These labor agents vied with Army recruiters who sought enlistments among the men, stationing themselves outside the village grounds after Nichols had denied them entrance. Caught in an ongoing dispute between Nichols and authorities at Camp Casey, a USCT facility near the village, a group of new recruits from among the "returned Haytiens" were, by Nichols's own description, "forcibly taken possession of" by his guards and brought back into Freedman's Village. There seemed no end to their displacement and injury. Nichols's confusion as to the returned emigrants' status—Haitian? American? Contraband? Recruit?—and thus his responsibilities toward them persisted. A week later, the superintendent sought clarification. Greene responded, "The returned Haytian colonists are on just the same footing as other Freedmen. If they labor they will be classed with laborers—if not, they will be classed with dependent Freedmen. You will please make a list at once of all the able-bodied single men in camp, who can be spared for service in the Q. Ms Dept. in this city and Alexandria, as I wish to deplete the camp, and have all employed to the most advantage of themselves and the Government."[80]

Officials' desires to deplete the camps around DC and Alexandria via employment and self-support were constant. In the context of competing demands for able-bodied men, the market in contraband labor increasingly focused on hiring and moving women out of the camps. Those who remained faced high rents, regulation, surveillance, and constant pressure to move on. Urging fellow New England Friends to see Washington, DC, and northern Virginia as mission fields among free people, one agent reported that the formerly enslaved suffered greatly and unnecessarily under military authority. The agent repeated the complaint of a woman "much better situated than many others" living in Freedman's Village, who said, "Don't feel as if I was free, 'pears like there's nobody free here."[81] This echoed the sentiments of contrabands living in Alexandria who resisted being relocated to the village at Arlington. Harriet Jacobs and Julia Wilbur were at constant loggerheads with Albert Gladwin on this issue, as with so many things. Wilbur noted, "Not one [contraband from Alexandria] in a hundred is willing to go to Arlington. The restrictions there are such that it is to them very much like going back into slavery."[82] The contrabands' resistance to coercive mobility thus hit several registers, marking a refusal to "go back" or return to something like the slavery they had fled, while resisting the present conditions and coercions of "free labor."

The bureaucratic archive of contraband management at Freedman's Village swells with labor requests, contracts, and travel documents, but it is simultaneously a powerful record of free people's resistance to the management of their lives and labors. In March 1864, a piqued Colonel Greene wrote to Nichols, "You are hereby requested not to give any passes to contrabands to visit this city, to see about their pay, as I am annoyed almost every day by some of them coming to me with the most trivial and groundless complaints; if there are any such to be made, they should come through you, and be submitted to this office in writing, where they will receive proper attention."[83] While some complained to Greene directly, others simply left jobs that were not wanted or turned out to be not as they had been described. One boy's journey from Freedman's Village to domestic work in the capital and back to the camp reads like a map of contraband Washington, showing both his resistance and continued regulation by military authority. Greene's chief clerk sent him back with a letter to Nichols: "The colored boy Daniel Makel whom I send over, says he left Freedmen's Village yesterday afternoon with a gentleman of this city to live with him as a servant, but when they arrived here, the gentleman told him he wished him to go to Pennsylvania to live with his mother—not being willing to go so far from his relatives, the boy left and went to Camp Barker from which he was sent here [Greene's office]."[84] Receiving constant pushback and negotiation from the formerly enslaved people whom authorities sought to mold and move as free laborers, military officials shared their suspicions with one another. "Charity Bonner, who was taken yesterday by Mr. Rickette was returned to him this morning, she stating that she expected to be confined quite soon and was unable to work, if that is really the case she had better not be sent out," explained a man from the Chief Quartermaster's office, sending Bonner back to Freedman's Village. He continued, "but if not [pregnant] she ought to be punished in some way for making that statement, she has been put out to service and returned several times and I thought she might have told this story in order to get back again. I have given her a pass to go over but thought it best to send you this note."[85]

Military authorities and the civilians working for them were not alone in their frustrations with contraband resistance and seeming imperviousness to instruction. Sojourner Truth lived and worked in Freedman's Village in 1864 as an agent with the New York–based National Freedman's Relief Organization. Military leadership believed that as a former slave herself, Truth might be a more effective teacher, that she would be heard in a way that they themselves and white reformers were not. She lectured and spoke with individual free people about moral living, domesticity, skills for wage work, and self-sufficiency. Truth confided to others that her message was not always appreciated. One audience demanded that she leave when she told them that living "off the government" was to live "in disgrace."[86] Writing to the feminist abolitionist Amy Post of her experiences in Freedman's Village from her new position at the Freedmen's Hospital in Washington, Truth explained that the "good" of the village had welcomed her counsel but that she was often rejected by "those who desire nothing higher than the lowest and the vilest of habits." Looking back on this time, Truth was described in the 1875 edition of her *Narrative* as being worried that contrabands would slip inexorably toward dependency and depravity because of their previous enslavement and that "they had never known that freedom meant anything more to them than being no longer obliged to serve a master, and at liberty to lounge around in idleness." Like so many other black reformers during the war, Truth drew sharp distinctions among herself, "good" contrabands, and the "idle" and "filthy," taking on the dominant terms of her day while seeking to dispel the prevailing notion, as represented by the Contraband Tax, that all black people were the same.[87]

In the midst of all of this movement, there was a major shift in authority at Freedman's Village when the civilian Superintendent Nichols was replaced by an officer of the Quartermaster division. As early as January, during Army investigations of Nichols's conduct and the transfer of Camp Barker residents to Arlington, Greene had suggested that problems might be solved, whether or not Nichols was guilty of the charges against him, by getting "citizen employees" out of camp administration and assigning "a commissioned officer to report to [Greene] for duty at Arlington." Such a man would need to be accountable for significant funds, properties, and disbursement, Greene continued, and so should come from the Quartermaster division. Furthermore, he concluded, the officer "should be a earnest sympathizer with the Administration in its emancipation policy."[88] Nichols had become an ongoing concern to the officers at Camp Casey. Around the same time that Nichols detained new recruits from among the people returned from Haiti, an officer for the Twenty-Third Regiment USCT complained that Nichols was an active impediment to recruitment. "What authority has Mr. Nichols to prevent the able-bodied men in Freedmen's Village from entering the service of the U.S. if they freely choose to do so? How far does his control extend beyond the line of sentries?" Nichols, for his part, charged that many recruits were bullied or coerced by soldiers and that he only sought to protect them. The superintendent of contraband in Alexandria made a similar charge, asserting that men and boys were being "kidnapped" by individuals seeking a bounty. It was, Gladwin claimed, "as barefaced and ungodly a trafficking in human beings, as that which has brought this terrible curse of rebellion and war upon us; and while it may be done professedly in the interest of the country, and against rebellion, it is really adding burning coals to the fiery indignation of a justly incensed Jehovah."[89]

Some of these tensions and Greene's concern were put to rest when Special Orders No. 114 assigned Captain John M. Brown, assistant quartermaster, to Freedman's Village and ordered Nichols to transfer to Brown all "public property in his charge."[90] Nichols was not relieved of his role with contrabands altogether, however, but moved to the camp and labor recruitment at Mason's Island. That had been Sojourner Truth's first stop in 1864, where she worked with Nichols before moving to Freedman's Village. Greene was soon to move on himself, promoted to assistant quartermaster general at the rank of brevet brigadier general and assigned to the Department of Ohio and the Cumberland, where he was to oversee the supply chain to Sherman.[91]

Village superintendents drawn from the quartermasters rarely remained in the position for more than a few months and confronted steady resistance from inhabitants. By late summer, a new officer, H. H. Howard, held the post and sought to establish his own authority. He suggested firing some noncontraband employees at the camp and replacing them with current inhabitants, both to save money and to get "off the rolls" free people who might support themselves, thus "gradually reducing the village to a nearer approximation, to a self sustaining establishment." Villagers bristled at the new regime, challenging military regulation, rent collections, and labor contracts. The new superintendent's letters show increasing exasperation, seeking "instructions as to the discharge of dependents from the village, the disposal of quarrelsome and turbulent renters," and whether he could "punish, and in what manner, dependents for insubordination, assault, or indecent or abusive language and conduct toward the civilian employees here." Some, he said, were so incorrigible that they should be banished from the camp. "I only desire authority to be able to remove them all."[92]

All of the promise that white northern observers had seen in Freedman's Village when it first opened was shaken by the following year, when *Harper's Weekly* reported,

> The village is a neat and extensive collection of frame-houses, erected especially for the use of such contrabands as, failing to provide for themselves, become a burden to the Government. The village is surrounded by farm land, which the negroes cultivate for their support. To Colonel Elias M. Greene is due the principal credit of thus assisting the negroes to help themselves. . . . All the smartest and strongest among the released slaves find employment as servants

of different kinds—barbers, teamsters, etc. But there is still a number
who fail to get employment, and thus Colonel Greene has tried to
make self-supporting on the Government lands, and so far with considerable success.[93]

Now presumed to be a burden on the state, Freedman's Village within
only a year was represented as a loafing collection of ineffectual and
ungrateful free people, not strong or smart enough and lacking in the
gumption to survive on their own. Some people suggested that life in
the village was simply too nice and the formerly enslaved who lived there
"too happy" to move on as its planners had originally intended.[94] Greene
had himself worried several months earlier that "so well satisfied are the
colored people with their present condition at Arlington, that they can
hardly be induced to accept service with private families or individuals
in this City and vicinity, and generally endeavor to return to the public
quarters provided for them."[95] Although dismissed by Meigs, an internal
Army investigation that summer called Greene and Freedman's Village
failures, charging "errors in theory: defects in practice" and concluding,
"We fail to see any improvement in the character or conduct of the
Adults. . . . Their erroneous idea that 'emancipation' signifies a claim
upon Government for support in idleness has been confirmed rather
than corrected."[96] Yet, despite increasing discontent, the moral rebuke of
locating a community of former slaves on the confiscated plantation of
Robert E. Lee remained compelling to most people—and became even
more so with the addition of the national cemetery that same summer.

Chapter 3

A NATIONAL CEMETERY

There can be no kindlier spot in which the soldiers of our love
may rest after the march and the battle. There can be no fitter
place in all the world, than the domain of the man who used such
power to destroy her, for the mausoleum of the nation.

—"A Woman in Washington" (1866)

WASHINGTON WAS OVERWHELMED by the injured, ill, and dying
from nearby forts and fronts, as it had been since the First Battle
of Bull Run. This escalated in the early summer of 1864 with Grant's
Virginia campaign. "Boatloads of unfortunate and maimed men are continually arriving," detailed one journalist. "All Washington is a great hospital."[1] In addition to the "boatloads" of white and black Union soldiers
and Confederate prisoners, significant numbers of formerly enslaved civilians continued to seek new futures in the District, facing many of the same
rank conditions and diseases. With the understanding that purchase of
the Arlington Estate by presidential order had given the federal government clear title to the land and the structures on it, Freedman's Village
gained some security, and a path was cleared for more permanent government use, such as a national cemetery. In May 1864, the graves of George
Washington Parke Custis and his wife, Mary, as well as those of many
whom they had enslaved or who had already died at Freedman's Village,
were joined by Union-soldier dead in burials on the grounds of Arlington.

The national cemetery, which today is synonymous with Arlington,
was the last of the plantation's wartime uses and to some people seemed

even its least. It was born of necessity and not a little vengeance on the part of its creator, United States Quartermaster General Montgomery C. Meigs, who sought to destroy the traitor Robert E. Lee by stripping his family of their plantation seat. If Meigs could not have the man's life in payment for the Union blood on his hands, he would take the life the general once knew by seizing his family's beloved Arlington and forever altering it. It was several years before Meigs saw special honor and unique privilege in burial there—before he made Arlington hallowed ground—and it took another war, reconciliationist patriotism, and imperial fervor for the rest of the country to fully acknowledge it as such.

James Parks, younger brother to Perry, the enslaved man Lee took to war as his body man, helped dig the first Union graves in what was soon to become the national cemetery at Arlington. Born into slavery on the very soil he now lifted to bury the war's dead, Parks was witness to and participated in the radical transformation of the Arlington Estate wrought by war, emancipation, Reconstruction, and reunion. Many years later, he described the plantation as it had been in G. W. P. Custis's last days. He recalled for journalists and historians the Lees' departures, how Robert left first to take his command of Virginia's military, and then Mary and the children left to escape Union troops. James Parks was among the enslaved still at Arlington when Union forces occupied the house and its lands overlooking the capital city across the Potomac. He remembered the occupation and the chaos of battered Union troops returning to Washington a month later after First Bull Run. He was put to work for the Army, first in building Forts McPherson and Whipple, part of the District's new defenses, and possibly Freedman's Village, where Parks lived for a time, and then as a grave digger and groundskeeper. Somewhere around twenty years old by May 13, 1864, Parks had seen a great deal.[2]

Private William Christman, Sixty-Seventh Pennsylvania Infantry, on the other hand, had not seen much of the war at all when he died in a Washington hospital and became the first Union soldier buried in Arlington that day. Around the same age as the man who dug his grave, Christman died at twenty-one of peritonitis after contracting measles. He had enlisted in the Army only two months prior in the town of Easton, stating his occupation as "laborer." He never saw combat. Like many who were interred at Arlington after him in the nineteenth century, Christman's was a poor man's burial with no ceremony, no honors, no family in attendance, and far from the Pennsylvania ground of his birth.[3] He was buried at the far northeastern edge of the plantation, distanced from the mansion, whose rooms, gardens, and yard were still home to Union officers and bivouacked troops.

The military cemetery at Arlington was made official on June 15, 1864. Secretary of War Stanton ordered that 200 acres comprising the "Arlington Mansion and the grounds immediately surrounding it are appropriated for a Military Cemetery, the bodies of all soldiers dying in the hospitals of the vicinity of Washington and Alexandria (after the grounds now used at Alexandria are full) will be interred in this cemetery." He charged the quartermaster general with executing the order, stating that it was to be done without "interfering with the grounds occupied by the Freedman's camps."[4] Over time, Freedman's Village would go from being respected as a morally profound use of the land and as part of a mission and obligation to free people meriting protection to being perceived as a hindrance to better use of valuable lands than providing a haven for idleness and black dependency.

Perhaps the clearest indication that the new national cemetery at Arlington held nothing of its later gravitas or power to bestow honor on the dead is the fact that no one considered burying Lincoln there after his assassination. There were many people in the District who thought the martyred president was best memorialized in the national capital, including some who thought he should be interred in the empty tomb beneath the Capitol dome that was originally constructed for George Washington. But no one seemed to feel that Arlington was a fitting place for the final rest of a president.[5] It was another century before an assassinated president was immortalized by eternal flame in front of Arlington House. Other Lincolns found their way to Arlington, however. The president's son Robert Todd Lincoln; Robert's wife, Mary; and their child and namesake grandson, Abraham Lincoln Jr., are all interred there together. The site was chosen by Mary, against her husband's express wish to rest near his father in Illinois. The Lincoln sarcophagus marks the cemetery's dramatic shift in prestige by 1926 and serves as a shadow presence within the cemetery, overwhelmed by the Lincoln Memorial (which can be seen from its east side) across the Potomac. Today, the site of President Lincoln's burial, Oak Ridge Cemetery in Springfield, Illinois, is the second-most-visited cemetery in the United States, after Arlington.[6]

In the aftermath of First Bull Run, the pressing need for an official policy on identifying, recording, and burying the Union battle dead became clear. The War Department directed that the Army's quartermaster assume responsibility for a mortuary system, initially focusing on hospital deaths. General Orders 33, of April 3, 1862, specified that this responsibility extended to the battlefield and outlined the requirements of commanders in the field to gather, record, bury, and mark Union graves "to secure, as far as possible, the decent interment of those who have fallen, or may fall, in battle." The qualification "as far as possible" allowed commanders wide latitude in how they chose to carry out the order, which suggested far more time, systematic action, and careful record keeping than usually occurred in the aftermath of battle.[7] Nevertheless, the federal government now assumed a mortuary responsibility that, combined with an executive mandate to acquire appropriate lands, resulted in the first national cemeteries in U.S. history. Fourteen were established by the end of 1862, including one at Alexandria and Washington, DC's Soldiers' Home National Cemetery.[8]

With the dedication in November 1863 of the battlefield cemetery at Gettysburg, it had become the most revered of all the wartime cemeteries and a model for those that followed. It was not a federal site or part of the official national cemetery system until 1870, however. Conceived and built by Pennsylvania state authorities, the cemetery was shaped by contributions from other states in honor of their own dead, as well as private commercial interests, including members of the board for the adjoining Ever Green Cemetery. Dedicated in 1855, Ever Green was part of the American rural cemetery movement that had begun with Mount Auburn in Cambridge, Massachusetts, in 1831 and had profound effects on the Civil War generation's expectations for their own "good deaths" and the role of mourning and memorialization in civic as well as family life.[9] Lincoln was himself an advocate of the rural cemetery, and his short address at the dedication still resonates. Describing the collection gathered at the battlefield, which only a few months earlier had been the "high water mark" of the Confederacy and northernmost scene of carnage, amounting to 51,000 casualties on both sides, Lincoln said, "We have come to dedicate a portion of that field, as a final resting place for those who here gave their lives that that nation might live." Lincoln made clear the mourners' and memorializers' roles while denoting their limitations: "We can not consecrate—we can not hallow—this ground. The brave men, living and dead, who struggled here, have consecrated it, far above our poor power to add or detract. The world will little note, nor long remember what we say here, but it can never forget what they did here."[10]

By 1864, the cemeteries in DC and Alexandria were near or at capacity, which resulted in the new cemetery at Arlington. Long interested in the fate of Lee's lands on the heights, Washington newspapers eagerly reported their new use in stories that were reprinted nationally. The *Washington Morning Chronicle* editorialized, "The grounds are undulating, handsomely adorned, and in every respect admirably fitted for the sacred purpose to which they have been dedicated. The people of the entire nation will one day, not very far distant, heartily thank the initiators of this movement." The paper continued, erroneous in the facts of the plantation's previous ownership but true to the legacies of George Washington it was intended to carry, "This and the contraband settlement established there are righteous uses of the estate of the rebel General Lee, and will never dishonor the spot made venerable by the occupation of Washington." In a subsequent story titled "Gen. Lee's Lands Appropriately Consecrated," which soon appeared in Chicago and New York papers as well, the *Washington Republican* reported,

Gen. Robert E. Lee, who commands the army of rebels, is fighting to enslave the black man. In view of this fact, a happy thought has occurred to the Secretary of War, which it gives us pleasure to record. *First* he ordered Col. Greene to organize the Freedman's Village, for the protection of the black man and his family, upon the Arlington Estate belonging to the rebel Gen. Lee. That village is a success. *Second* he has himself recently selected a site, upon the same estate for a national cemetery, for the burial of loyal soldiers who die in Virginia from wounds inflicted by Lee's orders!

The partisan paper's suggestion that the earth's consecration came in the combined presence of Freedman's Village and the cemetery held profound implications. It asserted the radical notion that seizure of rebel lands was itself a way to remake them, to turn them into monuments to the end of slavery as well as effecting the punishment of traitors and honoring the loss of those who fought to preserve the Union.[11] The making of a cemetery on Lee's plantation was both a vindictive act and a hallowing of ground that was fundamentally different from Lincoln's description of Gettysburg at the founding of that cemetery the year before. And the presence of Freedman's Village, already a year old and the continued residence of many former Custis-Lee slaves, troubled the equation of Union dead from elsewhere and hallowed earth.

The man who originated the plan to make Arlington a cemetery and who directed its development until his own death and burial there near the end of the century was none other than United States Quartermaster General Montgomery C. Meigs. His vision for the place was quite personal and most certainly punitive. Born in Georgia in 1816, Meigs grew up in Philadelphia, the oldest of ten children. After attending the University of Pennsylvania for a year, he received an appointment to the U.S. Military Academy at West Point. Meigs graduated near the top of his class in 1836 and joined the Corps of Engineers after a brief stint in another Army division. In 1837, he lived and worked with Robert E. Lee on corps projects along the Mississippi River. More than other people, Montgomery Meigs understood how much Arlington meant to Lee and his family. After subsequently serving in several northern posts, in 1852 Meigs was sent to Washington, DC, where he was first assigned to an aqueduct project and then to oversee construction already under way at the Capitol building, the latter assignment made by the new president Franklin Pierce's secretary of war, Jefferson Davis. Meigs's supervision of the Capitol extension included the addition of the new, grand cast-iron dome that visually defines the building today. The change in administrations in 1857 brought years of turmoil to Meigs's work as lead engineer on the Capitol project due to conflicts with the new secretary of war, who briefly pulled Robert E. Lee into their disagreements when he was home to deal

with his late father-in-law's estate.[12] Meigs was eventually removed from
the project and sent to a new post in Florida during the fall of 1860. When
the secretary was replaced, Meigs was vindicated and brought back to
Washington and his old post, in February 1861. By this time, seven
southern states had already seceded from the Union.

Construction on the Capitol continued for a time under Meigs's renewed
supervision, while the nation seemed to move inexorably to war. "Exciting
times, these," he wrote in his journal the night before Lincoln's inauguration. "The country trembles in the throes of death."[13] But in April, Meigs
was dispatched with an expedition to reinforce defenses at Fort Pickens on
an island near Pensacola, Florida; "there was no use in a Capitol unless we
had a country," Secretary of State William H. Seward told him.[14] His own
mission successfully completed without interference from a Confederate
fleet that remained anchored nearby, Meigs did not learn of the attack at
Fort Sumter until almost two weeks after it happened. By the time his ship
returned to New York City on May 1, regiments of newly enlisted troops
were headed south. "Thousands of men are hastening to Washington to
defend the capital against the rebels who threaten to take it," Meigs noted
before deciding there was more information than he could get down in
his journal entry. "History gets too full for me to follow it here."[15]

Meigs was back in Washington himself two days later. Having left the
city at the rank of captain in the Corps of Engineers, he was promised a
promotion and central role in the federal effort. Still waiting, Meigs was
home two weeks later when columns of soldiers marched past his house
on their way to occupy Alexandria and the Arlington Heights. They
moved down the street, he wrote, "with no music, every bayonet glancing
brightly in the moonbeams." Meigs watched them "with sadness" from
his window, he recalled, "to think that they were going to suffer for the
ambition and villainy of these——politicians of the South. How much
does Davis have to answer for?"[16] In June, Lincoln promoted Meigs to
brigadier general and made him quartermaster general of the Union army,
retroactive to May. The new quartermaster held nothing but contempt for
fellow West Point alumni who led the Confederacy and its military, including President Jefferson Davis, General Joseph E. Johnston (who had
resigned the position that Meigs now held to follow Virginia out of the
Union), and Robert E. Lee. Meigs was vocal in his belief that they were

traitors and should be tried and executed as such or at the least stripped of their rights and properties.[17]

Meigs wanted to ensure that Lee would never—could never—reside at Arlington House again. He was furious when he learned that the first burials in May, including Christman's, had not occurred around the mansion as he had directed but out at the far edge of the plantation. He later described that his "plans for the cemetery had been in some degree thwarted" in those earliest days, by "officers stationed at Arlington, some of whom used the mansion and did not like to have the dead buried near them."[18] After this discovery, Meigs personally oversaw the burial of several officers right next to the house along the rose garden border and designated an area abutting the mansion's grounds and running to the west and south for enlisted, white soldiers. This became the place of final rest for thousands, commonly known as the "Field of the Dead."[19] In the exchange of letters that formalized the national cemetery at Arlington, Meigs sought to have his designs made clear, writing to Stanton, "I have visited and inspected the grounds now used as a cemetery upon the Arlington Estate. I recommend that interments in this ground be discontinued, and that the land surrounding the Arlington Mansion, now understood to be the property of the United States, be appropriated as a National Military Cemetery, to be properly enclosed, laid out, and carefully preserved for that purpose, and that the bodies recently interred be removed to the National Cemetery thus to be established. The grounds about the Mansion are admirably adapted to such a use." Stanton echoed this request in the wording of his orders.[20]

Meigs's drive and fury burned hotter when bathed in his immense sorrow at the death of his son, John, who had survived the First Battle of Bull Run, returned to complete his studies at West Point at his father's insistence, and was serving as an aide to General Sheridan in the Shenandoah Valley when he was killed in early October 1864. With family in DC to care for his corpse, there was no suggestion that John Meigs would be buried at Arlington; that was still a place for poor unfortunates far from home and loved ones. After a service attended by Abraham Lincoln and Edwin Stanton, among others, John was buried alongside two younger brothers and an infant sister in the Oak Hill Cemetery in Georgetown.[21] This was not to be their final resting place, however.

U.S. Colored Troops (USCT) continued to be buried at the far northeastern edge of the plantation. They joined other black people who died in Washington-area hospitals, camps, and on the streets and perhaps a few from Freedman's Village, thus initiating the racial segregation of the national cemetery that persisted well into the twentieth century. Separated from the developing "upper cemetery" near the mansion by over half a mile of wooded ground and a stream, the plot seemed a lonely corner and nearly altogether separate cemetery for decades. During the close of the war and Reconstruction, it had its own sexton, whose report forms were printed across the top with "Contraband Cemetery, Arlington, Va.," rather than "Arlington National Cemetery."[22] The practice of interring black soldiers with contrabands at Arlington—of lumping together all black people, no matter their pasts, status, or the circumstances of their deaths—was a source of significant outrage among black veterans and activists, including Frederick Douglass and some members of the Grand Army of the Republic, after the war. The segregation of the site was not total, however, as William Christman and a few other white soldiers among the first burials were never relocated and remain at the front of the section.

The section is designated Section 27 in today's cemetery; the majority of the people buried there in the nineteenth century were civilians, numbering about 3,800, compared to 1,500 USCT. Initially given wooden headboards like most wartime burials, the graves are marked today by stones similar to those in the rest of the national cemetery, though they were added much later. They read "civilian" or "citizen." The people buried there were brought to Arlington in death because they were too poor or alone, and even those whose identities were known and recorded remained unknowns of a sort. This was not true of William H. Johnson, the former valet and barber to Abraham Lincoln. He was believed for years to have been buried in Arlington at Lincoln's instigation. The story of his 1864 death and burial heralded the president's principled decency and attachment to an individual black man, as it simultaneously denoted the power of Arlington as a place. But the true spot of that particular William Johnson burial remains unknown, for the man buried in plot 3346 of Section 27 is almost assuredly not the president's former servant.[23]

William H. Johnson had traveled in Lincoln's employ from Springfield to Washington in 1861. Within days of their arrival at the White House, it must have been clear to both men that Johnson was not accepted by other members of the staff, which included other black as well as white servants. Lincoln wrote to Secretary of the Navy Gideon Welles less than two weeks after his inauguration in hopes of securing a new position for Johnson, noting that Welles's employment of him would "confer a favor" on the new president. He assured Welles that the man had "integrity and faithfulness," adding, "the difference of color between him & the other servants is the only cause of our separation."[24] Lincoln finally succeeded in securing a position for Johnson with the Treasury Department as a messenger at the end of the year.[25]

Johnson was with the president as his body servant on the trip to Gettysburg for the dedication of the cemetery, a trip from which Lincoln returned with a mild but contagious form of smallpox. Johnson, who had cared for the president, died from the disease less than two months later, in January 1864. Although Lincoln denied in the press being the source of contagion, it is probable that he was. He also described paying for Johnson's coffin and burial. The story of Lincoln's actions soon entered the political sphere as a compelling example of his kindness and commitments to black people, appearing in a Republican campaign text during his run for a second term as president. Over the years, it gained greater significance and moral power as part of the canonization of Lincoln as the Great Emancipator. More than a century later, the editor of Lincoln's papers popularized the idea that Lincoln had buried Johnson in Arlington's Section 27, paid for his headstone, and had it inscribed, "citizen." It is, indeed, a profound and utterly affecting story, but it is a near certain impossibility. Johnson died several months before the first burials at Arlington and the plantation's designation as a national cemetery. Furthermore, headstones first replaced wooden headboards in that area in the late 1870s, when "citizen" and "civilian" were added by the Army to demarcate the graves from those of the soldiers in the same section. Yet the story persists, drawing energy from the meanings and national importance attributed to Arlington National Cemetery in the twentieth century.[26]

William H. Johnson joins the legions of Civil War–era casualties whose burial places are lost, in the records as well as in the ground. Despite common popular and official claims that the civilians of Section 27 are from Freedman's Village, their burial ground near the camp, perhaps abutting the Arlington slave cemetery, was apparently never moved as the Freedmen's Bureau had requested.[27] These graves of unknown location join many more of unknown identity buried in Arlington. Most were brought from shallow graves and trenches across Virginia and Maryland in a massive removal and reinterment campaign directed by the Quartermaster Division after the war's end. Taken together—the lost dead and those who were carefully found, and the graves neglected as a federal cemetery and memorials were built and maintained—their final rests provide a window onto the limitations of Reconstruction. As military authorities and civilian officials sought to shape the postwar American future through careful remembrance of some who had died in its battles, their racially blinkered visions were built into the landscape. The slave and Freedman's Village burial grounds that were lost through federal carelessness and long since overridden by the national cemetery provide as stark a reminder of slavery's ongoing centrality to Arlington's development as the cemetery's formal segregation.

In a report from the summer of 1865, Army Captain James M. Moore, assistant quartermaster, described his Washington, DC, office as responsible for the area's "national cemeteries and the burial of deceased soldiers and others in the service of the United States," concluding, "[it] is probably the most important of my specialties." In addition to describing his work in early June on the battlefields of the Wilderness and Spotsylvania Court House, where he supervised the identification, marking, and registration of graves of Union and "rebel" dead, Moore detailed measures taken to improve access, enclosures, and landscaping at the Old Soldiers' Home Cemetery, Harmony Burial Ground, "where," he said, "all soldiers dying of infectious diseases, and contrabands, are interred," and Arlington. Responding to public and veterans' concerns about the fates of the bodies of Union soldiers lost in battle or in hospitals, Moore argued, "the improvement of the national cemeteries has been a source of great gratification to all who visit them, and entirely dissipate the prevailing opinion of those living remote from Washington, that soldiers were irreverently or carelessly buried." He devoted the most attention to improvements at Arlington, concluding, "indeed, the place [is] so transformed as hardly to be recognized by persons who had previously visited it."[28]

Shortly after submitting this report, Moore was dispatched by Meigs to Andersonville, Georgia, and its notorious prison to identify, register, and disinter thousands of bodies from shallow trenches where Union soldiers had been forced to bury their deceased fellow prisoners of war. Those men had been careful to preserve identities on small tablets lining the trenches, and each was reburied in the newly enclosed fifty-acre national cemetery in his own plot with wooden headboards like those used in other military cemeteries. Seemingly staggered by the scene, and with a distinct quartermaster's view of the costs of war, Moore added that the 12,461 markers, including only 451 reading "Unknown United States Soldier," alone required 120,000 feet of pine lumber for their construction. Meigs submitted Moore's report with a note that this work and information "will, doubtless, be appreciated by the relatives and friends of those who have given their lives to their country."[29]

With no mandate from Congress or presidential policy, it was left to the War Department, which meant the quartermasters, to account for Union losses and make their final resting places known to relatives, friends, and the public. After quickly collecting information for all deaths registered during the war, a fraction of total losses, and attending to known sites like the Wilderness and Andersonville, in October 1865 the War Department started its more difficult mission: to locate, identify, disinter, move, and rebury hundreds of thousands of Union dead scattered across farmland, along roadways, and around townships that had only recently been fields of battle. The cemetery at Arlington, which had reduced its labor force in August from 300 to 40 people due to slowed work, became busy again as thousands of Union dead were moved there from lonely sites and mass graves in Maryland and Virginia.[30] Some people worried that the Lees could still claim Arlington and hoped that continued burials would discourage their return. That December, an assistant quartermaster reported that Robert E. Lee's brother Smith Lee had recently visited Arlington and had remarked to the superintendent "that the house could still be made a pleasant residence by fencing off the cemetery and removing the officers buried around the garden." Noting that Meigs had wanted all burials close to the house "so as to more firmly secure the grounds known as the national cemetery to the Government by rendering it undesirable as a future residence or homestead," the assistant quartermaster wrote that with "a thousand interments yet to be made, the views of the Quartermaster General can now be carried out."[31] Many thousands more soon followed.

Others still worried, including members of Congress who raised concerns about the use of the Arlington Estate while debating appropriations for the reburial program. One congressman noted that he "had received numerous letters from friends and relatives of deceased soldiers buried in the cemetery at Arlington Heights" who feared the property would be returned and that "the bones of the soldiers there might revert to the heirs of the arch-traitors."[32] They sought assurance that the government's title to the property was secure, which the secretary of war gave by detailing the purchase of the plantation after the Lees' failure to pay taxes. Newspapers addressed the concerns of readers while chronicling the debate in Washington, with statements like the *Hartford Courant*'s: "There is consequently no danger of the removal of the bodies of soldiers buried in the cemetery there."[33]

Congress approved the program, already under way, six months after it began with a joint resolution authorizing the secretary of war to take measures to "preserve from desecration" the graves of Union soldiers and to "secure suitable burial places" to be enclosed as proper cemeteries, "so that the resting-places of the honored dead may be kept sacred forever."[34] A few months later, *Harper's New Monthly Magazine* ran a long article by James F. Russling titled simply "National Cemeteries," in which the author called for immediate federal action to create a national system to appropriately honor the Union's "fallen heroes, the nation's martyrs, the republic's slain." Noting that the Army had not waited and describing the work already under way, Russling urged, "the nation, with a united voice, should call for these scattered dead of the Union army, whether white or black, to be disinterred from the places where they lie, and brought speedily together into great national cemeteries, where they may repose in peace and dignity beneath the aegis of the Republic while time endures." Of the cemetery at Arlington, the author notably concluded, it does not "approach to the dignity of a national cemetery in either design or execution."[35]

Beyond the honor of the individual dead and the places of their collective burials, Russling saw in a federal system the potential to broadcast the dignity and exceptional modernity of the restored Union to the world. Not only would bringing the dead together in every state where they fell stand as a "monument forever to the South, and to us all, of the crime and folly of Secession," but it would serve as "a standing exhibition to the world of the might and majesty of the Union, the dignity and power of a free republic, the sentiment and culture of a self-governing people." Before Russling ended his article with a verbatim reprinting of Lincoln's Gettysburg Address, he concluded that beyond realizing a responsibility to care for and memorialize the soldier dead, a substantial and centralized national cemetery system would stand as a monument to "let the American Government show" that it was "first of all modern nations."[36] It was not until the following year that Congress passed and President Johnson signed into law on February 22, 1867, an "Act to Establish and Protect National Cemeteries," turning wartime measures into enduring federal commitments.[37]

By this time, much of the work of reburial at Arlington had already been done. The secretary of war's annual report for 1866 stated that remains had been removed from "all points" in Maryland and Virginia within a thirty-five-mile radius of the capital and relocated to the national cemetery at Arlington. Writing to a friend in April that year, Mary Lee said,

Commercial stereograph card from the series "Views in Washington, DC," depicting part of Arlington National Cemetery around 1867. Viewing the card through a stereoscope would give the illusion of one image of graves receding into the distance.

"[I have] passed a quiet and tolerably comfortable winter, but my heart will never know rest or peace while my dear home is used & I am almost maddened daily by the accounts I read in the paper of the number of interments continually placed there."³⁸ The previous December, the oldest of the Lee daughters had gone to Arlington to see the state of things for herself, avoiding Thornton Gray when she saw him, for fear of being identified. "It was a very trying visit," she wrote, "more painful even than I expected." In the rose garden, she reported to her mother, "around the paling were the row of graves of which you have heard."³⁹

The secretary of war's 1866 report noted that the Quartermaster Depot of Washington had created a numbered list of all removals, with a book of accompanying sketched maps that showed where bodies or graves had been found, including central roadways and identifying buildings, features, and local land owners. The list linked the numbered sites on the maps to their new individual graves in Arlington. This was kept in the office of Assistant Quartermaster Moore, now a lieutenant colonel, so friends and family might locate their loved ones and, the War Department hoped, aid in the identification of bodies marked "unknown." The headboards themselves, whitewashed wood with black writing, indicated not only names and companies if known but also the place from which the body had been removed and the date of disinterment—each one a small testament to the work of the Army in recovery and care.⁴⁰

Moore estimated that his office had answered more than 5,000 letters that year seeking information about the burial places of the writers' family and friends or offering identifications in the hopes of reducing by one the number unknown. One such letter remains nestled within the pages of one of the volumes of *Sketches Showing Graves of Union Soldiers Whose Remains Were Exhumed and Removed to National Cemetery at Arlington, Virginia,* now collected with other records of the Office of the Quartermaster General in the National Archives and Records Administration building in Washington, DC. Sent to Moore on September 15, 1866, by Charles Wunderlich, who describes himself as recently a private with the Fourth New York Cavalry, Company H, the letter reads,

> I beg leave to let me inform you partially of the where abouts of
> one of our brave soldiers, of who left his life for our country on the

battlefield. He is buried on the road from Aldie to Middleburgh, Va., about one half mile from Aldie on the right hand side of the road near a beech orchard; on the left of the road is a small oak wood. His name is Alfred Fickel and belonged to Captain Snyder's Co (H) 4th NY Cav. S.V. Maybe the farmer living close to his resting place can instruct your command to his whereabouts. Dear Colonel, if it should be in your possible power to inform me of his permanent resting place after removal. You allways will have my most gratefullest thanks.

The letter is tucked next to a sketched map showing a lone grave, number 1799, in the middle of a triangle of land about a mile wide at the base, bordered by two roads, all labeled "Sketch showing grave on land of Wm. F. Adams near Aldie, Va." On the back of the letter are the initials "B.B." and "October 7, 1866," perhaps noting the date of either receipt or response. Across the front top of the letter is penciled a series of numbers denoting the body's original location, disinterment date, and new grave number in Arlington: "1799-95-7-2-E W, F Adams July 24/66." Whether slid into the pages by an archivist many years later or by "B.B." in October 1866, the map and letter together provide an intimate record of one living Union veteran's expectation of his military, government, and nation and a moment of transmutation, when a Civil War unknown was identified as the letter writer's friend and comrade Alfred Fickel, Fourth New York Cavalry.[41]

When the Federal Reburial Program concluded in 1871, more than 300,000 Union soldiers, sailors, and officers had been located and reinterred in seventy-three different national cemeteries at a cost of about $4 million. Of this number, 30,000 were members of the U.S. Colored Troops.[42] In a sign of the many ways in which emancipation only marked the beginning of black freedom struggles during the war, they were all buried in racially demarcated and segregated sections of the new national cemeteries. It was this relocation of thousands of bodies to Arlington in what came to be known as the "Field of the Dead" or, if they were black, in a distant segregated plot called the "Lower Cemetery" that began to shift the meaning of the landscape for the military. It was this program, and the marshaling of federal resources it represented, that began the process of making hallowed ground.

In the war's immediate aftermath, Arlington was a local cemetery born of military exigency and a potter's field from which many people sought to remove their loved ones closer to home. In describing the work of Moore's DC office, the secretary of war's annual report for 1866 had also noted that about 4,000 permits had been issued for the removal of bodies from national cemeteries near the city. In 1868, one woman describing a visit to the "Field of the Dead" stretching behind Arlington House wrote that one often found on the back of headboards "a statement that friends have 'removed the body' elsewhere. For, if money, patience, or effort possibly can restore the beloved dead to the family burying ground where friends can visit his grave and keep it green and flower-strewn, it will be done!"[43]

Those who could never be identified, remaining forever unknown, were perhaps most emblematic of collective loss and honor, prefiguring the place and effect of the Tomb of the Unknown Soldier, established in Arlington more than fifty years later. A significant portion of all the bodies moved and reburied under the federal program, 42 percent, were not identified. It is a staggering figure, to be sure, but not as large as might have been expected given the carnage, field burials, and the absence of formal identification measures. The identification of 58 percent of the dead was testament not only to the work of the Quartermaster Division but to measures of self-identification taken by individual soldiers and the efforts of surviving comrades to ensure that the fallen would not be forever lost. In a poem dedicated to the counting and accounting for the Civil War dead, Walt Whitman lamented, "And everywhere among these countless graves—everywhere in the many soldier Cemeteries of the Nation, (there are now, I believe, over seventy of them) . . . we see, and ages yet may see, on monuments and gravestones, singly or in masses, to thousands or tens of thousands, the significant word Unknown."[44]

In addition to thousands of individual headboards so marked, in 1866, Montgomery Meigs ordered the construction of a collective tomb for unknowns in the cemetery at Arlington, next to one of Mary Lee's flower gardens near the main house. Prompted by the state of the remains, described in the secretary of war's annual report as "such scattered bones and disorganized remains . . . as could not be identified for separate burial," the monument soon became a central memorial feature of the cemetery and its ceremonies.[45] Its large altar tomb, originally embellished with four Rodman guns mounted to point out from each corner and a central pyramid of round shot, sits atop a vault containing the partial and comingled skeletal remains of a reported 2,111 soldiers found at Bull Run and on land abutting the tracks of the Orange and Alexandria Railroad. With the vast majority coming from Bull Run, it was perhaps made all the more fitting by the fact that it had been losses at the first battle there that had originally prompted the assumption of a Union mortuary responsibility.[46]

The monument was initially designed to have a flat stone covering flush with the ground, but Meigs changed the plan after the vault was filled, requesting that an architect draft an altar tomb "of plain but good classic severe design" to carry an inscription authored by him.[47] Unlike Lincoln's address at Gettysburg, the inscription dwells on the importance of record keeping and the acts of the grateful in consecrating that ground: "Beneath

This circa-1900 photograph of the Tomb of the Civil War Unknowns was taken after the decorative elements were removed from the monument and placed around it. In the background, the Arlington House yard and the edge of the Gray family's quarters can be seen in the far left, while the Temple of Fame is to the right.

this stone repose the bones of two thousand one hundred and eleven unknown soldiers, gathered after the war from the fields of Bull Run and
the route to the Rappahannock. Their remains could not be identified,
but their names and deaths are recorded in the archives of their country,
and its grateful citizens honor them as of their noble army of martyrs.
May they rest in peace." The actions of the dead, no longer located where
they fell, are abstracted as general sacrifice, while the work of the living—
recording, archiving, gathering, thanking, and honoring—is carefully
denoted and itself memorialized. Within Lincoln's calculus of hallowed
ground, then, it is Meigs and his quartermasters "who struggled here"
and so "have consecrated it." The inscription dates the monument at September 1866 for the month and year of the sealing of the vault. Work did
not begin on the tomb until November.[48]

If the monument was intended to stabilize the remains by bringing
them together, their collection and known disorganization prompted
anger and significant anxiety among the wider public. Of chief concern
was whether the vault contained the bones of both Union and Confederate soldiers. As the work of removal and relocation in Virginia was
begun, the *New York Times* reprinted an article from the *Washington Star*
expressing fears that separating remains from their original context might
make their status impossible to discern: "in removing them it will be hard
to distinguish 'Union' from 'rebel' bodies." Even identifying scraps of uniform, buttons, or buckles could be deceiving, the article's author concluded, because "clothing affords an uncertain index of the politics of the
wearer, as necessity often compelled the Confederate soldier to don the
Federal blue."[49] The fact that the vault contained a jumble of parts compounded these fears and revulsion. Mostly intact unidentifiable remains
received individual burials, which was still far from the "good death" of
a well-tended grave visited by loving mourners but at least afforded some
eternal individuation. Writing of the vault before it was sealed, the *National Intelligencer* described its contents:

> A more terrible spectacle can hardly be conceived than is to be seen
> within a dozen rods of the Arlington mansion. . . . Down into this
> gloomy receptacle are cast the bones of such soldiers as perished on
> the field and were either not buried at all or were so covered up as to

> have their bones mingle indiscriminately together. At the time we
> looked into this gloomy cavern, a literal Golgotha, there were piled
> together skulls in one division, legs in another, arms in another,
> and ribs in another, what were estimated as the bones of two thousand
> human beings. They were dropping fragmentary skeletons into this
> receptacle almost daily.[50]

The horror of the scene beneath the "good classic severe" tomb stuck with
people, as evidenced by a reference in a fictionalized travel serial published in *Godey's Lady's Book* in 1873. Describing a visit to Arlington, the
central character declares, "There's a great moniment by the garden with
the bones o' more'n a thousand soldiers under it. They was gathered up
by pieces on the battle fields and brought here—an' then throwed all together in one great pit. For nobody could tell anything about the poor
bones—they was scattered helter-skelter, in all directions. Oh, what a terrible thing war is!"[51] By this time, many *Godey's* readers around the
country would have been well familiar with the cemetery's monument to
unknown Civil War soldiers.

These descriptions call to mind the photograph of a stretcher piled
with skulls, bones, moldering scraps of uniform, and one awful booted
foot, titled "A Burial Party, Cold Harbor, Virginia," from *Gardner's Photographic Sketch Book of the War*, published in two volumes in 1865
and 1866. The party referenced in the title refers to the five living black
men in the picture, four spread across the background in various acts of
digging and handling remains and one in the foreground, sitting right
behind the raised stretcher, his own booted foot visible beneath the
handles. Positioned to be just higher than the descending row of skulls,
the man both joins the line and sits apart from it—his intact, vital body
and his dark skin a stark contrast to the bleached skeletal remains. The
large skull beside the man, resting close at the height of his shoulder, has
been faced to the camera and appears to gaze at the viewer just as the man
does. While the accompanying text in Gardner's original publication explained, "This sad scene represents the soldiers in the act of collecting
the remains of their comrades, killed at the battles of Gaines' Mill and
Cold Harbor," over time the popular image was lifted from its context,
including the identification of the living men as fellow Union soldiers.[52]
Indeed, this was already in effect by late 1866. Original copies of Gardner's *Sketch Book* were in very limited circulation then, but some of the

images were translated as woodcuts or illustrations for publication in *Harper's Weekly*, including in November of that year "A Burial Party." Identified as a representation of a Gardner photograph but without his title, the new caption reads, "Collecting the Remains of Union Soldiers for Re-interment in National Cemeteries."[53] Transforming the image into an illustration of the entire federal reburial program, the caption introduces more distance between the dead Union soldiers and the black men collecting them.

It is notably impossible to identify the race of the soldier dead in either image. Like most bones, the remains are white. At once a potential commentary on death's equalizing or leveling qualities and the fundamental humanity of all people, this skeletal unknowability was underscored by the inclusion of black figures. In the context of stated concerns about the possibility of the comingling of Union and Confederate remains, it raised the obvious possibility that the promiscuous jumble of bones was racially mixed as well. This flew in the face of the enormous care that was taken in every other aspect of the reburial program to maintain racial segregation, a commitment so deeply ingrained that it was maintained in the

"Collecting the Remains of Union Soldiers for Re-interment in National Cemeteries," *Harper's Weekly*, November 24, 1866.

battlefield burials detailed in the quartermaster's records of the sites from which bodies were exhumed for removal to Arlington.[54] Like other U.S. Colored Troops, individual unknowns who could be identified as such were buried with a headboard reading "unknown" in the segregated section of the cemetery.[55]

In the pitched political struggles of the postwar moment, many Republicans looked to the national cemetery on the heights above the capital as the strongest argument for Radical Reconstruction, waving the bloody shirt before its endless ordered rows of white headboards atop Union graves. In an article published in the *Monthly Religious Magazine* the month of Andrew Johnson's impeachment, the Reverend John C. Kimball urged his readers to visit "the great cemetery of our soldiers, overlooking the city from Arlington Heights . . . not directly a part of Washington, but intimately connected to it." He described the many graves and the great vault of unknowns, calling to the living to uphold the just cause for which they died: "It is fitting to have them buried here in the soil they redeemed from its curse, and so near the great capital they died to save. Though dead, they yet speak. They pour a mighty purifying influence ever and ever over the broad river into the living city's heart. They rise up between the President and the rebel horde, to whom he would give again the rod of power. They admonish our legislators to be true and faithful to the great principles for which their bones are bleaching there." The government's living heart might beat in its democratic institutions, in the breasts of politicians, but its moral conscience was in the redeemed plantation soil of the national cemetery at Arlington. And should a legislator be moved to hinder Reconstruction, "let him go to Arlington Heights, and stand amid those acres of Federal graves,—let him listen to the pleading of their twenty thousand silent tongues to be firm and true."[56]

Three months later, in May 1868, Arlington was the scene of Washington's most elaborate ceremonies for the new national holiday, Decoration Day. Scrubbed of its origins as a ceremony first conducted by formerly enslaved South Carolinians and their northern white allies in 1865, the official northern holiday organized by the Grand Army of the Republic (GAR) called for the ceremonial decoration of all Union graves. Founded in 1866, the GAR quickly became the largest national organization of Union veterans in the United States and enormously influential in American politics and the Republican Party. Mirroring military organization in ranked leadership and "camps," the GAR was committed to the voluntary association of officers and enlisted, commemoration, and securing veterans' benefits.[57] While Kimball's moral appeal, "though dead, they yet speak," resonated, Decoration Day was largely a platform for the speeches and rituals of the living. With ceremonies crafted for people to revere the fallen and to share in collective grief and mourning, the holiday also provided a stage for political contests and controversy and for defining who and what was appropriate to honor.[58]

On that first holiday in 1868, James A. Garfield, a Union general in the war and congressman from Ohio who later became the president of the United States, addressed an enormous crowd of elected officials, dignitaries, veterans, and members of the public, young and old, from the portico of Arlington House. He spoke of the virtue and patriotism of "this silent assembly of the dead" who "for love of country . . . accepted death," while asserting the inadequacy of any words to really express their righteousness or the sorrow of the living. Garfield then pointedly marked the plantation history and Lee's previous residence in the place where the crowds of the dead and living now gathered. "This soil beneath our feet," he reminded, "was watered by the tears of slaves" and was now "sacred" to the capital. After Garfield concluded his address, the multitude followed a procession of children from the Soldiers' and Sailors' Orphan Asylum to the Tomb of the Civil War Unknowns. There the children sang a mournful song and a military band played, while others decorated the tomb with flowers and garlands. The *New York Herald* pronounced this combined scene "the most impressive feature" of the ceremony.[59] The *Boston Daily Journal* called it "most solemn and impressive" and found it "picturesque and full of poetical significance."[60]

This sentiment was echoed by *Harper's Weekly*, which illustrated its account with a pair of images labeled "Decorating the Soldiers' Graves—Ceremonies at Arlington, Virginia." One sketch depicts three women and two children affixing floral garlands to the "Unknown Soldiers' Monument at Arlington," while a man holding a bunch of flowers and a woman with a basket on her arm look on. All are dressed in formal attire, and the

UNKNOWN SOLDIERS' MONUMENT AT ARLINGTON.   ORPHAN CHILDREN STREWING FLOWERS ON THE GRAVES AT ARLINGTON.
DECORATING THE SOLDIERS' GRAVES—CEREMONIES AT ARLINGTON, VIRGINIA.—[SKETCHED BY C. M. THOMAS.]

"Decorating the Soldiers' Graves—Ceremonies at Arlington, Virginia," *Harper's Weekly*, June 20, 1868.

tomb itself is draped in American flags. The women and children at work in the foreground are clearly white, while the pair watching the decoration are cast in shadow, making it difficult to ascertain their race. The image highlights the differences between official, military-directed memorialization, on the one hand, and civilian mourning rituals, on the other. These were both highly gendered and usually complementary but also carried potential conflicts. In this case, the presence of women and children draping garlands on the large tomb that is already decorated with seven American flags and scattering flowers at its base casts them as grateful and grieving dependents, honoring the absent hero, valorous manhood, and the victorious nation that are all joined together in the monument's representation. This is reinforced by a neighboring image depicting "orphan children strewing flowers in the graves at Arlington." All of the figures except for one, his back turned to the viewer, are white girls.[61]

Decoration Day enabled the transformation of Arlington's Tomb of Civil War Unknowns from a localized repository of unsettled remains removed from specific locations in Virginia to a monument honoring the sacrifices and valor of all Union soldiers and the nation they fought for. The ritualization of the site facilitated these national attachments for the individuals who participated or witnessed them in person but also for the many thousands more who read about the Arlington ceremonies in their local papers or saw images like the ones in *Harper's Weekly*. This nationalization of the Tomb of Civil War Unknowns as a special and especially meaningful site of collective mourning and patriotism promoted the early individuation of Arlington from other national cemeteries. While the experiences of the monument and ritual and their physical location were not the same for the reader and the participant in situ, they had similar outcomes that were fundamentally defined by the space of Arlington and its uses.[62]

Despite the fanciful depiction of Arlington, an image appearing in *Harper's Weekly* the following year, "Soldiers' Cemetery at Arlington Heights, Virginia," further illustrates this early process. It offered readers a composition impossible to experience in the cemetery itself that includes many of the site's distinctive memorial features and frames its relationship to Washington, DC. At its center sits the tomb, in a near direct line with the Capitol building on the vista across the Potomac. To the left stands Arlington House in relative proximity to its actual relationship with the Civil War Unknowns Monument but shrunken by comparison. Across the entire foreground of the sketch, stretching beyond the frame of the image, are row upon row of identical graves that do not correspond to the actual layout of the cemetery. Notably, the two slave

"Soldiers' Cemetery at Arlington Heights, Virginia," *Harper's Weekly*, March 27, 1869.

cabins behind the house, and thus any reference to slavery, are missing altogether.[63]

From the beginning, Decoration Day's theater of patriotism and national belonging through public mourning of the military dead enabled distinct visions of various groups' attachments to this ideal. This was made stark in explicit prohibitions against the decoration of Confederate graves as well as the official neglect of the U.S. Colored Troops interred in the far-away "Lower Cemetery." Julia Wilbur, writing in her diary of that first Decoration Day in Arlington, described both of these aspects in a connected way. She had spent that morning at church and then working with a group of other women to create floral "crosses, wreaths & bouquets" for use at the cemetery later. When Wilbur headed home to await her ride out to Arlington Heights, she brought one of the bouquets with her to later decorate "if opportunity offered some *colored soldier's grave.*" The afternoon's ceremonies and somber spectacle of decorating the graves in the "Field of the Dead" moved her with "the solemnity & beauty of the scene," and Wilbur pronounced it in her diary to be "unlike any thing [she] ever witnessed before. Many a tear fell on those graves."[64]

But the official program had not presented Wilbur with the opportunity to place her flowers at the grave of a black Union soldier, and she noted that the crowd itself was largely white. "The colored soldiers are not buried in this part of the estate, but in the N.E. part," she recorded, along with "some white soldiers graves & the graves of the Contrabands who died & were buried at Gov. Ex. during the war." While noting that "the programme did not seem to apply to this portion of the Cemetery," Wilbur added that she "understood that a few persons white & colored" had taken flowers and offered a prayer there, and she herself "was not satisfied to leave without going there." In a sign of the distance between the main cemetery and the segregated portion down the hill, Wilbur remarked that she and her companions drove rather than walked to the graves. When she got to the other part of the cemetery, Wilbur discovered that the grounds had not been prepared, despite the thousands who were expected to attend and did, in fact, participate in Decoration Day at Arlington. It seemed as if the area had not been tended in a while: "the grass had not been cut, & it is very tall." A small section of soldiers' graves was made visible by the flags and flowers left by visitors before her, so Wilbur deposited her bouquet there "on the grave of an 'Unknown' & a few others" near it. "It seems a pity that a part of the Cem. must be detached from the rest," Wilbur concluded, adding, "In the principal cem.y there are 600 rebel graves. No flowers were allowed on them to day, although a few persons attempted it."[65]

Ultimately, the Army's refusal to allow anyone to decorate the Confederates' graves was small consolation in light of the racial segregation of the cemetery. Julia Wilbur was not the first or the last person appalled and motivated to action by this juxtaposition of black Union soldiers interred down the hill among the contrabands, while graves of the traitorous remained peppered among the honorable in the all-white main cemetery. While she understood the African American civilians constituting the majority of those graves to be contrabands, buried, she noted, at government expense, interments continued there well after the war and had been regular in the weeks surrounding her visit in May 1866. An assistant quartermaster noted in his accounting of a cemetery inspection a year later that burials in what he called "the contraband ground" were averaging three a day by the spring of 1867.[66] Nearly two years after the ratification of the Thirteenth Amendment, none of these black men, women, and children could actually fall within the category of contraband, but the ground they were buried in and its history continued to mark them as such.

While free people brought to Arlington in death were made something less than free in the "contraband ground" of the segregated cemetery, residents of the former contraband camp, Freedman's Village, continued to build their lives and communities in freedom on that ground. This included daily negotiations and conflicts with reformers, camp superintendents, Freedmen's Bureau officials, and various military authorities. The Arlington village had joined other contraband camps as the purview of the new Bureau of Refugees, Freedmen, and Abandoned Lands in March 1865. While there was general continuity in the daily life of the camp, this transfer of immediate authority brought heightened expectations for residents to demonstrate their self-sufficiency, free labor responsibility, and respectability—to show they were not dependent idlers.[67]

Records and correspondence relating to the management of Freedman's Village show the balancing of food, medicine, clothing, fuel, materials, and wages expended by the Freedmen's Bureau against the rents and labor gained from residents or work papers recorded. In 1866, officials constantly surveyed the community to distinguish the "able-bodied" from those who could not work and looked to expel the men and women whom they believed capable of labor but who were unemployed, along with other residents they deemed unruly. At the same time, a number of formerly paid jobs within the camp were newly categorized as unpaid chores that remaining residents should simply assume. One list from this period of able-bodied individuals and families to "be compelled" to leave the village in accordance with Freedmen's Bureau instructions included more than 200 entries.[68]

The Freedmen's Bureau's activities and particular surveillance of its showplace camp on the heights above the capital were motivated by wider struggles over the character of Reconstruction that were then raging in Congress. This included a fight for the Freedmen's Bureau's very existence, as Democrats railed against providing relief for black people and using white men's taxes to pay for it. A campaign poster for that year's Pennsylvania gubernatorial race blasted, "The Freedman's Bureau! An Agency to Keep the Negro in Idleness at the Expense of the White Man." Filled with specious accounting of tax dollars so used, the poster is dominated by a caricatured black male figure resting on his back beside scenes of white men laboring. The reclining man dreams of handouts from Congress, including good food, access to white women, and alcohol, and states in dialect, "Whar is de use for me to work as long as dey make dese appropriations."[69] A presumed exposé published the following year, *The Sights and Secrets of the National Capital* (1869), used Freedman's Village to make the same argument in slightly different terms. Describing inhabitants as vicious and unruly, the author, John B. Ellis, said the Freedmen's Bureau had "hard work to keep the negroes in subjection, and to enforce their orders" there. "Yet the establishment has done little for the permanent good of the black man," Ellis argued. "It has but encouraged his habits of idleness and dependence, and it would seem far better to abandon it as soon as possible, and thus relieve the country of the heavy load of taxation which its support renders necessary."[70] Erased from this picture of unearned benefits and federally encouraged black dependency was the Contraband Tax and rent collections that built and continued to sustain Freedman's Village.

While Freedmen's Bureau leadership and agents in the field were themselves motivated by concerns about black dependency and degeneration in freedom, they were determined to prove the lie to these images and estimations of black capacities for freedom. They argued for the government's ability to steward the recently emancipated and its fundamental obligations to do so. At Arlington, these efforts and investigations highlighted the many ways Freedman's Village and the national cemetery overlapped, other than sharing the acreage of the former plantation. Shortly after receiving instructions to begin evictions, the superintendent of Freedman's Village requested that two men and their families identified for expulsion be allowed to stay, "they being employed at the Arlington Cemetery." They were struck from the list, as Bureau Assistant Commissioner General C. H. Howard ruled that "freedpeople remuneratively employed in the Village or near it may be allowed to remain in the tenements."[71]

Throughout this time, Freedman's Village remained an ongoing draw for Washington elites and politicians, visitors from abroad, and the generally curious, as well as reformers and activists. In late December 1866, a multidenominational Protestant group in DC issued an "Appeal in Behalf of the Freedmen at Arlington Heights" to other congregations in the capital, Baltimore, Philadelphia, New York, and Boston, seeking assistance for "nearly one thousand freedmen . . . at Arlington Heights within sight of the capital of our nation" and in need of "the charities of the Christian public." A New Year's festival at Freedman's Village on January 5, organized to facilitate this giving, was marked by controversy due to increases in the number of evictions during the particularly cold winter. Organized by a minister and fellow Freedman's Village resident, public meetings of protest were held by members of the community, who also petitioned General C. H. Howard directly. Their letters questioned the fairness and abilities of village managers and sought more authority for the residents in community governance. Making counterclaims about the uses and abuses of black men's taxes, some argued that wartime Contraband Tax collections should be understood to have already covered their rents. Another claimed the government had an obligation to support the "poor women which husband & Son both have been Shot on battle field dead for our liberty."[72] The controversy prompted an investigation within the Bureau and reconsideration of some evictions, but little changed in terms of management, work expectations, or rent collections. And the leader of the protests was himself soon evicted.

The Freedmen's Bureau and village superintendent seemed ever more determined to drain the community of many of its inhabitants. At the January festival, General Howard spoke to these issues publicly and to the village residents directly. He celebrated them as "fellow-citizens," describing the power and thrill of it, as well as his own spare ability to capture in words what he knew it meant and how it must feel to the formerly enslaved. Then he turned to the responsibilities that came with the "full rights of manhood." Howard acknowledged obligations to care for the old, disabled, and sick. "It is right and fitting that they should receive their support now, and the Government has made some provision for such at this village," but he argued that citizenship meant that the rest must leave. "This rule seemed harsh to some of you," he said in a direct reference to recent protests, but it "was done that you might, by going elsewhere, be put upon a footing of real independence and prosperity."[73]

In 1868, the Bureau planned to close Freedman's Village entirely, but residents' requests for time to prepare opened the space and time for a new plan to emerge, one that meant less surveillance and greater self-determination for those who remained. A number of very old, sick, or disabled residents were moved to Freedman's Hospital in DC, while the rest were given the option to purchase their houses and rent plots of land for agriculture. Village residents rented about 600 acres surrounding the community. They continued to raise families and build churches and associations and for a while became an influential block of black voters in local politics. Many, including James Parks, rented land there while continuing to work in the cemetery, as did others who were formerly enslaved by the Custises and Lees. For much of this time, Parks worked as a gravedigger and groundskeeper alongside Selina Gray's brother Wesley Norris. This version of Freedman's Village was much larger in terms of acreage than was previously conceived and persisted on the heights above the capital long after the Freedmen's Bureau was closed in 1872.[74]

✯ ✯ ✯

The prominence of Decoration Day as a national holiday continued to grow, as did Arlington's role as a preeminent site for the ceremonies. The events of 1871 brought to a head many of the concerns that Julia Wilbur had raised about the neglect of black Union soldiers and the cemetery's segregation three years earlier. May 30 fell on a Tuesday that year. As usual, Arlington National Cemetery was the scene of one of the North's grandest official ceremonies of the day. A number of newspapers noted that the observance was marked by the closure of government offices and most businesses in DC, indicating the continued novelty and significance of the national holiday. The grandstand erected in front of the Custis-Lee mansion's portico looked out across the Potomac to the city and groaned beneath the weight of flags and bunting. President Ulysses S. Grant and several members of his cabinet were among the many dignitaries, elected officials, and citizens in attendance to honor the Union dead in speech and song and to place evergreen wreaths on the graves and strew flower petals. Describing the scene, the *Boston Journal* noted that Decoration Day fell almost ten years to the day from the night Lee's plantation was first occupied by federal troops. With Robert E. Lee's death in 1870, Mary and their children had redoubled efforts to regain Arlington House, focusing on the mansion rather than the land. They were joined by Senator Thomas Clay McCreery, Democrat of Kentucky, who made a much-derided attempt to introduce legislation to remove the cemetery and its many thousands of graves altogether and to restore the entire plantation to General Lee's widow.[75]

After the opening exercises, the crowd moved toward the garden to surround the Tomb of the Civil War Unknowns and to hear an address by Frederick Douglass, who was present at the invitation of the GAR post responsible for the day's events.[76] He urged the gathered mourners to resist appeals to the equal bravery and honor of Union and Confederate troops, a theme Douglass would broadcast ever more urgently as the Lost Cause gained purchase on national perceptions of the war and its aftermath. "Dark and sad will be the hour to this nation when it forgets to pay grateful homage to its greatest benefactors," he argued, continuing, "The offering we bring to-day is due alike to the patriot soldiers dead, and to their noble comrades who still live; for, whether living or dead—whether in time or in eternity—the loyal soldiers who perilled all for country and freedom, are one and inseparable."⁷⁷ Reprinting his speech in its entirety, the *Boston Journal* reported, "Mr. Douglass was listened to with marked attention and never have nobler or more patriotic sentiments been uttered on the sacred soil of the Old Dominion." The paper also noted, with not a little obvious glee, that "secesh sympathizers" who arrived to attempt to decorate Confederate graves in Arlington were prevented from making any "demonstrations in honor of the disloyal enemies of the dead soldiers of the Union."⁷⁸

Surely some people in the audience knew—as did Douglass himself— that this "dark and sad" hour was already upon them. After the ceremony's conclusion, a group walked down the hill to find the graves of U.S. Colored Troops in their distant, segregated area without adornment or formal recognition.⁷⁹ After an impromptu decoration with materials demanded from GAR organizers, a delegation that included Douglass was appointed on the spot to confront the secretary of war about the location of the USCT graves and seek their relocation among the rest of the Union dead up the hill. Douglass's own paper, the *New National Era,* had reported similar neglect the year before with "astonishment, grief, and indignation," remarking, "It is true that the bodies of both the white and colored soldiers are within the limits of the same cemetery, but separated by the distance of a mile, in an undesirable portion of the grounds; while with strange inconsistency, rebel soldiers" are buried among white Union dead. "We demand as an act of justice, that during the coming year an exchange be made, that the Confederate soldier have his place by the paupers of the State, among whom the colored soldiers now sleep, and the Union dead be placed side by side."⁸⁰ There were Confederate dead among the black civilian graves, too, which prompted more outrage and very different outcomes at century's end.

Beyond the segregation of the grounds and persistent official neglect, the affront to the USCT dead was compounded by proximity to black civilians whose burials reflected their dependence on the state, in contrast to the soldiers' roles as agents of freedom and protectors of the Union. It brought to mind a line from an earlier Douglass speech, his famous 1863 recruitment call, "Men of Color, To Arms." Then he urged black men, "fly to arms, and smite with death the power that would bury the government and your liberty in the same hopeless grave."[81] Now Douglass's derisive "paupers of the State" bore some discomfiting resonance with public perceptions of Freedman's Village failures. Black soldiers in an Alexandria hospital had made similar distinctions during the war when they protested the use of the contraband cemetery for USCT burials, demanding that the black military dead be moved to Alexandria's national cemetery. "We are not contrabands but soldiers of the U.S. Army," they argued. "As American citizens, we have a right to fight for the protection of her flag, that right is granted, and we are now sharing equally the dangers and hardships in this mighty contest and should share the same privileges and rights of burial in every way with our fellow soldiers, who only differ from us in color."[82] The assistant quartermaster responsible for the military cemetery in Alexandria supported their demand and, in a letter to Meigs, noted his own attempts to stop the practice by directing that all USCT be interred near their white comrades in "the military cemetery, keeping them in a separate portion."[83] Meigs endorsed the petition and ordered the bodies moved, which was completed in January 1865.

Now six years later, the request by Douglass and the ad hoc committee for a meeting with Secretary William W. Belknap at the War Department prompted an appeal from Belknap's office for more information from Meigs as the man still responsible for the national cemeteries. This time the quartermaster counseled leaving the bodies where they were and made a case for maintaining racial segregation at Arlington. His reply confirmed the fears of Douglass and others seeking equal recognition for black Union soldiers, dead and living. Explaining that an initial failure to follow his orders in 1864 had resulted in the burial of a number of white soldiers in the northeast corner, Meigs noted, "This was an error which I corrected as soon as I discovered it. A few whites only I think had then been interred in it, and when the collection grew larger on the hill these few were removed to repose with their comrades. The colored soldiers appear to have been left where so large a number of their own race had been interred, and thus this part of the grounds was generally devoted to the colored people, soldiers and refugees." While deflecting his own direct responsibility for leaving the USCT there, Meigs explained later in his letter why he believed it to be the most appropriate course, which should be stayed:

Among the colored burials are many women and children. The majority of those refugees buried by the care of the government were colored persons, and with them I presume that many colored soldiers have been buried. This seems now to be objected to. Some of the colored persons who attended ceremonies on the last Decoration Day objected—I scarce know to what. If it be ordered that all those buried in this part of the grounds shall be removed, or that only the remains of those who died as soldiers in hospital, or on the field, shall be moved, it can be done, though.

While removal and relocation was possible, Meigs urged against it in spirit and in terms of the expense. Somewhat disingenuously given the movement of white bodies that he had demanded and supervised earlier, the quartermaster concluded, "I regret always to move a body once interred in National Cemetery, believing that the dead, *once decently buried,* should have rest. These are buried among their own people, the whole of the colored persons buried at Arlington, were victims of the strife which brought freedom to their race in this century, and I believe that hereafter it will be more grateful to their descendants to be able to visit and point to the collective graves of these persons, than to find them scattered through a large cemetery."[84] Douglass would have shuddered at the soldiers' inclusion within the collective category of "victims." Given that no orders for disinterment were issued, it appears that Meigs was persuasive in his argument that decent burials for black and white people alike were segregated ones. While the War Department chose not to move the black soldiers' remains to the main cemetery, in 1871 it did approve the removal of eighty-nine sets of Confederate remains from Arlington for reburial in Richmond, Virginia's Hollywood Cemetery.[85]

In the early 1870s, two amendments to the National Cemetery Act of 1867 transformed the system by establishing the right to burial in a national cemetery for veterans who had survived the Civil War. In 1872, it was granted to "all soldiers and sailors honorably discharged from the service of the United States who may die in a destitute condition," which, like the network of National Homes for Disabled Volunteer Soldiers established in 1865, indicated a sense of expanding federal obligation to care for veterans who were unable to care for themselves or lacked family to support them. The next year, the law was amended again to permit the national cemetery interment of any "honorably discharged Soldiers, Sailors, and Marines," effectively tying the right to national cemetery burial to having served rather than any form of need. This expanded eligibility as a benefit of citizen-soldiery generated the need for significant new cemetery space. The decade witnessed the establishing of forty-seven new national cemeteries, many far from Civil War battle sites, including in Nebraska, New Mexico, and California. The new reach of veterans' benefits for burial and a coast-to-coast cemetery system was in some ways mirrored in expanding pension benefits, reflecting the work of the GAR and the prominence of living veterans in American political culture. It also signaled the increasing centrality to postwar nationalism of honoring the dead Union soldier and his valorous manhood. In an address to the GAR's national encampment in June 1877, Chaplain in Chief Joseph F. Lovering celebrated the bonds shared among the collected veterans and the larger meanings of their wartime sacrifices and ongoing endeavors: "It is permeated, it is saturated with the spirit of that love. That love is love of country. That religion is the religion of patriotism. Its altars are the graves of the unforgotten and heroic."[86] Meigs devoted much of the 1870s and 1880s to making Arlington patriotism's high church and most sacred terrain.

From the location of Arlington's graves and racial segregation to roadway names and the monuments, structures, and ornamentations that proliferated in this period, Meigs continued to have singular authority over the direction and design of the national cemetery. Secure in his knowledge of engineering and architecture, Meigs turned to others for advice in landscape design and planting, seeking assistance from Frederick Law Olmstead in 1870 and hiring the landscape gardener David H. Rhodes, whose many years of work at the cemetery had a lasting impact on the land.[87] In 1874, Meigs built a large amphitheater for the GAR's Decoration Day ceremonies not far from the Tomb of the Civil War Unknowns. Between 1879 and 1881, he oversaw design and construction of ornamental gates for the cemetery's primary entrances that incorporated materials from a condemned building that once held War Department offices. Along roadways, he added several plaques carrying stanzas from Theodore O'Hara's elegiac poem "The Bivouac of the Dead" (1847).

O'Hara's poem was originally composed for the dedication of a monument to some of his fellow Kentuckians killed in the Mexican-American War, but it gained enormous popularity in Civil War memorialization. The poem is composed of twelve stanzas, but the first was the most popular and was often reproduced to stand on its own, including on Arlington's McClellan Gate:

> The muffled drum's sad roll has beat
> The soldier's last tattoo;
> No more on life's parade shall meet
> That brave and fallen few.
> On fame's eternal camping-ground
> Their silent tents are spread,
> And Glory guards, with solemn round
> The bivouac of the dead.[88]

In 1884, Meigs added to the cluster near the mansion a memorial structure called the Temple of Fame. Located near the Tomb of the Civil War Unknowns, the temple anchored a new design and complete reorientation of the gardens, removing the last vestiges of the hands of Custis and Lee women and the enslaved people they directed. The temple was composed of marble columns salvaged from the demolition of the Patent Office Building and topped with a dome; all were engraved with the last names of Civil War heroes, mostly generals and Abraham Lincoln.[89] While the quartermaster did not include himself among the names on the Temple of Fame, one column of the McClellan Gate carries his name in gilt letters and the road running alongside Section 1, dedicated to graves of officers, is Meigs Drive.

By the 1880s, significant numbers of Civil War officers, many with subsequent experience in the Indian Wars, were choosing to be buried, or their families were having them buried, in Arlington, signaling the ways in which the cemetery was becoming a site of particular honor for members of the Civil War generation who survived to fight other wars or lived into old age. When the general and former president Ulysses S. Grant died in New York City in 1885 without leaving a definitive statement of his wishes for burial, other than his explicit desire that his wife be interred beside him in the future, many people argued he should be buried in the capital and suggested either Arlington or the Old Soldiers' Home cemetery. While New York City carried the day, it was not for want of trying among veterans and elected officials in DC, who balked at delays in building Grant's monument and again attempted to have his remains moved by an act of Congress in 1890. Facing a similar question as to which national cemetery "in" Washington was the most national and sacred for an esteemed general's final rest, Arlington's status seemed secured when General Philip Sheridan was buried there in 1888.[90]

The officers' burials were distinct from the iconographic rows of common headstones in the "Field of the Dead." Many were joined by their wives, who were often interred beside them in separate graves. This marked the beginning of Arlington's practice of allowing the burial of officers' spouses in the national cemetery. Enlisted men and their families were denied this option in national cemeteries until 1908, and then the order required that wives of the enlisted be interred in the same graves as their military spouses and only after the man's death.[91] The rule was later amended to include predeceasing minor children and unmarried daughters, predeceasing or subsequent wives, and eventually husbands. Today, if you walk the rows of graves from behind, you will see spouses and children listed on the backsides of the stones, where they are interred in the same plots with their military partners or parents. Officers enjoyed the right to headstones and monuments of unique design and size, which explains the visual diversity of Section 1 and other officers' graves throughout the cemetery. This became vexing to those who found the greatest beauty of the cemetery in its sections of stark uniformity, reflecting later nineteenth-century transformations in American cemeterial landscapes to favor open, park-like vistas and simple adornments and the professionalization of cemetery management.[92]

Meigs spent most of the 1880s simultaneously at work on his last great project in Washington, the Pension Building. The quartermaster general's influence on the logistics, facilities, and aesthetics of two key features of the expanded federal state emerging from the Civil War, military burial and pension benefits, was unparalleled and intersecting. It would be hard, in fact, to find another figure with a greater singular impact on the built environments and landscape of federal memory of the Civil War. As access to national cemetery burials expanded in the 1870s, so too did the numbers of veterans and their families receiving pensions under new qualifications that included conditions and disabilities acquired after the time of military service. It was not the universal service pension lobbied for by the GAR, but with 75 percent of all Civil War veterans earning a pension by 1900, it came close.[93] Tasked with designing and overseeing the construction of a fireproof structure large enough to house the burgeoning records and staff of the Pension Bureau, then about 1,500 employees, Meigs sought to create a monument to the Union war effort. Modeled after the Farnese Palace in Rome, the enormous rectangular red-brick building is three stories high with exterior dimensions of 400 by 200 feet, which is larger than a contemporary football field. The most notable feature of the building's exterior is a terra-cotta frieze running its entire perimeter between the first and second stories that depicts every aspect of the Union military in an endless line of troops and materiel on the march. Included among them, at Meigs's insistence, was a black teamster. "Most of the drivers of Baggage wagons were freedmen Blacks. . . . By all means make the driver a Negro full blooded," Meigs directed the sculptor. "I leave all the clothes to your taste, but he must be a Negro, a plantation slave, freed by war."[94] It is notable that Meigs sought to represent black contributions to the war effort as the work of civilian laborers, rather than soldiers.[95]

During this time of monument building and increasing sentiment that the cemetery at Arlington was made sacred by the bodies of the military dead and memorial landscape, the federal government's title to the property was in question. Mary Lee had made a rare visit to Arlington in June 1873 but could not bring herself to go inside the mansion, which was now the office for cemetery management. "I rode out to my dear home," she wrote of the visit later, "but so changed it seemed but as a dream of the past."[96] When Mary died five months later, her quest for the plantation's return was assumed by her oldest son, Custis Lee, who had been willed the property by his grandfather upon expiration of his mother's lifetime tenure. Rebuffed again by Congress, Custis Lee sued in 1877, claiming illegal seizure and subsequent federal use of the land and naming as defendants military personnel, cemetery employees, and the residents of Freedman's Village. Taking years to move through the courts and appeals process, the suit ended up being heard by the U.S. Supreme Court and decided in Lee's favor in October 1882. Rather than force the removal of thousands of graves and the military installation, Lee agreed to accept $150,000 for the land and transferred the deed to the United States, which was handled for the government by the secretary of war and Abraham Lincoln's son, Robert Todd Lincoln.[97]

None of this was much consolation for Mildred Lee, the youngest of the Lee children. Writing in the summer of 1890, she described visiting Arlington and standing amid the garden that she and her mother had so loved. "In place of the jasmine arbour, was a hideous white pavilion, with the names of Lincoln, Grant, Sherman, Sheridan, etc.," she lamented. "Everything was gone"—by which Mildred meant everything of her family and her own antebellum past, replaced by monuments to Union glory and mourning. Sounding much like her mother, Mildred continued, "Everywhere, as far as my aching eyes could see, graves, graves, graves, in memory of the men who had robbed me of my beautiful home." Her grandparents' graves were "neglected, unknown—almost hidden by the myriads of monotonous headstones," concealing the pair who to Mildred were alone among the thousands of dead at Arlington to "have a right to rest in peace amid its fragrant, flowering woods."[98]

The payment to Custis Lee and the clear title to Arlington safeguarded the cemetery and the fort but ultimately spelled the end of Freedman's Village, which was disbanded by the close of the decade. While various interests had periodically called for the community's dispersal, it persisted until it was finally overwhelmed by local political investments and land developers with different designs on the valuable land so close to Washington. By the 1880s, the *Washington Post* was sounding insistent calls for the village's closure after years of suggesting it was a threat to local communities and the capital city as a source of crime and contagious disease. The paper referred to the home-owning residents as "squatters"

and pronounced the community's original goal of "building up the freedmen" a failure. At one point calling for the land to be turned into a grand riverfront park, the *Post* argued,

> On this fertile plantation, under these apparently favorable auspices, the negro was expected to work his way to independence and reputable citizenship. One need only ride over the now dismantled and barren estate to see the practical result of that experiment. Perhaps it was too much to expect the colored man to emerge suddenly from servitude equipped with thrift and industry; perhaps the neighboring city held too many attractions for his gregarious nature; perhaps there was some flaw in the plan which looked so promising. At any rate it did not work, except to work out the land on which it was tried.[99]

Upon visiting Arlington in 1886, a writer for *Harper's Weekly* described the community as "numberless ragged plots in the last stages of negro agriculture" and claimed that "Negroes born in slavery on the old estate still tell of their extraordinary well-being 'befo' the wah.' "[100]

In 1887, residents were given notice of eviction by the War Department, with sixty days for compliance. Acting on behalf of the community, John B. Syphax petitioned the War Department for recognition of their understanding, "fully impressed upon" them by "Agents" of the government, that renters would "in some way . . . come to possess a valid claim to a part of Arlington," which led them to improve their lots and dwellings. Syphax also explained that many who remained in the village had been part of the ill-fated colonization attempt in Haiti and "were told, perhaps as an apology, that they would remain here." Acknowledging the seeming inevitability of the community's eviction, Syphax reminded the War Department of the community's collective work as soldiers and laborers and their years of paying rent and taxes—they "have been no unjust burden"—and requested payments to compensate for the loss of buildings and improvements.[101] On the basis of subsequent recommendations of the War Department and a census of Freedman's Village and valuation of individual holdings, Congress appropriated $15,000 for payments. James Parks, who was identified as a former "Custis slave" in the documentation, received $13.20 for his improvements. Wesley Norris, who was not so identified, received $48.50.[102] The map accompanying the

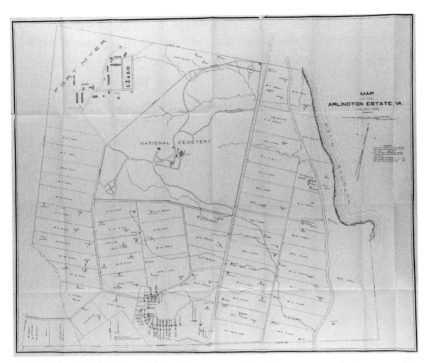

This map (January 1888) depicts the plots rented by residents of Freedman's Village and structures considered improvements for the purposes of determining compensations at eviction. The original dense cluster of Freedman's Village can be seen at the bottom, just left of center. The triangular lot beside it is the Syphax claim.

census inventory from the War Department depicts the cemetery nearly surrounded by Freedman's Village. With evictions under way, the cemetery annexed 142 acres in 1889, expanding its original allotment of 200 acres to 342.

Montgomery Meigs joined his family in Arlington at his death in 1892; James Parks helped prepare his grave. His wife, Luisa Rodgers Meigs, had died suddenly in 1879. Rather than place her next to their children in Oak Hill Cemetery, Meigs buried her in Section 1 and brought the children and several Rodgers relatives to be with her in Arlington. By this time, Meigs understood that the national cemetery that bore so much of his hand in creating and shaping it was where he wished to spend his own eternal rest. The quartermaster general managed his own burial like he had his various projects, from his work completing the Capitol dome in the 1850s to provisioning the Union military during the war and then building the U.S. Pension Building toward the end of his life. Meigs left very detailed instructions in his will: "I wish my body to be conveyed quietly and soberly to Arlington cemetery and placed in the marble sarcophagus over the grave of my beloved wife. Let the head be covered with plaster of Paris or hydraulic cement in fine powder duly tempered with water but not in such quantity as to incur any risk by swelling or fracturing the sarcophagus. Replace the lid securing it from infiltration of water through the joint and leave me to await the Resurrection."[103]

One of Montgomery Meigs's most enduring legacies was the radically transformed land itself. Under his influence, the national cemetery at Arlington had gone from a pauper's field to a place of honored military rest for the thousands who were moved there from far-flung battle graves and a generation of military officers who chose to be buried there. Meigs's creation of the Tomb of the Civil War Unknowns produced a site that became central to the capital's Decoration Day ceremonies. This elevated the tomb over time as a special place of collective mourning for visitors as well as those who read about the ceremonies in their local papers and the national press, which in turn began to cultivate a sense of Arlington's distinction among national cemeteries as a special site for Civil War remembrance. Additional monuments, such as the Temple of Fame and the amphitheater for Grand Army of the Republic gatherings, cemented these associations, while the eviction of Freedman's Village further distanced Arlington's memorial landscape from the emancipationist functions of the war and ongoing struggles for the realization of black freedom and citizenship.

Chapter 4

BRINGING HOME THE DEAD

The bringing home of the dead to the land of their
birth or adoption is regarded as an innovation
in the world's history of warfare.

—*New York Times* (1899)

IN 1892, the same year Montgomery Meigs had himself buried in Arlington, the remains of several Revolutionary War soldiers were reinterred in the cemetery after removal from the Presbyterian Burial Ground in Georgetown, which was slated for demolition. Like the period's quickened pace of Union officer burials in Section 1, the move signaled Arlington's already established distinction for the military. This was not yet the case for many elected officials or the public at large, however, despite the prominence of the cemetery in ceremonies for Decoration Day, later Memorial Day, and the burials of celebrated generals like Sheridan. The quartermaster's annual report for 1893 made this explicit in its request for congressional appropriations for cemetery improvements and urged an understanding of the cemetery's unique status: "In addition to its historical associations, the park abounds in rare natural beauty, and has been most carefully kept and improved. Few cities have so fine a park contiguous to their borders. Arlington Cemetery, where so many heroes lie buried, has become, like Great Britain's Westminster Abbey, the nation's 'Walhalla.'" Speaking of the ground as "consecrated" by the patriot dead and ripe with "hallowed associations and lessons" for all who visited, the quartermaster ultimately urged attention and the dedication of resources through appeals to Arlington's proximity to the capital.[1]

The Revolutionary War remains were joined in 1905 by those of fourteen unknowns who had died in the War of 1812, discovered during work on Washington, DC's historic Marine Barracks. These reburials continued the process of making Arlington uniquely national and hallowed through the relocation of military dead from other places and past wars. It also meant that by 1905, military remains from every American war had been interred at Arlington, the only national cemetery then or now to claim this distinction.[2] Broad perceptions of Arlington had shifted significantly for the wider public between the reburials of historic remains in 1892 and those in 1905. U.S. continental expansion through Indian removal, relocation, warfare, and white settlement had given way to overseas empire building in the Spanish-American War in 1898 and the ensuing war with the Philippines in 1899. Notably, almost 90 percent of the officers serving in the Philippines had experience in the Indian Wars, and many were Civil War veterans.[3] These new wars represented the first time that the president and military authorities interpreted post–Civil War federal mortuary policies to mean that Americans who died in battle abroad should be repatriated for burial. From 1899 to 1913, remains from Cuba, Puerto Rico, and the sunken wreck of the USS *Maine* in Havana Harbor were brought to Arlington. These were joined by military personnel who died in medical quarantine in the United States and then many more who passed away in their old age and claimed their rights as honorably discharged veterans for Arlington burials. While many who served in the Philippines were buried in Arlington later, most remains of enlisted people repatriated during that war but unclaimed were interred at San Francisco National Cemetery in California.[4]

This completed Arlington's evolution from being one among many national cemeteries in the nineteenth century to *the* national cemetery of the twentieth. What began in Union military exigency forged out of crushing sadness, loss, and rage was transformed within a few decades into a potent scene for sectional reconciliation, triumphant white supremacy, and imperial might. It was only in this context that the public began to perceive burial at Arlington as carrying some of the gravitas it has today.

The management of Arlington's landscape and organization of the built environment, including the placement of graves, made evident the contradictions and complexities of a liberal democracy celebrating itself through the "cult of the fallen soldier," as the historian George L. Mosse terms it.[5] The cemetery, like the nation it symbolized, was aggressively segregated by race, with a few notable exceptions, which remained official policy at the turn of the century. In addition came the segregation of Confederate remains in their own Section 16 and the segregation of women who were not spouses but had themselves served in the Spanish-American War as contract nurses. Distinct from the logic of racial segregation that framed black soldiers as unworthy of proximity, even in death, and unequal to other military personnel in their claims to heroic sacrifice, the Confederate and nurses' sections proclaimed their patriotic contributions and national inclusion by congregating them within the main cemetery.

These assertions of visibility and national belonging were mirrored in a range of monument-building campaigns and memorial gifts that proliferated in Arlington at the start of the twentieth century. Whereas the commemorative terrain of the nineteenth-century cemetery had been almost entirely directed by the Army, the new century brought artistic oversight and monument campaigns from various civilian organizations and patriotic groups, mostly women who sought to make their histories and contributions recognizable within the militarized nationalism and collective mourning at Arlington National Cemetery.[6] This began a series of struggles across the twentieth century to define women's military contributions, shaped by wider debates about the roles of women as service personnel, as fund-raisers for and builders of monuments, and as mourners, civilians, and citizens.

This new era of monument building within Arlington reflected the cemetery's prominence amid wider efforts to transform the national capital. Inspired by Pierre L'Enfant's original 1791 plans for the city and influenced by the neoclassical design and coordinated spaces of Chicago's 1893 World's Columbian Exposition, the Senate Park Commission published its plan, titled *The Improvement of the Park System of the District of Columbia,* in 1902. The plan created the city's definitive monumental core and National Mall on an axis from the Capitol to the Washington Monument to the space designated for the Lincoln Memorial. It included

a grand bridge across the Potomac, linking Lincoln's memorial to the national cemetery, with Arlington House understood as the axis terminus.
In 1909, L'Enfant was reinterred in front of the mansion overlooking the
capital. The Commission of Fine Arts (CFA) was established the following
year by Congress to guide implementation of the plans he had inspired,
and the CFA was given significant review authority over proposals for
monuments, public buildings, and changes to the landscape.[7]

The stunning vista from the vantage point in front of Arlington House
had long been one of the property's most notable features and became central to packaging the cemetery as a must-see part of any tourist's trip to
Washington, DC. In 1912, for $1.50, one could take the International Auto
Sight-Seeing Transit Company's tour of Arlington Cemetery, Fort Myer,
and the Virginia suburbs, departing from its Pennsylvania Avenue offices
three times daily for a round trip. The company's promotional pamphlet
provided a guide to the cemetery and its history with several photographs,
making it a souvenir in its own right. "Just as one may not comprehend
in its fullness the outward and material beauty of Washington who has
not looked upon the city as a part of the noble prospect from Arlington
House," the promotional narrative opened, "so he has not caught the finer
essence of what Washington stands for as the Capital of the Nation who
has not within the sacred precincts of Arlington Cemetery been brought
closer to the four years of sacrifice and felt his patriotism quicken at the
contact."[8] Washington's burgeoning tourist industry sold an American's
visit to the capital, which now included an obligatory trip to Arlington
National Cemetery, as nothing less than a pilgrimage. It was an opportunity to feel deeply one's patriotism, and nowhere was that more apparent
than among the graves and historical associations of the cemetery.

The publication of photo compendiums and guidebooks to Arlington
began in earnest at the close of the nineteenth century, reflecting shifting
perceptions, increased tourism, and growing reverence for the cemetery.
One of the earliest was *Historic Arlington* by Karl Decker and Angus Mc-
Sween, published in 1892 after the interment of the Revolutionary War
remains. "The fact that so little was known, or could be learned, by the
general public concerning Arlington caused the authors to undertake the

publication of this volume," they explained, adding that they felt "assured that its value to every student of American history, as well as to the many whose comrades and relatives lie beneath the Arlington sod, will be recognized and appreciated."[9] Tracing Arlington's plantation history from Custis to Lee as one of national significance, antebellum glamour, and benevolent slavery, the narrative ends with the removal of Freedman's Village in the aftermath of the successful Lee lawsuit and subsequent resale of the property to the government.

As was so often the case at Arlington, claims to historical continuity were embodied in the living presence and ongoing labors of people who had once been enslaved there. For Decker and McSween, this presence was Wesley Norris, still employed at the cemetery when they were writing their guide. The authors name and describe him as "an old negro, . . . one of the slaves of Mr. Custis, who was born on the estate and often accompanied his master on his long hunting expeditions. He was one of the squad of slaves that bore the body of the first master of Arlington House to his lonely grave in the deep grove west of the mansion, now marked by a crumbling stone shaft."[10] If Decker and McSween knew of Norris's experiences after his owner's death, they make no inferences. Rather, in their narrative, Norris is ever the faithful slave, always of the plantation's past, and forever bearing the bodies and histories of the dead.

The juxtaposition of living black people, both former slaves and their descendants, with the graves of white soldiers and former masters persisted into another photo-heavy guide to the cemetery published five years later. William Bengough's *United States National Military Cemetery Arlington* (1897) straddles the conventions of the photo book, commemorative history, and travel guide. Much of the narrative dwells on the cemetery's plantation past and illustrious white residents before the Civil War, while the photographs and their captions illustrate its contemporary memorial terrain. A number of the images include the figure of an unidentified adult black male, wearing a long overcoat and hat. He first appears in a picture of the Sheridan Gate, standing inside the cemetery and looking out across the Potomac toward the capital, the Washington Monument nearly centered between the pillars of the decorative entrance. The figure appears again ten pages later in a photograph of Section 1, labeled "Monuments to Officers." Just left of center in the image, he stands on a path bordering the section and gazes into the graves. The black man's presence, if not his identity, is finally explained near the end of the book in a photograph paired with the narrative's conclusion. With more distinctive features, larger, and now the clear subject of the photograph, the man sits on a bench in the foreground looking down to a plaque containing lines from O'Hara's "Bivouac of the Dead." Behind this scene stretches row after ordered row of the uniform headstones of enlisted men. The caption reads, "The most impressive sight of all, for here at once we see dimly what endless heartaches follow along each separate little stone in these long, long rows. Here lies the strength which was spent to give freedom to the black boy sitting here, representative of his race."[11] Whereas many others had suggested this link visually, as in Gardner's much-circulated "Burial Party" or in narrative accounts of former slaves and their children still working at Arlington, Bengough makes explicit the argument that white men sacrificed themselves for black men's freedom. These heroic soldier dead—notably not including members of the U.S. Colored Troops buried in a distant segregated area of the cemetery—were at eternal rest after giving freedom to black people, embodied in a "black boy," who is clearly a man, simply "sitting there."

"ON FAME'S ETERNAL CAMP-
ING-GROUND
THEIR SILENT TENTS ARE
SPREAD."

The most impressive sight of
all, for here at once we see dimly
what endless heartaches follow
along each separate little stone
in these long, long rows. Here
lies the strength which was
spent to give freedom to the
black boy sitting here, representative of his race.

An unidentified black man in Arlington National Cemetery beside a tablet carrying lines from Theodore O'Hara's poem "Bivouac of the Dead." The original caption to the right of the image links the living man's freedom to the dead, white Union soldiers interred behind him. From William Bengough, *United States National Military Cemetery Arlington* (1897).

Beside this picture on the opposite page, Bengough's narrative concludes with "Arlington's Lesson" for all who visit the cemetery. "Mute
tongues are these which teach brotherhood and love to all who make this
pilgrimage, for in the cause of unity they gave up all they had," he writes,
"and only by following humbly in their spirit and promoting the great
brotherhood of man can we carry forward the work which they began."[12]
These words are necessarily tied to the depiction of black freedom and
who paid its costs in the photograph beside them. This version of Arlington's lessons in reconciliation focuses on interracial brotherhood via
white paternalism, rather than the narrower claims to sectional unity and
white-supremacist nationalism that came to dominate the cemetery's terrain and popular associations by the end of the century. The pilgrim is
twice embodied here, in the author behind the camera and in the black
man he depicts moving through the cemetery, each with his own part of
the lesson to learn. This notion of brotherhood had been signaled earlier
in the text in the caption to a photograph of the North Slave Cabin, describing the structures and scene behind the mansion as presenting "a
view of slavery days which is far from disagreeable" and noting the cabin's current occupation by cemetery laborers and "their children, white
and black, [who] play in freedom together around the doors," thus
grounding a vision of interracial possibility in a romantic renarration of
the history of slavery.[13]

While some people like Bengough looked to Arlington's Civil War history and memorial landscape for reassurance of white honor, black gratitude, and clearly defined racial hierarchy as a path toward the future, for
many more, the cemetery was an ideal stage for exhibiting, and thus
enacting, more exclusive nationalism in the sectional reconciliation and
martial fraternity of white men secured through the Spanish-American
War. Memorial Day ceremonies at Arlington on May 30, 1898, took on
added significance in the context of war with Spain, which had at that
point been ongoing for a month. Speaking to the crowd, Senator John M.
Thurston, Republican of Nebraska, struck the note of sectional unity,
shared patriotism, and common military valor that was predominant in
wartime rhetoric and later commemorations. Standing on plantation

land that had been transformed by defeat amid the monuments and memorials to Union victory and honorable sacrifice, Thurston proclaimed, "What an inspiring sight to see those who once fought against each other now rallying around under one flag, exalting and rejoicing that the azure field of the union banner holds in equal honor every star of statehood, and singing together the rearranged music of the Union—'Yankee Doodle' and 'Dixie'—the favorite airs."[14] Although black troops glorified themselves in battle and made their own claims to fitness for full political and civil rights through their abilities as soldiers in Cuba and Puerto Rico, the mingling strains of "Yankee Doodle" and "Dixie" were a rearranged anthem evoking the national fraternity of white men and based on a revised history of the Civil War.[15]

As the last in a long line of Civil War–veteran presidents, William McKinley drew on that war and its aftermath in his approach to the dead of the Spanish-American and Philippine-American Wars. Believing that the greater the time between death and proper burials, the greater the likelihood of significant numbers of unknowns, McKinley directed the secretary of war to locate, identify, and mark swiftly all American military graves in Cuba and Puerto Rico. Similarly shaped by the policies and experiences of that earlier war, a proper burial in this case was taken to mean repatriation to American soil for interment. Again, this mortuary responsibility fell to the quartermaster and the newly created Burial Corps, largely composed of civilian morticians and laborers directed by military officers. With the end of battle and the signing of the armistice with Spain in mid-August, the Burial Corps headed to the Caribbean to identify, disinter, and prepare American remains to be transported back to the United States. This policy was extended to the Philippines with the start of the "insurrection" there in January 1899 after Filipinos declared independence as a free republic, rather than accepting the status of U.S. possession as outlined in the Treaty of Paris.[16]

But it was the dead of the Civil War that McKinley had in mind when he went to Georgia in December 1898 for the Atlanta Peace Jubilee. The celebration was designed to honor American victory in the war with Spain and to promote congressional authorization of the Paris treaty and its grant of U.S. colonial possessions. In his address at the Georgia House of Representatives, McKinley appealed to regional unity and martial fraternity as the basis of national glory and strength. Like the senator from Nebraska before him, the president appealed to metaphors of patriotic song and collectively raised voices: "Sectional feeling no longer holds back the love we bear each other. Fraternity is the national anthem, sung by a chorus of forty-five States and our Territories at home and beyond the seas," he intoned.[17] This focus on new national anthems reinforced notions that the deep embodiment of patriotism and military honor was shared among white men alone.

The president then thrilled many people by stating that the federal government should assume some responsibility for Confederate graves as it had long attended to the Union dead. "The national cemeteries for those who fell in battle are proof that the dead as well as the living have our love," he explained, stating that it was now time "when in the spirit of fraternity we should share with you in the care of graves of Confederate soldiers."[18] McKinley's promise sparked quick work among members of the United Confederate Veterans (UCV) and their compatriots in Washington, DC, and was the genesis of the Confederate Section in Arlington National Cemetery. This meant the start of another federal reburial program simultaneous to the repatriation of overseas war dead. These missions and their outcomes necessarily became entangled in the ongoing transformation of the cemetery's terrain and national meanings.[19]

By January, press reports of the War Department's plan to repatriate bodies from Cuba and Puerto Rico presumed that Arlington would be the ultimate destination of many. The *Chicago Tribune* assured readers that every deceased returnee not claimed by loved ones "will be cared for by Uncle Sam and buried in one of the national cemeteries, probably Arlington," adding that it was "the most beautiful of our national cemeteries." Assuredly beautiful, in the minds of many people, including the author of this article, Arlington was largely a place for the unclaimed—a default measure rather than first choice. Much of the article was devoted to the careful casket-sealing process employed by the War Department to ensure that there was no release of "tropical microbes" within the United States or risk of a typhoid or yellow fever outbreak. This meant that family and friends had to refrain from opening caskets in order to see their sailor, soldier, or nurse and had to trust in the identifications made by the Burial Corps before the bodies were transported home. "Care is being taken that no other than the proper body can possibly be delivered to the relative or friend making application," explained the *Tribune*. "Uncle Sam is aware that any uncertainty in this respect would cause unabatable uneasiness and distress." Recognition of concern and the high stakes for proper identifications ultimately had to stand in for complete assurance, as the unknowns of the Civil War continued to haunt the military engagements of the present. Further cementing connections between the recently dead of this new war with their predecessors, the article concluded by noting McKinley's promise to care for Confederate graves and the investigations under way to facilitate that process.[20]

From late March to June 1899, 1,222 bodies were shipped to the United States from the Caribbean in a mission widely lauded as emblematic of American exceptionalism and modernity as a nation. "The bringing home of the dead to the land of their birth or adoption is regarded as an innovation in the world's history of warfare," explained the *New York Times*.[21] Quartermaster General Marshall I. Ludington expounded in his annual report for that year, "It seems proper to remark here that this is probably the first attempt in history where a country at war . . . has undertaken to disinter the remains of its soldiers who . . . have given up their lives on a distant foreign shore and bring them by a long sea voyage to their native land for return to their relatives and friends, or their reinterment in the beautiful cemeteries which have been provided by our Government for its brave defenders."[22] Others found heroic precedent and profound democratic associations in classical history and stories of the returned Athenian dead of the Peloponnesian War, just as they had with the creation of the national cemetery system three decades earlier. Repatriation of the dead was claimed as an innovation of empire, seeming even more distinctive with the onset of the Second Boer War in October 1899 and the eventual interments of thousands of British Imperial forces in South Africa. This war prompted the first widespread distribution of military identification discs in the British Empire, with the express purpose of making possible the individuation of the deceased. In the American context, the Army chaplain tasked with overseeing mortuary responsibilities and identifications in the Philippines, Charles C. Pierce, is credited with suggesting the use of similar discs, precursors to today's "dog tags."[23]

The first military transport from the Caribbean arrived in the harbor at New York City on March 29, carrying the remains of 686 people. Crowds gathered at the pier to watch the unloading of the solemn cargo, some waiting to collect their own lost loved one. The *New York Times* noted that more than half of this number, mostly unclaimed, would "be buried in the National Cemetery at Arlington, remaining in the service so to speak, encamped in the bivouac of the Nation's dead." In this instance, burial at Arlington transformed the remains that were unknown or without family or friend as belonging to the larger collective of the nation. For this *Times* author, the representation of the nation forged in battle was understood to be particularly inclusive, making clear that while dominant and supple, the white reconciliation narrative was never totalizing. The military transport, returning from victory carrying those who paid its individual costs, was a microcosm of the country, sailing in "under the shadow of Liberty's statue." Perhaps unaware that they would ultimately rest in segregated areas of the cemetery, the author celebrated the comingling of black and white soldiers beneath the decks, "stowed in the promiscuous comradeship of the dead." These new immigrants' parents or themselves had made earlier passages under the Statue of Liberty's gaze. "Side by side or piled on top of each other were names suggesting widely different nationalities and races," the jumble "a strange conglomeration of the nations of the earth brought together with the common object of defending the rights of their common country."[24] This distinction in the outcomes of military service—between the segregated claims of mostly native-born black men to national belonging and the assimilation into national whiteness of the foreign-born and their children—became far more pronounced in the First World War.

The 359 caskets bound for Arlington were carried south on a specially designated train, decorated for official mourning; nearly a third of its deceased passengers were unknowns.[25] While some were claimed by family for private services upon their arrival in Virginia, most were buried in the national cemetery on the afternoon of April 6, 1899. Flags all over the capital were flown at half staff; federal offices and courts were closed at noon. Rows of caskets encased in wooden boxes, each covered by a single, large American flag, were lined beside awaiting graves, freshly dug in the new

Spanish-American War section of the cemetery, Section 22. They were guarded by two artillery detachments, which kept vigil along with a large crowd that had arrived early in hopes of securing good vantage points for the ceremonies. The collective funeral service was attended by President McKinley and his cabinet, numerous elected officials, and several foreign dignitaries, who all arrived with a large military escort.[26] This scene was replayed again at the end of the year when 151 sets of remains from the USS *Maine*—referred to as the "Maine Martyrs"—arrived by ship at Newport News, Virginia, and were sent via train to Arlington for burial with honors and presidential witness on December 28.[27] The bodies of many other sailors remained entombed within the wreck of the *Maine* at the bottom of Havana Harbor. It was another decade before they joined their comrades at the national cemetery.

Creating both a narrative history of the cemetery and a guide to its most notable interments and memorials, John Ball Osborne described his interest in writing *The Story of Arlington* (1899) as being "prompted by the fact that [his] brother, an officer of the United States Army and a hero of Santiago, sacrificed his life in the War with Spain and was laid to rest at Arlington."[28] William Headley Osborne was buried among other Spanish-American War dead near the Revolutionary War remains in Section 1. A lieutenant in the First U.S. Cavalry, the younger Osborne contracted typhoid fever while serving in Cuba. He returned to the United States and died in Camp Wikoff at Montauk Point, New York, where many who served in Cuba and Puerto Rico were sent to protect families and local communities from potential infection by "tropical diseases." The brothers could trace their genealogy to the Revolutionary War and the earliest days of the nation through both parents. Their father, Edwin Sylvanus Osborne, was a Pennsylvania attorney when he enlisted with the Eighth Pennsylvania Regiment in 1861. He was appointed judge advocate after Lee's surrender and was a central figure in investigating and drawing up the charges against Henry Wirz, the commander of the notorious Confederate prison camp at Andersonville and the only Confederate military figure tried and executed for war crimes. The senior Osborne returned to his legal practice in Pennsylvania, served in the National Guard, and was commander of the Grand Army of the Republic, Pennsylvania Department. He was elected to Congress in 1885 and in retirement returned to Washington, DC, where he died shortly after the publication of his son's book. He was buried in Arlington near William; his wife, Ruth, joined him there several years later.[29]

It was these family legacies to which John Ball Osborne appealed in his presentation of Arlington's history and its importance to the nation and the military. Although he had already served as United States consul in Belgium and held the position of joint secretary of McKinley's Reciprocity Commission when writing his book, Osborne listed after his name only his memberships in the Society of the Sons of the Revolution and the Military Order of the Loyal Legion (as the son of a Union officer) and the Columbia Historical Society, authorizing his martial and historical knowledge despite his professional experience in neither area. These associations also enhanced his claims to Arlington's status as a site of common military honor and reconciliation:

> Arlington—a name synonymous with deathless patriotism and graven upon the hearts of more Americans than that of any other spot on the globe. Indeed, not even hallowed Mount Vernon is so rich in historic associations, for Arlington is at once the old home of the adopted son of George Washington, who, with tender recollections of the personality of that illustrious man, linked the past with the present century; the former home of the principal actor in the drama of the "Lost Cause," and as such endeared to all Southerners; the last resting-place of thousands of heroic defenders of the Union, and therefore cherished at countless firesides in every Northern State; and, finally, the eternal bivouac of hundreds of gallant martyrs of our recent war for suffering humanity, by whose solemn advent Arlington has been consecrated anew as a truly *National* Cemetery.[30]

In arguing Arlington's importance as a memorial landscape for all Americans made "truly *National*" by the Spanish-American War burials, Osborne simultaneously celebrated the regionally or historically specific associations that the site still nourished and stitched together. He detailed the April mass burial of "the very large contingent of martyrs," concluding that their "chief glory [is that] their patriotism knew no geographical lines within the limits of the Union, so that henceforth these new-made graves at Arlington, where children of the North rest eternally beside comrades of the South, will symbolize a rehabilitated and solidified nation."[31] More than martyrs to the global reach of American power and freedom, for Osborne the returned bodies nationalized Arlington's sacred ground and associations, each fresh grave a testament to national rehabilitation through war and the certain valor of another generation of men in uniform.

For Osborne, this national space, embodied literally in the landscape of graves, included African Americans, if mostly confined to separate places. He notes Arlington's racial segregation among the historic graves as well as in the new Spanish-American War section, also indicated on the map included at the end of the book. Unlike the white officers buried together in Section 1 or at the head of the April interments, he identifies "three colored officers" from black regiments who were buried "in the southern section of the cemetery."[32] Osborne's book includes at the end a section on "colored soldiers," describing the Civil War graves of USCT and noting the presence—and the notable defiance of this standard segregation—of Alexander T. Augusta and Orindatus S. B. Wall in Section 1. He goes on to describe black service in segregated regiments in Cuba and Puerto Rico, including a long testimonial from a white officer proclaiming their fine soldiering, "bravery, coolness, and patience," which earned the admiration of all who saw them. In describing their presence in the national cemetery and making a case for black valor and "gallantry" in the Spanish-American War, Osborne describes shared effort and certain possibilities for biracial martial alliance within a hierarchy that nonetheless falls short of the horizontal relationships of fraternity. Yet this version of martial nationalism in all of its limitations is ultimately drowned out by the volume's overarching narrative of white sectional reconciliation. A short section on "Confederate soldiers" interred at Arlington immediately follows this discussion of black troops and closes the book. Osborne gives the final word to President McKinley, quoting from his 1898 address in Atlanta: "Every soldier's grave made during the unfortunate Civil War is a tribute to American valor."[33]

One of many books on Arlington National Cemetery now in the collections of the Virginia Historical Society in Richmond, the Osborne edition held there, signed and specially dedicated by the author, additionally serves as a unique object of sectional reconciliation. It is dedicated in the author's hand with "complements" to "Dr. Samuel E. Lewis, Commander, Charles Broadway Rouss Camp," United Confederate Veterans (UCV). Osborne, Lewis, or an archivist later has also underlined Lewis's name in the book's printed acknowledgments, where it appears without UCV identification. Lewis was the leading figure in efforts to locate all Confederate graves in and around Washington, DC, and have the remains reinterred in a specially designated section of Arlington. He would have been actively at work on this plan as John Ball Osborne was writing and publishing his book.

Perhaps even more than the location of Confederate graves, the company they kept in their eternal rest was Samuel Lewis's overriding concern. The Rouss Camp, capitalizing on its location and political access in the District, was a particularly activist chapter of the UCV with Lewis in the lead. Under the auspices of its historical division, and with his own and other Confederate veterans' future interments in mind, Lewis had already begun a survey of Confederate graves in the area when McKinley's promise provided a new platform for action. While the work of Ladies Memorial Associations (LMA) had resulted in the removals and reburials, mostly in deeper Virginia and the Carolinas, of more than 200 sets of remains, Lewis's team initially located 136 Confederate graves, mostly in Arlington and scattered around the capital, and then 128 in the Old Soldiers' Home Cemetery in DC proper. The group petitioned President McKinley on June 5, 1899, to support the removal of all the bodies and their reinterments together in a designated section of Arlington. Of the graves in that cemetery already, the petition noted, they "are scattered about the cemetery, principally in three straggling groups, distanced from each other." Offensive in itself to Lewis and others on the team, it was more the fact they are "intermingled" with Union dead, "citizens, quartermaster's employees, and negro contrabands" that caused them to feel that the Confederates were "singularly misplaced."[34] Furthermore, the similarity of their headboards with the civilians reinforced their indecipherability. In other correspondence, Lewis made clear the racial and martial specificities of the offense, noting that the thin marble stones over Confederate graves "bear no mark whatever to distinguish them from the Contrabands and Refugees, whose graves are marked by exactly the same description of stones." This was even worse at the Soldiers' Home Cemetery, he complained, where dead Confederate prisoners had been interred near Union soldiers but with different headstones "matching the Confederate Dead, the Contrabands and Refugees and Arlington."[35] McKinley endorsed the Arlington Confederate section plan and the federal relocation of the bodies, but funding the measure could only come from Congress. On June 6, 1900, Congress appropriated $2,500 for removals and relocations to Arlington but delayed the project's commencement so that relatives wishing to claim the deceased for burial elsewhere could if they wished.[36]

To the surprise of some in Washington swift resistance to the plan emerged from within the world of Confederate patriot groups themselves, which threatened to end the process before it fully began. Confederate women's organizations, particularly those associated with the work of Ladies Memorial Associations and Richmond, Virginia's Hollywood Cemetery, resented the UCV's intrusion on their decades of work to care for, build monuments to, and when possible, "repatriate" the Confederate dead to their home states. Moreover, they were particularly suspicious of the aims of the men of the Rouss Camp, accusing them variously of being out of touch with or careless of the wishes of all Confederate veterans, of succumbing to Washington myopia, of patronage seeking, and of being driven primarily by their own desires for Arlington burials in the future.[37] As a struggle over who was the best custodian of the Confederate past and national identity, the yearlong conflict was pitched, widely publicized, and broadly revealing of the gendered politics of memorialization. It made clear the ways in which Arlington had become so thoroughly federalized and associated with the Union for many people, despite its plantation past and connections to General Lee. If the dead were to be uprooted, they should be sent home, the women argued, never imagining that home to be Arlington. If they were not to be sent to home ground, some of the women concluded, then they should at least be sent to the grand cemetery in Richmond where so many other Confederates both eminent and average were at rest. In September 1900, a founding member of Richmond's first United Daughters of the Confederacy (UDC) chapter and a fierce opponent of the Arlington plan, Janet H. W. Randolph, proclaimed, "We want our dead and notwithstanding the extreme generosity of the Government in allowing Dr. Lewis out of *Our Taxes* the magnificent sum of $2500.00, we are going to have our dead."[38]

When it appeared that the women might actually convince Secretary of War Elihu Root to halt the plan, Lewis and his allies mobilized an intense campaign to undermine their arguments, question their abilities, and demonstrate broad support among veterans for their plan. Hilary A. Herbert, a Confederate veteran and former secretary of the Navy under Grover Cleveland, who did much to promote the Arlington burials, noted in a letter to Lewis that if the women were successful and the remains removed to locations further south, they "would be giving up the Capital of what is now our common country, entirely to the Union dead."[39] Lewis and his Rouss Camp prevailed ultimately; 267 Confederate bodies were interred in the new section at Arlington by 1902, arranged in rings around a central, monument-ready mound. Their headstones were designed to be distinct and easily recognizable, with pointed tops rather than the shallow curve of those marking the federal dead of the Civil War and all subsequent conflicts. As men and women of various Confederate patriotic organizations struggled over whether Arlington National Cemetery was an appropriate place to honor their dead and broadcast their contemporary identifications, another new heredity-based women's group was successfully stewarding the cemetery's first memorial gift from such an organization that same year.

The Spanish-American War Memorial given to Arlington by the National Society of the Colonial Dames of America was intended not only to mark the sacrifice of the soldiers and sailors freshly interred in that war's designated section but also to make tactile, public, and permanent the work of American women in supporting national war efforts and mourning the dead. This is made clear in the memorial's inscription, framing the monument as a gift twice intended, first to the dead and then to all American women who were not Colonial Dames: "To the soldiers and sailors of the

United States who gave up their lives for their country in the war of 1898–99 with Spain this monument is dedicated in sorrow, gratitude, and pride by the National Society of Colonial Dames of America in the name of all the women of the nation. 1902."[40] Nearly fifty feet tall, the granite memorial is composed of a column capped by a Corinthian capital on which rests a globe. An eagle with wings outstretched, cast in bronze, perches on the world. In a nod to the specific aims of the Colonial Dames, a band containing thirteen stars for each of the original colonies is wrapped around the globe. Forty-eight stars representing each of the states encircle the monument's base. Describing the monument effort in a later organization history, the Dames noted with pride, "It is the first monument ever erected in the National Cemetery at Arlington by a society of women, and stands on a commanding site."[41] Here, the Dames marked themselves as active participants in the proclamation of American power and as stewards of honor, all based on their own hereditary authority. Two years later, they added to this gift—and their own presence in Arlington—a hand-printed, leather-bound record book containing the names of all soldiers and sailors who died in the Spanish-American War, "placed in a marble, fireproof case, in the Lee Mansion." Federal authorities added an inscription making clear that the book was not an official record of the dead but contained "the names of the soldiers and sailors of the United States who died during the war with Spain, in 1898, irrespective of their place of burial. It is not a public record, but is presented as a Memorial by the National Society of the Colonial Dames of America."[42]

Established in 1891, the National Society of the Colonial Dames comprised several self-governing state-based societies all dedicated to historical preservation and the promotion of the national foundations and patriotic legacies drawn from the original thirteen colonies, to which all of its members could document an ancestral link. The Colonial Dames were part of a wave of lineal societies established in 1890s America that also included the Daughters of the American Revolution, the Society of Mayflower Descendants, the Order of the Founders, the Descendants of the Signers of the Declaration of Independence, and the United Daughters of the Confederacy. In the context of entrenched legal segregation and yawning disparities in wealth, representation, and opportunity between the rich and poor, white and nonwhite, and native-born and the more recently immigrated, the proliferation of genealogical societies was part of wider efforts to consolidate American identity as essentially white, deeply rooted, and, literally, carried in one's blood. As preservers of national heritage, the groups' members saw themselves as defenders, not only against the "forgetting" of preferred origin stories but also against national degeneration. Their veritable worship of ancestors and bloodlines wove easily with eugenic commitments to physical perfectibility and social engineering as the century turned.[43] This included the multivalent appeal of Theodore Roosevelt's "Strenuous Life," at once a Progressive imperialist call for military readiness and action as well as an entreaty to the development of individual white bodies beautiful and persevering.[44] As the Colonial Dames described it later, their members' blood ties to the past carried duties in the present and future: "*Not Ancestry But Heredity:* Not pride of birth but a sense of obligation to it: that we may not only descend from distinguished forefathers but ascend, 'building yet nobler mansions' on the foundation they have laid."[45]

The Dames understood their memorial gift as a natural continuation of their support of the American war effort against Spain. Society members from various states were active in relief work, donated funds for medical supplies, and took special interest in the sick and wounded aboard the Navy's new hospital ship, the *Solace*. In 1900, the women decided they should complete their "service by a suitable memorial to the soldiers who fell."[46] While the monument was expansive in its message, it also addressed some very specific concerns of the women who fund-raised and worked for its construction. Relationships between the national and state-based societies and their various leaderships were often complicated. The monument campaign was the national society's first significant effort under its own auspices: "It is interesting to notice that the first public project which the National Society undertook . . . had nothing to do with the Thirteen Colonies. It was a monument at Arlington to the soldiers and sailors who died in the Spanish American War, and it was an act of patriotism relating wholly to modern times."[47] Significantly, the women chose the ground at Arlington to articulate the distinction of the national society as a separate entity. More than this, they chose Arlington to promote their place and authority in martial nationalism, to insert themselves as women with particular contributions and commitments to white fraternity.

By the time President Theodore Roosevelt presided at the monument's dedication on May 21, 1902, the tides of public opinion had turned against the war in the Philippines. The Anti-Imperialist League and others had been attempting to publicize American war atrocities and systematic uses of torture, including the "water cure," today's "water boarding," since 1899. Early 1902 saw the circulation of more detailed information and American casualty numbers at nearly 4,000 dead and 3,000 wounded. A Senate investigation on the conduct of the war and administration of the occupation government in the Philippines had begun in January. At the dedication of the monument, Roosevelt focused on Cuba, where formal U.S. occupation had officially ended the day before with the seating of the republic's first president. "It is eminently appropriate that the monument should be unveiled to-day," he explained to the crowd, "the day succeeding that on which the free republic of Cuba took its place among the nations of the world as a sequel to what was done by those men who fell and their comrades in 1898."[48] This was followed in the speech by public recognition of Cuba's outgoing military governor, U.S. Army Brigadier General Leonard Wood. Wood was soon sent to the Philippines, where he led attempts to pacify the predominantly Muslim southern provinces long after the war's declared end on July 4, 1902.[49]

Roosevelt was saving his comments on the Philippine war and behavior of American troops there for his Memorial Day address about a week later, making him the first sitting president to do so. Newspapers and periodicals published around the country had long covered Arlington's Decoration Day and then Memorial Day ceremonies for their readers. With a planned address by an embattled wartime president, rather than the senator or congressman who had become the common feature at Arlington by the end of the century, a big audience and wider circulation of the speech's text were guaranteed. Roosevelt meant for it to be one of the great orations of his young presidency, profound in its moment and part of a lasting legacy.[50] Even more than broadcasting the president's message, Arlington's landscape of military sacrifice and Civil War memory itself formed part of his argument.

By all accounts, the crowd that day was enormous, far exceeding previous Memorial Days and the capacity of the amphitheater. Ceremonies began at noon with the Fourth Battery artillery firing a national salute.

The procession then marched first to the Tomb of the Civil War Unknowns, which was decorated while the Marine band performed with a choir. Everyone then dispersed to decorate individual graves, including those in the new Confederate section. When the president arrived, all converged on the amphitheater as the band played "Nearer, My God, to Thee," and someone read Lincoln's Gettysburg Address. Roosevelt's speech opened with words of thanks to the men of the Union, to whom, he said, the nation owed everything, as did the world, for securing "the future of mankind as a whole."[51] Roosevelt claimed for Union veterans the achievement of a united country. "You left us the right of brotherhood with the men in gray, who with such courage, and such devotion for what they deemed the right, fought against you." But even more than this, "you left us the memory of how it was achieved," which would "stand as the wisest of lessons to us and our children and our children's children." With this reference to the lessons of the Civil War generation, to the lessons of Arlington's collected dead and the living veterans gathered for tribute, Roosevelt turned to the Philippine War. He called it "small but peculiarly trying and difficult," and in it, the stakes were not just "the honor of the flag" but "the triumph of civilization over forces which stand for the black chaos of savagery and barbarism." The American troops fighting this war, Roosevelt said, still aiming his remarks to the Civil War veterans of the crowd, "are your younger brothers, your sons," who had proven themselves worthy and deserving "of the support of all men who are proud of what you did." While recognizing American acts of atrocity and assuring that the guilty would be prosecuted, Roosevelt couched these admissions in larger arguments that they were "wholly exceptional" and "shamelessly exaggerated."[52] The president urged the gathered crowd to recall the criticisms and invective hurled at Union leaders, policy makers, generals, and troops during the Civil War and criticized contemporaries who decried actions overseas while failing to do anything about the horrors of lynching in the United States. These last interconnected points prompted southern Democrats, many of whom opposed annexation of the Philippines, to accuse Roosevelt of "waving the bloody shirt."[53]

Despite this, and the agreement of some Republicans who offered regrets for the sectional direction of the speech, the president's ultimate appeal derived from the reconciliationist narrative's foundations in white fraternity and the shared valor of good soldiers. It was authorized by Arlington's specific funereal and memorial landscape, which had recently become so emblematic of that story, while serving fundamentally as an overwhelming reminder of the costs of war. For above all, Roosevelt said, the soldier's commitment, purity of patriotism, and willingness to die when so called on should always be unequivocally supported and celebrated, particularly by those who did not share their service and had little understanding of their experience. "Let those who sit at ease at home, who walk delicately and live in the soft places of the earth," refrain from judgment, Roosevelt argued with characteristic emphasis on the manly moral character, or lack of it, revealed in physicality. "Let not the effortless and the untempted rail over-much at strong men who with blood and sweat face years of toil and days and nights of agony, and at need lay down their lives in remote tropic jungles to bring the light of civilization into the world's dark places."[54] One needed only look at the new Spanish-American War Memorial shaft, piercing the sky and marking the section to the south of the amphitheater and its dense cluster of Civil War monuments, to be reminded of recent sacrifice.

Memorial Day events in Arlington the following year felt momentous to some people but did not generate the crowds or the publicity of 1902. President Roosevelt was not there; he marked the day with a speech in Wyoming, at the tail end of a two-month tour of western states and national parkland largely devoted to conservation.[55] Instead, the speaker was the former U.S. postmaster general and current editor of the *Philadelphia Press* Charles Emory Smith. Smith sang the collective praises of the Union and Confederate dead and described the Civil War as "necessary to make us a true nation" and a step in the "natural evolution" toward global power as the "world's best peacemaker and most potent influence . . . for arbitration, humanity, and civilization." But some work remained unfinished, Smith argued, as a "race has been emancipated from slavery and yet not admitted to the privileges of freedom."[56] In this, Smith urged his audience to see sectional unity and white fraternity as a path toward addressing the issue, which he framed as the Booker T. Washington–inspired concerns of educational and industrial opportunity, stopping short of calling for political rights or social equality.

Whether the Confederate veterans and their supporters in the audience were much persuaded by Smith is unknown. What they recalled of events in Arlington in 1903 was that the following weekend marked the first Confederate Memorial Day ceremonies in their designated section after the completion of reinterments. Men and women from Confederate veteran and patriotic groups gathered to decorate the graves and listen to orations of southern glories, the Lost Cause, and sectional unity and new national strength. One speaker invoked Robert E. Lee and Abraham Lincoln together as national heroes and concluded that it was most fitting that this "spot of earth," Arlington, with all of its connections to Lee, was the scene of realized fraternity. All veterans, he said, could now "repair to this spot and over the graves of all who lie here swear eternal allegiance to our country and our flag."[57] When the speeches were done, the crowd marched in procession to the Tomb of the Civil War Unknowns and placed there a large floral shield, as "a tribute to Northern valor," Hilary Herbert described later. It carried a phrase from McKinley's 1898 Atlanta address: " 'In the Spirit of Fraternity,' June 7, 1903."[58]

In this spirit, Roosevelt had sent a large floral arrangement earlier that day from the White House to decorate the Confederate section. This began an annual tradition of presidential recognition of the Confederate dead through flowers or a wreath sent to Arlington's Section 16. In 2009, this tradition ran headlong into the first Memorial Day of the new presidency of Barack Obama, when scholars petitioned the country's first black president to end the practice. They argued that the presidential gift not only glorified the Confederacy through official recognition but also authorized the warped historical views of slavery, Reconstruction, and segregation represented in the section and the violent, white-supremacist reconciliation politics that produced it. In the midst of the ensuing controversy, the art historian Kirk Savage suggested a compromise in a *Washington Post* editorial. Noting that it seemed unlikely that the president would choose not to send the wreath, Savage also questioned the historical and political efficacy of tying the issues of slavery and thwarted black freedoms only to the South and individual Confederate soldiers. "The crime of slavery was interwoven not only into the Confederacy but into the fabric of the American nation, into the Constitution, our economic system and wars of territorial expansion across the continent," he explained. "To single out the ordinary soldiers of the Confederacy as beyond the moral pale does not help us come to grips with slavery's more profound role in American history."[59] Rather, Savage suggested, the president should send two wreaths, one to the Confederate section in Arlington and the other to the African American Civil War Memorial honoring the men of the U.S. Colored Troops, dedicated in 1998 and located in Washington, DC's Shaw neighborhood at the U Street Metro stop. This is ultimately what President Obama chose to do.[60] While effective, the compromise highlighted Washington's—and the nation's—very different geographies of Civil War remembrance and commemoration as they intersected with the stark racial segregation that has long characterized the capital city. Whereas Section 16 is a carefully defined portion of the national cemetery, decorated by a central monument that remains one of Arlington's taller memorials, and is included in every map or tourists' guide to the cemetery, the graves of USCT in Section 27 enjoy no similar distinction. As in 1903, the geography of Arlington in 2009 mattered; with no obvious equivalent in the national cemetery, the compromise highlighted the localizing and ongoing segregation of black Civil War remembrance.

On May 2, 1905, a crowd gathered in what was then still mostly an open field of green, edged by young trees, for the dedication of the Spanish-American War Nurses Memorial, sited at the head of the new section dedicated for nurses' burials generally. In a picture taken that day, a row of headstones and the tall, eagle-topped shaft of the Spanish-American War Memorial can be seen in the background. While the Colonial Dames had celebrated their monument's dedication in 1902 as the first of its kind from a women's organization, the Society of Spanish-American War Nurses had begun fund-raising for their own memorial in 1899. But the monument they envisioned was radically different in its aim, which was to liken the work of wartime nursing to soldiering in battle. This was not to be a monument to the roles of women as national mourners and keepers of memory but to skilled caregiving women as valorous military actors. The nurses' aims intersected with the work of women's suffrage activists such as Julia Ward Howe who pointed to the nurses' service in the war as evidence of their worth and due, querying, "Should they not be counted among the citizens of the great Republic?"[61] In November 1899, the society began mailing circulars and publishing its call in periodicals such as the *Trained Nurse and Hospital Review* publicizing the monument plan and seeking support from other groups of organized nurses, particularly those with their own histories of service in the Spanish-American War. The monument, they explained, was to be erected for "those who died at their post, giving their lives as gladly to their country as did the soldiers who died on the field of battle." The aim of the memorial from its inception was to make visible the similar sacrifice of women, perhaps even nobler than that of the soldier, the society suggested, because it was freely given without the "glamour of glory" or expectation of fame in battle. Their work was physically and emotionally difficult and dangerous; "they died that others might live; and to us who love their courage and their zeal remains the privilege of fitly honoring their memory." A fit memorial meant its placement in Arlington National Cemetery. The society called this work of commemoration a privilege but made clear that it was also a necessity, as no one else was likely to do it. "All ages and nations have honored the heroes who have died in the front of battle, but this will be the first memorial of its kind erected to women."[62] The nurses, in honoring their dead, sought to promote their own contributions.

The leading figure behind the monument campaign was the society's president, Dr. Anita Newcomb McGee. Charismatic, fierce of will, and politically and militarily connected, McGee had a profound impact on the development of nursing within the Army that began in the war with Spain. McGee hailed from an elite, scholarly family in Washington, DC, and her medical education and work as a physician lent her significant authority with military leaders, in part because she was not herself a nurse but a doctor. McGee had encouraged the U.S. surgeon general to employ only trained, professional nurses for military service and offered herself as an agent for selecting them. In this capacity, she drew from her leadership role in the Daughters of the American Revolution (DAR) as much as, if not more than, her medical knowledge. In April 1898, McGee and her committee composed of other DAR members in the Washington area began reviewing applications for nursing contracts, considering applicants within three criteria: professional credentials, character, and physical health. Like the women of the Colonial Dames, McGee and her compatriots in the DAR believed that ability, morality, and patriotism were hereditary. Soon McGee oversaw this process from her own position in the War Department as acting assistant surgeon for the Army.[63]

Despite McGee's efforts to singularize the process, nurses came to their work in the Spanish-American War through various means and institutions. This included trained African American nurses from institutions like Washington's Freedmen's Hospital and the Tuskegee Institute, Red Cross volunteers, nuns from several religious orders, independently hired women near American camps like the one in Montauk, and a number of black women who were not professional nurses but were believed to be immune to yellow fever. While nursing as a caregiving act and as a job never lost its gendered associations with women, men had long been part of wartime nursing and were also evident in small numbers in 1898—a fact that raised questions for the monument campaign later.[64] But if the presence of men in professional nursing seemed unusual at century's end, the presence of women among the overseas military dead was remarkable. In an account of the return to New York Harbor of the first American military remains from Cuba and Puerto Rico, the *New York Times* noted, "Some little stir was occasioned later among the group of spectators on the pier when the first body of a woman was brought ashore."[65] Unidentified by name in the article, she was described as a contract nurse who had died at her post in a Santiago Army hospital.[66]

Efforts to make a trained nurses' corps permanent within the Army were simultaneous with the start of the Arlington monument campaign and impossible to delink from it. Congressional hearings were held in 1899, but the Army Nurse Corps did not become reality until February 1901 with the passage of the Army Reorganization Act. It was many more years before the all-women Nurse Corps represented a ranked part of the military with avenues for advancement and access to the full range of veterans' benefits, including pensions.[67] But one benefit that had been gained early and widely publicized among the intersecting professional communities and organizations was the Spanish-American War nurses' option for an Arlington burial.[68] This remained somewhat tenuous, however, as it was not understood to be a veterans' benefit, nor did it operate in the same way. The possibility of national cemetery burials for nurses was reported as the War Department began the process of repatriating remains from the Caribbean. The *Chicago Daily Tribune* noted that along with all honorably discharged service personnel, Army nurses were eligible "if they are in a destitute condition," suggesting that this was a matter of necessity for women who were lonely and alone, rather than an honor.[69] In the Society of Spanish-American War Nurses' 1901 report on the status of the monument campaign, McGee noted that while the site in Arlington had been selected and funds raised, the project was in limbo without the secretary of war's authorization. "Fortunately," she assured, "the monument question does not affect the distinguished right of burial with the army and navy in beautiful Arlington" for honorably discharged Army nurses, a right that had been secured with creation of the Nurse Corps.[70]

By the next annual meeting, which was held in Washington, DC, the monument plan was fully authorized and well under way. Official events included a trip to the cemetery for a guided tour led by the superintendent and an opportunity to inspect the nurses' section. Recalling a moment still familiar and affecting for many visitors to Arlington today, the report noted that the group passed a funeral cortege for men who had recently been killed in the Philippines. "The plot assigned to the Spanish War Nurses has a beautiful site," the reporter continued, "and in the corner of it the ground has already been prepared for the erection of the monument which this society proposes to erect to the memory of their deceased comrades."[71] This use of the term "comrades" further cemented the women's desire for the monument to mark the explicit military sacrifice of women who had died and their own martial contributions and potential future sacrifice.

Who was included exactly within the category "comrade" became a point of concern the following year. As McGee gave her presidential address at the 1903 annual meeting held at the Presidio in San Francisco, she noted that the original plan for the monument had been to honor all contract nurses who died in 1898 during the war. This had included not only trained nurses but also African American "immunes," Catholic sisters, and male contract nurses. No nurse killed in 1898 had been interred in Arlington in 1899 when the monument campaign began, however, nor had the nurses' section existed. This, McGee argued, meant that the question of who was to be honored by the memorial remained open.

McGee's claim seemed largely prompted by a recent report from the War Department showing that four nurses serving in 1898 had since been interred in the section; two were "untrained 'immunes,'" suggesting they were African American women, and the other two were men. "It is evident that our society does not care to erect a monument to the nurses actually buried in Arlington," McGee stated matter-of-factly, indicating the racial, gendered, and educational specificity of "comrade." "It is also evident," she continued, that "although many of us hope one day to have the honor of lying in our National Cemetery, that we cannot at this time erect a monument to ourselves." Of course, this is exactly what the women were doing, but propriety seemed to counsel denial. A resolution was put before the members present for a vote: should those honored by the memorial include all contract nurses, be limited to women ("whom we could more properly call 'our comrades'"), or be further limited to "trained nurses," which to their mind excluded most black women and Catholic nuns.[72] While the results of that vote were not included in the report, the stated list of deceased nurses honored by the memorial printed in 1905 included no men but did contain women identified in the following categories: "Graduate Nurses and M.D.s," "Immune Nurses," "Sisters of Charity and of Mercy from St. Joseph's Academy, Emmitsburgh, MD.," and "From Mount St. Agnes' Convent, Mount Washington, Baltimore Co., MD."[73]

While the society publicized the names of these women and their affiliations, the monument itself did not include them. Standing about seven feet high, the monument is composed of rough-hewn granite and topped by a Maltese cross, the society's emblem, inscribed with "U.S.A." at the center and the society's name around the four arms. The front carries the inscription "To Our Comrades," surrounded by a bas-relief of palm fronds topped by a laurel wreath. The back side includes an inset bronze plaque reading, "In Memory of the Women Who Gave Their Lives as Army Nurses in 1898—Erected by the Society of Spanish-American War Nurses." While President Roosevelt and the secretary of war declined their invitations to the dedication, a number of notable figures were on hand to honor the women, including a member of the Japanese Legation, the commander at Fort Myer and several other officers of the Army and Navy, the past and present commanders of the Spanish-American War

Veterans, the president-general of the DAR, and many nurses, active and retired, from various societies and institutions. Among the latter group were six women from the DC area who had worked as nurses during the Civil War. The palm-branch features of the monument were echoed in the site's decorations. A flagstaff of bamboo from the Philippines was erected beside the monument, and the ground before it was covered with enormous palm branches from Cuba and Puerto Rico. Marking the familiar ground of Virginia with the exotic flora of overseas battlefields served to remind those who were in attendance of the far-away scenes of the women's service. The day's main address was given by the commander of the veterans' organization, himself a physician, who asserted that based on his experience as both a soldier and a doctor, "and with all due credit to the soldier, the nurse who gives up her or his life in the performance of duty is more of a hero than is the soldier."[74]

More often, the early twentieth-century memorial work of women in Arlington remained defined by gendered conceptions of domesticity and public mourning. This was clearly evidenced in the United Daughters of the Confederacy's campaign for a Confederate monument in Arlington, which began the next year. Speaking at the cornerstone-laying ceremony in 1912, William Jennings Bryan put it plainly in his praise of the UDC's efforts: "Woman—last at the cross and first at the sepulcher—holds undisputed sway on occasions like this."[75] At the monument's dedication two years later, another speaker lauded the UDC for its tireless work and achievement in providing this "gift" to the nation, noting that in many ways it was a monument to the UDC women, and to all southern women, for "when the monument to their heroes stood unveiled before the world in the nation's burial ground [it was] . . . a tribute to woman's undying devotion to true manhood and valor."[76]

With approval from William Howard Taft, the former civil governor of the Philippines and now the secretary of war, in 1906 the women set to fund-raising and securing an artist and design for a monument at the center of Section 16's concentric rings of Confederate graves. While those in the organization who had campaigned against the creation of the section in the first place retreated from those criticisms, the UDC women continued to promote themselves as best suited to memorialization, historical preservation, and the crafting of appropriate public honors for the Confederacy—an argument that they, too, now brought to Arlington. This included continually reinforcing that idea among themselves, as both motivation and reassurance. A fund-raising letter aimed at women across the chapters of the UDC in early 1909, more than two years into the campaign, opened, "We begin a new year full of life and hope, with the sacred duty of perpetuating in imperishable stone, in Arlington Cemetery, the story of heroism of both the living and the dead"—making clear the importance of such a monument to the living, to the women of the UDC reading that letter, to all southerners across time, and to future visitors to the cemetery. "Many who lie in Arlington, who bore the crimson flag with such dauntless courage, *deserve* that the women of our Southland should rear a fitting memorial in testimony of their love and reverence. Shall the stranger in our midst find a monument to every hero but the *Confederate Soldier?*"[77] The Confederate Monument, created by the sculptor Moses Jacob Ezekiel, himself a Confederate veteran and today buried at its base, would not just glorify the soldier but carry figural representations of every aspect of the Confederate effort as Ezekiel and the women of the UDC imagined it.[78]

The UDC held its annual convention in Washington, DC, in 1912, the first outside the former Confederacy, to coincide with ceremonies laying the cornerstone for the monument in Arlington. Opening the meeting in Continental Hall, donated for the UDC's use by the Daughters of the American Revolution, the women were addressed by the lame-duck President Taft. Like many before him, the president appealed to the racial nationalism and shared military valor of sectional reconciliation, realized, he said, in the election just days before of the southerner Woodrow Wilson, the Confederate meeting in the federal city, and the soon-to-be-erected monument in the national cemetery.[79] "No son of the South and no son of the North, with any spark in him of pride of race, can fail to rejoice in the common heritage of courage and glorious sacrifice" shown in the Civil War and so honored, he claimed.[80] When Cordelia Powell Odenheimer, the UDC's vice president, took the podium, she celebrated the memorial work of the UDC as especially important to making public spaces "historic land, filling it with monuments," which would "speak forever." She then turned to the new Confederate Monument, which many people believed to be the most notable memorial achievement of the UDC to date: "Just across the river lies beautiful Arlington. Arlington! The very name will be a memorial forever to the South's knightliest son, Gen. Robert E. Lee."[81] While Taft had dwelled on the reconciled nationalism of northern and southern white men made visible in the cemetery, Odenheimer urged the room to see that land as essentially Lee's and thus as fundamentally theirs. Within a decade, many members of Congress agreed with Odenheimer, as Arlington House was designated a memorial to the Confederate general.

At the monument's dedication two years later, General Bennett H. Young, commander of the United Confederate Veterans, expressed some amazement at the sight before him. "As one looks around in this Federal cemetery he can but question if the exercises of this hour are real, or if they be but the phantom of some dreamer's imagination." While for many people this moment was a nightmare and a stark reminder of how far the cause of black freedom had been pushed from official memories of the war and their nationalist formations, it was no dream. "We are here to dedicate on the Nation's ground, on the space reserved for its most renowned and illustrious dead, a Confederate monument," Young continued. "In its inception, its construction, its location, and in its mission, this structure stands in a class by itself."[82]

At thirty-two feet high, with tiers bursting with figural representations, the monument remains one of the more distinctive memorials within the cemetery. It is topped by a white female figure in draped classical attire, representing the South. She wears an olive wreath and holds another in her left hand made of laurel, which she offers to honor the Confederate dead at rest below. The figure leans on a plough and hook, literal representations of the biblical inscription beneath her: "They have beat their swords into plough-shares and their spears into pruning hooks." An inscription at the base blends Lost Cause justification with calls to valor and nationalism through ennobled suffering: "Not for Fame or Reward—Not for Place or for Rank—Not Lured by Ambition—Or Goaded by Necessity—But in Simple Obedience to Duty—As They Understood It—These Men Suffered All Sacrificed All Dared All—And Died." The monument's midsection is wrapped with a frieze composed of life-size

"Confederate Memorial, Arlington Cemetery," ca. 1914–1920.

figures in various groupings, representing the men and women of the South facing war and marking their contributions. Included among them are two black figures, one an enslaved woman depicted as a "mammy" and the other an enslaved man marching into war alongside his master, renarrating black military service as faithful slavery. As many speakers remarked that day, the monument also carried a permanent reminder of the women who made it possible, indicated in another inscription at the base: "To Our Dead Heroes—By the United Daughters of the Confederacy," thus marking the UDC women's place in sustaining a living Confederate nationalism through memorialization. Or as UDC President-General Daisy McLaurin Stevens put it at the dedication, "this monument will be not only a memorial of the past, but a symbol of the present and future."[83]

As the adornment of the Confederate Section was under way, Arlington received the last USS *Maine* remains and the ship's mast for a memorial. The simultaneous repatriation of bodies from overseas suggested a similar sort of homecoming for the former rebels, making manifest in the land popular assertions that shared white valor and racially exclusive nationalism were the central legacies of the Civil War. Embraced among the heroes of Arlington and so visibly honored, the Confederate dead joined those who were more recently lost in American wars for empire in a fight, as Roosevelt had put it, for "the triumph of civilization" over the forces of "the black chaos of savagery and barbarism." Before the decade's end, many more American soldiers were lost in faraway battles, this time in Europe in a war that seemed in some senses to represent savagery's modern triumph and a Pyrrhic victory. Some of the lost, including only one American of unknown identity, were brought home to Arlington.

Chapter 5

OUT OF MANY, ONE UNKNOWN

That which takes place to-day at the National Cemetery
in Arlington is a symbol, a mystery, and a tribute. It is an
entombment only in the physical sense. It is rather the
enthronement of Duty and Honor. . . . He—this spirit
whom we honor—stands for the unselfishness of all.

—*New York Herald* (1921)

THE REPATRIATION POLICY that had been lauded as a sign of the
nation's exceptional patriotism and modernity at the turn of
the century became a logistical and diplomatic nightmare in the face of a
world war that brought more significant losses in Europe and the resistance of allies to American plans to repatriate their dead. While U.S.
military remains were scattered across several countries, the vast majority were buried in battlefield graves throughout France. A month after
the first American Expeditionary Forces had arrived there, the Army
established the Graves Registration Service (GRS) within the Quartermaster Division in August 1917, successor to the Burial Corps. The
retired Army major and chaplain Charles C. Pierce, who had managed
registration and burials in the Philippines, was called back into active
duty to handle the work in Europe.[1]

The interpretations of Civil War and Reconstruction-era military
mortuary policies that led to the return of remains from the Spanish-
American and Philippine-American Wars, combined with the expectations they had generated among military personnel and civilians, now

provided the basis for Secretary of War Newton D. Baker's promise to return the dead for burial at home. In September 1918, the *New York Times* reported the news under the headline "To Bring Back Our Dead—Burials in France during War Will Be Only Temporary."[2] How and when these repatriations were to happen was left unclear and became the source of significant conflict within the War Department, the American public, and abroad.[3]

Eventually, a policy was set to return all remains requested by next of kin to any location in the United States at no cost to the family. Those remains that were not requested, because their loved ones wished them to remain in Europe or because they were unidentifiable, would have their rest in American-managed, national "Fields of Honor." Making a request from families the prompt for repatriation marked a significant departure from the earlier policy of returning all remains to the United States and providing national cemetery burials to any not claimed for private interments. It shifted the register of the nation's obligation to care for the military dead by placing the responsibility for the decision to repatriate on the bereaved living. This raised the larger issue of to whom the military body ultimately belonged, the government or family?

Another result of this policy was the 1921 interment of an unknown American soldier from the First World War and the creation of the Tomb of the Unknown Soldier. More than anything else, the grand ceremonial burial of the otherwise unidentifiable body of an American soldier solidified Arlington's identification as a singularly national and representative terrain made sacred by military sacrifice elsewhere. In a travel guide published the following year, the journalist and popular historian Minnie Kendall Lowther explained, "Here all heroes of all ranks and of all wars, from the Revolution to the great World War, share, alike, in this embracing mold, so close to the heart of the great country they gave their life blood to preserve."[4] The creation of the tomb, arguably the heart of the cemetery today, was shaped in large part by the War Department's inability to fulfill its promise to collect and repatriate every American body from the battlefields of Europe.

This was, of course, not the first memorialization of unknowns in Arlington. While clearly inspired by the state funerals and memorials for unknown warriors in Britain and France the year before, generations of

Americans had looked to the Tomb of the Civil War Unknowns as a distinctly moving and emblematic site of patriotic commemoration. At the turn of the century, it had been infused with new importance as a place for demonstrating sectional reconciliation, the martial fraternity of white men, and strength through sacrifice. The racial and national attachments made possible by the Civil War monument persisted with the Tomb of the Unknown Soldier in 1921.[5] The war had started with an uncharacteristic call from W. E. B. Du Bois for African Americans to "Close Ranks" and temporarily set aside the fight for racial justice in order to support a unified war effort and demonstrate shared patriotism.[6] Like the military generally, however, the strict maintenance of racial segregation in Arlington and continued relegation of black workers and soldiers to positions of subservience reinforced associations of Americanism and honor with whiteness. This was reinforced by the start of a movement to make Arlington House a national memorial to the Confederate Robert E. Lee simultaneous with the creation of the Tomb of the Unknown Soldier and the eulogizing of James Parks as a faithful slave when he was interred in the national cemetery at decade's end.

The often-ghastly tasks of disinterment, transportation, and congregation of remains in central cemeteries in Europe had been disproportionately performed by thousands of African American soldiers whose segregated labor battalions were assigned to grave duty. Photographs of their labor necessarily call to mind the better-known images of black gravediggers during and after the Civil War fifty years earlier. Yet while this work was generally understood as an example of the worst duty tasked to the least valued within the service, two black activists argued that because care for the dead was such important work, the generals and the GRS had—in spite of themselves—conveyed the deeper humanity, morality, and patriotism of black soldiers. In the war memoir *Two Colored Women with the American Expeditionary Forces* (1920), Addie W. Hunton and Kathryn M. Johnson explained that reburials were a "gruesome, repulsive, and unhealthful task," isolating the units on scattered and long-abandoned fields of battle, but it was "sacred" work to ensure an honorable rest for the soldier dead. Indeed, Hunton and Johnson argued, the American cemeteries in France could themselves be seen as monuments to honorable black military service, as "strong and indisputable evidence" of the "devotion and loyalty and matchless patience and endurance" of the living black soldier. Perhaps it was Providence that selected black men for this duty, they concluded, as "just another means . . . to hasten here at home the recognition and enforcement of those fundamental principles" of democracy.[7]

Whereas repatriation of the First World War dead was a question and became the subject of significant controversy, the policy was assumed by officials and the public alike from the start of America's entry in the Second World War two decades later. The First World War had been called "Great" in its reach and hailed by some people as the "war to end war," but the next conflagration presented the strains of two overseas theaters and enormous numbers of missing, wounded, and dead. Beyond casualty figures, the conditions and technologies of battle were vastly different, which meant the qualities of death were, too. World War II marked the first American war in which military battle losses outstripped the numbers killed by illness or accidents away from the front. Of the 405,399 U.S. military personnel killed in the war, 291,557 were combat deaths.[8] When taken together, the number of people killed during World War II—military and noncombatant; Allied, Axis, and nonaligned—surpasses eighty million souls worldwide in a horrific testament to the human costs of total war in the twentieth century, as well as the staggering impacts of the Holocaust, aerial bombardment, incendiary weapons, and the dawn of the Atomic Age.

As had been the case since the policy's origins in the nineteenth century, repatriations of American military remains could not begin until after the war was over. Until then, the GRS worked to locate, identify, and collect the dead in temporary cemeteries spread across three continents. When returns were authorized by Congress in 1946, the War Department issued a pamphlet titled *Tell Me about My Boy* to explain the process to surviving family members and their options for repatriation or overseas interment. Their "boys" had sacrificed their lives for their country, reassured the pamphlet, but "the Government now feels it is the right and privilege of the next of kin to decide where these valiant dead shall rest."[9] In the early days of crafting military mortuary policy after the Civil War, Montgomery Meigs once argued, "all care for the dead is for the sake of the living."[10] Pitched struggles among civilian authority, the military, and the families of the dead and missing during World War I changed that care into the "right and privilege" of the living and forever transformed Arlington National Cemetery.

While Great War Allies shared national commitments to mark through registration and single burials the individual sacrifices of average soldiers as well as officers, for the Europeans this was a relatively new practice of the modern, imperial nation-state.[11] The British and French discouraged the American promise of repatriation and resisted compliance. Concerned about the impact on the morale of the British public, for whom virtually no friend or family was spared losses, authorities in the United Kingdom balked at the plan. Some feared that it would raise expectations in Britain and its empire for similar repatriations. The British maintained a strict and long-standing policy of not returning enlisted men's remains, glorified in Rupert Brooke's 1914 poem "The Soldier," which opens,

> If I should die, think only this of me:
> That there's some corner of a foreign field
> That is forever England. There shall be
> In that rich earth a richer dust concealed.[12]

France responded that facilitating the American policy was impossible and quite clearly the very least of the country's current concerns. The French terrain had been physically devastated by the war, and Allied and enemy bodies from several countries were scattered everywhere in battle graves and newly sprung cemeteries. Setting aside the strain that such mass removals of remains would place on the French rail system and shipping, already taxed in the context of the demobilization of the living, one more grisly prospect was too much to consider. As a French official put it to the GRS in April 1919, all of France "would become a veritable charnel house if such extensive exhumations" occurred. Despite these protests, the French eventually relented after several rounds of negotiations over the next two years.[13]

Meanwhile, American officials and the public were divided on the issue of repatriation, with various organizations emerging to catalyze opinion on both sides. The most prominent of these was the Bring Home the Soldier Dead League and, on the antirepatriation side, the American Field of Honor Association. The latter was composed of several political officials, including former president Taft, and such unlikely allies as the American Federation of Labor president Samuel Gompers and the railroad magnate Cornelius Vanderbilt. The newly formed American Legion, the largest organization of American Great War veterans, and the Gold Star Mothers groups, precursors to the national organization incorporated in 1928, both remained somewhat neutral on the issue, deferring to the individual choices of grieving families. The most influential voice against repatriation from the American Field of Honor Association was none other than the commander of the American Expeditionary Forces himself, General John J. Pershing. The general argued that could the dead speak, they would wish to remain where they fought and fell. "The graves of our soldiers constitute, if they are allowed to remain," Pershing argued in a cable to the War Department, "a perpetual reminder to our allies of the liberty and ideals upon which the greatness of America rests."[14] The graves of U.S. soldiers would represent the nation abroad, proclaim its honorable sacrifice, and territorialize the reach of its global power.[15]

Pershing's argument echoed earlier military descriptions of American burials in France. An article in the Army's official newspaper, *Stars and Stripes,* published shortly after Secretary Baker made his repatriation promise, described the American cemetery at Suresnes, just outside of Paris, as "a little plot of earth that is as much American as is the National Cemetery at Arlington or the hallowed ground of Gettysburg."[16] Beyond equating the cemeteries as similarly consecrated by the presence of the military dead and hallowed by Civil War associations, the article, titled "Tender Hands Care for Graves of A.E.F.," was itself largely focused on assuring readers of the devoted attention the graves received from grateful French women. The American men, far from forgotten, were ensured public acts of mourning that conformed to the living's expectations of female nurture. Not only were comparisons to Arlington a central means for making overseas Fields of Honor desirable to the American public, but the cemetery itself became a model for their design.

Despite the authority, greater access to publicity, and persuasiveness of those who were against repatriation, a majority of people with deceased loved ones buried overseas expressed wishes for the return of their remains. Two weeks after the publication of the *Stars and Stripes* article, Secretary Baker said that given the option of leaving the dead buried in France or returned to the United States "for reinterment at Arlington or any other designated National Cemetery" or to any part of the United States for private burial, the nearly unanimous response among the relatives had been repatriation for burial at home. "Over and over again," he said, "the relatives have written: The Government took our boy away; it can do no less than return to us his precious body." Baker was responding to a query for an article in *Frank Leslie's Weekly* titled "Should We Bring Home Our Soldier Dead?" The piece opened with Theodore O'Hara's poetic assertion from "Bivouac of the Dead" that American soldiers should not have their final rest among "stranger steps and tongues" but should find their "fitter grave" in their "own proud land's heroic soil."[17]

It was around this same time that the first suggestions emerged for the ceremonial burial of an unknown American soldier, inspired by plans already under way in France and Britain. The new technologies of modern warfare deployed in the Great War, combined with the conditions and awful intimacies of trench fighting, resulted in all-too-common losses of identity and bodily integrity among the dead, exploded or incinerated beyond recognition or, as the historian Thomas W. Laqueur describes, "fragmented, beaten into the mud as the war moved back and forth over them."[18] While casualty figures for American forces were much lower than those of their Allied counterparts, reflecting different resources, battlefront experiences, and a much shorter time at war, the Great War resulted in enormous numbers of unidentifiable dead and missing people for whom no remains were ever found. Of 1,075,293 British war dead, for example, 180,861 were unknown and 336,912 missing, compared to 1,622 unknown out of 116,516 American military dead.[19]

Regardless of the relatively small numbers, national pathos and concern for the fate of the American unknowns loomed no less large. In a Memorial Day plea to the nation's bereaved mothers to leave their sons at rest overseas, Elizabeth Robinson, the wife of Charles L. Robinson, the president of the Colt Firearms Company in Hartford, Connecticut, and mother of a son killed in action at Belleau Wood and buried in France, urged special consideration for unknowns. "To remove the known dead would be unjust discrimination against the many unknown dead, who made the supreme sacrifice and cannot be honored by name," she said. "If the unknown dead alone were left, they would be forgotten."[20] Robinson's concerns carried an inherent criticism of the War Department's policy tying repatriation to the initiating request of family members, ensuring that unknowns could not be returned. She, too, praised the care that American cemeteries received in France and remarked on the presence of many French women in mourning clothes honoring the fallen there.

On Armistice Day, November 11, 1920, Britain and France held simultaneous ceremonies, turning the anniversary of 1918's victory, the historian Philippe Ariès has argued, into a "day of the dead."[21] The British Unknown Warrior was interred in Westminster Abbey, after a long funeral procession that included the Cenotaph at Whitehall, inscribed simply to "The Glorious Dead," while France's Unknown was interred at the base of the Arc de Triomphe. The British Unknown was the imperial nation's only repatriated body of the war. When first approached with the idea for a similar event and memorial in 1919, U.S. Army Chief of Staff General Peyton C. March was unenthusiastic. He felt sure that given time the Graves Registration Service would be able to identify all of the American fallen.[22] Furthermore, he saw no place comparable to Westminster Abbey or the Arc de Triomphe for such a ceremony; Arlington did not yet seem an equivalent to him, as it had already come to for so many others in the Army and among the civilian public.[23]

If not exactly sharing March's sentiments, a number of people believed there were better places than Arlington National Cemetery for an unknown's interment. On November 19, 1919, the executive chairman of New York's Victory Hall Association presented Secretary Baker with a request from the association for an unknown American soldier to be sent from France for burial in its planned New York City memorial building. Incorporated earlier that year, the association was collecting subscriptions for an enormous multifunction Victory Hall to honor the state's world war veterans, living and dead, on what was then an empty block across from the newly reconstructed Grand Central Terminal. It was to be decorated with bronze plaques bearing the names of the dead, while serving the living as a headquarters for the American Legion, and it would include a large auditorium, music and sports venues, and exhibition spaces. The source of significant controversy and decried by the future New York City mayor Fiorello LaGuardia as a crass real-estate scheme, the building project was ultimately abandoned.[24] Baker rejected the New Yorkers' request for an unknown and made clear that any subsequent appeals from state or private organizations would be similarly denied. The *New York Times* editorialized twice in favor of Baker's decision, first lauding his refusal to allow a precedent that might lead to the "scatter" of the unidentified dead "in loneliness all over this great land" and a week later encouraging the burial of a single American unknown in a "shrine [that] should be in the National Cemetery at Arlington, where the bravest lie, men of the South as well as men of the North, who fought for the Stars and Stripes."[25] Less than two weeks later, the Great War veteran and new congressman from New York Hamilton Fish Jr. introduced legislation for the selection and return from France of an unknown American soldier to be reinterred in a tomb in Arlington's Memorial Amphitheater, which had just been completed.

Far more epic in scale and seating capacity than the nineteenth-century amphitheater constructed by Meigs, the new structure was located near the Spanish-American War section of the cemetery. In 1908, the GAR had petitioned Congress for a larger facility, noting that Memorial Day crowds far exceeded the capacity of the extant structure. In subsequent hearings, one GAR member urged, "Arlington is not for today; it is not for the Grand Army of the Republic alone; it is not for the Spanish War veterans alone, but during all time as long as this nation lasts Arlington will be unique and will be the burial place for our soldiers."[26] This new location represented both a geographic and a chronological shift of centers within Arlington's memorial landscape away from Civil War structures and graves toward honoring those who were lost in wars of the twentieth century. Declared by the *Hartford Courant* to be "the most splendid mortuary monument ever erected by any nation" and to particularly "eclipse" the Arc de Triomphe, the enormous classical structure was described by the paper as a monument to democracy because it was located in Arlington, the epitome of the American national cemetery system, which was the "most democratic on earth." With honorable military service the only requirement for interment, Arlington was defined, the

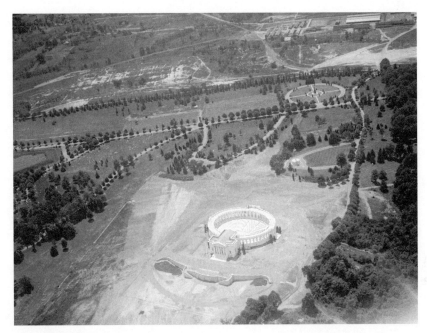

Aerial view of Arlington National Cemetery, 1919. Visible structures and memorials, from top to bottom: Fort Myer reserve; the West Gate, which was the primary entrance to the cemetery until the completion of Memorial Bridge; the Confederate Section with memorial at the center; the mast of the USS *Maine*; and, to the left amid the trees, the Spanish-American War Monument; and Memorial Amphitheater.

newspaper rejoiced, not by rank, wealth, or birth but by "equality of service and sacrifice."[27] Despite the structure's vaunted modernity, the first funeral service conducted in the new amphitheater was for the Confederate veteran and sculptor Moses Jacob Ezekiel, after which his body was interred at the base of the Confederate Monument that he created.

Representative Fish wanted the ceremonial burial of the American unknown to happen on Memorial Day 1921, but the date in May was rejected as being too soon and the possibility of interring a body that could have been identified too great. In the midst of this, the *New York Times* took a new editorial direction, rejecting the cemetery at Arlington because it was neither appropriately national nor reverential enough for such a solemn patriotic exercise. Rather, the Unknown Soldier should be laid to rest beneath the Capitol rotunda, "a shrine of the American people" and far more heavily trafficked by visitors due to the "irresistible impulse of interest and patriotism." The editorial argued that while "all America" eventually found their way to the Capitol, many would never set foot in Arlington, which "being a military cemetery by dedication, can hardly be the 'Westminster Abbey of America's heroic dead,' to use an expression of Secretary Baker." Writing a month before Ezekiel's funeral, the *Times* editorial concluded that the cemetery was not sufficiently national because it would always be seen as a cemetery for the Union dead of the Civil War, potentially eliciting feelings of disunity rather than "the noblest sentiments of humanity [and] love of country" that should attend an unknown. For this reason, the *Times* also counseled against Memorial Day for the ceremony, with all of the holiday's Civil War connotations, and urged the anniversary of Congress's war declaration, April 6, instead.[28] Fish persisted in pushing for Memorial Day, appealing to the new president William Harding's secretary of war, but was similarly rebuffed. Ultimately the tomb was placed in Arlington, and the service happened on Armistice Day, November 11, as it had in Britain and France. In October, Congress declared the day a national holiday, marking the origin of the United States' contemporary pair of holidays for honoring military service and sacrifice, Memorial Day and Veterans Day.

As the new administration took office, Congress passed legislation funding the repatriation of the requested dead in March 1921. The American Commission on Military Remains had concluded its work the year before, identifying cemeteries in which most of the American dead had already been congregated to be turned into permanent "Fields of Honor" and tasking their beautification and management to a War Memorial Council. This formed the basis of the American Battle Monuments Commission (ABMC) established by Congress in 1923. Ultimately, 45,558 bodies were returned to the United States for burial, while 764 were sent to family in various European nations of the deceased soldiers' birth, at a cost of about $30 million. The bodies of 30,922 Americans remained in European cemeteries that eventually became the purview of the ABMC.[29]

As plans were being made for American cemeteries in France, members of the War Memorial Council worried that Arlington would be neglected.

Their concern was compounded by the passage of legislation on April 15, 1920, that made a national cemetery burial available at no cost to any honorably discharged soldier or sailor "who served or hereafter shall have served during any war in which the United States has been or may hereafter be engaged."[30] Writing to members of Congress on behalf of the council, Charles Moore, chairman of the Commission of Fine Arts (CFA), said that in addition to the 2,000 to 3,000 interments from the recent war expected in Arlington in the near term, many more would follow. "Unless means shall be taken at once to carry out in the new areas the same general scheme of planting that has made Arlington beautiful and endeared it to the American heart, the result will be over-crowding of graves, and such lack of planting as will destroy the present fine character of the place, while at the same time it will be dishonoring the memory of the boys who died in the World War." The CFA and Quartermaster General Harry L. Rogers had a ready plan but needed Congress to fund it. "It is right to spend millions of dollars on the American Cemeteries in France," Moore concluded, "but at the same time we should not neglect the National Cemeteries at home."[31]

Included with the letter was a copy of the report concerning Arlington's distinction among national cemeteries and its future plans and needs, which had been developed over the previous few years by the CFA and quartermaster general. In terms of uniqueness, the report stated that first and foremost, "Arlington is a national shrine," with a "sacred character [that] should be protected and fostered." This included keeping it free from "self-assertive or grotesque" monuments, like those of many officers in Section 1 that Moore abhorred. Rather, he said, "quiet, simplicity, reverence should prevail." For Moore, this desired character for the land was largely to be achieved through landscaping, the maintenance of park-like greenways, and the careful locating of new sections of graves so the entire cemetery would not seem crowded. But in addition to being a shrine, Moore noted that "Arlington is also a historical place," by which he meant the histories of George Washington Parke Custis and Robert E. Lee. Renovation of the "mansion house and grounds to restore its original character" was the priority on this front. Exactly what constituted the plantation's "original character," however, would be the source of significant controversy as work got under way a few years later.[32]

Arlington's third needful quality and, in Moore's estimation, of near equal importance to the first two was its place in the "great central composition of Washington extending from the Capitol through the Mall to the Monument and on to the Lincoln Memorial, whence the Memorial Bridge already authorized by Congress" will cross the river and connect to the cemetery. The bridge corresponded with the Army's long-standing wish for better means of transportation to the cemetery from the capital, and when it was finished in 1932, it effectively shifted the cemetery's primary entrance away from the gate near Fort Myer on the west and opposite side. The end of the report was echoed in the letter to congressmen, noting that not only had the recent war brought many new graves to the cemetery, but "it has also given to more than a million men the right" to a burial there in the future. "The present appropriation for all the 83 National Cemeteries is $250,000 a year," he concluded. "Arlington alone will need more than that entire sum annually."[33]

The American Unknown was selected in France on October 24, 1921, from among four bodies exhumed from each of the American cemeteries there. By the time an infantry sergeant chose the Unknown by placing a bunch of roses atop his casket, it had been made impossible to know from which cemetery the remains had been drawn, further erasing any identifying circumstances of the soldier's death. The roses remained with the casket and were buried with it in the crypt at Arlington, which was also dusted with a layer of soil from France, two physical reminders of the place where the Unknown fell. Solemn ceremony attended the body—the only American unknown repatriated from Europe—on every point of the journey home to the United States. This included being carried up the Potomac River, past the cemetery, to the Washington Navy Yard aboard the USS *Olympia*. It was the last official service of Admiral Dewey's famed warship from the Battle of Manila Bay in 1898, effectively linking the Unknown of the Great War to the Spanish-American War and the Philippines. On November 9, a procession led by a cavalry band playing "Onward Christian Soldiers" brought the Unknown to the Capitol, where he lay in state the next day in the rotunda atop the Lincoln catafalque. The line for viewing was still so long as the appointed end approached on the night of the tenth that it was kept open until midnight. By then, an estimated 90,000 people had passed through to pay their respects.[34]

The procession to Arlington began the next morning at eight o'clock, at which point an artillery unit stationed at the Washington Monument commenced firing a single shot every minute until the end of the funeral ceremonies. Like Americans all over the country, members of the unit paused at noon and bowed their heads for two minutes of silence. The ceremonial gunfire and moment of silence attending the Unknown's burial enabled awareness and participation for people in Washington and around the nation who were not witness to the events themselves. In the weeks before, the Motion Picture Theater Owners of America had pledged their cooperation with the president in publicizing the two-minute silence across the country, promoting its "direct and constant communication with the American public."[35] Trade journals publicized the organization leadership's suggested slide text to be shown before films across the country, including, "Stop all activities for silent prayer on Armistice Day, Friday, November 11, between 12 noon and 12:02 p.m. as an unknown American hero is to be buried at that time in Arlington Cemetery."[36]

Following the caisson carrying the Unknown, the cortege included President Warren G. Harding, former president and then chief justice of the U.S. Supreme Court William H. Taft, and former president Woodrow Wilson, who was too ill to walk, along with General Pershing, the cabinet, members of the House and Senate, and several state governors. In some ways removed from the rest in a horse-drawn Victoria carriage, driven by two liveried African American coachmen, Wilson's ailing body seemed emblematic of his failure to get the Treaty of Versailles, including U.S. participation in the League of Nations, ratified in Congress and of his party's landslide defeat at the hands of Harding and the Republicans the year before with their platform of a "return to normalcy" and nonintervention. Harding's policies, not Wilson's, would imbue the ceremony and official stated meanings of the Unknown's sacrifice. This was compounded by the fact that the president's international Conference on the Limitation of Armament was set to open the next day. In addition to participating military leaders from Britain, France, and Belgium, the ceremonies for the Unknown were attended by several foreign dignitaries and national representatives gathered for the arms-reduction talks—turning the ceremonial burial of the Unknown into a kind of opening ceremony for the conference.[37]

Complementing the formal representatives of the government and military, the cortege included a long list of veterans' groups, women's auxiliaries, lineal societies, civic organizations, the Red Cross, National War Mothers, and several Catholic, Protestant, and Jewish organizations. The veterans' groups represented service in every war since the Civil War, including Confederate veterans, as well as two associations defined explicitly by ethnicity or race, the Jewish Veterans of the World War and Colored Veterans of the War.[38] The parade itself became a spectacle of the body politic produced in the ritual of honoring an unknown, parading behind that singular body.[39] Like earlier visualizations of the relationship of the dead to the liberties, identities, and citizenship of the living, this performance of national belonging and patriotism became a key feature of the monument, embodied in the act of laying a wreath at the tomb. The practice began almost immediately after the 1921 burial and had been prefigured in more limited ways by similar acts at the Tomb of the Civil War Unknowns.

Once the cortege reached the amphitheater, the Marine Band played Chopin's "Funeral March" as the Unknown's flag-draped coffin was moved from the caisson to a catafalque near the speakers' stand. A choir of men in white robes sang "The Son of God Goes Forth to War," while walking up into the balconies among the colonnades. The president and his wife entered just before noon, and all stood for the national anthem and a prayer. A bugle signaled the start of the national two-minute silence, after which Secretary of War John W. Weeks opened the speakers' portion of the funeral: "We are gathered not to mourn the passing of a great general or other conspicuous person, but an unknown soldier of the republic, who fought to sustain a great cause, for which he gave his life." Weeks went on to impress on the crowd the meaning of the event, the truths evident within its unknowns: "Whether he came from the North, the South, the East or the West, we do not know. Neither do we know his name, his lineage, or any other fact relating to his life or death, but we do know that he was a typical American who responded to his country's call and that he now sleeps with the heroes."[40] While Weeks did not elaborate on what constituted a "typical" American, the ceremonies and reporting surrounding the body's journey to Arlington made clear the presumption that it was not only male but also white and Protestant.

While those who had invitations filled the amphitheater, the entire cemetery was packed with nonticketed attendees. Many could still hear the speeches, as the ceremony marked one of the first uses of amplification for such an event through a device called the Bell Loud Talker. The equipment also enabled simultaneous broadcasts via telephone lines to crowds gathered in New York City, Chicago, and San Francisco—one of the first national broadcasts of its kind.[41] A precursor to the civic and political power of radio, as well as a technological touchstone, the broadcast of the Unknown's memorial would also be cited later in arguments for the use of coaxial cable for national television transmission in the 1940s.[42] As a special place, Arlington National Cemetery consistently seemed to inspire innovation in order to expand its reach while bringing it closer to individual Americans no matter where they were. This, in turn, made the cemetery all the more distinctive and central to American cultures of patriotism and national identity.[43]

President Harding followed Weeks and began his address with a similar appeal to the essential American character of the Unknown, choosing the metaphor of private domesticity rather than region in his depiction of a dispersed nation made one symbolically through the unidentifiable body. After noting, "He might have come from any one of millions of American homes," Harding moved immediately to an unknown mother, one among many "wondering today, finding a touch of solace in the possibility that the Nation bows in grief over the body of one she bore to live and die, if need be, for the republic."[44] The linking of the unknown young man and the unknown mother who had given him birth enabled a range of national attachments and made clear the necessity of women's mourning and maternal care to appropriate military honors. This was echoed in the amphitheater's seating, which included a section designated for families of the missing or unidentifiable dead, leaving a *New York Times* journalist to wonder if the "nearest kin of the boy who was this day honored by all America" was not sitting there near him.[45] The following year, a new tradition began on Mother's Day with a tribute at the tomb in honor of the unknown mother.[46]

"Crowd at Burial Ceremony of the Unknown Soldier in Arlington Cemetery," 1921.

Harding's address suggested that the unknown mother could also be in a faraway place and not in America at all. "In this body there once glowed the soul of an American, with the aspirations and ambitions of a citizen," he explained, adding, "He may have been a native or an adopted son; that matters little, because they gloried the same loyalty, they sacrificed alike." The 1917 Selective Service Act had transformed the composition of the armed forces. While acknowledging the significant numbers of new immigrants who enlisted or were drafted into service, Harding was clear to frame the Unknown as a "citizen," which limited the list of potential countries of origin and sustained his presumed whiteness. Two months before the United States entered the war, Congress had passed the Immigration Act of 1917, which extended the restrictions of the Chinese Exclusion Act (1882) to include all non-U.S. insular territories of the South Pacific, Southeast Asia, South Asia, and much of the Ottoman Empire (today's Middle East and Turkey). Added to this vast territorial restriction was a literacy test for all seeking entry to the United States and statutory exclusions of anarchists, "idiots, imbeciles, feeble-minded persons, epileptics, insane persons," those with contagious diseases, the physically disabled, "paupers," "vagrants," and anyone considered sexually deviant, including prostitutes, polygamists, and homosexuals, among others.[47] By law, none of these people were considered fit for naturalization, none presumed capable of embodying the "soul of an American." These new immigration restrictions intersected with official and popular domestic campaigns against "hyphenated Americans" and the promotion of English education, Americanization, and the politics of "100% Americanism," as did the passage, a month later, of the Jones Act, which reorganized territorial governance and granted U.S. citizenship to residents of Puerto Rico, making them eligible for the draft. While Puerto Rican soldiers of African descent were posted to predominantly African American segregated units, others were dispersed across divisions, indicating the complex racializations of Latinos in the early twentieth century. In May 1921, with support from Harding, Congress further restricted immigration by instituting a system of quotas limiting the immigration of any nationality to 3 percent of the number of immigrants from that country listed in the 1910 census, which significantly reduced southern and eastern European immigration. The religious and racial contours of this quota system were made even clearer with the Immigration Act of 1924, which shifted the calculation to 2 percent of those listed in the 1890 census. When Harding spoke of the patriotism of America's adopted sons to the gathered mourners in Arlington on November 11, 1921, he was still talking about white men.

Throughout Harding's address, he attributed not only unmitigated patriotism to the Unknown but total confidence in the nation for which he perished. Added to this was confirmation of Harding's own postwar commitment to normalcy's return through nonintervention in foreign affairs and an end to modern warfare: "This American soldier went forth to battle with no hatred for any people in the world, but hating war and hating the purpose of every war for conquest." In the "maelstrom of destruction and suffering and death," the Unknown "fired his shot for the liberation of the captive conscience of the world." Before Harding concluded his remarks with an impromptu recitation of the Lord's Prayer, he described the funeral as a moment for all to commit themselves to "a better order for the living" through their tribute to the unknown dead. "Standing today on hallowed ground, conscious that all America has halted to share in the tribute of heart and mind and soul to this fellow American, and knowing that the world is noting this expression of the Republic's mindfulness, it is fitting to say that his sacrifice, and that of the millions dead, shall not be in vain."[48]

When it was time for the burial service at the tomb itself outside the amphitheater, the Marine Band played "Our Honored Dead," and another procession made its way behind the casket. After prayers and several wreath layings, Chief Plenty Coups of the Crow Nation removed his headdress and placed it on the casket, before addressing the crowd. "I feel it an honor to the red man that he takes part in this great event," the chief remarked to the gathered mourners, "because it shows that the thousands of Indians who fought in the Great War are appreciated by the white man. I am glad to represent all the Indians of the United States in placing on the grave of this noble warrior this coup stick and war bonnet, every eagle feather of which represents a deed of valor by my race."[49] Plenty Coups was an advocate of Indian military service as a path to recognition, respect, and citizenship, and his remarks likened the valor of the Unknown to that of Native American veterans but did not suggest that the body within the casket might himself be Indian. Rather, the occasion of the Unknown's burial provided a platform for claiming national belonging and shared patriotism while asserting a kind of limited resistance to total assimilation or refusal to merge into the representative body about to be lowered into its tomb.[50]

While the *New York Times* opened its reporting of the day's events by describing the Unknown as a "boy whose very namelessness symbolized" all Americans who died in the war, the paper quickly moved into suggesting that the body symbolized much more, something individually felt, collectively expressed, and harder to put one's finger on. "The dead boy's funeral" was a "benediction, a spiritual something whose very realities were less apparent than the thoughts they conjured." The crowd wept, not in simple sorrow, the paper explained, but "carried away by the symbolism of patriotism which this unknown American embodied."[51] Although the ritual was borrowed from antiquity and the recent ceremonies of European allies, the Unknown of the First World War provided a remarkably literal enactment of the U.S. motto, *E Pluribus Unum*—"Out of Many, One."

From the simultaneous broadcast of the speeches to later newspaper accounts and the newsreels that quickly replaced didactic slides urging two minutes of national silence before feature films, the power of the Unknown to bond the many and elicit shared feelings of national honor, sacrifice, and grief extended well beyond his burial. Or as one newsreel company put it, "Here was something in which every man, woman, and child who claims Americanism shared, in spirit if not in presence."[52] The federal government had taken great care to accommodate multiple film crews along the parade route, in the amphitheater, and overlooking the tomb itself, "so that the unprecedented scenes of solemnity will be presented before the people of the country as vividly and realistically as possible by way of the screen."[53] Trade publications and fan magazines gave thrilling accounts of cameramen and editors speeding through Washington in cars and rushing to planes to get the story and images out. Later advertisements and testimonials for various news agencies promoted their speed and the power of the moving image, or "celluloid newspaper." Pathe News had edited reels of the entire ceremony from cortege to burial in New York City theaters by nightfall; Universal International Newsreel announced its national reach with ads reading, "Four Days to the Coast."[54] Writing for *Picture Play Magazine,* one journalist concluded, "Never was an important ceremony impressed more vividly on the composite mind of the entire nation."[55]

Of course, the sense of connection, or "composite mind," generated in combined expressions of mourning and patriotism—feelings of nationalism, shared sacrifice, and intimacy among strangers—had been common to Arlington for some time, facilitated by federal action, the transformation of the landscape, and the ritualization of public mourning for the military dead. As the plantation-turned-cemetery was transformed into hallowed ground through the relocation of bodies, its national associations had intensified at the turn of the century as the site was loosened from its predominantly Union Civil War connotations. All of this paled in comparison, however, to the effect of the 1921 reburial of a single unknown from the First World War, to the depth and reach of the national sensibilities "embodied" in that "spiritual something," which would

thereafter be forever associated with Arlington. Where before the interment of certain American bodies had changed the meaning of the land,
after 1921 Arlington's ability to change the meanings and identifications
of the bodies buried within it, its status as the nation's "most hallowed
ground," was secured.

While the Unknown's carefully protected anonymity was intended to ensure the body's universality and to abstract the conditions of death to
unquestionably glorious sacrifice, much was known and assumed about
the body within the tomb. That it was male and military was taken for
granted, making stark the limitations embedded within the notion of the
universal American subject and citizen. The Unknown's whiteness and
Protestantism were assumed and expected but could not be taken for
granted in the same way, as the range of mourners, resistance, and overt
counternarratives quickly made clear. The "imagined community" of
white Americans produced at the Tomb of the Unknown Soldier was
never uncontested, nor could it fully contain the dissident voices and desperate sadness it sought to assuage. Challenges had begun with the official ceremony itself and the presence of religiously and racially diverse
veterans' organizations whose markedly distinct bodies threatened the
ceremony's spectacle of unanimity.

The next funeral held in Memorial Amphitheater after the Unknown's
made stark the exclusions and racial segregation foundational to the national honor and citizenship celebrated at the tomb, and defining Arlington's landscape. At the same time, the service and its location enabled
challenges to these policies as no other place in America could, a fact not
lost on Harding's advisers, who had counseled against allowing the amphitheater's use as an invitation to protest. On Friday, June 1, 1923, thousands lined the streets of the capital and crowded into the amphitheater
to honor the life and work of Colonel Charles Young, who had achieved
the highest rank of any African American in the U.S. military on the eve
of the Great War but had not been deployed to Europe with the American Expeditionary Forces. Grand Memorial Day services, including an
address from the president, had just been held there on Wednesday. Now

crowds of Americans streamed into the cemetery again, only this time they were almost entirely black.

Charles Young was born into slavery in 1864 in Kentucky, a border state excluded from Lincoln's Emancipation Proclamation, and grew up in Ohio, where his family fled to freedom and his father had enlisted in the U.S. Colored Troops. After becoming the third black student to graduate from West Point in 1889, Young served in the American West with the Ninth Cavalry, one of the pair of famed segregated regiments formed after the Civil War, known along with the Tenth Cavalry as the "Buffalo Soldiers." In 1894, he was assigned to lead the new Military Science Department at Wilberforce University, where he became lifelong friends with his fellow professor W. E. B. Du Bois. After serving as the first black superintendent of a national park in 1903, then an army position, Young was assigned as the military attaché to Haiti, stationed in the Philippines, and then sent as attaché to Liberia. When he returned to the United States, he was posted with the Tenth Cavalry Regiment along the border with Mexico. In 1916, the Tenth formed part of the Punitive Expedition under the command of Brigadier General John J. Pershing and organized to capture the Mexican revolutionary Francisco "Pancho" Villa.[56]

Young distinguished himself in battle and stepped in briefly to command the Tenth Cavalry when its white commander took ill—making him the first African American officer to lead the black regiment in its fifty-year history. Thus, the newly promoted lieutenant colonel expected to go to war in Europe in command of a black regiment for the also-promoted Major General Pershing. Having championed Young with the promotion board, Pershing also expected as much. In 1917, however, Young was medically retired at the rank of colonel because of a heart condition. This development conveniently alleviated high-level concerns about the possibility of white officers having to serve under him and the likelihood that combat service in France would lead to his swift promotion to general. Young fought his forced retirement, including making a highly publicized June 1918 ride on horseback from his home in Ohio to Washington, DC, in only sixteen days. Wearing his uniform, Young sought to demonstrate his strength and endurance as a cavalryman to prove his fitness for duty.

In November, he was returned to active-duty status just as the Great War ended and sent back to West Africa and his intelligence post as military attaché to Liberia. In early January 1922, Young died from kidney disease and heart failure while on a mission in Lagos, Nigeria, where British colonial authorities buried him in the European section of Ikoyi Cemetery.[57] The colonel's wife, Ada, said her husband had always "wanted to occupy a soldier's grave at Arlington" and requested the repatriation of his remains, which took over a year.[58]

Young was a military hero, author, and leading figure in the NAACP and antilynching activism, and news of his death was received with enormous sadness and not a little anger across diverse communities in the United States but was framed as a particular loss to African Americans. While describing Young as "beloved by all his countrymen," a Kalamazoo, Michigan, newspaper qualified that he "was a patriotic figure among the colored people." Whereas just two months before, the nation had mourned the Unknown as the "heart of the Nation," the midwestern newspaper now explained that Young's "death saddened the hearts of all Afro-Americans and many memorial services have been held all over the country in his honor," including one by an all-black American Legion post in Kalamazoo.[59] Mainstream newspapers and white journalists reported the "imagined community" of black America that was produced and made visible in services across the country. Working through black churches, organizations, clubs, and newspapers, a coordinated national observance of Young's birthday occurred on March 12, 1922, becoming an annual tradition in many communities. Noting that President Harding and General Pershing both approved of the plan, the *Washington Post* reported, "Memorial services for Col. Charles Young who died recently in Lagos, Nigeria, will be held Sunday by colored people all over the country."[60] Harding and Pershing sent official messages to the services, the general paying tribute to Young's "exemplary military character," adding that "he should ever be an inspiration to his people," and the president writing of his "high opinion" of Young.[61] So notable was the racial specificity of the memorialization that diverse attendance at a service became remarkable. Portland's *Morning Oregonian* described a memorial in San Francisco, where Young had served as a captain in a black regiment at the Presidio earlier in his career: "That race feeling is a thing apart with them is shown by the action of the several San Francisco, Cal. American Legion posts in turning out almost en masse for the funeral of Colonel Charles Young, one of the few negroes to graduate from West Point."[62] This was a rare occurrence, however, as "race feeling" and the overwhelming sense that Young's military heroism was "a thing apart" predominated.

Fueled by anger drenched in grief, pride, and activism, this sense was true in some ways for the black press and among many African American veterans, as well. The black-owned *Tribune* of Savannah, Georgia, published a poem during the week of memorial birthday observances for Young that imagined his arrival in heaven—"Blow, Bugles of Heaven, a hero advances"—and described his fight with, rather than for, America. "'Twas he who endured every slight and foul insult, / Defending his manhood, his god, and his race," the poem reads, leaving notably absent his nation.[63] Writing in the NAACP's magazine the *Crisis*, Du Bois was furious, charging that his friend had been purposely sent to his death in Africa. "They sent him there to die," Du Bois raged. "They sent him there because he was one of the very best officers in the service and if he had gone to Europe he could not have been denied the stars of a General. They could not stand a black American General." He concluded his obituary, "He is dead. But the heart of the Great Black Race, the Ancient of Days—the Undying and Eternal—rises and salutes his shining memory: Well done!"[64] When Young's body was finally returned to the United States over a year later, the *New York Amsterdam News* ran a front-page story headlined "Col. Young's Body Arrives Here."[65] Before Young's remains were sent on to Arlington, an American Legion post named in his honor hosted a memorial service in the Great Hall at City College, with Du Bois and Assistant Secretary of the Navy Theodore Roosevelt Jr., the former president's oldest son, providing the central eulogies. Roosevelt Jr. had been instrumental in gaining the use of the amphitheater for Young's funeral after the War Department and some in the Harding administration balked. Speaking first, Du Bois scandalized some and energized others in the crowd by renewing his charges against the military and government as Roosevelt Jr. looked on, concluding that Young had died of "a broken heart."[66]

Fast on the heels of Memorial Day events and drawing on much of the ceremony for a state funeral, Young's funeral began with a cortege to

Arlington through the streets of the capital. In addition to friends, family, pallbearers, and the traditional riderless horse, with empty boots reversed in the stirrups, the procession included veterans, various civil organizations, and students; to a person, almost all were African American. Thousands lined the streets to mourn the loss and celebrate the colonel's achievements and contributions. The *New York Times* described the funeral and crowds, noting that Memorial Amphitheater "had not been used for a like service for an individual officer or man since the burial of America's Unknown Dead. The negro population of Washington made the occasion of Colonel Young's funeral one of demonstration in respect to his memory, negro schools being closed for the day, and thousands gathered along Pennsylvania Avenue and Arlington."[67] Writing of the service in the *Crisis,* Du Bois called the honors hollow and representative of nothing so much as the hypocrisy of the president and military, which now honored a man they had so abused while he was alive. "The last sad ceremonies over the body of the late Colonel Young bring forward the old and familiar phases of Caucasian propaganda in the United States."[68]

Like the Tomb of the Unknown Soldier, Young's grave became a pilgrimage site within the cemetery. Writing of the new monumental headstone placed at his grave in 1926, the *Washington Post* noted, "it has become the practice of all negro organizations which convene [in Arlington] to lay a wreath on it."[69] Benjamin O. Davis Sr.—who was sent to the Philippines instead of France in the Great War—ended up becoming the first black general in the U.S. Army in 1940. His son, Benjamin O. Davis Jr., was the fourth black graduate of West Point, after Young had been the third nearly fifty years before. Davis Jr. went on to command the famed Tuskegee Airmen during World War II and followed in his father's footsteps when he became the first black general in the U.S. Air Force in 1954 and the first black four-star general in American history in 1998. Both are buried in Arlington.[70]

While the CFA and Quartermaster Division had been working for some time on plans to restore Arlington House "to its original character as a distinctive house of its historic period," it remained largely empty and used primarily as offices for cemetery administration in the early 1920s.[71] The period they had in mind was the early republic and G. W. P. Custis's heyday. Prompted by a visit to Mount Vernon and the restoration efforts of the Mount Vernon Ladies Association in 1921, Frances Parkinson Keyes, the wife of Senator Henry Wilder Keyes, Republican of New Hampshire, sparked a popular effort for renovations at Arlington that ran contrary to the Army's and CFA's aims. Devoting part of her popular *Good Housekeeping* column, "Letters from a Senator's Wife," to the "shocking neglect of the Lee Mansion" in federal hands compared to the women's private stewardship of the first president's plantation, Keyes made clear that Arlington was to her most associated with Robert E. Lee and the late 1850s, not Custis. "Whatever our opinions and traditions may be," she concluded, "we all realize now that Robert E. Lee was one of the greatest generals and one of the noblest men who ever lived. To every American woman the abuse of his home must seem a disgrace; to every Southern woman it must seem a sacrilege."[72]

With a national platform and significant influence in Washington, Keyes helped marshal renovation efforts toward the memorialization of the Confederate general. In 1924, Congress's Joint Committee on the Library held hearings on the "restoration of Lee Mansion" and, on March 25, 1925, passed a joint resolution authorizing the work, which President Calvin Coolidge promptly signed into law. Charles Moore remained vocally opposed to the direction of these efforts, arguing that the house should be restored to represent "the first fifty years of the Republic" and called "Arlington House" or the "Custis Mansion." Conceding its importance to Lee's history, Moore suggested that the parlor where Robert and Mary wed could be restored to that moment in his honor.[73] Despite Moore's efforts, the 1925 legislation directed the house to be returned to the "condition in which it existed immediately prior to the Civil War" and "occupancy by the Lee family" and the procurement of as many of the Lee furnishings as possible. This was all tasked with no appropriation of funds to the Quartermaster Division and the War Department, which retained jurisdiction of the site. The resolution opened with a celebration of sectional unity before dwelling on the representative qualities of Lee as an American hero due great honors, which were "compelling factors in cementing the American people in bonds of patriotic devotion and action against common external enemies in the war with Spain and in the World War, thus consummating the hope of a reunited country that would again swell the chorus of the Union."[74] Sixty years after the surrender of Robert E. Lee to Ulysses S. Grant at Appomattox Court House, the national apotheosis of Lee seemed complete, as a congressional act spearheaded by Republicans not only attributed to him posthumous victories in the Spanish-American and First World Wars but credited the Confederate general with unifying the nation, illustrated by a quote from Abraham Lincoln's first inaugural address. This association of Lee with Lincoln was manifested on a grand scale with the completion of Memorial Bridge linking their memorials and pulling the commemoration of Lee into the capital's monumental core.

This celebration of Robert E. Lee as national hero and emblematic American was more than some people could bear, and Moore was far from alone in his resistance to the restoration plan. In August 1925, the national encampment of the GAR closed its annual meeting in Grand Rapids, Michigan, with a scathing protest to the legislation, which would "make that house in the midst of our sacred dead a shrine to" the man who "sought to destroy" the republic they "died to save." The GAR called the plan "an insult and a disgrace to the Nation, to every grave in Arlington Cemetery," and adopted a resolution urging repeal of the law and continued use of the mansion for cemetery administration. Making it "a memorial to Lee" not only was a "desecration" of the cemetery, the resolution concluded, but would undo decades of reconciliation as it would "destroy the friendship which has heretofore existed between the Blue and the Gray."[75] That same month, the CFA was asked to supervise the project, which allowed Moore to redirect plans toward the earlier period. This introduced a tension within the restoration that persisted for several years between its guiding periodization and popular perceptions of the site as a monument to Robert E. Lee.[76]

Just as quickly, the Tomb of the Unknown Soldier itself became a potent site for challenging the very patriotic narratives and military sacrifices it was designed to valorize. One could see this in the use of the memorial as a platform for challenging increased immigration restrictions in 1924, juxtaposed with the Ku Klux Klan's celebration of those very limitations at the site a year later. In attempting to persuade fellow congressmen to vote against the changes to the quota system introduced in the 1924 legislation, Peter F. Tague, Democrat of Massachusetts, said, "I stood awhile at the tomb of America's Unknown Soldier, the last resting place of him, whom we know not, nor whence he came. Standing there, with bared head, I wondered if in life he was an Italian, an Irishman, a Jew, a Nordic, a Slav, or what." Tague set the scene of patriotic mourning, pulling on the emotional power of the tomb and its location to frame his dissent: "I thought of what a travesty of American ideals it would be if in passing this bill we would prevent coming to America the unknown mother of our revered unknown soldier."[77] Notably, the congressman's list, before ending with the open-ended "or what," was limited to national or ethnic groups generally considered white. His concern for the immigration status of the Unknown's mother sustained the tomb's predominant dyad of gendered sacrifice for the nation, the soldier giving his life after his mother gave him to the service, as well as racial exclusion. Despite opposition from Tague and others, the 1924 bill passed and was signed into law by Coolidge. Support for greater immigration restriction had come from many quarters, including the Ku Klux Klan, which had been active in its second iteration since 1915, promoting "100% Americanism" and seeking to protect the national character and culture from immigrants, Jews, and Catholics, as well as African Americans, through ballot boxes, fear, and violence. With more than four million members nationwide by 1924, including a significant number of local, state, and federal elected officials, the Klan was in the mainstream of American politics and represented one of the largest social and reform movements of the early twentieth century. When the Klan marched on Washington in 1925, surrounding events included not only the burning of an eighty-foot cross from the heights of Arlington not far from the cemetery but also a formal wreath laying at the Tomb of the Unknown Soldier.[78] While standing on opposite sides of the immigration issue, Tague and members of the Klan each drew on the same patriotic symbolism, authority, and moral heft of the Unknown and his memorial in the national cemetery.

It was in this context that the War Department and CFA sought assistance from some who had been enslaved at Arlington as they looked to restore the mansion, slave quarters, and yard to antebellum conditions. In December 1929, the Army's lead architect on the project, Luther Leisenring, walked the property with Selina Gray's daughters, interviewing them on two separate occasions. Before that, James Parks had provided assistance. Parks had worked at the cemetery until June 1925, for sixty-one years since he had helped dig the first federal graves in 1864. Sometime after the final dispersal of Freedman's Village, Parks moved into a small cabin near the cemetery's south entrance. Records from his application for retirement benefits show that he was briefly employed as a laborer with the cemetery's landscape gardener again in October 1928 "for a particular purpose in connection with the restoration of the Arlington Mansion."[79] By then, Parks was approaching ninety. An officer with the Quartermaster Division later described hiring him so he would be available for questions relating to the property as they arose. Parks provided a significant amount of detail that continues to guide interpretations, particularly concerning the slave quarters and summer kitchen, gardens, and mansion exteriors. He also provided information about Custis's Arlington Springs resort and led at least one journalist in 1928 to the old slave cemetery where his parents and other family were buried. By that time, the graves were on land in the Department of Agriculture's Experimental Farm, largely neglected but undisturbed.[80]

In thanks for Parks's assistance and in light of the fact that he had never lived or worked anywhere but the Arlington Estate, the secretary of war issued an order at the end of the year making it possible for him to one day be buried in the national cemetery as a civilian. The country's largest circulation African American newspaper, the *Chicago Defender*, reported the order with some of Parks's history. The article described Parks's grandfather George Clark, who had cooked for the Custises and who had lived, Parks said, to be 110 years old. " 'Uncle Jim' does not expect to live to that age," the article concluded.[81] Parks died the following summer and was buried on August 23, 1929, with honors in a western section near the cemetery's wall abutting Fort Myer, at the opposite side of the former plantation from the old slave cemetery. He had outlived two wives but left behind many children and grandchildren, including five who had served in the First World War.[82]

In death, the formerly enslaved man who had experienced so much change, joy, and pain at Arlington was transformed into the epitome of the eternally faithful slave. Eulogies to "Uncle Jim" in the white-owned press described the passing of the "last of the home folks" and detailed Parks's affection for Custis and connection to Lee, his work at the national cemetery, his trustworthiness in contributions to renovations, and his "remarkable and photographic mind for an old man of his race." He had been "received into the earth of the old Virginia plantation from which he sprung." This was all presented as evidence of Parks's fidelity across the decades to Arlington and its owners. Little was said of his family other than to remark upon its size—twenty-two children—and the recent military service of some. The obituaries marveled at all Parks had seen in his lifetime but understood him only as a witness to the histories of Custis, Lee, and the plantation, to the changes in the lives of white people.[83]

A year after Parks's funeral, this version of his story was immortalized for posterity on his grave marker, erected by the American Legion. Roughly the same height as a regulation national cemetery headstone, the marble monument is wider, with a broad rectangular face carrying a bronze plaque, angled up for ease in reading from a standing position: "James Parks—An Interesting, Respectful, Kindly Old Negro: Born a Slave at Arlington House Estate About 1843. Dies Arlington County, Virginia, August 22, 1929. He Belonged to George Washington Parke Custis, Proprietor of Arlington Estate from 1781 to 1857. 'Uncle Jim' Lived and Worked at Arlington Practically the Whole of His Long and Useful Life. In Appreciation of His Faithful Service the Secretary of War Granted Special Permission to Bury His Mortal Remains in This National Cemetery. Requiescat In Pace." The *Washington Evening Star* reported the American Legion's gift with a picture of the monument under the heading "In Memory of Fidelity" and said that Parks "would have been very proud of the honor, because he was a rare and courtly old fellow, . . . a page out of the past."[84]

The attorney and popular historian Enoch Aquila Chase, who wrote extensively about Arlington's past and the cemetery, composed Parks's epitaph. It was Chase who had popularized the "Uncle Jim" moniker in 1928 and had crafted his story as one of timeless faithful slavery within the contexts of benevolent white mastery. Chase reported, "[Parks] assured me he had always been well treated and knew nothing to the contrary with respect to the other slaves." Chase often referred to Parks as an embodiment of antebellum days who seemed to step out from one of Thomas Nelson Page's "stories of the Old South."[85] Ten years later, Chase credited himself with being the person "who discovered 'Uncle Jim Parks,' 'The Last of the Home Folks,' and made him famous." In the sense that Chase had created the figure of faithful "Uncle Jim" Parks, his boast of discovery was largely true.[86]

Published in 1932, the second volume of John Dos Passos's *U.S.A.* trilogy juxtaposes the official and vernacular narratives of the Unknown Soldier's valor and universality with an insistent focus on the specific body within the tomb and the horrors it experienced, not only in war but in the very processes of anonymity and sanctification. The section, titled "The Body of an American," opens with lines from the enacting legislation, run together, nearly unintelligible: "Whereasthe Congressoftheunitedstates Byaconcurrentresolution-adoptedon the4thdayofmarch lastauthorizedthe Secretaryofwar to cause to be brought totheunitedstatesthe body of an American . . ." Dos Passos then moves to the scene of selection in France and the assault on the senses of the "reek of chloride the lime and the dead," as the unknown is picked, "enie menie minie moe." He asks, "how can you tell a guy's a hundredpercent when all you've got's a gunnysack full of bones, bronze buttons stamped with the screaming eagle and a pair of roll puttees?" But Dos Passos has already answered his own question with a soldier's preceding call: "Make sure he aint a dinge boys, make sure he aint a guinea or a kike." The narrative moves through various homes and occupations that might have been part of the Unknown's biography; it describes his Army physical and naked body parts, fondled and examined, his induction and the manipulation of his body in the transformation from civilian to soldier: "Atten'SHUN suck in your gut you c—r wipe that smile off your face." Dos Passos details the number of ways the soldier might have become separated from his identification tag, and the drunk quartermaster who might have lost his service record, before describing the Unknown's death in sickening detail, when "blood ran into the ground" and "brains oozed, . . . licked up by the trenchrats, the belly swelled and raised a generation of bluebottle flies, and the incorruptible skeleton, and the scraps of dried viscera and skin bundled in khaki."[87] The entire section dwells on the body, its senses, orifices, pleasures, trials, death, and decay, to remind the reader of what is concealed in the tomb, abstracted beneath its ritual, classical aesthetic, and seeming impenetrability.

While this is perhaps the most famous literary evocation of the Unknown, Dos Passos was far from the first writer to suggest that the tomb was a monument to national exclusion, hypocrisy, warmongering, and corruption. The NAACP executive secretary and poet James Weldon Johnson had already looked within the tomb in "Saint Peter Relates an Incident of the Resurrection Day," begun in 1927 but finished in 1930 while Johnson was furious at the segregated accommodations and treatment of African American Gold Star Mothers on War Department trips to visit gravesites in France. His poem re-creates a version of the 1921 cortege to Arlington as a parade of the risen, responding to a call for all patriots and "100% Americans" to come and escort the Unknown to heaven. Johnson describes the collection responding to the call, made up of members of hereditary groups, the Klan, and veterans from every war, including the Sons of Confederate Veterans. The parade rushes to the cemetery in fear that the Unknown will have ascended before they can get there, only to discover him still struggling to get out of the tomb— an image of the symbol and monument so sturdy and immobile that the man cannot get out from beneath it—and set about helping to break him free. "Through it, at last, his towering form loomed big and bigger—/ 'Great God Almighty! Look!' they cried, 'he is a nigger!'"[88] There is stunned silence before an eruption; what should they do? Klansmen suggest burying him again in a scene that turns the patriotic parade—the national community produced in the act of collectively honoring the Unknown—into a lynch mob. As the crowd dithers, the black soldier climbs to heaven singing an old spiritual.

While Dos Passos and Johnson focus on the man beneath the tomb, the African American playwright and author May Miller explores the place of the unknown mother in order to challenge not only the racially exclusive versions of citizenship and national belonging solidified in the memorial but also its gendered contours. In doing so, she replicates the popular mother-son dynamic of shared martyrdom and the centrality of female mourning to nationalism to focus on the particular experience of black women. Miller sets her play "Stragglers in the Dust" (1930) at the Tomb of the Unknown Soldier just before the cemetery closes for the night. The first scene opens with Nan, a black domestic worker tasked with shining the brass fixtures in Memorial Amphitheater, sitting beside her scrub pail and rag, looking at the tomb and the river and capital city beyond it. She is approached by a middle-aged white man named Mac, the cemetery watchman, who encourages her to finish up as it is almost closing time. Nan says she would rather stay, as her son Jim is there and she wishes to be near him: "All Ah got is heah." Mac expresses surprise that he has never heard that Nan's son also works at the cemetery and is even more surprised when she corrects him and explains that her son is buried in the Tomb of the Unknown Soldier. The watchman's mistake marks the general assumption that the valorous military bodies that lie in Arlington are white, while the laboring bodies that bury them are black. Images of the tomb's construction itself had played on this narrative, depicting an all-black crew building the original crypt. Nan describes Harding's words of patriotism and sacrifice from the 1921 funeral, to which Mac replies, "Yes, I heard that, but Nan, they weren't talking 'bout your Jim. Why they don't even know who that soldier is—he's unknown. It wasn't about your Jim they were talking." Mac's assumptions deepen here, as he insists not only that the Unknown could not be a black soldier but also that black soldiers were generally not included in the patriotic heroics they were "talking 'bout." This racialized distance is reinforced by his persistent use of the phrase "your Jim," as opposed to "the country's"—or "our"—Unknown. Nan insists that Jim is the Unknown; but she does not demand his recognition because she knows "dere'd be them dere as wouldn't want Jim tuh stay dere cause he's cullud," and she does not want him moved again. In fact, she thinks he might have been better off left in France. Nan leaves, and the scene shifts to a conversation between Mac and a white politician who has come looking for his veteran son, "a straggler," who was traumatized by his war experience and has been haunting the amphitheater "with his ghost-like face." When Mac describes the conversation he just had with Nan, the politician responds,

Black men constructing the Tomb of the Unknown Soldier of World War I, ca. 1921.

if the Unknown were black, "what a terrible joke on America!" The politician's son believes the Unknown is the black soldier who died saving his life in France: "[He is a] black Nigger too who stole my place. He caught the shell aimed at me! He holds the tomb meant for me!"[89] It is a stark depiction of the idea that demonstrations of black heroism and military valor rob white men of the power of their racial privilege and representational authority.

Miller revisited the theme in a short story published near the end of World War II, "One Blue Star" (1945). In it, an unidentified mother of a young black man who has just been drafted feels herself connected to black mothers across history who have sent their sons to war. She becomes the mother to Toussaint L'Ouverture, Crispus Attucks, and Nat Turner, among others. Her story ends in Arlington at the Tomb of the Unknown Soldier: "And here again I am, my dark form silhouetted against a vast white amphitheater, marble columns rising behind me and below me flowing the lazy Potomac; but I see none of this. The omnipresent thing is the severe white sepulcher, and I claw and claw to scratch my way to the carrion flesh within. Can he be mine, too? He might; he well might."[90] It is her "dark form" contrasted with the tomb, her living maternal body, that makes visible the possibility that the nation's universal body is black. While the constant presence of various groups laying wreaths at the tomb made the site a permanent theater for the performance of patriotism and national belonging through public mourning and acts of honoring the Unknown, the "unknown" mother's visible body gave specificity to the manufactured anonymity of the tomb.

The presence of military guards stationed at the tomb—living, uniformed expressions of state power and authority—carried their own appeal to martial fraternity with the Unknown Soldier while serving as visual reminders of what he had been in life. In the years immediately following the 1921 ceremonies, there was no common public script or clear expectation for behavior at the tomb. While visitors with wreaths came regularly in small groups or as representative bodies, and commercial photographers captured the ceremony, others wandered the deserted amphitheater or sat on the low-slung first version of the tomb to rest their feet and take in the view. The tomb became a popular site for picnickers, its squat rise seeming a fine table. The War Department received a number of complaints about behavior at the tomb and requests for its protection. The burial of the Unknown may have cemented Arlington's status as hallowed ground, but these complaints suggested that the touring public still needed a policing presence to train appropriate reverence among the living. The American Legion appealed to the Army to place a regular sentry at the tomb to discourage its disrespectful uses for leisure and lunching, as well as loud talking, laughing, smoking, and men's neglect to remove their hats. The War Department resisted this kind of regular duty, erecting a fence around the tomb instead, but relented in the face of added pressure from the White House and Congress. In 1926, soldiers from Fort Myer were tasked with daily guard duty during the cemetery's operating hours, which placed living military personnel at the site but did not yet constitute the elite honor guard or precise ceremony of today's Tomb Guard.[91]

"First Permanent Guard at Tomb of Unknown Soldier, Arlington, Va.," March 25, 1926.

While the presence of a guard discouraged visitors from sitting or stepping on the tomb, it became far more difficult to do so once the larger permanent memorial was completed and opened to the public in 1932. As Congress was prodding the Army to place sentries at the site in 1926, it had appropriated $50,000 for the completion of the monument and authorized a formal design competition that opened in 1928. This resuscitated debates about the meaning and symbolism of the Unknown that had simmered for years. These debates were largely focused on whether the Unknown Soldier's burial site was a symbol of war or peace, whether it broadcast national power and greatness or vulnerability and loss. With the tomb linked in the Harding administration's original ceremony with disarmament and nonintervention, some people feared it had come to represent the awful costs and ultimate futility of the First World War, making it primarily a place of advocacy against future military engagements.[92]

The design selected in 1929, submitted by the architect Lorimer Rich and the sculptor Thomas Hudson Jones, carried traces of these controversies but was primarily devoted to martial honor. It was stark white and funereal, with a heavy solidity and plain classical lines, reminiscent of Meigs's plan for the Tomb of the Civil War Unknowns: "of plain but good classic severe design."[93] The new memorial incorporated the original tomb as its base for a rectangular, sarcophagus-like monument of marble; it is eleven feet tall, roughly seven feet wide, and thirteen feet long. The western end of the tomb, facing the amphitheater plaza, carries the inscription, "Here Rests in Honored Glory an American Soldier Known But To God," while the other end bears three classically adorned figures in relief, two female and one male, representing Victory, Peace, and Valor. Each side is decorated with three inverted laurel wreaths set between four relief columns.

The first Armistice Day after the new tomb's completion was to be its formal dedication. Instead, it became the scene of protest when veterans disrupted the secretary of war's address by walking out to honor the fallen of the Bonus Marchers in the capital earlier that summer. Thousands of Great War veterans, calling themselves the Bonus Expeditionary Force and struggling in the early years of the Depression, had come to Washington with their families seeking early payment of service bonuses scheduled for 1945. Denied by Congress and President Herbert Hoover, many remained encamped on the Mall, near the Capitol building. After police failed to evict them and killed two veterans in the struggle on July 28, 1932, Hoover sent in the Army. Led by General Douglas MacArthur and including his aide and the future president Major Dwight D. Eisenhower and a tank unit commanded by Major George S. Patton, they drove the Bonus Marchers out of the monumental core into Anacostia and burned their largest camp there to the ground. The horrifying spectacle of veterans and their families brutalized by their own military in the midst of a presidential election year helped assure Hoover's landslide defeat by Franklin Delano Roosevelt three months later.[94] Occurring just days after that election, the November 11 ceremony dedicating the new Tomb of the Unknown Soldier was not attended by Hoover. Word that some American Legion posts intended to leave the event en masse had been reported earlier in the press, as had their plans to march from the amphitheater to the graves of the two men who had been killed, William Hushka and Eric Carlson, who had both been buried in Arlington.[95] On the second anniversary of the "Battle of Pennsylvania Avenue," the Veterans of Foreign Wars (VFW) held memorial exercises at the men's graves and then placed a wreath at the Tomb of the Unknown Soldier.[96]

The year 1932 had opened with the completion of Memorial Bridge and a new broad avenue leading from it to the base of the rise up to Arlington House. Situating the plantation house as the terminus of the capital plan's axis from the Lincoln Memorial, the bridge not only shifted the primary entrance to the cemetery but also transformed the vista from Washington. It had long been marked by the mansion's presence on the heights, but the monumental thoroughfare now trained the eye directly toward the house. This facet of the construction had been highlighted in a front-page story and photograph in the *Washington Star,* headlined "Clearing Way to Arlington House," that depicted the mansion framed between two unfinished pylons.[97] The mansion's pride of place, forecasted by Charles Moore and the CFA years earlier, signaled its new status as a de facto federal memorial.

While work on Memorial Bridge had been under way and the Unknown's permanent memorial taking shape, women in the Army and Navy Nurse Corps began pursuit of another monument in Arlington to honor their own service, perhaps motivated by their lack of inclusion in the tomb's representation of "universal" military sacrifice and valor. The idea for a memorial in the cemetery's nurses' section, or Section 21, came in 1928 from an Army nurse serving in the Philippines; she also made the first donation of one hundred dollars to kick off the fund-raising. With a site selected through the help of the sculptor Gutzon Borglum, on a break from his work on Mount Rushmore, the Corps continued to raise funds for several years. In 1937, the superintendent of the Army Nurse Corps, Julia C. Stimson, who had been the first woman to earn the rank of major after her service in the First World War, explained the goals for the memorial in a letter to the CFA. While Section 21 already had the monument to the Spanish-American War nurses at its tip, she noted, the Corps sought to add its sculpture to a different area, among the more recently interred, who had been military personnel, not civilian contract employees. "The idea is to have some kind of simple but

Aerial view showing the axis from the Lincoln Memorial across Memorial Bridge to the Hemicycle and Arlington House, January 1935. The island visible in the Potomac River to the right had by this time been designated Theodore Roosevelt Island. During the Civil War, it was called Mason's Island and was the location of a "contraband" camp, among other uses.

impressive indication," she explained, "that the place where it is erected is dedicated to former members of the Army and Navy Nurse Corps."[98]

Unlike the rough-hewn granite of the Spanish-American War nurses' marker, the new monument dedicated on November 8, 1938, brought a uniformed female figure into Arlington's memorial and martial terrain. The monument's design appealed to the gendered frames of women's service, casting nursing as natural to women and feminine, distinct from other parts of the military but no less honorable. Carved in white marble and located "within sight of the Tomb of the Unknown Soldier," as the *Washington Herald* was careful to note, the figure stands on a short pedestal in a nurse's cloak and hat on a slope near a copse of cedars, overlooking rows of graves.[99] At nearly ten feet high, the figure appears even taller because of the rise. The *New York Times* described the memorial

Members of the Army and Navy Nurse Corps pose with the monument to their service on the day of its dedication in Arlington National Cemetery, November 8, 1938.

as "heroic in size and symbolic in character," designed to be a "timeless representation of the spirit of nursing."[100] This included careful avoidance of any aspect of the uniform that might specify historical period or service branch, facilitated by the statue's modernist lines and aesthetic.[101] The sculptor, Frances Rich, said she sought to depict "the gentleness, kindness, and willingness to serve, which nursing represents."[102] This was a common note in descriptions of the monument and ceremony, which dwelled on the softness, tenderness, and quiet beauty that the memorial—and the Nurse Corps—brought to the cemetery. Superintendent Stimson concluded her remarks at the dedication, "Inspired by the beauty of this quiet place and by . . . the lives of useful loveliness of those of our sisters who lie here, [Rich] has carved in immortal marble a symbol of the spirit of nursing. With renewed dedication to that spirit, we present this guardian of our comrades in their eternal sleep, and as an inspiration to all who devote their lives to the service of others."[103] Rich was the daughter of the popular actress Irene Rich, a fact that never went without notice in coverage of the new memorial and added an extra layer of glamour

and the feminine to the commemoration of the Army and Navy Nurse
Corps.

In 1933, the mansion, slave quarters, and immediate surroundings had
been classified together as a "miscellaneous memorial" distinct from the
cemetery and transferred by executive order from the jurisdiction of
the War Department to the National Park Service and the Department of
the Interior, much to the chagrin of military authorities and Charles
Moore at the CFA. This brought new oversight and guiding principles to
the restoration and interpretation of the site and created an NPS island
within the cemetery.[104] It was the front edge of much larger fights among
federal agencies over the use of Arlington lands. Conflict reached a cre-
scendo in 1941 when large tracts of the Department of Agriculture's Experimental Farm, once Freedman's Village land, were repurposed for
the construction of a new War Department headquarters. Originally designated for the farmland abutting Memorial Bridge, the site was shifted
south toward the airport after Secretary of the Interior Harold L. Ickes
charged that the Army's plan would "spoil the setting of such national
symbols as the Arlington Lee Memorial."[105]

Ultimately taking a smaller corner of the Arlington Estate, the War Department broke ground on September 11, 1941. Europe had been at war
for two years already, and the United States' official entry in the Second
World War was just on the horizon, with the Japanese attack at Pearl
Harbor on December 7. The rest of the agricultural land was soon dedicated to an annex for Fort Myer and an apartment complex called "Arlington Farms" with housing for 7,000 unmarried women who were drawn
to the capital for war jobs and service in the armed forces auxiliaries. This
shift in the new War Department location meant that residents of Queen
City, the neighborhood community built by former Freedman's Village
residents after their eviction from the Arlington Estate, were once again
displaced by federal order and the military. Construction of the new
building was swift in the midst of war; by February 1943, Queen City was
gone, and the War Department occupied its new central headquarters,
the Pentagon.[106]

✯   ✯   ✯

Just two days after the attack at Pearl Harbor, the Quartermaster Division advised including a statement in condolence telegrams that specified no remains would be transported from outside the continental United States until after cessation of hostilities, when they would be repatriated for final burial, if possible and only if requested by next of kin. The War Department quickly adopted the policy. By the end of the week, the United States was officially at war with Japan and Germany.[107]

While mortuary policies remained the same in both world wars, the conditions of battle, challenges of recovery and identification of remains, and logistics were radically different. The number of Americans serving in World War II, as a multifront conflict in two overseas theaters, was enormous compared to the earlier war. Mobilized quickly with the help of the draft, which had been reinstated with the Selective Service Act of 1940, more than sixteen million Americans served in the armed forces between 1941 and 1945. Nearly 300,000 were killed in battle, about 10,000 of whom remained unknown.[108] As the war progressed and casualties mounted, military leaders briefly considered a policy change in the late summer of 1943. The new proposal would have required the total number of next-of-kin requests for the repatriation of bodies from a given location to reach 70 percent before any bodies from that area would be returned. If that figure was reached, all remains, whether or not they had been requested, would be sent back to the United States; if not, none would be returned at all. The plan was ultimately rejected under the assumption that the American public would never accept it.[109]

By the war's end, tens of thousands of American military dead were spread across nearly 300 temporary cemeteries throughout Europe, North Africa, Asia, and the South Pacific. Changes in technology and the conditions of fighting presented new difficulties in recovery and identification as aerial bombardment campaigns and the use of heavy artillery destroyed bodies or made them disappear altogether. Unlike the fierce intimacies of World War I's trench warfare, the technological innovations of the Second World War introduced new levels of physical and conceptual distance between strategists, troops, sailors, and pilots and their targets, which were often civilian populations. This was perhaps never more apparent than America's use of two atomic bombs on Hiroshima and Nagasaki that ended the war with Japan in August 1945.[110]

Anticipating the start of repatriations, the *Washington Post* marked Armistice Day 1945 with a long article on the policy. It described the GRS's process of concentrating remains for identification and return or interment in an American cemetery overseas. "There is little doubt that the great majority" will be returning, the writer argued, since the "sentiment for bringing home the war dead is much stronger than it was 27 years ago." This he attributed in part to how disturbing it was that some World War I cemeteries had fallen under German occupation and the physical devastation of Europe, making pilgrimages to the graves of loved ones difficult to mount. But the sense of greater demand for repatriation seemed in his estimation to stem mostly from the racial geography of the war— most Americans did not want to leave their dead in "remote" Asian locations or visit them there.[111] This prediction was ultimately borne out in the statistics of return and development of new ABMC cemeteries, which were limited to only two in the Pacific—one in Honolulu, Hawai'i, and the other in Manila, Philippines—compared to eleven in various European countries and one in Tunisia along the Mediterranean coast.[112]

The return of remains commenced when the policy was made law in May 1946, providing repatriation at the request of next of kin for any American who had died since September 3, 1939, when Britain and France had declared war on Germany. Congress mandated completion of returns within five years, after which time the still missing would be declared dead and appropriate benefits made available to their families. Shortly after legislating the repatriation policy, Congress passed an additional law in June calling for the War Department to select an unknown from World War II to be interred at Arlington on Memorial Day 1951, the year all repatriations were set to conclude.[113]

On April 6, 1948, the Army's Third Infantry Regiment, more commonly known as the "Old Guard," was reactivated in a grand ceremony on the Capitol Plaza after having been deactivated with so many others following World War II. Broadly tasked with the security of the capital, the new iteration of the storied regiment, with a history dating back to the earliest years of the nation, was to now be the preeminent ceremonial unit of the military, based at Fort Myer, just outside Arlington National Cemetery. This included responsibility for funeral honors in the cemetery, state funerals, the transfer of repatriated bodies at Dover Air Force Base after 1955, and, most famously, the twenty-four-hour, 365-day-a-year guarding of the Tomb of the Unknown Soldier. While the longer history of tomb security had included a round-the-clock presence since 1937, today's precision and tradition of the elite Tomb Guard unit dates to this moment.

The reactivation of the Third Infantry was the opening event for a massive Army Day parade along the National Mall from the Capitol building to a review stand where President Harry S. Truman and military officials waited, situated between the Washington Monument and the Ellipse. More than 150,000 people lined Constitution Avenue to salute and cheer the parading veterans and active-duty military and to witness the "Famed Third" marching again. While the *Washington Post* reported with an air of disappointment that there was not much big weaponry on display, "perhaps as a symbol of the reduced peacetime Army," it did note that a "Negro detachment of the Ninety-Fourth General Service Engineers . . . drew interest" with their large construction equipment. The paper's subheading, "Negro Group Draws Eyes," suggested it was the soldiers of the segregated unit, as much as their heavy trucks and cranes, that prompted the most notice.[114]

Less than two weeks before the Army Day holiday, the NAACP had issued a "Declaration of Negro Voters," listing demands adopted by twenty different black organizations, which included, "as an all-important immediate step," an insistence that "every vestige of segregation and discrimination in the armed services be forthwith abolished."[115] This was part of an escalated postwar extension of the "Double V" campaign to desegregate the military and industries with government contracts. Three days later, A. Philip Randolph, who had organized the March on Washington Movement in 1941 that resulted in the creation of the Fair Employment Practices Committee by executive order, testified before the Senate Armed Forces Committee. Truman issued Executive Order 9981 committing the government to desegregating the armed forces on July 26, 1948, establishing the mandate, if not immediate implementation.[116] In the coming months, Arlington went from being a central location for the national maintenance of racial segregation to the scene of its official challenge by the federal government and armed forces. But in April, the Army still paraded its racial segregation and funneling of black troops into labor battalions down Constitution Avenue.

The country was primed for the return of the "Famed Third" in articles and publicity as Army Day approached. The *Washington Post* detailed the history of the regiment from its 1815 origins, populated by "Valley Forge veterans," to getting its "Old Guard" moniker from General Winfield Scott. It described the careful selection of 1,200 men for the unit, with a preference for those with combat experience who conformed to exacting physical requirements of height and weight—their precise ceremony embodied in their uniform appearance. It went without saying that all were white. After April 6, the Military Police and ceremonial unit at Fort Myer would be known as the First Battalion and Ceremonial Company, Third Infantry, respectively.[117] The men of the Third drew the pay of combat infantry—their active-duty combat status standing as a barrier to the racial and gender integration of the unit long after official changes to armed services' exclusions.

In addition to Army Day events in Washington, the Department of Defense, which had replaced the War Department in the military reorganization of the National Security Act of 1947, sent more than a hundred "top brass" around the country to give public addresses on the need for preparedness and civilian commitments to defense in the face of the Soviet Communist threat. While the holiday dated back to 1928 and was set on April 6 to mark U.S. entry in the First World War, it had been an official national holiday dedicated to preparedness, a strong peacetime military, and raising public interest in national security only since 1937. By 1948, it not only was an opportunity for parades but provided a platform for promoting the new obligations of Cold War citizenship. Speaking in Providence, Rhode Island, Army Lieutenant General W. S. Paul argued, "The day has passed in which the armed forces of a nation can accept sole responsibility for its security. National security in 1948 is the business of every person living in this nation." Army Day speakers generally campaigned for a two-pronged strategy of bigger military budgets and greater vigilance on the part of all Americans.[118] The reactivation of the Third Infantry, with its primary commitment to ceremony and legacy, provided a well-drilled, historical face to this defense, exhibited on the nation's sacred ground at Arlington National Cemetery before the altar of the Unknown's tomb. The most iconic ceremony of the cemetery today was conceived as an early spectacle of Cold War militarism and patriotic vigilance.

That same year witnessed the creation of another new tradition at Arlington when Gladys Vandenberg, wife of the first chief of staff of the newly formed U.S. Air Force, discovered that some airmen were being buried in the cemetery with no family in attendance. She vowed that no member of the Air Force "would go to his grave alone," and she began attending every funeral.[119] Soon overwhelmed by the number of funerals, Vandenberg enlisted the help of friends from the Officers' Wives Club, which marked the beginning of the Arlington Ladies. Over the years, every branch of the service but the Marines formed its own group, all committed to ensuring that every military funeral in the cemetery would have a female civilian mourner in attendance. While not visible to the touring public like the Tomb Guards, the four branches of Arlington Ladies continue their service today. Most of the funerals they visit now are attended by the deceased's family and friends, marking the Ladies' presence more as representatives of the wider family of the service and the maintenance of gendered rituals of mourning and remembrance. If, as one documentary recently put it, the Tomb Guards are "for many visitors . . . the face of Arlington," the Ladies are the face of care for the grieving.[120] These living people, the Tomb Guards and the Arlington Ladies, help cement the meanings of the dead through their proximity and specific actions grounded in the dominant gender politics of bodies and honor in postwar America.

The summer of 1948 also saw the passing of General John J. Pershing, with his grand funeral at Arlington befitting both his popularity and stature and reflecting his rank of general of the armies conferred by Congress after World War I. It is the highest possible rank of the U.S. armed forces and one that Pershing still shares with only one other, George Washington. The general's grave, on the other hand, was a testament to the leveling possibilities of the national cemetery to which many people have appealed over time but that have never fully described the memorial

landscape of Arlington. At Pershing's request, a simple regulation headstone marks the grave where he rests among the dead of the First World
War in Section 34.

With ongoing repatriations of World War II remains, these years were
marked by the constant occurrence of military funerals across the country
and a spike in weekly interments at Arlington. As the mandated May 1951
burial of a new Unknown swiftly approached, military authorities remained undecided on how to go about it. Clear on the date, the law had
left otherwise open the logistics of selection and burial, stating only that
the Unknown should be placed beside or near his comrade from the First
World War. This sparked discussion about whether to construct a second
tomb. The idea was ultimately rejected in deference to the central place
of the existing Tomb of the Unknown Soldier in popular perception,
which by then included the Old Guard sentries and ceremony. Planners
feared that a new site and monument would introduce too much uncertainty about where to lay wreaths or hold official ceremonies.[121] The decision to add another unknown body from a different war to the same
tomb enhanced the memorial's place in the cemetery and patriotic imag-
inary. More than this, it promoted the idea that the specific conditions of
individual wars were unimportant to the larger nationalist aims of vener-
ating military sacrifice and valor; it cast all wars and all American military personnel as equally honorable.[122] Memorial Day 1951 did not see the
interment of a World War II Unknown, however. It was several more years
before he found his rest in Arlington, as plans were halted by the start of
another conflict in Asia during the summer of 1950. When the Unknown
of World War II was buried at the tomb, another from the Korean War
joined him.

Chapter 6

FOR US, THE LIVING

Now in this time and in this place our concern is not the honor of
a dead soldier—for that honor is his and no man can take it from
him. Our concern is for our country, if we fail here we bring
dishonor on ourselves.

—*The Arlington Case: Robert Thompson, Story of an
Unburied Soldier* (1966)

O N JUNE 4, 1948, two soldiers from the 442nd Japanese American
Regimental Combat Team, a segregated unit that served in the European theater of World War II and included many recruits from internment camps, were buried in Arlington to wide national press and fanfare.
Privates First Class Fumitake Nagato and Saburo Tanamachi had been
killed in the Vosges Mountains in France in October 1944 as part of the
442nd's famed rescue of the "Lost Battalion." Described in the press as
"the first interments of Japanese-Americans in the history of the cemetery,"
the men's joint funeral, prompted by their families' next-of-kin requests,
was organized by the Department of the Army with assistance from the
Japanese American Citizen's League (JACL). As such, beyond marking
the honor due the fallen of the highly decorated combat unit, the funeral
became an official postwar assertion of proven Nisei Americanism and a
celebration of national inclusivity bolstered by the assimilationist politics
of the JACL. These joint efforts were made nationally visible in the funeral
itself, which brought together not only the grieving families, JACL, and
ceremonial acts of the Old Guard but also military leaders, members of

Congress, and other representatives of federal authority, including the honorary pallbearer Dillon S. Myer, head of the War Relocation Authority, the office responsible for managing Japanese American internment.

Arlington literally and symbolically provided the grounds for authorizing this particular constellation of postwar Japanese American citizenship claims. At the funeral, scheduled for the week after Memorial Day, high-ranking military officers acted as pallbearers and speakers, while many of the congressmen, officials, and community leaders invited by the JACL served as honorary pallbearers, offered eulogies, and laid wreaths at the graves. The Army chief of chaplains performed the military service, which was followed by a Protestant ceremony in Japanese performed by a minister of Japanese descent. General Jacob L. Devers, chief of Army field forces, who presented Nagato's mother with the precisely folded flag from her son's coffin, said of the Nisei men, "There is one supreme final test of loyalty to one's native land. This test is readiness and willingness to fight for and, if need be, to die for one's country. These Americans and their fellows passed that test with colors flying."[1] Between his words lay the implication that the will to self-sacrifice and bravery was the test of loyalty for those in whom it could not be presumed because of their race or ethnicity and that definitive proof came only in death. Representative Ed Gossett of Texas, an honorary pallbearer, similarly argued, "They glorified and helped to save American institutions. They also glorified Japanese American citizenship. Our nation is doubly proud of them."[2]

Every account of the men's funeral in the mainstream press identified their participation in the "Lost Battalion" rescue, but only one made any reference to the histories of internment that shaped their segregated service. Fumitake Nagato's family had adopted Arlington, Virginia, as their home during the war, which meant that the *Washington Post* adopted Nagato as a kind of local son. The paper provided more extensive coverage of his biography in life than others, which noted only the conditions of his heroic death. Twenty-six years old when he was killed in France, Fumitake Nagato had been born in Los Angeles County, California, where his parents "ran a farm" in the Imperial Valley. The Nagatos had all moved to Arlington in 1943, when they "were evacuated from their West Coast home along with thousands of other Japanese-Americans to a relocation center in Arizona before going to Arlington." Employing common euphemisms for eviction, coerced relocation, and incarceration, the *Post*'s description of the family's agricultural past in California as "running" a farm similarly suppressed questions about potential losses of property—and who was now "running" their farm—in the story of their eastward travels. Fumitake's surviving siblings were described as thriving and similarly dedicated to the nation; a brother was also in the military, then serving in Korea as part of occupying U.S. forces, a married sister worked at the Treasury Department, and their younger brother, Lincoln, was a student at Thomas Jefferson High School.[3] Saburo Tanamachi hailed from Texas, like most of the members of the "Lost Battalion" he had lost his life saving. While his family did not have an immediate experience of internment, his service in the segregated unit had been defined by it.

The story of the Nisei soldiers' burial was folded into a developing official narrative of racial inclusivity and democratic promise nurtured in military service and protected by the federal state. This was markedly different from the segregated burials of Arlington's recent past, from the separate and subservient places for nonwhite people in the nation and its armed forces that were taken for granted in the 1923 funeral of Colonel Charles Young, for instance. Nagato's and Tanamachi's interments twenty-five years and another world war later were shaped by the particular histories of anti-Asian racism, Japan-U.S. relations, immigration restriction, and wartime incarceration. But they also signaled new federal responses to the untenable contradictions of having fought the "Good War" with a racially segregated military and Cold War assertions that the United States was a beacon for freedom and democracy around the world while so many people obviously enjoyed neither within its borders. Arlington became the scene of several high-profile burials of nonwhite service personnel that enabled a corrective story of progress and democratic social change, while simultaneously asserting that these were already the foundations of American character. The nation's most hallowed ground was recast as a terrain of inclusion and meritocracy distinct from other parts of the country, while exhibiting its true national values. In this official antiracist story, Arlington was once again a model for the rest of the country on honor, citizenship, and the management of race.[4]

The versions of integration and liberal reform promoted at Arlington made clear the narrow parameters of the Cold War state's antiracism,

however. It proffered limited inclusion via military service—and sacrifice—
in order to contain more radical democratic activisms. While this new
direction was framed as organic and exceptional to the United States,
springing from the hallowed ground within the cemetery's borders,
government directives and military policy had not prompted it. Rather,
assertions of federal antiracism were largely reactions to ongoing pressure from activists, many of whom were veterans, amplified by Cold War
foreign-relations concerns and movements for decolonization.

Arlington remained a landscape shaped by slavery, however, and its
plantation history and segregated graves were persistent reminders of the
shaky ground on which these narratives rested. The summer of 1963
marked a turning point in the cemetery's uses and meanings, with the
burial of the assassinated Mississippi NAACP leader Medgar Evers and
then of President John F. Kennedy after his own murder. Evers was eligible for an Arlington interment because of his service in World War II,
and his funeral was transformed into a national memorial for a martyr of
the modern African American civil rights struggle. Distinct from the pro-
ductive abstractions of the Unknown Soldier, long framed as the heart of
an embodied nation unified through patriotic mourning, the horrific details of Evers's death became in his Arlington rites the basis of calls for
moral reckoning, engendering, many people hoped, a collective national
conscience ready to change. It was this version of the nation embodied
in the national cemetery to which Evers's wife, Myrlie, appealed in her
1967 memoir, *For Us, the Living.*[5] Likewise, the decision to bury President
Kennedy in the cemetery a few months later shifted the emotional register and memorial function of the cemetery dramatically.

Alongside subsequent escalation of the war in Vietnam and intensified
antiwar activism, struggles for economic, racial, gender, and sexual justice proliferated within and around the edges of the cemetery in the 1960s
and 1970s. As a terrain of military death and the nation's most hallowed
ground, Arlington authorized powerful moral arguments about the war
and the nation's future from a range of often-contradictory perspectives.
Although Arlington had only recently been celebrated as iconic of liberal
citizenship, American democracy, and the assimilation and integration
of diverse populations, it became a staging ground for national debates
about the substance and failures of democracy, who or what presented

the greatest threats to it, and acts of political radicalism. It became a place for questioning the durability of national bonds forged through war and the real impacts of liberal reform. Martin Luther King Jr. had spoken of these bonds as a hollow and "brutal solidarity" in his first direct public argument against the Vietnam War in 1967 at an event organized by Clergy and Laymen Concerned About Vietnam (CALCAV). Describing the war's disproportionate toll on the young men of poor and nonwhite communities and gutting of resources for domestic poverty programs, King argued, "And so we have been faced with the cruel irony of watching Negro and white boys on TV screens as they kill and die together for a nation that has been unable to seat them together in the same schools. And so we watch them together in brutal solidarity burning the huts of a small village, but we realize they would hardly live on the same block in Chicago."[6] Ten months later, in some defiance of the Army, which had refused permission for a memorial on the grounds that it was a "partisan" event, and a court of appeals order upholding the Army's ruling, King led more than 2,000 members of CALCAV in a quiet march through Arlington to the foot of the Tomb of the Unknown Soldier for a long silent prayer. The silence was only broken, one reporter noted, "by the clicking of heels and sharp commands of the changing of the Army honor guard at the tomb above them."[7]

In 1949 and 1951, the Mexican American infantryman Felix Longoria and then the American Indian Army sergeant John R. Rice had highly publicized Arlington burials after each had been denied funeral services by private operators in their hometowns because of their race. Longoria had been killed during the last months of action in the Philippines in the summer of 1945. With his body set to arrive in San Francisco from overseas on January 13, 1949, Longoria's widow, Beatrice, was refused service by the one funeral home in their community of Three Rivers, Texas, as she attempted to make her husband's arrangements. Understanding that he would ultimately be buried in the town's "Mexican cemetery," she had hoped to use the funeral home for the memorial service. The reason given by the manager for his refusal, the *New York Times* reported, was that "white people object to the use of the funeral home by people of Mexican origin." Hector V. Garcia, founding director of the Mexican American veterans organization American GI Forum, contacted the newly elected Texas senator, Lyndon B. Johnson, for assistance, arguing that the actions in Three Rivers were "in direct contradiction of those same principles for which this American soldier made the supreme sacrifice in giving his life for his country and for the same people who now deny him the last funeral rites deserving of any American hero regardless of his origin." Founded in 1948, the American GI Forum became a primary vehicle for Mexican American civil rights activism, in part due to the publicity of the Longoria case, inherently defining claims to fully recognized rights and social justice through military service. Johnson was quick to suggest a national cemetery interment in Arlington, "where the honored dead of our nation's wars rest," or the Fort Sam Houston National Cemetery in San Antonio, noting that neither he nor anyone in the federal government had authority to compel the services of private undertakers. Beatrice Longoria chose Arlington for her husband's final rest.[8] Some press coverage of the Longoria case included similar experiences confronted by the families of Japanese American soldiers in California and Illinois.[9]

Whereas reports of the burials of Nagato and Tanamachi in 1948 had focused on their status as "firsts" in the cemetery and confirmations of their loyalty and fitness for inclusion through heroism, narratives of the Longoria funeral highlighted national belonging versus localized prejudice. They sought to contain the racial discrimination experienced by some nonwhite veterans as a situational, not a national, problem, one that could be federally and militarily remedied, personified in the granting of honors and a place in hallowed ground at Arlington. This was summed up in the New York Times front-page headline "GI of Mexican Origin, Denied Rites in Texas, to Be Buried in Arlington." Of course, the national cemetery had itself only ended racially segregated burials six months earlier, prompted by Truman's executive order to desegregate the armed forces. While the executive order was still being resisted by military leaders in early 1949 and was several years from full implementation, the highly publicized act of federal remedy to local harm in Longoria's burial resonated with Truman's order as well as his party's recent Dixiecrat revolt, when southern segregationists ran Governor Strom Thurmond of South Carolina for the presidency. Sgt. Rice's interment in 1951, headlined in the *Times* "Indian Hero Is Buried in Arlington Ceremony after Being Refused Interment in Sioux City," had similar effects.[10] But unlike the Japanese American soldiers of World War II or the African American service personnel whom Truman had in mind with his executive order, neither Longoria nor Rice had served in a formally segregated unit.

John Rice, a World War II veteran who had served for most of the war in the Pacific, became a casualty of the Korean War. Born on the Winnebago Indian Reservation in Nebraska in 1914, Rice attended the state's Genoa Indian Industrial School, part of the federal boarding-school system aimed at assimilating Native American youth by removing them from family and reservation communities. Military service was common among graduates. The first boarding school had been founded in an old Army barracks in Carlisle, Pennsylvania, in 1879 by Army Lieutenant Richard Henry Pratt, a Union Civil War veteran and career military man serving in the Indian Wars at the time. Carlisle provided the model for later nineteenth-century institutions and changes in federal Indian policy to focus on assimilation, or, as Pratt put it in 1892, "Kill the Indian in him, and save the man."[11] Pratt retired as a brigadier general and was buried along with his wife in Arlington's Section 3 in 1924. They rest beneath a large monument inscribed at the base, "Erected in Loving Memory by His Students and Other Indians." John Rice enlisted in the Army in 1941. Shortly after his discharge in 1945, he met his wife, Evelyn, who was white, in Winnebago through his brother, who was married to her sister. Rice reenlisted in 1946 and served at various posts in the United States and overseas, including a period as a military escort for the repatriated bodies of World War II dead. During this time, John and Evelyn had three children, two girls and a boy. In August 1950, Rice was sent to fight in Korea. He was killed two weeks later, on September 6, in the battle of Pusan Perimeter.[12]

Battle conditions in Korea confounded the usual practices of the Graves Registration Service, particularly where establishing temporary cemeteries was concerned. In March 1951, the Defense Department shifted to a policy of "Concurrent Return," requiring no next-of-kin requests and repatriating all remains while military operations were ongoing. "We are going to evacuate the honored dead as fast as we possibly can," explained Far East Command Quartermaster Brigadier General Kester L. Hastings.[13]

The policy shift had been prompted in part by public outrage and charges of elitism after Lieutenant General Walton H. Walker, commander of the Eighth U.S. Army in Korea, was killed in a jeep accident and immediately brought home for burial in Arlington, escorted by his widow and son, who was also on active duty. The wife of a soldier lost in battle several months earlier, just one day after John Rice had been killed, expressed the sentiments of many in a letter to President Truman: "I'd like to know if a soldier's high rank, made him better to be brought home right away for a safe burial, than for my Sgt. first class husband. If I had my way, and could get to Korea, I'd accompany my husband's body home, too."[14] The new policy was motivated by disastrous public relations, battle conditions, and the lack of clear victories or ground gained, and many people welcomed it. The delays of the old process were such that repatriations of the Korean War dead began while some who lost loved ones in World War II still waited for their remains.[15] Concurrent Return became the standard military mortuary policy for all subsequent conflicts, a definitive aspect of the Vietnam War in particular, and remains the policy for repatriations today.[16]

Rice's body was sent back to the United States under the new policy in August, arriving in California before being escorted home to Winnebago. In the meantime, Evelyn had purchased a cemetery lot in the Memorial Park Cemetery, just across the border in Sioux City, Iowa. John Rice's funeral was held there on August 28, 1951, but cemetery management refused to bury his body when they surmised that he was an Indian after being prompted to ask questions by the composition of mourners at his graveside. The cemetery's bylaws included a "Caucasian only" rule, which had clearly seemed beside the point to the person who sold the plot to Evelyn, assuming the white widow's husband had also been white. Evelyn said she had not noticed the clause in the contract but added, "When these men are in the army, they are all equal and the same. I certainly thought they would be the same after death, especially in a military section of the cemetery."[17]

President Truman learned of the events in Sioux City the next day from his military aide Major General Harry H. Vaughn, who had represented the president at Longoria's funeral two years prior, and telegrammed Evelyn Rice with the offer of an Arlington burial. The *New York Times* reported Truman's swift action, noting that Rice would be "the second soldier buried at Arlington National Cemetery under such circumstances," the first being Longoria, and added, "it would not be surprising if Mr. Truman chose to attend to demonstrate anew that racial prejudice is abhorrent to the American system of democracy." Truman was committed to equal rights for all, the story continued, working "vigorously . . . even at the cost of splitting the Democratic Party."[18] Evelyn Rice accepted the president's offer, and the Department of the Army set about planning the service and transporting her husband's body to Virginia. Messages had also been sent to the mayor of Sioux City and the management of the Memorial Park Cemetery expressing Truman's dismay at the situation; these messages were similarly reported. In an editorial praising the president's actions, the *Washington Post* quoted one of the telegrams: " 'The President feels that national appreciation of patriotic sacrifice should not be limited by race, color, or creed.' Nothing more need be said."[19] In the midst of largely glowing press accounts and editorials, some Republicans charged Truman with politicizing the circumstances surrounding Rice's burial, noting that an Arlington interment had always been available to him, while another paper suggested that if the president wished to do something for American Indians, he should address reservation poverty.[20] The *Washington Post* published a letter from Mike Masaoka, national legislative director of the JACL, who had been instrumental in organizing the joint funeral for Fumitake Nagato and Saburo Tanamachi in 1948. In it, Masaoka argued that Rice's experience was "not without its parallel right here in Washington, DC," where Japanese American service personnel had been recently denied interment at a private cemetery. Noting that a bullet made no distinctions among the races, Masaoka praised Truman and concluded that if race did not prohibit some Americans from serving their country, "why should it be a prohibition away from the battlefield against free men being interred together and honored in their last bivouac?"[21]

Four years later, another Native American military hero, the reservation-born Pima Ira Hayes, was interred in Arlington amid a deluge of national publicity that dwelled on very different narratives of Indian citizenship. On November 10, 1954, the U.S. Marine Corps War Memorial was dedicated on federal land just outside Arlington National Cemetery, composed of a central bronze sculptural representation of Joe Rosenthal's Pulitzer Prize–winning 1945 photograph of Marines raising the American flag at Mount Suribachi in the Battle of Iwo Jima. Three of the men who had participated in the moment captured by Rosenthal—Rene Gagnon, John Bradley, and Ira Hayes—sat in the front row looking at representations of themselves as thirty-two-foot-high bronze figures—the larger-than-life sculpture an apt symbol of the many ways the photograph had taken on monumental proportions in the culture, as well as the way its narratives of victory, diversity, and American greatness had swallowed so much of the men's lives and individual war experiences. Less than three months later, Hayes was found dead in the desert near his parents' home on the Gila River Indian Reservation in Arizona. The press reported the cause as exposure and alcoholism. Ira Hayes was thirty-two years old.[22]

Mainstream reporting invariably told Hayes's story as one of incredible tragedy stemming from his continued identification with his reservation and inability to assimilate, reflecting Cold War transformations in federal Indian policy. Thrust into the spotlight for war bonds and publicity tours, he was a reluctant public figure who had initially wished for his identity as one of the men in Rosenthal's picture to remain unknown. He expressed feeling unworthy of the hero label and mourned the men who had not survived the war, three of whom had also participated in the photograph. While some accounting of the toll of this kind of celebrity seeped into mainstream obituaries, most articles focused largely on his many arrests for public drunkenness and the cause of death as evidence of Hayes's "inability to find a place for himself in the white man's peacetime world."[23] This "inability" to assimilate was largely framed as personal failure rather than choice and was situated in the reservation where his parents and siblings still lived; he "wandered from his reservation home and back again."[24] The *Chicago Tribune* explained the Marine's death—under the subheading "Firewater His Downfall"—as caused by his inability to control himself, to fully master his own nonwhite body: "The man who never quailed before enemy fire never learned to cope with or leave alone the firewater of his own country."[25] A day after reporting his death, the *New York Times* announced, "Ira Hayes, the tragic Indian Marine, will rest in Arlington Cemetery."[26] If reservation land had facilitated his embodied downfall, the ground at Arlington would ensure Hayes was always a hero, always honored, which, in turn, would ensure the continued sanctification and national resonance of Rosenthal's image of Marines raising the flag on Iwo Jima.

Five months later, in honor of the ninetieth anniversary of Robert E. Lee's surrender at Appomattox Court House, described in the legislation only as the "cessation of hostilities between our States," Congress passed Public Law 107, officially designating what it called the "Lee Mansion" a national memorial to the Confederate general. For years, there had been some disconnect between popular perceptions of the site as commemorative of Lee and guiding interpretive frameworks that understood the mansion to be emblematic of the early national period. Official brochures for tourists were already well tipped toward Lee, however. A 1941 NPS brochure had called the site the "Lee Mansion National Memorial" and blurred the restoration's chronological intents by describing the aim as reproducing "the condition in which it existed prior to the War Between the States."[27] The new legislation, passed in late June 1955, left no question as to the meanings of the mansion and its immediate surroundings as a historic site. Linking to the Appomattox anniversary, the law draws an odd equivalence between the honor historically bestowed on Ulysses S. Grant and overdue to Lee, in arguing that the Union general had been "highly honored by becoming President of the United States, but the other, Robert E. Lee, has never been suitably Memorialized by the National Government." This would now be remedied, as "the Congress of the United States does hereby express its humble gratitude to a kind Providence for blessing our nation with leaders of true greatness who, like Robert E. Lee, have been able to see beyond their times, and by whose vision, guidance, and wisdom this Nation has gone forward to a place of world leadership as the unfaltering and powerful champion of peace, liberty, and justice." Custis and the deeper past of the "magnificent manor house" were not to be displaced, however, as the legislation mandated a new name for the site, the "Custis-Lee Mansion, The Robert E. Lee Memorial."[28] This legislative use of the anniversary was a precursor to the deluge of Civil War centennial plans and events to come. It also signaled the ways in which the civil rights movement and calls for a Second Reconstruction would become entwined with that public memory when young Emmett Till was murdered later the same summer.

A decade after Congress had first authorized the selection and interment of a World War II Unknown at the tomb in Arlington, prompting by veterans' organizations led to new legislation and a reactivation of efforts. The plan now included the selection of an additional Unknown from the Korean War, with ceremonies set for Memorial Day 1958. The Korean War Unknown was selected first from unidentified remains that had been interred at the National Memorial Cemetery of the Pacific in Hawai'i, known as the "Punchbowl" because of its distinctive natural setting in a volcanic crater. That body was transported to the military installation at Guantanamo Bay, Cuba, where it was transferred to a warship along with two candidates for the World War II Unknown, one from the Pacific and the other from the European theater, although neither was identifiable as such by that time. After a decorated Navy enlisted man chose the World War II Unknown by placing a wreath of carnations on the casket, the other body was sailed into open water and buried at sea.

Official ceremonies for the two new Unknown Soldiers were similar to those for the first in 1921, with some notable differences that reflected the military reorganization of 1947 and significant growth of the Defense Department in the context of the early Cold War. The Unknowns lay in state for public viewing in the rotunda for two days. The bodies were switched halfway through so that both could spend a day resting on the Lincoln catafalque. The cortege carrying the Unknowns to Arlington from the Capitol comprised three separate march units, each fronted by commanders and a different military band. The first included cadets from West Point and the Naval Academy and active-duty personnel from each of the branches: Army, Marine Corps, Navy, Air Force, and Coast Guard. These groups were followed by another, labeled in planning documents as "Service Women." While each of the branches had established women's reserves during World War II that became part of the regular armed forces with the Women's Armed Services Integration Act of 1948, the active-duty processional segregated all of the women together at the end rather than have them march with their branches. The second march unit comprised groups from the national guards and reserves of each branch. The third included representatives of three major veterans organizations: the American Legion, Veterans of Foreign Wars, and American Veterans. These three parade units were followed by a special honor guard, color guard, and group of clergy, who were followed by the caissons carrying the coffins of the Unknowns, flanked by pallbearers. Next came the honorary pallbearers, the secretaries of the Treasury, Defense, Army, Navy, and Air Force, the justices of the Supreme Court, the Speaker of the House, the dean of the Diplomatic Corps, cabinet members, and state governors. President Dwight Eisenhower and Vice President Richard Nixon did not march but met the Unknowns and their cortege at the amphitheater. Just as in 1921, a shot sounded every minute from a regiment stationed at the Washington Monument, which paused only to observe the national moment of silence.[29]

The day was stifling hot, and many people required medical attention after collapsing in or along the parade route or during ceremonies at the amphitheater. This included at least forty service personnel in the cortege and a Supreme Court justice, as well as hundreds of attendees and parade watchers. Much of the press coverage remarked on the heat and those who were felled by it. Evidence of living bodies' fragilities seemed heightened by the occasion and setting. One person seemed notably unfazed, however, according to the *New York Times:* "The President's capacity for standing at attention and sitting in prayerful attitude during the long ceremonies was notable. Others fanned themselves with their programs." Moving on to the many who suffered from heat-related incidents, rather than merely showing signs of their discomfort, the journalist added, "Many did not display the 67-year-old President's stamina."[30] This was generally attributed to the fact that the president was himself a military hero or, as the *Boston Globe* put it, also "an old soldier."[31] The remarks were also pointed commentaries on Eisenhower's health in the aftermath of a heart attack that had necessitated a month-and-a-half-long hospitalization in late 1955 and another hospitalization after surgery and a stroke in November 1957.[32] While the ceremony seemed long to many who fanned themselves in the heat, there was a marked economy to the program compared to the events of 1921. There was no eulogy, and the president spoke only twenty-six words as he placed on each coffin the Unknowns' Medals of Honor: "On behalf of a grateful people I now present Medals of Honor to these two Unknowns who gave their lives for the United States of America."[33]

Like the Army Day speeches of a decade earlier, the Unknowns were drawn into narratives of Cold War vigilance and nationalism shaped by a state of constant threat and potential subversion. A long article in the Sunday *New York Times Magazine* published a week before the Memorial Day ceremonies laid out these distinctions while drawing connections to the original Unknown of World War I. "It has sometimes seemed that the dead of the first war laid down their lives in vain, for there had to be a second against the same enemy, and that the dead of the second war failed, too, since within a few years it was necessary to go into battle against a newer tyranny." But those sacrifices were not in vain, the story argued, because the "United States speaks for peace with a stronger voice today" because of them. These dangers and particular sacrifices could no longer be understood as the express domain of military personnel, however. "The nature of war has changed. The sacrifices it may demand are of a more inclusive kind. There are no refuges for the old, for children, for the infirm and the weak. The days when only strong men of military age were endangered have past forever. Men have at their command inventions that may destroy all that makes life on this earth beautiful. Except one thing: courage, which abides forever. That may be the final lesson of this tomb, as it will henceforth be, of the Unknown Soldiers."[34] Beyond the potential for mass destruction, within the fraught politics of domestic containment where anyone was a potential threat, everyone had to be a Cold Warrior.

While framed as a universal body, the midcentury Unknowns remained inherently male and white in popular and official understandings. This was in spite of the fact that the face of the military had changed significantly between the 1921 and 1958 interments at the tomb. Formal racial segregation in the armed forces was a thing of the past, if far from gone in practice and the culture. Women were permanent parts of the armed forces and had served as nurses and clerical and administrative staff in significant numbers during World War II, the Korean War, and the peacetime military. Yet, tellingly, the Unknown's presumed status as a combat death necessarily excluded female service personnel.

In the context of Cold War sexual politics, the Unknowns of World War II and Korea were also presumed to be heterosexual. While this had been the case in 1921 as well, the concern was more pronounced by the 1950s. Much of the policy architecture for military discharges and exclusions of men and women thought or known to be gay and lesbian was crafted during World War II and in postwar benefits and draft regulations. This was well known in the wider public, including the use of "blue discharge" forms for administrative separations of "undesirables" outside the formal courts martial process to expel gays and lesbians. Named for the color of the paper on which they were printed and instantly recognizable in a file or application, the discharges not only meant ineligibility for all veterans' benefits, including national cemetery burials, but also made it difficult to find employment in the private sector. Campaigns to enlist women during the war and then to make permanent their roles in the branches had elicited particular scrutiny from champions and critics alike of any behavior deemed abnormal or unwomanly by the dominant gender expectations of the day.[35]

A popular set of images taken at the Tomb of the Unknown Soldier by a photographer for the Office of War Information in 1943 illustrates these concerns and the political uses of Arlington to steel against them. They all depict a young sailor and civilian woman, both white, in romantic poses at the tomb. While suggesting what the World War I Unknown might have lost in his sacrifice, the images are not maudlin. Rather, they celebrate wholesome, all-American young people and link them to the patriotism and national honor enacted at the Tomb of the Unknown Soldier. There is no doubt in the composition of each photo that the two are romantically attached. They hold hands and stand close, and in one image the sailor kneels on one knee, holding the woman's hand and gazing up at her, as if he is proposing marriage. The photographs are overtly heterosexual and affectionate but not lurid. The young woman is casually dressed in a skirt and plaid shirt, bobby socks, and flat shoes, and she is notably not in the uniform of the women's naval auxiliary, the WAVES. Images such as these, which later became enshrined in popular

"Sailor and Girl at the Tomb of the Unknown Soldier, Washington, DC," May 1943.

celebrations of the "Greatest Generation," both indicate the way in which normative heterosexuality was taken for granted as a core aspect of honorable nationalism and reveal some of the cultural and political work that cemented those associations.[36]

Military investigations and purges were joined in 1950 by similar initiatives aimed at civilian employees of the federal government. In February of that year, Senator Joseph R. McCarthy, Republican of Wisconsin, made his infamous claim to have a list of Communist Party members who were knowingly employed at the State Department, "traitors" protected by the Democratic administration, he charged, and the cause of American "impotency" in the Cold War.[37] In the coming days, McCarthy added that many were "flagrantly homosexual" and "very unusual" and shared certain "tendencies," melding the figures of the Communist and the homosexual in a threat made all the more pernicious by their ability to hide in plain sight. At the end of the month, a deputy undersecretary testified in an open Senate hearing that ninety-one State Department employees who had been fired as security risks were homosexuals. Politicians and the press had a field day. This merging of political and sexual subversion, partisan politics, popular fear, and titillation generated widespread purges across the civil service, which one historian has termed the period's "Lavender Scare."[38] In early 1953, newly elected and the first Republican in the White House since Franklin Roosevelt defeated Herbert Hoover in 1932, Eisenhower signed Executive Order 10450. It replaced Truman's 1947 Loyalty Review program for federal employees with a new set of requirements that expanded the category of "security risk." For the first time, dismissal of federal employees and the decline of civilian employment applications were explicitly mandated for "sexual perversion," as was already the case in the military.

This period also saw the emergence of the earliest gay and lesbian civil rights organizations in the United States, including the Mattachine Society, founded in 1950, and the Daughters of Bilitis, founded in 1955. As in other post–World War II civil rights activism, veterans were heavily represented among these activists, as were appeals to recent military service in order to make claims for inclusion earned and full and equal participation in American life. The 1955 inaugural issue of the *Mattachine Review* included an open letter to a U.S. senator written by an anonymous official in the California Republican Party, the writer's name withheld so as not to jeopardize his job. The letter urged the senator to rethink his position on "sex variants" and national security through an appeal to common patriotism and honorable sacrifice illustrated by the presence of gay men among the military dead of World War II. "Thousands of graves in France; many, many thousands more graves on South Pacific Islands and beneath the seas," he wrote, "contain the sad remains of men who were brave soldiers, airmen, sailors and marines *first* and homosexuals second. They were no less brave, they did no less to win the war for democracy, than did their heterosexual compatriots." The letter goes on to note the ongoing military service of gay men that goes unrecognized as such, their willingness to sacrifice all bringing honor to their country but specifically to all gay Americans. "But the democracy for which they did fight and die, and still fight and still die, and will yet fight and yet die, denies them and us our rights."[39] The anonymous letter writer's focus on the dead who were lost or never repatriated introduces an element of distance that signals the double sacrifice of death and the erasure of one's identity as gay. By referencing only those who might have become the soldiers interred at the Tomb of the Unknown Soldier in a letter to which he cannot sign his name, the writer links the national shrine to the processes of being made unknown by the state.

As some Americans began the organized struggle to serve openly as gay and lesbian in the military as a path to liberal inclusion and sought the recognition as honorable Americans and patriots enacted through mourning, the first African American Tomb Guard began walking the mat. Fred Moore earned his place among the elite unit in March 1961, just shy of the centennial of the start of the Civil War. He was already serving with the Third Infantry Regiment in a different capacity when, the story goes, during an official visit to place a wreath at the Tomb of the Unknown Soldier, Kwame Nkrumah, the longtime pan-African leader and recently elected first president of the Republic of Ghana, asked President John F. Kennedy, also recently elected, why there were no black men among the Tomb Guards. As a pointed remark on the domestic inconsistencies of American Cold War claims to champion individual rights and freedoms abroad, Nkrumah's question prompted fast action from Kennedy, who demanded diversification of the Army's premier ceremonial unit. Moore was reassigned to training for the guard, excelled where so many before him and since have fallen short, and became the unit's first black member.[40]

Reporting the importance of Moore's status as a first some months later in an essay devoted mostly to photos, *Ebony* magazine noted the presence of more black men in the regiment generally since Kennedy's action, including the first black officers. *Ebony*'s images of Moore at the tomb chronicle the shift in the site's visual registers of national inclusion enacted by his presence, by a black male body in the role of the living uniformed man as mirror of the Unknown's potential past and identity. Two of the *Ebony* images directly address the wider pedagogical function that a black guard held for the viewing public at the ceremony. In the first, Moore stands at the end of the mat, clearly performing his twenty-one-second pause while facing the tomb. Two white boys who could be brothers, their light hair in short buzz cuts, stand near Moore but obviously outside the cordon, squinting in the sun and similarly looking toward the tomb. The youngest boy, in short pants in the picture's foreground, stands at attention, hands stiff at his sides and chest outthrust. The caption beneath the photo reads in part, "Ramrod posture of Moore is copied by little admirer of military procedure among tomb's visitors." While appealing to a charming, gentle aesthetic, the photo's narrative is a powerful representation of white youth looking to a black man as a model for behavior and honor, as a model soldier and American. This is reinforced by the image just beneath it, taken from a greater distance. The tomb's corner is visible in the foreground at the photo's right edge. The mat, almost in its entirety, is centered in the picture, and Moore, walking his paces, is centered on the mat. The ring of viewers several people deep who surround the central action, watching carefully, are described in the caption: "Tomb visitors, some 8,000 of whom see Moore each duty day during peak of tourist season, line famous site to witness ceremonial changing of guard."[41]

On the afternoon of March 3, 1963, just after four o'clock, Park Service guides at the Custis-Lee Mansion were surprised by a visit from President Kennedy. He spent about fifteen minutes in the house, taken through by the guide on duty in the central hall, Paul Fuqua. Kennedy conversed easily with Fuqua about the Civil War and the cemetery's history and asked questions about Lee writing his resignation from the U.S. Army in the house. NPS leadership was particularly pleased that the guide at the front desk had taken the opportunity of the president's visit to tell him about the agency's Mission 66 initiative to increase the visitors service infrastructure across the system by 1966. Leading Kennedy and his small party out of the mansion and toward the edge of the grass to take in the famous vista, Fuqua described the history of Memorial Bridge and its intended role to link the Lincoln Memorial and Custis-Lee Mansion. Kennedy looked out at the capital as evening approached and said, "I could stay here forever."[42]

The night that the Mississippi NAACP field director Medgar Evers was assassinated in Jackson, he and his wife, Myrlie, had watched separately as Kennedy addressed the nation on television about the need for federal civil rights legislation. The president's administration had proven mostly a tepid ally and common bystander as various groups within the civil rights movement pressed direct-action campaigns, from sit-ins and freedom rides to city-specific movements in places like Birmingham, Alabama, and Jackson, Mississippi. In the main, activists remained committed to nonviolence while confronting escalating white resistance and brutality. The nation and the world had been horrified by images of police dogs and fire hoses turned on children in Birmingham the month before, to which Kennedy referred in his June 11 address as impossible to ignore. The primary occasion for the president's televised remarks was his act earlier that day federalizing the Alabama National Guard to enforce the desegregation of the University of Alabama, while the state's governor, George Wallace, staged his infamous "stand in the school house door" in Tuscaloosa.

It was seven o'clock in the evening in Jackson when Kennedy went on the air. Myrlie Evers and the couple's three children were at home. Medgar was still working, with a mass meeting at the New Jerusalem Baptist Church to attend later that night. Direct-action work in Jackson was taking its toll on Evers, and fellow activist Ed King recalled that at the church that night he had seemed "very sad and very tired."[43] With several people still to see and work remaining, Evers did not pull into his driveway until around twenty minutes after midnight. The kids were still awake and excited to see their dad when they heard his car pull onto the gravel drive and the doors open as he gathered a box of T-shirts and paperwork to bring inside. Then gunfire cut through everything. Myrlie ran to the door to find her husband face down near the steps, where he had staggered after being shot in the back, his keys in his hand, "trying to come home," she said. He was still alive but could not speak. Blood was "everywhere— everywhere," as were the shirts that had gone flying, each one screened with the demand "Jim Crow Must Go!"[44] Myrlie held Medgar's head and screamed, his children screamed, and neighbors appeared to help, one putting him in the car to go to the hospital. Medgar Evers died there fifty minutes later, in the early morning hours of June 12, 1963.[45]

Jackson erupted in mass demonstrations, which were met with police violence and hundreds of arrests over several days. This force could not contain the rage of black mourning and the desire to continue Evers's work evidenced in the streets of Jackson, however, and only helped to further broadcast it through the press around the country and the world.[46] Myrlie Evers recalled in her grief seeing one young activist wearing an NAACP shirt reading, "White Man, You May Kill the Body but Not the Soul."[47] Thousands attended the funeral service on Saturday in Jackson, including Martin Luther King Jr. and other movement leaders. Mourners came together in a march afterward that transformed the cortege into protest, their voices lifted in song, including "Before I'd be a slave, I'd be buried in my grave, and go home to my Lord and be free!" The march was similarly met with brutal resistance and more police violence, as a number of marchers were arrested.[48]

By that time, it was known widely that Evers would not be interred in Jackson. Myrlie had planned to bury her husband in the family plot in the city's "Negro Cemetery," about ten minutes from their home. Medgar had been elected to the national board of the American Veterans Committee shortly before his murder. A veteran of World War II who had been drafted in 1943, Evers earned two Bronze Stars for his service in the invasion at Normandy and northern France. As for many who filled the ranks of the postwar civil rights movement, his experience in the segregated military had shaped his outlook in powerful ways. Now the progressive veterans' organization suggested to Evers's wife that he should be buried in Arlington rather than in Mississippi. The NAACP activist Ruby Hurley encouraged her to consider it, "pointing out that many more people could visit the grave if it were near Washington and that it would be a tribute to Medgar."[49]

The day after the Jackson funeral, as Sunday papers around the country reported the events that had followed as a "riot," Evers's body was sent to Washington by rail. It was greeted at Union Station by a large contingent of activists from various organizations, including members of the NAACP, the Southern Christian Leadership Conference (SCLC), the Congress of Racial Equality (CORE), and the Student Non-Violent Coordinating Committee (SNCC). More than 500 people marched along crowded streets behind the hearse that carried Evers's body to the funeral home. Unlike events in Mississippi the day before, one paper called the event "quiet, orderly, and solemn."[50] Marchers distributed fliers depicting

Evers and reading, "He Sacrificed His Life for You," reinforcing both his place as a martyr and the political meanings of his memorials. Speaking of the days to come, the Washington NAACP director told the *Post*, "There will be no trouble. The only troubles here will be troubled consciences." This, he explained, was because every person who witnessed or heard of the Arlington rites would have to ask, "What [have I] done personally to stamp out this awful shame of the United States of America?"[51]

Over the next two days, thousands attended the viewing at the John Wesley AME Church, while many more continued to read or hear about it in the press. On Wednesday morning, June 19, a long parade of cars followed the hearse carrying Evers to Arlington for an eleven o'clock funeral, which was broadcast nationally on the radio. As the line of vehicles slowly made its way through the city, roadsides were lined with people paying their respects. The procession paused at the Lincoln Memorial. "It was on that ride that I decided I was right to agree to have him buried in Washington," Myrlie said later.[52] There was a short service at the Fort Myer Chapel before the funeral moved into the national cemetery. Stephen Gill Spottswood, a bishop in the AME Church and part of the national leadership of the NAACP, addressed the collected mourners. "I hope Medgar Evers will be the last Black American to give his life in the struggle to make the Constitution come alive," he said, calling on the power of one black man's sacrifice, as the last in a long line of sacrificed black Americans, to give life to national ideals. Evers died, Spottswood said, in order that all black Americans might be free to "share in the full fruits of democracy," and in doing so, Evers "laid down his life for all Americans."[53]

Medgar Evers was buried with full military honors and lauded as an American military hero, but throughout the service he was eulogized more pointedly as a fallen soldier in the civil rights movement. In attendance were 2,000 people, including a number of elected officials and various members of the Kennedy administration. Mickey Levine of the American Veterans Committee said, "No soldier in this field has fought more courageously, more heroically, than Medgar Evers. We pledge that this fight is not ended. We shall go to the Congress; we shall go to the people; he shall not have died in vain." Evers had drawn this connection himself while he was still alive: "If I die it will be for a good cause. I've been fighting for America just as much as the soldiers in Vietnam."[54] Roy Wilkens gave the last words: "Medgar Evers believed in his country; it now remains to be seen whether his country believes in him." And then the people who were gathered at the gravesite sang "We Shall Overcome." Myrlie said, "It rang out over the graves of so many who had given their lives for their country, I steeled myself and held my head high and looked up at the trees with the sun sifting through the leaves and was thankful that Medgar was buried here, near the nation's Capitol. For the first time in my life, I had a sense of pride in being a real American and not merely a second-class citizen."[55] The ground and graves at Arlington facilitated Myrlie Evers's feeling of pride and belonging as a "real American," as they had for so many others over the years, but they did so through the dissident script for national sacrifice represented in her husband's funeral. Medgar Evers's grave and the family, friends, and allies who gathered to mourn him hallowed that earth anew and with a different meaning. This alternative narrative of honor and patriotism had significant impact beyond the funeral itself, including among tourists in the cemetery that day. A journalist interviewed a woman he described as "a blond-haired visitor," who stood in the shade of a nearby oak tree with her family and watched some of the funeral. "We just came from the Lincoln Memorial," she said, "and I feel miserable inside."[56]

Associations between the two assassinated figures separated by a century and now framed as fighting and dying for the same cause were persistent and often politically pointed. Myrlie Evers's 1967 book was as much a fierce cry to keep pressing the conscience of the nation as it was a story of the Evers's marriage, family, activism, and the loss of husband and father. In it, she and her coauthor, William Peters, draw heavily on overt and subtle comparisons to Lincoln. Myrlie describes going through her husband's things, returned from the hospital, after she got home from Washington. Among the items was a five-dollar bill from his pocket: "On the bill was Lincoln's face, and on Lincoln's face was Medgar's blood." The comparison provides the title for Evers's book, which opens with a pair of epigraphs linking a eulogy for Medgar in 1963 to Lincoln's address at Gettysburg in 1863. Rather than focus on hallowed ground and memorial as so many had before, however, Myrlie Evers's book draws out the necessity of the living to fight on, as presented in the president's address: "It is for us, the living, rather, to be dedicated here to the unfinished work which they who fought here have thus far so nobly advanced."[57] From the funeral and news coverage to the later work of this memoir, connections to Lincoln and the president's martyrdom reinforced the idea of Evers's martyrdom and drew a long line back to the enslaved and the Civil War in the struggle for black freedom.

With the FBI closing in after a fingerprint had been lifted from a rifle found near the spot where police believed the shooter hid, Byron de la Beckwith turned himself in on June 23, 1963, and was arrested for Evers's murder. Beckwith was a Klansman from Greenwood, Mississippi, a town about ninety miles north of Jackson that had once been the headquarters for the White Citizens' Councils that were established to stop implementation of the *Brown v. Board of Education* decision in the mid-1950s. Like Evers, Beckwith was also a veteran of World War II; he had served in the South Pacific. He was tried twice for the crime in 1964, both times ending in a mistrial when all-white juries would not convict him. Beckwith was finally convicted of Evers's murder in 1994. Key evidence in the case had been gained by exhuming Evers's body, which was done secretly in the early morning of June 3, 1991.[58]

When Myrlie Evers learned that President Kennedy had been shot, she was at the hairdresser's, getting ready to leave for speaking engagements in Chicago and New York. She wept and "couldn't speak," she recalled, likening the feeling to the moment when she "heard the shot that killed Medgar." She rushed home to be with her daughter, who was out of school with a cold. Like so many other Americans the afternoon of November 22, 1963, the pair was watching television when Walter Cronkite announced that Kennedy was dead. Charles Evers, Medgar's brother who was now Mississippi's NAACP field secretary, telephoned the house. He was overwhelmed and noted that he had just seen the president on Veterans Day in Arlington. Kennedy had shaken Charles's hand and asked how Myrlie and the children were doing. Now, Myrlie thought, she needed to send a condolence letter to Jackie.[59] In the days and months to come, many people in the movement linked the assassinations of the two men, their widows, and their Arlington funerals. New York City's largest circulation black newspaper, the *Amsterdam News,* noted that Beckwith's first trial date had been set at a hearing in Jackson while Kennedy was being buried in the national cemetery, under the headline "Evers Also Buried in Arlington."[60]

Also like Evers's burial there, Arlington National Cemetery was not the first location that came to mind for Kennedy's final rest. Many people assumed he would be buried in the family plot in Brookline, Massachusetts. Secretary of Defense Robert McNamara argued that the president should remain in Washington, however, and that he should be buried in Arlington. This would make Kennedy the second president interred there; William Howard Taft was the first in 1930. The only president buried within the city limits of the capital today is Woodrow Wilson, who was entombed at the National Cathedral in 1924, although some people had hoped he would be the first president to rest in Arlington.[61] The cemetery's superintendent, John C. Metzler Sr., offered three possible sites, including the eastern slope below the Custis-Lee Mansion with the unobstructed view of the capital that Kennedy had so admired just months before. This was the site Jackie ultimately selected the day after her husband's murder. By this time, she had already settled on many of the funeral details, including modeling it after Abraham Lincoln's and incorporating a silent drill for the fallen by cadets from the Irish Army. The president had witnessed the ceremony and been notably moved by it during his official visit to Ireland that June. Her request for an eternal flame similar to the one marking the French Tomb of the Unknown Soldier beneath the Arc de Triomphe did not come until the next afternoon, less than twenty-four hours before the burial.[62] Meanwhile, an estimated 300,000 people lined the route from the White House to the Capitol, where Kennedy's body was taken to lie in state on the Lincoln catafalque in the rotunda. Many thousands waited throughout Sunday afternoon and evening to pay their respects, as about seventy people passed by the coffin every minute. When the line outside was still thirty blocks long and roughly four people abreast at the appointed closing hour of nine p.m., it was decided to keep the viewing open through the night.[63]

While Monday's funeral procession from the Capitol to St. Matthew's Cathedral for the requiem mass and then to Arlington was similarly thronged, millions more around the country, as well as internationally, watched the events as they happened on television. By 1963, more than 85 percent of American households had at least one television, and an estimated 93 percent of those tuned in to the funeral on November 25.[64] Kennedy's assassination was a landmark televisual event, from the initial coverage of the shooting and announcement of the president's death to his funeral three days later. This included the alleged assassin's own murder, which was witnessed by millions when it was captured during NBC's live broadcast and aired shortly afterward by CBS.[65] Arlington National Cemetery had long been a site for the collective imagining of a national community through mourning as a physical location and represented in newspapers, images, newsreels, radio broadcasts, and tourist ephemera, but the simultaneity and broad accessibility of the live TV broadcast amplified these qualities to new levels.[66] The broadcast of the World War I Unknown's burial in 1921 had signaled the possibilities, both in the desire to air the event at all and in its subsequent impacts on the country and the cemetery itself. But where the Unknowns of World War I, World War II, and the Korean War were supposed to represent everyone because they could be identified as no one, the national trauma and drama of the handsome young president murdered and the spectacular grief of his glamorous wife and small children created for most Americans a sense of direct connection and personal loss in Arlington. In this sense, the Kennedy funeral shared more with the Arlington rites of Colonel Charles Young and Medgar Evers.

Amid an event that produced a number of iconic images of mourning, including stoic Jackie in her black veil and little "John John" saluting his father's casket on the caisson, the journalist Jimmy Breslin drew on an old story at Arlington for his famous account of the funeral. His much-reprinted and still revered *New York Herald Tribune* story was told through the eyes of the black man who dug Kennedy's grave. Clifton Pollard was called in that Sunday morning on his day off. "Why, it's an honor for me to be here," he replied when Metzler apologized for bringing him in.[67] Pollard's honor is the article's organizing refrain, not only as he makes similar statements to others but also in terms of his character and his own history of World War II military service. Breslin returned to the cemetery for a *Saturday Evening Post* story marking the anniversary of

Kennedy's death in 1964. That story closes in another conversation with Pollard, who describes attempts to keep the grass lush around the gravesite in a dry season. "He is just a gravedigger who tries, and he is not very important," compared to all of the "big people" who run for office or publish books in the martyred president's name, Breslin writes, but "when you come down to it, the gravedigger worrying about the parched grass on the grave shows more dignity than all of them."[68]

Whereas Wesley Norris and James Parks had been transformed in story and image into perpetually faithful slaves forever tied to the land and in service to white men's honor and legacies, Breslin's depiction of Clifton Pollard and his labor was quite different. Yet its emotional registers and powerful everyman appeal remained shaped by those racial narratives, slipping into grooves made deep with repetition. As an honorably discharged veteran of World War II, Clifton Pollard was himself buried in Arlington in 1992; his widow, Hattie, joined him in 2010. Pollard's standard military headstone is so different from "Uncle Jim's," but, like Parks, he is buried near the community in which he had long roots. Pollard was born in Pittsburgh, but his family moved to Arlington when he was young. He graduated from the area's segregated high school named for Sally Norris's son, Edward C. Hoffman, and located near the cemetery: the Hoffman-Boston School.[69]

Kennedy's original gravesite was located precisely on the axis line between Arlington House and the Lincoln Memorial. Cemetery officials and the Army were also careful to place it outside the boundary of the land around the mansion managed by the National Park Service. A short, white picket fence was built around the grave and its eternal flame, creating a twenty-by-thirty-foot enclosure. This was a temporary measure, as plans for a larger, permanent memorial were soon under way, to be designed by the DC architect John Carl Warnecke. On the evening of December 4, after the cemetery had closed, the remains of two infant children, who had died before their father, were reinterred on either side of the president. News coverage of these burials included reports that the Defense Department had approved a Kennedy family plot of three acres for the new memorial and future interments. Disconcerting to read in light of Robert F. Kennedy's assassination and his own Arlington funeral just four years later, the *New York Times* noted that the Army had paved the way for similarly eligible family members to be buried in the plot, naming Robert and Edward explicitly.[70] Jacqueline Kennedy Onassis was interred beside her first husband and their children in 1994, and Senator Edward "Ted" Kennedy joined his brothers there in 2009.[71]

Two days after the funeral, Lyndon B. Johnson gave his first address to Congress as president of the United States and called for a different kind of memorial to Kennedy: passage of the Civil Rights Bill. "No memorial oration or eulogy could more eloquently honor President Kennedy's memory than the earliest possible passage of the civil rights bill for which he fought so long," he insisted.[72] Kennedy's assassination led many people to find historical resonance in Abraham Lincoln's presidency and murder, including the framing of both as martyrs to the cause of African American freedom. Strengthened by the context of Civil War centennial commemorations, this was structurally compounded in the funeral and the location of the Kennedy grave in line with the Lincoln Memorial, from which its eternal flame was clearly visible on the heights across the river at night.

For others, particularly those who were in the movement, it was the life's work and martyrdom of Medgar Evers that most demanded the legislation and was now associated with the president's assassination. Poppy Cannon White, the widow of the NAACP's Walter White, used her *Amsterdam News* column the following week to outline several connections between the two men's deaths, with a particular emphasis on the grief and grace shared by Myrlie Evers and Jackie Kennedy, "Two Heroines." One "great difference" between the two women, she concluded, was the fact that Mrs. Kennedy would never need to worry about her financial future or her children's educations. A gift to the NAACP's fund for the Evers family would be a fitting memorial to both men, she argued, and would "make certain that the eternal flame lit by Jacqueline Kennedy beside the grave of our President will also help to lighten and brighten the sad darkness that still lies heavy over such states as Mississippi."[73] Evers's grave was already a site of pilgrimage and reflection, and many individuals and groups now visited both sites. They often brought memorial wreaths, enacting engagement with the graves that mirrored the performance of honor and civic belonging embedded in the common practice at the Tomb of the Unknown Soldier.[74]

✯ ✯ ✯

Media coverage of Kennedy's funeral brought millions of people to Arlington through their televisions and resulted in massive increases in the number of daily visitors and a jump in requests for burials. Some of this was to be expected, as increases had occurred after other major public events and funerals since the burial of the World War I Unknown in 1921. No one was prepared for the magnitude of the rise and the multitudes that followed in the wake of JFK's funeral, however. By early January, the cemetery was already reporting a fourfold increase in requests for burial information, and thousands were going to the gravesite every day in a near constant flow of people.[75] This, in turn, raised visitation statistics for other sites in the cemetery, particularly the Custis-Lee Mansion and the Tomb of the Unknown Soldier. The *Los Angeles Times* added to this list: "Some, mostly civil rights groups, stop off to lay a wreath at the grave marked: Medgar W. Evers."[76] In the eyes of some people, the tourism associated with the influx was degrading to the meaning and sacredness of the Kennedy site and surrounding cemetery. In the midst of the late-summer crush, when most who saw the grave had to wait in line for more than an hour to get close to it, the *Washington Post* published a long article titled "Grave Not So Hallowed Now: Tourists Turn Kennedy Shrine into Just Another Capital Sight."[77] In addition to noting the public unveiling of plans for the permanent memorial, at the one-year anniversary of the president's assassination the *New York Times* reported that a record 7,740,000 people had been to the grave in Arlington, more than visitation at the Lincoln Memorial and Washington Monument combined.[78]

It is possible that Selina Gray's great-grandson and his family can be counted among that number, visiting on the same day that they posed for pictures in front of Arlington House. The date stamped on the front of the photographs in the commercial developing and printing process is January 1964. While the images themselves could have been captured any time before then, they clearly depict late autumn or winter. Everyone wears a coat and hat, although none seem to be especially cold. Henry and his son both wear their topcoats open enough at the neck to reveal pressed shirts and ties. It is possible that the family dressed up to visit the final resting place of their recently assassinated president. If so, they would have been able to see his fresh grave and crowds of other mourners just down the hill from the grand portico of Arlington House.[79]

The escalation of burial requests by veterans' families was worrisome to cemetery officials, who had already been confronting significant crowding at Arlington. By the time of Kennedy's burial, measures were under way to acquire a large tract from the Fort Myer reserve for new cemetery sections.[80] Arlington's space concerns were mirrored in the fears of elected officials in Washington and around the country who believed that the national cemetery system as a whole was inadequate to meet escalating demand. The House Committee on Interior and Insular Affairs investigated the issue in 1962, making recommendations for expansion across the system alongside new restrictions on eligibility requirements. Congress was compelled to act, the subcommittee report explained, by the fact that fifty-two bills requesting new cemeteries or enlarging existing sites were already on the calendar, while executive departments seemed complacent and the Bureau of the Budget had stated its opposition to any expansions. The report gave statistics on eligible Americans, whose numbers had surged in the aftermath of mass mobilization for World War II, the fast-on-its-heels Korean War, and new eligibilities for reservists and ROTC cadets who perished while on active duty, among others. These statistics were paired with dire projections for rates of veteran deaths and expected dates for extant cemeteries to reach capacity, noting that a number of states had no national cemetery within their borders at all. The subcommittee also reported the dramatic difference in average costs for private burials as opposed to those in a national cemetery, which provided the site, interment, service, and headstone at no charge to the family—differences amplified the following year in Jessica Mitford's exposé of the funeral industry and runaway best seller *The American Way of Death*.[81] The situation at Arlington lent new urgency to the congressional recommendations in 1964, and prompted the Army's decision to clear for new gravesites the last undeveloped section within the cemetery's 420 acres—a twenty-six-acre tract of historic old-growth forest behind Arlington House dating to the turn of the nineteenth century. Superintendent Metzler Sr. argued that without the land, Arlington National Cemetery would be forced to close in three years. Met with public outcry and significant resistance from the Department of the Interior, the plan was shelved and much of the tract transferred to National Park Service management.[82]

The cemetery's space issues remained and worsened with Johnson's escalation of the war in Vietnam the following year. After his election to the presidency, the steady creep of American "advisers" in Vietnam became full-scale escalation with the bombing campaigns of Operation Thunder beginning in February 1965 and the introduction of combat troops in March. By the end of the year, 184,000 troops were in Vietnam. That number rose to 385,000 in 1966, 486,000 in 1967, and peaked at over 500,000 in 1968. By the cease-fire of 1973, about 3,403,000 U.S. military personnel had served in Southeast Asia.[83] A large percentage had been drafted, which over time grew in proportion to those who enlisted. This trend was reflected in casualty figures as well. For example, 16 percent of American war dead in 1965 had been drafted, compared to 43 percent in 1970.[84] More than 58,000 Americans were killed in the Vietnam War.

In February 1967, the Pentagon stunned the American public with an announcement that most veterans would be barred from burial in Arlington under new regulations effective immediately. Citing continuing growth in requests after Kennedy's funeral, combined with the passing of greater numbers of eligible veterans from the World War I and World War II generations, officials said that Arlington would run out of space by the end of the year. In these dire circumstances, as plans for expansion got under way, new eligibility requirements for Arlington would be restricted to those dying on active duty, Medal of Honor recipients, retired military, and those eligible for national cemetery benefits who had been elected to federal office or held certain high-level government positions, and their qualifying family members. With this change, veterans and their families who had been roughly 70 percent of Arlington's burials in the past were no longer eligible. The rest of the national cemetery system, the Army assured, would remain open to all honorably discharged veterans and qualifying family, meaning there was no change in benefits. Nevertheless, protests from organized veterans' groups were immediate, as was pressure to find new solutions.[85] From this point on, space concerns and fears that one day in the not-so-distant future Arlington would be "full" plagued managers, the military, elected officials, and many in the public.

Concurrent Return remained the official policy, and repatriation had a profound effect on public opinion and popular memories of the period. On average, it took about seven days for remains to be returned to the United States after military personnel were killed.[86] This meant that bodies were continually coming home and sometimes shown in the process of collection, transport, or arrival on television and in publication. Commonly referenced later in the trope of "body bags on the evening news," this imagery became notably more pronounced in memory and subsequent policies relating to the draft and uses of the military than it had been at the time.[87] The policy of Concurrent Return also meant that the bulk of military funerals occurred before the war was over. Popular understandings of the Vietnam War and its costs were shaped by the constant presence of the dead.

The Cold War amplified concerns that an individual body could carry an identity, politics, or history into Arlington National Cemetery that might pollute or poison its hallowed ground. Similar sentiments had shaped the racial segregation of the cemetery's past and lurked around the creation of the Confederate section despite being drowned out by reconciliationist celebrations of the shared honor of white men. Now heightened fears of internal subversion and constant calls for vigilance in the face of potentially unrecognizable enemies, such as secretly gay or Communist government employees, came to include men and women in uniform and concerns that the outward signs of national honor and service could contain or even hide subversive aims. This was perhaps never more clearly illustrated than in Richard Condon's 1959 political thriller *The Manchurian Candidate* and its popular 1962 film adaptation, in which a Korean War hero and Medal of Honor winner is actually a brainwashed, sexually perverse, sleeper agent for the Soviets working to effect a quiet coup of the U.S. government.[88] In Arlington, these concerns came to a dramatic and controversial head when the widow of a decorated World War II hero and major figure in the American Communist

Party, Robert G. Thompson, sought to have her husband interred there.

Thompson had been among the eleven leaders of the Communist Party USA (CPUSA) convicted in 1949 under the Smith Act, interpreted to equate their membership and roles in the party with conspiracy to advocate the overthrow of the U.S. government. He had been a proud Communist for most of his adult life. Thompson fought in 1937 and 1938 with the Abraham Lincoln Brigade in the Spanish Civil War, part of the international volunteers who mobilized to support Spanish Republicans against the fascist Nationalists led by General Francisco Franco. In 1941, Thompson was drafted into the U.S. Army and served in the Pacific, where he earned the Distinguished Service Cross for "extraordinary heroism" in action in 1943.[89] When the 1949 convictions were upheld on appeal, Thompson was given a sentence of three years in federal prison, rather than the five years that others got, in recognition of his distinguished service history. But he failed to appear for sentencing in New York City and was tracked down only in 1953, outside Yosemite National Park in California. After being held at Alcatraz, Thompson was returned to New York, sentenced to four additional years for contempt, and incarcerated. He was released in June 1957, after four years and five months in prison. Robert Thompson died in Manhattan of a heart attack at the age of fifty on October 16, 1965.[90] His widow, Sylvia, sought to have his ashes interred at Arlington in a quiet ceremony with no military honors. She later explained that she and her husband were opposed to the war in Vietnam and did not wish the guns used there to be a part of the funeral service. Superintendent Metzler's letter approving the interment was dated January 4, 1966. At Sylvia's request, the funeral date was set for January 31.[91]

The story of Thompson's imminent Arlington burial broke nationally a week before the scheduled funeral, under blaring headlines such as "Red to Rest in Arlington" and "Burial of US Red, Convicted in 1949, to Be in Arlington."[92] Some veterans' organizations promptly made protest to the Army and the White House, while Representative Charles E. Bennett, Democrat of Florida, led a public charge against the burial, arguing that the national cemetery's hallowed ground would be "bespoiled" by the remains of a Communist. The Army's general counsel passed the question to the Justice Department. In a conversation with the president the day after the news went public, Attorney General Nicholas deB. Katzenbach told Johnson that Thompson's eligibility seemed clear and incontestable under current policies, noting that a quick change in the regulation would be problematic and obviously "aimed at this one fella." While Katzenbach told Johnson that they could defend the Arlington interment and proceed, the president was concerned about the politics of giving "a communist a hero's burial" and told Katzenbach to speak with McNamara and to "be positive that this is what [they] want to live with all through the campaign." That prospect was "a little bit frightening," Johnson concluded, ending discussion on the matter.[93]

Three days later, the attorney general issued an opinion stating that Thompson was not eligible for an Arlington burial under existing Army regulations, which excluded from national cemeteries anyone convicted of a crime and sentenced to five or more years in prison. Katzenbach had to add Thompson's sentence for contempt to his original three years for the Smith Act conviction to reach the five-year threshold. On the basis of the opinion, the Defense Department reversed its ruling and denied Sylvia Thompson's request. At the same time, the Pentagon changed the policy to specify that from that point forward, no one convicted for subversive activities would be eligible for national cemetery benefits, irrespective of sentence length. Representative Bennett cheered the decision, noting that any other "would have been an affront to the noble young men who have given so much of their lives to our country."[94] The scheduled funeral was by this time only four days away, and Thompson's cremated remains were already at the cemetery. Expressing regret "for any distress" that Sylvia Thompson "may have had because of conflicting advices," the Army's general counsel now asked her to let them know where to send her husband's ashes.[95]

While some people celebrated or were at least relieved, the decision sparked controversy and was widely derided as an affront to the military honor, democracy, and American values it was aimed to protect. "Barring the ashes of my husband, a war hero, from Arlington Cemetery, is an incredibly immoral and illegal act," Sylvia charged. "The Pentagon has yielded to political ghouls. Are they now saying that Arlington is only for political conformists?" In a similar vein, the *New York Post* queried, "A loyalty oath for the dead?"[96] The *Washington Post* editorialized that "the majesty of the United States is marred" by the refusal to bury Thompson, which also failed to acknowledge the cemetery's history and the diverse lives and actions of the dead who were honored for their military service over many years there. "Good men and bad men alike lie at rest in Arlington. Men of every faith—and of no faith—slumber there. In this cemetery, created on the estate of Robert E. Lee, there is, as indeed there should be, a Confederate Monument, erected by the Daughters of the Confederacy in honor of the South's dead heroes—men who believed it honorable and right to take up arms against the United States. And there rests there, too, in honored glory—whether in life he had been valiant or craven—an American soldier known but to God."[97] Another DC paper quoted George Washington: "When we assumed the soldier, we did not lay aside the citizen," noting that the words were themselves enshrined at Memorial Amphitheater, and charged that the Pentagon and Justice Department had laid aside Thompson's citizenship and rights to an unpopular political opinion. "Not all men who rest in Arlington are saints," the editorial concluded. "They are human beings, good and bad, strong and weak, brave and not so brave at all. We honor them as soldiers nonetheless. And so, too, could it have been with citizen Thompson."[98] The next day, Senator Robert F. Kennedy of New York, Katzenbach's predecessor as attorney general, for whom he had served as deputy, read the editorial into the *Congressional Record* and denounced the decision.[99]

In March, with legal representation from the American Civil Liberties Union (ACLU), Sylvia Thompson sued the Department of Defense for an arbitrary change of policy and infringement of her husband's rights to free speech and association. A week before, United States Chief Justice Earl Warren, who was himself to be interred at Arlington in 1974, had signaled from the bench his own disagreement with Katzenbach's opinion. Regardless, the district court judge hearing the Thompson case upheld the Pentagon's decision, arguing, "It would be abhorrent to many people that a man convicted of conspiracy to overthrow our Government by force and violence should be buried among our honored war dead." Sylvia and the ACLU appealed the ruling, while the *Washington Post* argued that a Defense Department victory would only "compound the injury it has done to its own honor and the significance of Arlington Cemetery."[100]

✯   ✯   ✯

As the Thompson case continued to work through the courts, Sylvia's role as a widow determined to honor her husband's wishes, his military heroism, and his political beliefs, as well as her own, was increasingly highlighted. This intersected with heightened attention to women's activism for and against the war in Vietnam, framed through their roles as the mourners of soldiers, particularly as mothers. On Mother's Day in 1967, two different groups of organized women converged on Memorial Amphitheater and the Tomb of the Unknown Soldier to assert their opinions and maternal authority. About 150 members of American War Mothers, an organization founded in 1917 for women with sons on active duty and recent veterans, convened in the amphitheater to hear an address by a Republican congressman from Idaho and to demonstrate their support not only for their sons in uniform but for the war itself. Representative George V. Hansen spoke of the costs of freedom and argued that the "draft-card burners deny any personal responsibility to the country that has given them so much. The disloyal will always be with us," he concluded, "but their pitiful outcries will be drowned out by men such as your sons."[101] As Hansen spoke, a similar number of activists from the Mother's Day Committee, a group affiliated with the Spring Mobilization Committee to End the War in Vietnam, popularly known as "the Mobe," stood around the Tomb of the Unknown Soldier in mostly silent protest. The diverse group of black and white women included some from the local area who identified themselves as members of Women Strike for Peace, a national pacifist organization dating back to 1961.[102] The group had gathered at the Lincoln Memorial to walk en masse across Memorial Bridge into the cemetery. As they marched, they distributed leaflets to onlookers that explained, "Because we are mothers who create life, we will no longer permit war lords to take that life."[103]

For the women of the Mother's Day Committee and the *Post*'s reporter on the scene, their stance against the war intersected with arguments that structural racism undermined patriotic assertions of America's fight for freedom abroad. The story dwelled on references to the particular sacrifices of black mothers, who disproportionately sent their sons to Vietnam. A spokeswoman for the group from Louisiana started short remarks that were mostly drowned out by a low-flying jet from the nearby airport before she was asked to remain silent by a Tomb Guard. She later told the reporter that she had spoken against "the deaths of black men and all men killed in Vietnam and all wars because this country is not the kind of democracy it talks about being."[104] One of the front-page article's accompanying images depicted an African American woman singing "over the grave" of Medgar Evers, visually reinforcing the linkage of movements for African American civil rights and against the war in Vietnam, a connection drawn with ever greater frequency in the spring of 1967, including in Martin Luther King Jr.'s remarks at Riverside Church from the month before. Along with King's arguments and the controversy they sparked, *Post* readers were probably reminded of the paper's recent coverage of the aftermath of the boxer Muhammad Ali's refusal to be inducted into the U.S. Army at the end of April.[105]

Despite the women's conflicting visions of the war in Vietnam, "personal responsibility," and sacrifice, both groups drew on the equations of motherhood, gendered honor, and mourning that had animated the site of the Tomb of the Unknown Soldier since its creation in order to ground their claims to special authority. Six months later, activists from the emergent women's liberation movement used Arlington as grounds for challenging these gendered arguments for tying women's voices to their biological capacity to have children and recognizing their citizenship only through the subordinate roles of mother and wife.

In the fall of 1967, members of Women Strike for Peace joined a number of other women from pacifist groups, the New Left, and the civil rights movement in a broad coalition led by Jeannette Rankin to stage a mass women's antiwar protest in Washington on the opening day of Congress, January 15, 1968. By then eighty-seven years old, Rankin had been the first woman elected to that body as representative from the state of Montana in 1916; she was then reelected in 1940. A lifelong pacifist, Rankin was the only member to vote against American participation in both world wars, casting the lone vote in 1941 against the declaration of war with Japan. Activists now rallied behind her and her history in a coalition dubbed the Jeannette Rankin Brigade (JRB) and prepared to converge on Washington in the new year to demand that Congress act to end the Vietnam War. Their call to participate encouraged women to come wearing all black in symbolic mourning; 5,000 ultimately answered it.[106]

Some who responded were women from the New Left in the nascent movement for women's liberation, distinct in its aims from the liberal inclusion and equality sought by feminists like those in the National Organization for Women (NOW), founded in 1966. More than petitioning Congress, the liberationists went primarily to appeal to the other women to stop "playing upon the traditional female role in the classic manner . . . as wives, mothers, and mourners."[107] Pointing to the place of these same gendered narratives in supporting militarism, national sacrifice, and patriarchy, they argued that only by rejecting the authority of "traditional womanhood" could they dismantle cultures of war. To reinforce and publicize their claims more broadly, the women's liberationists issued their own invitation to the JRB to join a radical countercongress on the spot and to attend a funeral for traditional womanhood in Arlington National Cemetery that night. The funeral oration, published later in New York Radical Women's foundational text *Notes on the First Year* (1968), identified Arlington as the obvious location for such a protest: "We must bury [Traditional Womanhood] in Arlington Cemetery, however crowded it is by now. For in Arlington Cemetery, our national monument to war, alongside Traditional Manhood, is her natural resting place."[108]

By the end of the year, a three-judge panel for the U.S. Court of Appeals for the District of Columbia, which included future Supreme Court chief justice Warren E. Burger, overturned the decision of the earlier court and ordered that Robert Thompson's qualification for an Arlington burial must be honored. His ashes were interred there in January, almost three years to the day from the date of his originally scheduled funeral.[109] So much had transpired just since the JRB protest and Burial of Traditional Womanhood, which had been followed less than two weeks later by the start of the Tet Offensive. The joint action by the People's Liberation Armed Forces of South Vietnam (PLAF), known to most Americans as the "Viet Cong," and North Vietnamese armed forces had had a dramatic effect on American public opinion about the war. Many Americans, including some inside the Johnson administration, concluded that it was unwinnable by any traditional measure of military success and must be negotiated to a conclusion. Reports in March that General William Westmoreland, commander of U.S. forces in Vietnam, had requested more than 200,000 additional troops to assure victory only escalated popular suspicions that American soldiers were fighting and dying for a grand delusion. At the end of the month, Johnson went on national television to announce a partial end to bombing campaigns over North Vietnam and his decision not to seek or accept the Democratic nomination to run for another term as president, in the hope of restoring unity and shielding the party enough from what was widely understood as his war to hold onto the presidency in November. Four days later, Martin Luther King Jr. was assassinated in Memphis. Over the next several weeks, more than one hundred cities across the country erupted in grief-fueled uprisings, or "race riots," which King had once called "the language of the unheard."[110] Then in June, Robert F. Kennedy was assassinated while campaigning for the Democratic nomination in California and was laid to rest near his brother in Arlington. Brutal and chaotic scenes of antiwar protest met by police violence in the streets outside the Democratic National Convention in Chicago followed in August. Events there had shown the growth and increasing diversity of the American antiwar movement, energized by the radical activism of students and working people around the world and domestic movements for self-determination of organizations such as the Black Panthers, the Puerto Rican Young Lords, and the American Indian Movement. Eisenhower's former vice president, Richard M. Nixon, narrowly won the presidency in November with promises of domestic order and an "honorable end to the war in Vietnam" and a late-campaign commitment in mid-October to end the draft.[111] Robert Thompson was buried in Arlington less than two weeks after Nixon's inauguration.

As one controversy was settled through the courts, another conflict over the line between citizen and soldier erupted in Arlington, this time concerning public statements made by an active-duty member of the Tomb Guard. On February 9, 1969, the *Louisville Courier Journal* published an interview with Sgt. Michael C. Sanders, a Tomb Guard from Kentucky.

The interview had been conducted on-site in the elite unit's fabled head-quarters beneath Memorial Amphitheater. The paper reported Sanders saying, "I am very much opposed to our Vietnam involvement and, I think, so is everyone else on duty here." While not so different from some of Nixon's campaign arguments or recently stated rationales for the new administration's policy of Vietnamization, Sanders's remarks struck a nerve because he was a Tomb Guard and because he had suggested that others among them felt the same way. Six weeks later, he received orders of transfer to combat duty in Vietnam, despite the fact that he had less than a year remaining of required service for his medical education and that he had been assigned to the Old Guard due to medical issues related to his hearing and asthma. Sanders later testified in court that his commanding officer had told him that General Westmoreland, Army chief of staff since being replaced as commander of American forces in Vietnam the previous June, had personally initiated his transfer.[112] In May, Sanders sued Westmoreland and the Army for infringement of his right to free speech, charging that his reassignment was retaliation for his public statements.

The Sanders case was reported early in the alternative military press, which had been growing since 1967. Produced and distributed on bases and in GI coffee houses by various groups of active-duty personnel, re-cent veterans, and draft resisters in exile, these papers provided a coun-terpoint to official military periodicals such as *Stars and Stripes,* as well as to the mainstream press. They were overwhelmingly antiwar, critical of the Pentagon and military leadership "in country," and attuned to the connections of domestic inequalities and the experience and conditions of military service, and they often sought to pierce popular images of the ever-loyal warrior patriot. Given the place of Arlington, the Unknown Sol-dier, and living Tomb Guards in promoting those images, the reassign-ment of Michael Sanders in apparent retaliation for airing his opinion was of particular interest. At least one alternative paper, *Dull Brass* from Fort Sheridan, Illinois, published the story before it broke in the regular press. "The Antiwar G.I. is Everywhere!" the article opened, framing the Tomb Guard as an unexpected place to find a critic of the war and thus indica-tive of how widespread such sentiments were among the military. This was echoed in "Screwed! Model G.I. to Vietnam for Anti-War Views," published in the first issue of *We Got the Brass,* produced in Tokyo, Japan, by the Second Front International, a group that described itself as "G.I.s, Deserters, and Resisters in Europe, united by our opposition to the mindless war in Vietnam and the pawn of that war, the U.S. Army."[113]

Coverage in the mainstream media similarly dwelled on the sergeant's role as a Tomb Guard. This included a spot on the NBC evening newscast on May 23, the day most Americans first learned of Michael Sanders. Airing after the first commercial break and a short report on casualties from the just-ended battle for "Hamburger Hill," the story interspersed Sanders's press conference with footage of the changing of the guard at the tomb, including audio of the ceremonial admonition to show respect by remaining standing and silent.[114] Many press accounts also noted Sanders's recent duty as part of Mamie Eisenhower's military escort for the state funeral of Dwight Eisenhower, who had died in March. The ceremony did not include rites at Arlington, as the former president and general left express wishes to be buried in his childhood home, Abilene, Kansas.[115] Carl Bernstein, who with Bob Woodward soon went on to break the Watergate scandal, covered the Sanders story for the *Washington Post;* the story stretched out over several weeks. While arguments from the Army insisting that Sanders's reassignment was routine had been weak, the sergeant did not win his case in court. After a new health examination and declaration of fitness for combat, he left Washington in mid-June for West Coast embarkation and by July was in Pleiku City, about 230 miles northeast of Saigon, with an Army Advisory Team. In December 1969, Sanders was discharged from the military and returned to the Washington area to take up study at the University of Maryland.[116]

Had Sanders still been part of the Old Guard in July, it is likely that he would have seen eighty-two-year-old Rebecca Shelley standing barefoot just beyond the cordon surrounding the tomb, wearing a veil and mourning black. For a week, she stood silent vigil against the continuation of the war in Vietnam, sometimes joined by other people holding placards reading, "Vigil for Vietnam War Dead," "Too Many People Have Died," and "End the War, Rebuild Our Cities." Shelley decided to speak on the eighth day of her protest, calling out over the plaza while the guard walked, "Spirit of the Unknown Soldier! Rise from out of your tomb! Your far-flung comrades mobilize!" This prompted the guard to act, and

Superintendent Metzler ejected Shelley and her two fellow protesters with the help of police. Tourists looked on and took pictures, the protest becoming part of their experience of the cemetery, as Metzler explained to Shelley and the others that they were violating posted regulations against demonstrations and unapproved ceremonies in the cemetery. A policeman escorted the elderly activists to their car, returned their placards, and took the name and address of each before telling them to leave. Like Jeannette Rankin, Shelley had been active in American pacifism since before the First World War and an activist for most of her adult life. After marrying a German national in 1922—shortly before the Cable Act went into effect, ending the legal mandate that American women who married non-American men automatically lost their citizenship and took on the nationality of their husbands—Shelley had spent two decades seeking reinstatement of her citizenship. The tourists and military personnel who saw her now, many years and several wars later, did not know that history. To them, she seemed just an old woman, just another antiwar demonstrator. "I am in mourning, I'm barefoot and wearing black, while our boys are dying in Vietnam," she told a journalist. "I saw the pictures in *Life*—those beautiful boys—they're all my sons."[117]

The Sanders case signaled a deluge of veterans' antiwar activism to come in which Arlington National Cemetery figured prominently, transforming its terrain of ennobled military sacrifice into an argument against the war and its human costs. Members of Vietnam Veterans Against the War (VVAW), founded in 1967, and other recent veterans were heavily represented among the thousands who marched on Washington in November 1969, organized by the New Mobilization Committee to End the War in Vietnam. The central demonstration was preceded by a three-day action called the March Against Death—A Vietnam Memorial to "symbolize and pay tribute to the Americans and Vietnamese who have been slaughtered in Vietnam." Starting in the morning on November 13, individuals carrying signs with the names of the dead and communities in Vietnam that had been destroyed began marching from Arlington National Cemetery past the White House to the Capitol, where the placards were placed in a large coffin to be delivered to Congress during the November 15 march. While the action's inclusion of the Vietnamese dead sought to expand the frame of lives that should be mourned, its incorporation of Arlington and the individual names of American military dead kept the focus primarily on the latter.[118]

Like the period's earlier calls to transform grief into action and change, the March Against Death highlighted the responsibilities of the living. In reporting the somber action later, the alternative *G.I. Press Service* noted that several marchers were relatives of servicemen killed in Vietnam. It quoted one mother, "Our son, who would very willingly have given his life for freedom, in fact gave his life for a government that was suppressing freedom. We are speaking for the silent majority of those who have died."[119] Her reference to a "silent majority" of the dead was a direct counter to Nixon's use of the term responding to mass walkouts across the country the month before for the Moratorium to End the War in Vietnam. Rattled by the size and diversity of the liberal Moratorium movement, Nixon had appealed to the country on television, calling on what he believed was the majority who supported his policies to make themselves known. Inspired by the speech, enormous pro-Nixon and prowar demonstrations were organized under the umbrellas of National Unity and Honor America Week to coincide with Veterans Day and to counter the antiwar march on Washington just before it started. This included one of the largest crowds anyone could remember for ceremonies at the Tomb of the Unknown Soldier.[120]

Arlington was the starting point of another protest the following April when VVAW staged a weeklong encampment and series of antiwar actions in the capital. Named for recent operations that had included controversial "incursions" into Laos, Dewey Canyon III—A Limited Incursion into the City of Washington was distinct from earlier protests in being composed only of recent veterans. The protest is mostly remembered today for its affecting conclusion, when hundreds of decorated Vietnam veterans and family members of the dead lined up to individually throw their medals and ribbons over police barricades onto the Capitol grounds, but its controversial start at the cemetery was widely reported at the time. In the days leading up to the well-publicized action, Nixon denounced the VVAW, claiming that few were actual veterans, and ultimately tried to keep them out of Arlington and evict them from their camp.

The administration's promised resistance to the VVAW action began at Arlington on the morning of Monday, April 19, the opening date selected because it was the anniversary of the first battles of the Revolutionary War at Lexington and Concord. Hundreds of veterans marched across Memorial Bridge from West Potomac Park carrying wreaths for the cemetery, including two for the Tomb of the Unknown Soldier, one to honor the American military dead, and another to mark Vietnamese losses. When the VVAW arrived at the main entrance of the cemetery, Superintendent Metzler locked the gate and refused them entry. Some yelled furiously, while others pleaded in frustration. As the marchers turned to head back into Washington, one man had to be pulled away by others as he yelled, "Does a vet have to be dead to get into Arlington?"[121] After press coverage of the lockout and conversation with Metzler, the VVAW was allowed into the cemetery the following day to hold what the superintendent now referred to as its memorial service. Placing two wreaths under a tree near the entrance, one marked "Allied" and the other "Indochina," about 800 veterans and family members knelt silently to the ground, some saluting but most raising clenched fists of protest.

Near the front of the thwarted first march to the cemetery had been the VVAW organizer and future U.S. senator, Democratic presidential candidate, and current secretary of state John Kerry. He had carried a wreath for the grave of his Yale classmate and friend Richard "Dick" Pershing, who was killed in combat in February 1968. A second lieutenant in the 101st Airborne and grandson of General John Pershing, Dick Pershing is buried next to his grandfather. Kerry learned of his friend's death while on his own first tour of duty in the Navy, and he spoke later of the comfort he had taken from hearing about the Arlington burial "that spoke of the great continuum of duty, honor, and country."[122] Now Kerry and others saw that continuum in their own sense of duty to speak against the war in Vietnam and the national ability of the cemetery to amplify their protests. The Dewey Canyon III action introduced many people in America to John Kerry when he testified before the Senate Foreign Relations Committee near the end of the week about the meanings of the protest. "How do you ask a man to be the last man to die in Vietnam?" he queried. "How do you ask a man to be the last man to die for a mistake?"[123]

Chapter 7

KNOWNS AND UNKNOWNS

The tomb itself demands the attempt. No war memorial is more
meaningful to more Americans than the Tomb of the Unknowns.
It cuts across generations and decades with equal power. It
affirms the greatest sacrifice ever made.

—*USA Today* (1998)

O N THE FIFTIETH ANNIVERSARY of the interment of the first Unknown from World War I, President Nixon laid a wreath at the tomb
and addressed the gathered crowd. Unlike previous years, November 11,
1971, was not Veterans Day, so the event was dedicated solely to the monument itself and its meanings. Following implementation of the Uniform
Holiday Act, Veterans Day had fallen on a Monday two weeks earlier.
With the aim of creating three-day weekends, the law had similarly moved
Memorial Day from May 30 to the last Monday in May, which also happened for the first time in 1971. While the long Memorial Day weekend
remains a part of the national calendar, the change to Veterans Day proved
so unpopular that it was shifted back to November 11 before the decade's
end.[1] Nixon said nothing of these changes but devoted his remarks to the
history of the tomb and its importance to the country, reading its more
recent uses back in time as eternal intents and fundamental American
values. Resting before him, he explained, the Unknowns' "skins may be
black or white or red or yellow; they may have been young with their lives
before them, or they may have had full lives already; their religions we
do not know; the homelands from which their ancestors came we cannot

know." This flowed into an appeal to the site's ability to represent the best and most honorable qualities of the country: "In the American ideal, none of these things was essential to the quality of life they were able to seek. In death, the ideal is realized—those who lie here are equal in the sacrifice they made, equal in the contribution they made, equal in the honor we bear them." In centering the "ideal," Nixon implied that the memorial's image of the country could be different from its realities, that only in sacrificial death, abstracted from its conditions and distanced from individual identifications, was that ideal truly "realized." The speech was aspirational but tinged with sadness about the state of the nation beyond Arlington's gates and an unpopular war still ongoing. Nixon concluded with the suggestion that one day soon an unknown from the war in Vietnam might take his place among the honored dead "on this hallowed hill."[2]

With the interments of the World War II and Korean War Unknowns in 1958, in which Nixon had been an official participant as vice president, came the presumption that every American war would carry a similar honor. The tomb was now the country's most visible place for honoring military service and sacrifice and for feeling patriotism's swell, and many Americans expected it would always be added to after future wars, that it was a memorial for "hereafter." As the Vietnam War ultimately showed, the tomb held such power in the national imagination that the failure to inter an unknown was tantamount to dishonor. Expectations for a perpetually inclusive Tomb of the Unknown Soldier sat uneasily with mounting frustrations about new restrictions on eligibility for Arlington burials that excluded a majority of veterans. The new qualifications had been enacted in 1967 to stave off a space crisis, and the cemetery's subsequent history, perhaps even its central drama up to the present moment and recent expansion plans, has been the struggle to find more acreage and new ways to maximize available land for burials and, after 1980, inurnments.

The dynamic of inclusion and exclusion that had long defined Arlington's terrain of individual and collective honor and national belonging merged with these scarcity concerns into a heady blend—or toxic brew— of competing claims to various kinds of benefits. The broader environment of continued rancor and devastation over the war in Southeast Asia, dramatic changes in the composition of the military following the turn to an all-volunteer force, and popular debates about entitlements, welfare, and government spending all were reflected in the cemetery and its various uses. Hanging over much of this was popular nostalgia for World War II and its impact on the country, including the sense that it had been a "good war," which had come with very good benefits and wide honors for those who fought in it.

Whereas Nixon saw a diverse nation made one and equal in the ideal represented by the Unknowns and hoped to attach some of the tomb's aura and honor to the Vietnam War, activists with Vietnam Veterans Against the War found a different moral symbol there. The August 1971 inaugural issue of the group's alternative paper, the *1st Casualty*, included a cartoon depicting a number of exhausted, defeated-looking men of various races standing in line at an unemployment agency. It illustrated an article describing the work of a new VVAW committee, the Veterans Action Group, organized to review veterans' benefits and make recommendations for reform; the committee's stated goal was to "improve existing benefits to at least equal those of WWII." A simple caption to the cartoon reads, "The Unknown Soldier, 1971."[3] Shifting the meaning from the unidentifiable honored dead to unseen living veterans, the cartoon equates the Unknowns with official neglect, while the inclusion of the year signals novelty in the problem. The cartoon's visualization of a diverse military, of men integrated in their struggle for benefits at home as they had been in battle, drew on narratives of military egalitarianism, as well as arguments about the disproportionate impact of the draft and enlistment on nonwhite men and the poor. The former had been heralded at the beginning of that summer in one of the many articles about Arlington that always appeared in the mainstream press in the lead-up to Memorial Day: "The Arlington Burials: Portrait of U.S. Diversity." The latter was reinforced in the VVAW's argument that black and Puerto Rican men were also disproportionately given dishonorable discharges for drug possession and other common infractions, making them ineligible for the benefits that did exist.[4]

Rather than the ground of integration and assimilation heralded after World War II, Arlington became in the post-Vietnam era a terrain for marking and managing multiculturalism; it became a "portrait of U.S.

diversity." In the social and political upheavals of the period, including the transformation of the military with the end of the draft in 1973, Arlington National Cemetery was itself a common field of battle in struggles over citizenship, soldiering, and the shape of future military engagements. While many people continued to look to the cemetery's hallowed ground as a place to make their own national contributions known, these efforts more often demanded simultaneous recognition of difference and diverse ways of belonging. Arlington became a more complex landscape in constant tension with its stated demonstrations of unity and shared national honor. In this context, the figure of the Unknown and the tomb became even more powerful symbols.

The difficulties of making arguments for liberation in Arlington, rather than the freedom of mere inclusion, were evident in the American Indian Movement's (AIM) thwarted attempt to hold a ceremony at the graves of Ira Hayes and John Rice in 1972. In the fall, activists began a caravan from the West to Washington, DC, collecting more participants as they traveled. Set to arrive a week before Election Day, they planned to present both presidential candidates, Richard Nixon and George McGovern, with a twenty-point set of demands for changes in federal Indian policy, greater tribal autonomy, and recognition of land and treaty rights granted but ignored since the nineteenth century. They called the action "The Trail of Broken Treaties." Like the VVAW encampment the year before, AIM members planned to start their week of action in Arlington at the graves of Hayes and Rice, but were denied entrance when they arrived on November 2. The Department of the Army refused their request, explaining that the planned service was not primarily religious or memorial but "closely related to other activities of a partisan nature being conducted this week outside the cemetery."[5] This and other official barriers led the activists to occupy the Bureau of Indian Affairs building the next day. They also appealed the Army's decision concerning Arlington in federal court. Dennis Banks, an AIM cofounder and one of the caravan's primary organizers and spokespeople, told journalists that AIM only wished to honor "Indian people who died serving in wars for this country" and were being forced into the courts to do so.[6] The Army's ruling was affirmed by a U.S. district court judge but overturned on November 5 by a three-member panel of the court of appeals. The justices found unanimously for the activists' right to hold their service in Arlington on religious freedom grounds but did so in a narrow way that did not challenge the Army's regulation, only its interpretation of the rule in this instance.

AIM promptly informed the press of its plans to hold the service in "honor of Indian war dead" just after noon the next day, when a court-ordered stay was set to expire. Speaking at a press conference that night, Dennis Banks described the event in greater detail. "The ceremonies will be special services," he explained, "held for the Indian veterans and all Indians that have died for the cause. They will be spiritually led by the medicine man to correct the wrongs the country has done to us."[7] Among the veterans to be honored were the more than 42,000 Native Americans representing about one hundred different tribal communities that had served recently in Southeast Asia. But at twelve o'clock the next day, the activists remained in the BIA building expecting a violent attempt at their forced removal by police. This was ultimately avoided through a negotiated end to the occupation three days later, by which time Nixon had been reelected to a second term.[8]

In an action premised on righting the historical wrongs of broken treaties and seeking autonomy and self-determination, AIM framed its demands as moral by pointing to the Indian lives sacrificed for a nation that failed to honor them. This was made more complicated by their indigenous rights claims, which necessarily existed prior to the nation, conveying the deeper past of the cemetery's land as originally home to Algonquian-speaking Indians. While the AIM action was unique for its historical actors and moment, it forecasted a set of tensions and contradictions that characterized official and popular uses of the cemetery from the end of the war in Southeast Asia to the invasion of Iraq in 2003. AIM's message that the government had failed to honor promises of the past, and continued to, resonated for many people.

Nixon's suggestion that an unknown from the war in Vietnam might one day join the Unknowns in Arlington inspired cemetery management and some members of Congress to begin making preparations. Representative

Hamilton Fish IV, a Republican from New York and son of the man who had initiated the original legislation to inter the World War I Unknown, advocated authorization and appropriations for an additional crypt in June 1972. It was an appeal to unity and honor, he said, for "despite diverging opinions on the wisdom of this conflict," Congress should show "that these boys and their families will not be forgotten."[9]

Plans for the Vietnam Unknown carried one very significant hitch, however, in that many people believed the war would end without producing any unidentifiable remains. Months before Nixon's speech, reports of the Army's record of identification had noted the unlikelihood of an unknown, and Pentagon officials made an immediate statement after his remarks that there were "no unknown dead in the Vietnam war."[10] While pointing to advances in forensic methods of identification, Memorial Affairs consistently attributed its perfect record to the Concurrent Return policy and the rapid evacuations made possible by helicopters. Removing remains immediately from the front, with records of battle, location, and personal effects, to mortuary facilities for processing made identification far easier than the temporary field burials and postwar processes of collection, identification, and repatriation of the past. One man who had been with Army mortuary services since World War II said that he hoped a Vietnam crypt in Arlington would remain empty. "I would be very happy," he explained, because "it would spell success for the program."[11] For many years, it seemed he would get his wish.

That Nixon and his advisers, Arlington management, and members of Congress pressed on in their plans for a Vietnam Unknown in spite of this probability indicated not only the appeal of the tomb as a symbol of national honor and collective patriotism but their desires to harness that power in order to mold the unpopular war's legacy. With the Paris Agreements of January 1973, American offensive operations in Southeast Asia officially ended, followed by a rapid demobilization of remaining forces. Back in Washington, sweeping changes in military organization, veterans' benefits administration, and efforts to limit executive war powers began in Congress, against the backdrop of the Senate's televised Watergate hearings and cresting scandal. The National Cemeteries Act of 1973 transferred all active national cemeteries except Arlington and the Soldiers' and Airmen's Home cemetery from the Department of the Army to the

Veterans Administration. It also included a provision directing the secretary of defense to identify remains from Southeast Asia for interment at the Tomb of the Unknown Soldier.[12] Less than two weeks later, on July 1, 1973, the president's draft authority was allowed to expire, a victory for Nixon since it fulfilled his campaign promise from five years before to end the draft. This was the beginning of America's All-Volunteer Force (AVF), which was a triumph for free-market advocates in and around the Nixon administration as much as for antidraft activists on the left.[13] As the ceasefire continued to deteriorate in Vietnam, Congress passed the War Powers Act over Nixon's veto in early November.

With plans to place the new crypt directly in front of the tomb in the space between the Unknowns from World War II and the Korean War, construction was already under way. It had been included in a scheduled renovation of Memorial Amphitheater set to add a broad terrace above the tomb site to accommodate the crowds of tourists coming to see the changing of the guard, by then averaging about 4,000 a day.[14] Pentagon officials described the new crypt as providing "for the possibility the remains of an unknown from the Vietnam War may be found," when recovery teams could return to old battlefields after the war.[15] The amphitheater project was part of a larger expansion plan for the cemetery to add another 200 acres of ground for burials and a new columbarium that could accommodate tens of thousands of cremated remains. Cemetery spokespeople argued that if they got appropriations for all of the work and land acquisition, the Army could loosen some of the stringent and incredibly unpopular eligibility rules enacted in 1967.[16]

By the time the new crypt was completed in 1974, Nixon had resigned the presidency, and there were still no unidentifiable American remains from Southeast Asia to place in it. With the obvious vulnerability of South Vietnam in the absence of significant U.S. support, the postwar sweeps described by earlier Pentagon spokespeople now seemed unlikely in the near term. In March 1975, the tomb was capped with a slab of white marble similar to those on either side of it. By this time, the North Vietnamese army, which had opened the year with a massive offensive, occupied several South Vietnamese provinces and was pushing on toward the capital, Saigon. A week before the last American helicopter lifted from the U.S. embassy in a wild evacuation as the city fell in April, cemetery workers removed the marble and covered the new crypt with the same red-granite pavers used across the rest of the plaza, leaving no sign of the empty grave beneath it.[17]

From the moment construction began to add a crypt for a Vietnam Unknown, the search for remains to inter within it was entangled with pressure to locate and bring home the missing, many of whom were believed by family, friends, and allies to still be alive and imprisoned in Southeast Asia. With roots in a 1967 organization of wives of missing aviators and other officers from bases in California, the National League of Families of American Prisoners and Missing in Southeast Asia remained the most prominent organization lobbying for continued attention to the issue from elected officials, the Pentagon, and the wider public. As outspoken critics of President Gerald Ford's 1974 amnesty plan for war dissenters, which tied clemency to terms of national service and demonstrated loyalty, the league drew sharp distinctions between the men who "suffered and bled," particularly those left behind, and those it said "deserted and fled."[18] The argument that protesters and antiwar advocates of various types garnered more attention than veterans became characteristic of the organization as it gained greater political purchase with the coalescing New Right. Staunchly anticommunist and socially conservative, league members often linked the figures of Vietnamese captors abroad with a bloated but negligent federal government and radicals at home as mutual culprits in the victimization of American POWs and MIAs and the degradation of national honor.[19]

On August 5, 1975, the public's attention to Arlington was shifted from the Tomb of the Unknown Soldier to the plantation house up the hill. The front portico of "Arlington House, the National Memorial to Robert E. Lee," renamed three years earlier, was host that day to President Ford's signing of a bill to "restore posthumously full rights of citizenship" to Robert E. Lee. Prompted in part by an earlier discovery of Lee's notarized Oath of Allegiance in the National Archives, the effort had recently become enmeshed with congressional attempts to pass amnesty legislation. While those who sought immediate and unqualified clemency for war dissenters pointed to a comparative lack of conditions attached to the returns of former Confederates historically—or to Ford's speedy pardon of Nixon more recently—the Lee citizenship law passed easily and provided a platform for linking difficult reconciliations of the past to contemporary ones. One of Jimmy Carter's first presidential acts after his election in 1976 was suspending the service requirement for clemency toward dissenters, which the Democrat from Georgia justified in part through appeals to his "historical perspective" as a southerner. "I know at the end of the War Between the States there was a sense of forgiveness for those who had not been loyal to our country in the past," he said, urging similar consideration now.[20]

While Memorial Affairs continued to insist that the absence of a Vietnam Unknown in the crypt was a good thing, a sign of the military's success and a reassurance to families of the lost, the vacant chamber conveyed a lack of closure. It seemed an apt symbol for the moral and political ambiguities of the war and its outcomes. The Pentagon explained the decision to cover the crypt as a measure to keep the public from believing a Vietnam Unknown was already there. Yet many people understood the act to be an expression of shame, an attempt not only to forget about the war and its domestic rancor but also to forget the individual men who fought in it. Members of Congress from both sides of the aisle pressed the issue, introducing legislation renewing their mandate to inter an Unknown twice in 1976 and again in 1977. In 1978, George McGovern, still a senator after his 1972 run for the presidency, made a direct appeal to the secretary of defense that garnered more publicity.[21] For disaffected veterans and many families and friends of the missing, the hidden crypt represented one more broken promise and the failure to honor those who had served in the Vietnam War.

In an effort to ameliorate these concerns, the Army announced plans in 1978 for a large bronze plaque in Memorial Amphitheater reading, "The People of the United States of America Pay Tribute to Those Members of Its Armed Forces Who Served Honorably in Southeast Asia during the Vietnam Conflict." During official Memorial Day services the following year, Max Cleland, head of the Veterans Administration, placed a wreath at the plaque similar to those at the Tomb of the Unknown Soldier. A decorated Army veteran who lost both legs and an arm in a grenade explosion in Vietnam in 1968, Cleland entered politics as an advocate for veterans and was appointed to the VA by Carter. In remarks on behalf of his agency and the administration, Cleland argued that Vietnam veterans deserved as much respect as those who fought in earlier wars and described public scorn and neglect as more injurious than the physical wounds sustained in battle. Denied the mantle of returning heroes, he continued, "all soldiers who fought in Vietnam are unknown."[22]

Jan C. Scruggs used the same Memorial Day to announce the creation of a Vietnam Veterans Memorial Foundation to raise money and secure a central location in the capital for a public monument. Himself a veteran of the war, Scruggs was a therapist who worked with other recent vets in the DC area. From the start, he understood the memorial as an act for healing on many levels, individual, emotional, and political, which was clear in the title of his later coauthored text *To Heal a Nation: The Vietnam Veterans Memorial* (1985). By Veterans Day in November 1979, Scruggs had enlisted congressional support for legislation providing a federal land grant. In a personal essay about his battles in Vietnam and afterward, Scruggs invoked a well-known poem from World War II called "The Young Dead Soldiers Do Not Speak," by the Librarian of Congress and War Department official Archibald MacLeish. Scruggs used a short version of the last line of the poem for his title, "We were young. We have died. Remember us," and closed his piece with more: "They say, Our deaths are not ours: they are yours: they will mean what you make them."[23] Framing Scruggs's wish for contemporary recognition for veterans through popular memories of the "Good War's" broad support in benefits and public honor for those who fought, the poem came to describe the dynamic between remembrance of the dead and recognition for living veterans that characterizes Maya Lin's eloquent memorial design. Yet while Veterans Day 1979 was a broad platform for Scruggs and others, most of the nation's attention was focused on Iran and the plights of more than sixty American hostages being held in the U.S. embassy in Tehran. The crisis was still fresh and unfolding—Carter announced the embargo on Iranian oil that Veterans Day—but it ultimately went on for well over a year.

On April 24, 1980, a secret rescue mission to retrieve the hostages, Operation Eagle Claw, ended in disaster in the desert outside Tehran due to equipment malfunctions and a helicopter collision with a C-130 transport plane, killing eight men. Carter's first official statement to the American public, broadcast early the next morning, announced their deaths but said nothing of their bodies. Later news coverage explained that the remains of the three Marines and five Air Force crewmen lost in the accident had been left behind in the urgent need to evacuate the living and because it had been impossible to retrieve the dead from still-burning wreckage. Like the ongoing hostage crisis, the bodies left in Iran reinforced growing popular opinions of Carter's weakness and the country's victimization and humiliation. This resonated with heightened discourse about how to honor Vietnam veterans and concerns for those still missing, kept visible by the MIA/POW movement. It fueled a braided narrative of vulnerability compounded by inept leadership that infused coverage of the failed rescue mission, including remarks from ABC's evening news anchor, Frank Reynolds: "We tried, we failed, and we have paid a price: the bodies of eight young Americans still lie in the Iranian desert, victims of a daring and tragic end to the rescue mission in Iran."[24] Despite the shift in context and geography, the helicopters and frantic evacuation were all too familiar.

The situation deteriorated further when the return of the men's remains was not forthcoming despite initial assurances from the Iranian president. The bodies and charred equipment were moved to Tehran, where members of the Revolutionary Guard denounced the folly of the rescue attempt and proclaimed dire consequences for Carter, punctuated by an exhibition of the bodies near the occupied U.S. embassy. Speaking at a press conference the next day, President Carter described the "ghoulish action of the terrorists and some of the Government officials in Iran . . . who displayed in a horrible exhibition of inhumanity the bodies of our courageous Americans."[25] Delays and disagreements among Iranian officials persisted for days while a Catholic archbishop from Greece waited in Tehran to receive the remains and transport them to a Red Cross facility in Switzerland, where they were to be transferred to American authorities for repatriation. Nearly two weeks after the American public had first learned of the thwarted rescue mission and its losses, the "Valiant Eight," as the press had dubbed them, were on their way home.[26]

On the morning of May 9, Carter gave the eulogy at a memorial service for the men, held in Arlington's Memorial Amphitheater before family members, top civilian and military officials, and more than 2,000 gathered mourners. The men's bodies were still at Dover Air Force Base, where the work of identification was under way. Three sets of remains were ultimately not individually identifiable or distinguishable from one another. They are interred together under a single headstone in the cemetery. In speaking of the men's courage and valor, the president explained, "They chose a life of military service when it offered very little glory in their land," framing their sacrifice as all the more noble because it was offered with no assurance of the affections or respect of their countrymen. They served because their nation needed them, Carter argued, and because it was right. To bring this Vietnam-drenched point home, the president turned to the Civil War and Robert E. Lee's decision to resign from the U.S. Army and join the Confederacy, calling it emblematic of the difficult choices confronted by members of the military: "It's fitting that we should remember them here in this place where Americans have long paid tribute to those who died for our country—those who were known and honored, those who were unknown; those who lie in unmarked graves, even across the sea, and those who are buried here. This very land once belonged to General Robert E. Lee. Like these eight men, he was a soldier whose affection for his home and family called him to a life of service that often meant hardship, loneliness, and long separation from those he loved and even from the Nation which he most loved."[27] Carter offered the cemetery's landscape of honorable sacrifice as evidence of martial valor's immutable quality, even when unrecognized in one's own time, the sacrifice made truer when given with no expectation of individual glory.

The presidential contest that followed centered on restoring those expectations of glory for all Americans. On July 1, 1980, Jimmy Carter signed legislation designating three acres on the Mall for the Vietnam Veterans Memorial. Two weeks later, the Republicans selected Ronald Reagan as their candidate to challenge Carter and chose George H. W. Bush as his running mate. With promises to "provide the strong new leadership America needs," Reagan's campaign was built around the theme and rallying cry "Let's Make America Great Again." In an early campaign event that summer, Reagan called the Vietnam War a "noble cause" and expressed dismay to members of the VFW that the country had "dishonored the memory" of all American troops who died in it "when we gave way to feelings of guilt as if we were doing something shameful, and we have been shabby in the treatment of those who returned."[28] Reagan's appeal to national pride without hand-wringing helped bind a set of ideas about small government, military strength, free markets, and traditional values that proved durable and winning, carrying the Republicans back into the White House.

The next time Max Cleland addressed a Veterans Day crowd at the Tomb of the Unknown Soldier, he took the occasion to announce his impending resignation as head of the VA, given Reagan's election the week before. Indicating the mix of nationalism, social issues, and concern about government spending that drew so many Americans to Reagan's message, some people at the ceremony who had supported Carter in his first run for the presidency explained their turn away from him now. Thomas Wincek, cofounder of an organization of veterans in business called the Grey Berets, explained his switch to Reagan: "As his administration went on, Carter continually put vets' problems on the back burner behind women, minorities, gays, and Vietnamese refugees. We became 'the Boat People.'"[29] Wincek likened recent federal measures addressing gender and racial discrimination in employment and education through training programs to pushing veterans out of the nation they had served and making them seem foreign to their own country, animated by his particular ire for programs aimed at Southeast Asian refugee resettlement and community development.[30]

Thomas Wincek was among those who had founded the Grey Berets on the previous Veterans Day at Arlington in 1979, the new organization punctuating its claims to represent benefits earned with the cemetery's landscape of military sacrifice that was also a monument to certain federal obligations. They argued that American tradition and law provided additional benefits for those who had honorably served in its wars and made them "the top priority in government programs" because they had "earned these entitlements by their military service." This was not about denying the rights and claims of others, the men assured, but insisted that they would "not stand idly by when the priorities of the government are directed toward these groups to the exclusion of veterans." The Grey Berets' statement continued, reinforcing the positioning of Vietnam veterans as distinct from other categories of people recognized in federal programs: "We are fed up with 'Boat People,' gays, Cambodians, women and minorities having priority over disabled and Vietnam veterans."[31] The possibility that these categories might overlap for veterans who were women, gay and lesbian, and not white was not accounted for here, despite some references to "men and women who served" in the group's literature and a black man pictured among the founding activists.

As had been the case since the Civil War and before, the valorous citizen-soldier was still presumed to be white and male, his honor reinforced by his independence, self-reliance, and care for his dependents. This historical framing was reiterated in the masthead of the national veterans' paper that carried the Grey Berets' founding announcement on its front page. The privately operated *Stars and Stripes National Tribune* used a quote attributed to Abraham Lincoln as its statement of mission to readers: "To Care for Him Who Shall Have Borne the Battle and for His Widow and His Orphan."[32] The Grey Berets' frustrations and claims to priority in federal resources echoed a long history of organized veterans' politics, advocacy for pension and other benefits expansions, and swift reactions when these things were curtailed. At the same time, they were molded by more recent contests over the legacies of the New Deal, the Great Society, and the upheavals of feminism, gay liberation, and various forms of racial and ethnic cultural nationalism, which were all oversimplified as "identity politics" in the 1980s and 1990s. In this context, the ongoing struggle to delimit the deserving from the undeserving, and the earned entitlement from the handout, intersected with some of the fiercest political fights of the day, in which the newly elected President Reagan was said to be leading a revolution. Testifying before a Senate select committee on veterans programs in the Small Business Administration, Wincek argued, "You are told if you serve honorably and survive, these entitlements will be given to you when you get out; it is the other half of your paycheck."[33] To fellow veterans, he made clear, "We're not talking about welfare."[34]

From the very start of Ronald Reagan's presidency, he grounded his vision for the future of the country, for making America "great again," in Arlington National Cemetery. He was the first president to be sworn into office and deliver his inaugural address from the west side of the Capitol building, looking out across the National Mall toward the Potomac River, rather than the east side facing the U.S. Supreme Court and Library of Congress. Reagan incorporated the shift in venue and the new vista it afforded into his address. In closing, he pointed to the monuments along the Mall dedicated to great men and presidents before him and then, following the sight lines of the central axis, kept going: "Beyond those monuments to heroism is the Potomac River, and on the far shore the sloping hills of Arlington National Cemetery, with its row upon row of simple white markers bearing crosses or Stars of David. They add up to only a tiny fraction of the price that has been paid for our freedom." He suggested that national greatness ultimately rested with the quieter heroism of the average citizen embodied in the soldier. While so much of his campaign had drawn on the recent legacies of the Vietnam War, he now turned to the First World War in illustration: "Under one such marker lies a young man, Martin Treptow, who left his job in a small town barbershop in 1917 to go to France." Treptow served with the Forty-Second Infantry "Rainbow Division" as a runner carrying dispatches across fields of battle. He was killed as he neared platoon command with a message on July 29, 1918, during the Battle of the Ourcq River. In his breast pocket, comrades found a small diary, stained with blood, in which the young private had written a pledge, which Reagan now recited with one small but significant change in wording. While Treptow's first line was reported at the time as reading, "America shall win the war," Reagan began, "America *must* win the war," putting emphasis on the need for action to secure victory, rather than its inevitability, and lending a sense of urgency for contemporary listeners. He continued with the rest of the recitation: "Therefore I will work, I will save, I will sacrifice, I will endure. I will fight cheerfully and do my utmost, as if the whole issue of the struggle depended on me alone." While assuring listeners that the dangers confronting Americans in 1981 would not require them to make Treptow's ultimate sacrifice, Reagan argued that all should adhere to his pledge and perhaps most importantly share his faith in the country's fundamental capacity for greatness.[35]

Reagan was not the first person to appeal to Treptow's legacy in hopes of motivating Americans not only to a sense of responsibility but also to patriotic self-assurance. The story of the young man's death and discovery of his blood-stained pledge had been reported almost immediately in *Stars and Stripes* during World War I, circulating in the military's official paper as inspiration to those who were still fighting. Within months, it was made part of the Federal Reserve's domestic war-bonds campaign on a poster depicting the final lines printed beside a large drawing of a dead soldier, slumped against rubble, his youthful face upturned. Bold red letters across the top of the poster read, "Pvt. Treptow's Pledge," while the bottom urges, "You who are not called upon to die—subscribe to the Fourth Liberty Loan."[36] Sixty years later, his story was still moving, accessible, and inspiring—so much so that the fact that Martin Treptow was not actually buried in Arlington, or any national cemetery, barely limited popular appreciation for the speech when it was reported the next day. Martin Treptow rests in the city cemetery in his hometown of Bloomer, Wisconsin.[37]

Three months later, the Arlington funeral of the boxer Joe Louis (Barrow) struck similar themes in celebrating the World War II hero as an American exemplar of progress and inclusion. He is buried in Section 7A along a heavily trafficked roadway leading to the Tomb of the Unknown Soldier, under a large headstone adorned by a bas-relief of the boxer in trunks and gloves, rather than a military uniform. Nicknamed the "Brown Bomber" after defeating the German Max Schmeling for the world heavyweight championship in 1938, Louis spent his military service with the segregated Army on a public-relations boxing tour, entertaining troops on bases in the United States and abroad. Under the 1967 eligibility requirements, he did not qualify for burial in Arlington, but Reagan provided a highly publicized executive dispensation. Six hundred people, including Louis's fellow politicized athlete Muhammad Ali, attended the funeral. The president could not be there, as he was still recovering from an attempted assassination in March. Instead, the secretary of defense read Reagan's remarks, in which the president lauded Louis as a "considerate and soft-spoken man" outside the ring and a courageous competitor within it. He demonstrated "an instinctive patriotism," Reagan explained, which infused Louis's accomplishments to make him a great American

figure for all time. Joe Louis's "career was an indictment of racial bigotry," Reagan argued, "and a source of pride and inspiration to millions
of white and black people around the world."[38] The president celebrated
Louis as an agent of change and evidence of the realized promise of
America, suggesting that the racism he confronted was in the past and
had long ago been remedied.

In conception, Joe Louis's funeral, resulting from presidential intervention, was reminiscent of the early Cold War burials of Nagato, Tanamachi,
Longoria, and Rice, but its meanings and implications were not easily
contained. During the war, the "Brown Bomber" meant very different
things and was a different sort of hero to black and white people, particularly in the context of the "Double V" campaign linking victory abroad
to fully realized black citizenship—to victory—at home.[39] The same
was true now, several decades later. One observer noted that Arlington
was "best known as the site of the Tomb of the Unknown Soldier, but in
his own quiet way Joe Louis was an unknown soldier, too."[40] His interior
life, opinions, and politics were concealed in soft speech, consideration,
and courage in the ring, the writer contended, in order to survive the
abuses of segregation and persistent racism.

Hearing Reagan's celebratory words of bigotry defeated, others might
have found it difficult not to recall his decision to start his national cam-
paign the previous year in a very different landscape of death and racial
memory. Stumping at the popular stop for politicians on August 3, 1980,
Reagan had assured the all-white crowd at the Neshoba County Fair in
Philadelphia, Mississippi, of his abiding commitment to "states' rights,"
not far from where the bodies of the murdered civil rights workers James
Chaney, Andrew Goodman, and Michael Schwerner had been found on
August 4, 1964. Shortly after Louis's funeral, Reagan nominated Clarence
Thomas, a fierce critic of affirmative action, to the position of assistant
secretary for civil rights in the Department of Education. This was the
start of federal appointments for the black conservative attorney that led
the next year to his Equal Employment Opportunity Commission
(EEOC) directorship and then a seat on a U.S. district court before his
confirmation to the United States Supreme Court in 1991.[41] Thomas filled
the vacancy created by the retirement of Thurgood Marshall, who had
argued several landmark civil rights cases as lead attorney for the NAACP,

including *Brown v. Board of Education of Topeka* (1954), before his own initial nomination to the federal bench. When Marshall died in 1993, he was buried in Arlington's Section 5.

By 1982, the military's Central Identification Laboratory in Honolulu had only four sets of unidentified remains from the Vietnam War. Although Reagan and some of his advisers were ready to move forward with the interment of an Unknown at that time, the president was persuaded to wait by arguments from the League of Families and others in the POW/MIA movement that the four might still be identified. This was, in fact, the case for two sets of remains. When one of the remaining pair was ruled "probably" not American in 1984, only one potential unknown was left, X-26, prompting the administration to act despite the continued reservations of some people. The skeletal remains had been recovered by a South Vietnamese army patrol near An Loc in 1972 alongside material evidence that included pieces of a flight suit and an ID card. When the remains were deposited in an Army mortuary in Saigon, the ID card was no longer with them, although the record of it having been found was. On their arrival at the facility in Hawai'i in 1976, investigators maintained the remains' designation as B.T.B. (believed to be) Michael J. Blassie, first lieutenant, U.S. Air Force. Later analysis made others less sure, however. The remains seemed inconsistent with Blassie's height and age at disappearance, among other things, so investigators changed the designation to unknown, X-26.[42]

With the decision to proceed with the interment of a Vietnam Unknown, the Reagan administration moved quickly. On April 13, 1984, Secretary of Defense Caspar Weinberger announced the selection of the Unknown and his Arlington burial on Memorial Day. The secretary simultaneously assured families and friends of the missing that their loved ones would not be essentially buried along with him and that finding the nearly 2,500 servicemen still unaccounted for remained the highest priority.[43] After a dedication ceremony at Pearl Harbor on May 17, the Unknown was taken by ship to San Francisco and then flown to Andrews Air Force Base in Maryland, where he was received on Friday, May 25, by the joint chiefs, General Westmoreland, and representatives of several veterans' organizations. While the flag-draped remains had traveled eastward, workers retrieved the marble crypt cover that had been removed in 1975 from storage beneath Memorial Amphitheater and readied it for use, including engraving it with the dates "1958–1975." The Vietnam Unknown was taken to the Capitol to lie in state on the Lincoln catafalque just as the others had before him.[44] President Reagan opened the viewing with short remarks, describing the Unknown as "the heart, soul, and spirit of America."[45] Writing in his diary later, the president noted his participation alongside the first lady, adding, "It's impossible to describe our thoughts when you stand before that casket."[46] After the ceremony, the couple left for Camp David, returning on Monday morning for the service in Arlington. During that time, tens of thousands passed through the rotunda to pay their respects to the Vietnam Unknown, averaging about 2,000 people an hour.[47]

The cortege to Arlington began at noon on Memorial Day. The day was gray and overcast, with occasional moments of rain to break the humidity. A horse-drawn caisson carried the Unknown's coffin down Constitution Avenue, which was thronged with spectators. As it passed the Vietnam Veterans Memorial, a line of fifty-six veterans holding flags from every state and U.S. territory dipped them in unison. The affecting moment not only made visible the particular participation of those who had served in Southeast Asia but also incorporated Maya Lin's memorial, which, while the source of much controversy from the moment of her design's selection, had already assumed a central and transformative place in Vietnam remembrance and public memorial cultures generally.[48] Whereas official participation of veterans in the 1958 ceremonies for the Unknowns from World War II and Korea had been mostly limited to the large, mainstream organizations such as the Veterans of Foreign Wars, American Legion, and Gold Star Mothers, the groups included formally in 1984 were many and diverse. More reminiscent of the 1921 cortege and funeral, these organizations were defined by categories including the race, religion, ethnicity, gender, specific battle experience, or disability of their memberships.[49] This did not reflect a return to the deeper past, however, but demonstrated official incorporation of public expectations for multicultural representations.

After the cortege had made the turn around the Lincoln Memorial and began moving across Memorial Bridge to the cemetery, a group of about 300 Vietnam veterans in their old jungle fatigues, Boonie hats, and blue jeans stepped into the end of the procession about a quarter of a mile behind the caisson carrying the Unknown. Moving in loose formation, the men marched as one of their number played "Amazing Grace" on the bagpipes. Two others carried iconic black POW/MIA flags with the motto "You Are Not Forgotten" as a kind of standard for the unit. While so many groups had been included in the ceremony, these men were denied formal participation when they applied, by the logic that they were already represented by other organizations. No one tried to stop the men now, and they seemed a welcome presence to the crowds that lined the approach to the bridge and that cheered and clapped for them. "By God, it's time we cheered them," a woman from Baltimore told an Associated Press reporter, wiping tears from her cheeks. "I don't know whether I'm happy or sad."[50] The official military history of the Vietnam Unknown's selection and state funeral describes the men as "insist[ing] on falling in" and "a reminder, however subdued, of the protests that had once seemed as much a part of the Vietnam War as the effort to defeat the enemy."[51] Once inside the cemetery, they joined the crowds of people around large-screen televisions who were not among the ticketed guests in the amphitheater or the early arrivals closer to the tomb site.

When Ronald Reagan addressed the gathered mourners in and around the amphitheater and across the nation watching the events live on television, he sought to impress on them the gravity and glory of the moment. His eulogy centered on themes of national and personal healing, pride in the country and its military, and national unity forged in moving forward from difficult histories, all through the interment of an Unknown. Throughout, Reagan took care to declare his administration's and the nation's unflagging commitment to securing a full accounting of the missing in action. He urged their families and friends not to see the Unknown as a symbol of closure and forgetting. "We write no last chapters," he soothed. "We close no books. We put away no final memories." The eulogy's references to healing and renewed unity recalled the protests of the past, but Reagan distanced the Unknown from any possible reservations about the war or its aims. While so much could not be known about the man whose remains were to be placed in the crypt, he explained, "We do know, though, why he died. He saw the horrors of war but bravely faced them, certain his own cause and his country's cause was a noble one; that he was fighting for human dignity, for free men everywhere."[52]

After the official ceremonies ended and all of the dignitaries were gone, people continued to visit the casket resting in front of the tomb and crowded the plaza deep into the evening. When the cemetery closed at 8:30 p.m. and all were gone, Arlington's superintendent, Raymond J. Costanzo, and the commanding general of the Military District of Washington lowered the casket into the crypt, and cemetery employees placed the marble cover. As the official history describes the day, "By 11:30 P.M. all work was done. The Unknown was at rest."[53]

Ultimately, it was Reagan's successor, former vice president George H. W. Bush, who claimed to have finally "kicked Vietnam Syndrome." Celebrating victory in the air and ground war in Iraq in Operation Desert Storm and praising the military in a March 2, 1991, broadcast on the Armed Forces Radio Network, he cheered, "The specter of Vietnam has been buried forever in the desert sands of the

The three crypts to the west of the Tomb of the Unknown Soldier containing the Unknown of World War I are, from left to right, the Unknown of World War II, the crypt for the Unknown of the Vietnam War, which has been empty since 1998, and the Unknown of the Korean War.

Arabian Peninsula."[54] At the Tomb of the Unknown Soldier on Veterans Day later that year, Bush linked that victory to the kind of national healing and recognition for Vietnam veterans that Reagan had promised in 1984. "We owe a special debt to the men and women of Desert Storm. . . . They freed a captive nation and set America free by renewing our faith in ourselves. And in this victory America rallied behind those who served in Desert Storm, and in a wonderful way, they rallied behind those who so proudly served in Vietnam. It was long overdue, and it was good for the Nation's soul."[55]

Amid the surge in public commemorations that followed the 1982 dedication of the Vietnam Veterans Memorial, including the interment of the Vietnam Unknown, members of the American Veterans Committee began working for a monument in the capital to honor all women of the past, present, and future U.S. armed forces—for their own "hereafter." The shift to an all-volunteer force in 1973 had led to swift and dramatic changes in the general composition of the U.S. military, with increased enlistments of women of all races and non-white men. Where women had represented 1.3 percent of the armed forces in 1971, by 1979 they constituted 7.6 percent. By the time the American Veterans Committee started their women's memorial initiative, women represented about ten percent of the military overall.[56] In 1985, the committee incorporated the Women in Military Service for America Foundation (WIMSA) and joined congressional allies in seeking a federal land grant for their monument. After some resistance from others in Congress and various federal agencies, who often cited the Vietnam Women Veterans Memorial project that was already under way as fulfilling the group's commemorative aims, the legislation was passed on November 6, 1986, and signed into law by Ronald Reagan.[57] Brigadier General Wilma L. Vaught, who had recently retired from the Air Force as the highest-ranking woman in the U.S. military, was elected foundation president the following March and set about fund-raising and finding a suitable location for the new memorial.[58]

While the design competition was still some years away, the foundation settled on a set of guiding principles and central aims for the memorial.

In addition to paying tribute to all women who had served in the military, were currently serving, or would serve in the future, it would "tell the story of their dedication, commitment, and sacrifice," which included illustrating "their partnership with men in defense of the nation." This latter signaled a strategy to soften or limit overt associations with feminism, particularly in the context of the recent defeat of the Equal Rights Amendment in 1982. Broadly, the foundation argued that its monument would make military women's "historic contributions a visible part of our national heritage" and inspire other girls and women to similar service in the future. These goals were to be met through a living monument, blending commemoration and function and including a visitors' center, meeting rooms, exhibit spaces, an auditorium, and the means for building an archive of individual women's narratives of military service.[59]

The present-day site of the Women in Military Service for America Memorial near Arlington's main entrance, which incorporates the Hemicycle at the end of Memorial Drive, did not appear on the original list of possibilities generated by the National Park Service. The NPS showed Vaught several locations in or near Washington, DC, mostly along roadways. Many were in areas of low foot traffic and distant from concentrations of tourists. It was Vaught who first asked about the Hemicycle after a day of looking at other locations, one of which was near the Pentagon abutting National Airport. The structure forms a decorative terminus to Memorial Drive and was part of the original plans for Memorial Bridge, pulling its classical lines and commemorative themes up to the cemetery and base of the hill capped by Arlington House. Officially marking the far edge of the National Mall and not a part of the cemetery, it met the federal land requirement of the legislation. Its indeterminate status, neither managed by the Army nor recognizable by the 1980s as part of the Mall, had contributed to the site's general neglect and damage over time. It was in need of cleaning and restoration and, with its empty niches and decayed grandeur, seemed a bit forlorn, despite its prominent location.[60]

Vaught and others quickly settled on the Hemicycle as WIMSA's best option. It would give the women's monument pride of place along a key axis of the monumental core from the Lincoln Memorial to the cemetery, in line with the eternal flame of Kennedy's memorial and Arlington House.

Moreover, its need for restoration served as an additional point of persuasion. Vaught later explained, "Not only is there great relevancy between this site and the purpose and features of the planned Memorial, but also this site gives the women of the Armed Forces and their supporters an opportunity to 'meet a need' as they have done throughout this nation's history, i.e., restore and complete the Hemicycle and enhance the entire Memorial Gate area."[61] Vaught underscored that women's service had always been the product of volunteering. No woman had ever been conscripted, but many had served as critical personnel in every war. These arguments intersected with the gendered terms of care work and nursing that had long characterized representations of women's military service.[62]

The winning design for the memorial was a proposal called "The Candles," submitted by the architects Marion Weiss and Michael Manfredi of New York City. It featured ten signature glass spires across the top of the Hemicycle that would glow at night, lit from within. WIMSA described the design to members and funders in its spring 1990 newsletter, announcing, "We Have a Winner!"

> Imagine pausing at night on Memorial Bridge over the Potomac River. Lights are glowing softly in the distance. Ten soft points of light guide the eye upward to the eternal flame of John F. Kennedy's gravesite, and toward Arlington House. Ten points of light proclaim the legacy of 1.6 million women who answered the nation's call for the defense of freedom. By day, ten spires of glass reflect the sun's light forming a radiant crown of liberty atop the treasured Hemicycle Wall at the entrance to Arlington National Cemetery. The Hemicycle, once neglected, now stands proudly. This is a place of honor for all who serve the country.[63]

With a design WIMSA felt appropriate to the location and reflective of the need to make visible the military contributions of women, the organization now confronted earning approval and shepherding the renovation and building project to completion while raising significant funds to do it. This required continued negotiating of the wants and jurisdictions of several federal agencies, including the Department of the Interior,

National Park Service, National Capital Planning Commission, Commission of Fine Arts, and a new superintendent at Arlington, not to mention foundation members, potential funders, and more than a million active-duty servicewomen, reservists, and veterans whom they sought to honor.

The building plan that eventually emerged from this process bore little external likeness to the original "Candles" design. To wide complaints about the spires and lighting scheme, several members of various agencies and commissions had added concerns that the plan included too much alteration to the Hemicycle's structural face and disruptive exterior landscaping. Over the next two years, Weiss and Manfredi edited their design in response to this input.[64] The ten spires were replaced with large plates of glass installed almost flat to the roof and etched with quotes from servicewomen throughout American history. The architects described the plates as "pages" carrying individual stories and memories that would come together across the top of the memorial in a unified whole. Stairs to the terrace level where one could walk close to the cemetery's grassy rise, gaze at Lincoln's memorial across the bridge, watch others pour into the cemetery from the Metro, and read the glass plates were shifted from central niches of the Hemicycle to recessed ends, reducing their visibility. Landscape designs that were found to be in conflict with other plants and trees around the Hemicycle, making the site stand out from its surroundings, were scaled back.[65]

At every turn, most external features suggesting that something other than the Hemicycle was in that location were removed, and no permanent signage outside the building designates it the Women in Military Service for America Memorial. In many ways, the Commission of Fine Arts, National Capital Planning Commission, and others ensured that WIMSA's aim of visibility on the cemetery's landscape could not be achieved.[66] Its internal, multifunction spaces for presentations, meetings, and exhibits, the bookstore, and facilities for collecting individual women's stories remained, however, and with them the ability to facilitate personal and community development among active-duty servicewomen and veterans, to grow the archives, and to exhibit women's military histories. Since the dedication of the memorial on October 18, 1997, it has become an active public space and popular event venue. As of early January

The central structure in this image is the Women in Military Service for America Memorial, dedicated on October 18, 1997, formerly the Hemicycle. The Kennedy Memorial and Arlington House are visible in the background.

2016, it has collected the registrations and individual stories of 259,224 servicewomen.[67]

As General Vaught, the architects, and others at WIMSA worked toward final approval of the memorial, they confronted a number of changes in management and the built environment at Arlington. In January 1989, a new Visitors Center to be followed by a large parking deck opened near the cemetery's main gate—and the Hemicycle—along Memorial Drive. Still in use today, the facility replaced a "temporary" structure that had been hastily constructed after Kennedy's burial in order to accommodate the new crowds in the cemetery. In the constant calculus of seeking new space for graves and balancing those needs with the cemetery's other uses, the superintendent had noted of the estimated $11 million construction project that demolishing the old visitors' structure and parking lot was making space for 9,000 more gravesites, increasing overall availability by more than 7 percent.[68]

Two years after the opening of the visitors' complex, a new superintendent came to Arlington, although for John C. Metzler Jr. it was more like a return. Metzler's father, John Sr., had been the most well-known and storied manager of the cemetery since Montgomery Meigs's day. An Army sergeant who served in World War II, John Sr. was superintendent of Arlington from 1951 to 1972, overseeing among many others the burials of the World War II and Korean War Unknowns and President Kennedy and managing the significant changes and growing number of burial requests and tourists that followed. He was buried in Arlington in late May 1990, just months before his thirty-nine-year-old son and namesake stepped into the superintendent's position. In January 1991, the younger Metzler and his family moved into the Superintendent's Lodge within the cemetery's grounds where he had spent his entire childhood and lived until he was nineteen. Metzler had been a little boy when Kennedy was buried and attended the funeral with his father. After serving in Vietnam, he went into the family business of cemetery management, working for the VA and eventually becoming the area director for cemeteries in the Northeast. Those who were working to finalize plans for the women's memorial found Metzler sometimes difficult in his possessiveness of the cemetery and its surroundings, a sense of ownership undoubtedly shaped by the fact that it had been his childhood home.[69]

The efforts to make women's military service visible as a part of Arlington's story of national honor and sacrifice was mirrored in simultaneous work by local community members, including a number of descendants, to publicize Arlington's diverse African American histories represented by the graves of U.S. Colored Troops and civilians in Section 27. On October 11, 1991, they gathered in the section once known as the "Lower Cemetery" with the commanding general of the Military District of Washington and invited guests to plant a memorial tree and hold a service for the men, women, and children buried there and to honor all African Americans who fought in the Civil War or lived in Freedman's Village. While the archives point to a cemetery for village residents elsewhere, now lost within the national cemetery like the graves of many people once enslaved there, Section 27 had been long associated with Freedman's

Village. It served as the only physical trace of the community's existence, along with the curve of Clayton Drive into Jessup Drive on the
opposite side of the cemetery near the notch of the old Syphax claim. The
following year, the group returned to dedicate a memorial tablet beneath
the tree, describing it as an honor to "African Americans of the Civil
War," and a call to remembrance and recognition of debts to earlier generations: " 'Lest We Forget, We Stand on Your Shoulders'—Dedicated in
Memory of the United States Colored Troops, Citizens, Freed Slaves,
and Contraband of Freedman's Village by the Descendants and Friends."[70]

The tablet made clear the intent to honor and the group's desire to mark
the antebellum and Civil War–era roots of contemporary black communities in the city of Arlington, but could not make the history of
Section 27's graves more visible to cemetery visitors. Flush with the
ground, the tablet is hard to see from the street and further marginalized
by the fact that tourists are discouraged from walking among the graves in
higher-traffic areas of the cemetery. The tree's unrecognizable meaning
without the tablet, which is itself almost invisible to those who do not already know of its existence—not unlike the WIMSA memorial—is a fitting symbol of the troubled embrace of black Civil War remembrance
and Reconstruction's memory in Arlington.

The community and descendant activism that produced the memorial
did prompt increased foot traffic and interest in the section, however,
which led to bigger changes. More people became aware of the neglected
condition of what had once been the racially segregated section of the cemetery, a condition that reflected the wider neglect of black histories at the
site. The issue drew the attention of Representative Louis Stokes, Democrat of Cleveland, Ohio. A World War II Army veteran who had gone
to college on the GI Bill, Stokes was the first African American elected
to Congress from his state in 1968. Three years later, he was a founding
member of the Congressional Black Caucus. Stokes was appalled by what
he found in Section 27 during a visit in 1990 and began working to change
it from his position as chairman of the House Appropriations Subcommittee on Veterans Affairs and Housing and Urban Development. When
Superintendent Metzler came to represent Arlington's budget requests in
1992, the hearing turned into an investigation about Section 27. Stokes
confronted Metzler with pictures showing the section's broken headstones

and overgrown grass and weeds, and he charged neglect. Stokes demanded a real accounting and change, and the subcommittee mandated a progress report and Metzler's return by the end of the year.[71] Stokes was joined by counterparts in the Senate, which resulted in greater attention from the Department of the Army, including grounds work, replacing almost 1,000 markers that were either deteriorated or did not correspond to the regulation headboards of the rest of the cemetery, and adding Section 27 as a point of interest on the cemetery's tourist map and brochure in 1993.[72] This was the first time the large collection of African American military and civilian graves and existence of the old "Lower Cemetery" were made officially known to the touring public. Among twenty-one "Points of Interest" highlighted on the map, "Section 27, dedicated to U.S. Colored Troops and residents of Freedman's Village," is listed as number nineteen, right after the Confederate Monument.[73] While Metzler had been clear in his 1992 testimony that it was doubtful that any Freedman's Village residents were interred in the section, and that the location of the village cemetery was unknown and presumed covered over by more recent military burials, the map misidentifies the civilian graves as belonging to villagers. This reinforced popular and official misconceptions of the section's history, only recently remedied in cemetery publicity. Notably, however, the most recent version of the walking map, published in March 2015, does not list Section 27 as a point of interest for visitors.[74]

Congressionally enforced attention to Section 27 in the early 1990s coincided with efforts by the National Park Service up the hill at Arlington House to facilitate greater awareness of the histories of slavery and emancipation there. This included the popularization of Selina Gray as the "Keeper of the Keys." In 1995, longtime Arlington resident and community advocate Evelyn Reid Syphax was successful in getting a county historical commission marker for Freedman's Village erected near its former location just outside the cemetery and at the edge of the original Syphax claim. The late Evelyn Reid Syphax was descended from Freedman's Villagers and a Syphax relation by marriage. Today, her son Craig Syphax is the second president of the Black Heritage Museum of Arlington, of which she was a founder, continuing the work of creating accessible public histories of Freedman's Village and black lives in slavery and freedom at Arlington, including Syphax family legacies.[75]

✶ ✶ ✶

Short markers and memorial trees and tablets like the one in Section 27 proliferated across the cemetery in the 1990s, installed by private organizations and individuals to honor the service of various people defined by a wide range of military actions and wars or group identifications, civic affiliations, and patriotic causes. Some memorials were historically corrective as well as celebratory, such as the Buffalo Soldiers Centennial memorial dedicated on July 1, 1998. The short granite marker is faced with a bronze plate reading, "Dedicated to the Buffalo Soldiers 9th and 10th Cavalry, and the 24th and 25th Infantry Regiments (Colored Troops) For Valiant Service in the Spanish-American War. They charged up San Juan Heights and El Caney, Cuba with Teddy Roosevelt and the Rough Riders." It is located in Section 22 beside the Rough Riders Memorial dedicated in 1907 to the white men of the storied First U.S. Volunteer Cavalry led first by Leonard Wood and then Roosevelt, and most famous for its role in the Battle of San Juan Hill. The dark granite monument is roughly fourteen feet tall and towers over the Buffalo Soldiers memorial.[76] Yet the two markers make an obvious pair, with the newer one serving as a reminder not only of the black military service that made victory and the subsequent glorification of "Roosevelt's Rough Riders" possible, but also the white supremacist narratives of reunion and empire that left the black troops' contributions and valor unacknowledged.

Seeking their own historical correction and recognition for honorable military service and sacrifices for the United States during the more recent war in Southeast Asia, Lao Veterans of America (LVOA) dedicated a memorial tree and marker in Section 2 in 1997. Predominantly Hmong in membership, the memorial was the result of the organization's many years of seeking recognition for service in the CIA's "secret war" in Laos. It is dedicated to "the U.S. Secret Army in the Kingdom of Laos 1961– 1973 in Memory of the Hmong and Lao combat veterans and their American advisors who served Freedom's cause in Southeast Asia." The inscription continues, "Their patriotic valor and loyalty in the defense of liberty and democracy will never be forgotten," followed by "you will never be forgotten," in Lao and Hmong.[77] The memorial is simultaneously an appeal to the national belonging and honorable citizenship of all Hmong-American communities developing from postwar refugee resettlement and secured through military service. The death in 2011 of General Vang Pao, the CIA-trained leader of Lao forces, revealed the limits to Arlington's embrace of Hmong veterans from the Vietnam War, however. With the support of several congressmen from his adopted home state of California, Vang Pao's family petitioned the Pentagon for an Arlington burial waiver. The denial of the request prompted Representative Jim Costa, Democrat from Fresno, California, to argue, "Many [Hmong veterans] paid the ultimate sacrifice and our nation owes a debt of gratitude to General Vang Pao and these patriotic individuals. Their service should be honored."[78] In drawing a line around recognized American military service and sacrifice that excluded the Hmong—excluded refugees—the Army's actions carried echoes of the Grey Berets' stark distinctions between earned and unearned benefits, between entitlements and gifts.[79] At the same time, the waiver rejection highlighted the fundamental lack of equivalence between state-directed military honors and community-sponsored memorial work within Arlington National Cemetery.

As efforts to mark the military contributions and histories of diverse populations in Arlington were under way in the 1980s and 1990s, lesbian and gay servicepersons and activists turned to the Tomb of the Unknown Soldier to make evident their own exclusions from the category of honorable service and stage different claims to visibility and national belonging. At the burial of the Vietnam Unknown in 1984, President Reagan had voiced a question on many people's minds: who was he? "We'll never know the answers to these questions about his life," Reagan concluded. Three years later at the March on Washington for Lesbian and Gay Rights, activists laid a wreath at the tomb to mark the ways in which the lives and military service of gay people had been made unknown by the ban on their service and the secrecy they were therefore required to work and live under. Since Air Force and Vietnam veteran Leonard Matlovich had come out on the cover of *Time* magazine in 1975 and been subsequently discharged, the activism of lesbian and gay military personnel and their allies was increasingly pronounced in the broader culture.[80] It also prompted the entrenchment of military leadership. In 1981, the Pentagon issued even more restrictive language in its ban on gays and lesbians, stating that "homosexuality is incompatible with military service."[81] As the HIV/AIDS crisis escalated across the 1980s, this appeal to the symbolic power of the Unknown Soldier became enmeshed with the activist cry "Silence=Death." The movement was drenched in grief and generated new forms of collective and political mourning as it pressed the public, government, and medical communities on questions of care, obligation, and the contours of what constituted an honorable life worthy of national grief.[82]

The issue of open service by gays and lesbians in the military became one of the most divisive in American politics after newly elected President Bill Clinton attempted to make good on a campaign promise to end the ban. Confronted with vehement public opposition and fierce resistance from the Pentagon, activists devoted much of the 1993 March on Washington for Lesbian, Gay, Bisexual, and Transgender Rights to rallying support. One of the action's central events was a "Requiem for Unknown LGB Soldiers." Not long after, on November 30, 1993, Clinton signed into law the "Don't Ask, Don't Tell" policy, intended as a compromise. It ended military investigations and formal questioning of recruits and service personnel about their sexual practices and partners, but kept in place—and in some ways made stronger—the demand that LGBQ people in the military remain unknown through silence and self-policing.[83]

One of the most outspoken critics of the policy was longtime activist, World War II veteran, and founding member of the Washington, DC, chapter of the Mattachine Society Franklin "Frank" Kameny. Honorably discharged after the war, Kameny had used his G.I. Bill benefits to earn a doctorate in astronomy. Hired in the summer of 1957 by the Army Map Service as a civilian employee, Kameny was called back to Washington in December from a job in Hawai'i and fired for being gay. Investigators for the U.S. Civil Service Commission had found evidence of his arrest in 1956 for "lewd and indecent conduct." Kameny fought the dismissal, first within the commission and later in the courts, as America buried its World War II and Korean Unknowns in 1958. When his petition to the U.S. Supreme Court was denied in 1961, he turned to activism and direct action, much of which focused on federal exclusions and discrimination in the military.[84] When Kameny died in 2011, ABC's Washington-centric Sunday-morning news program *This Week* used an undated piece of interview for its memorial segment in which Kameny explained, "Every year on Memorial Day I conduct a wreath-laying ceremony at the Tomb of the Unknowns in Arlington Cemetery to commemorate all of our country's dead including the many tens of thousands of gays who died in our country's wars."[85] The repeal of Don't Ask, Don't Tell, signed by Barack Obama in 2010, had just gone into effect the month before Kameny's death.

Today, Frank Kameny and Leonard Matlovich are buried near each other in Washington, DC's Congressional Cemetery, a privately operated cemetery with an old and illustrious history in the capital and a number of famous burials, including J. Edgar Hoover. Matlovich died from complications due to AIDS in 1988. His headstone, which he designed before his death, is made of black marble similar to that used for the Vietnam Veterans Memorial. Two pink triangles mark his birth and death dates, while the central space reads, "A Gay Vietnam Veteran," and beneath that, "When I was in the military they gave me a medal for killing two men and a discharge for loving one." Matlovich's name is engraved elsewhere on the gravesite, but this set of symbols and identifications challenge the very frameworks of unknown gay and lesbian service, while linking the state oppression it represents to the genocidal brutality of Nazi Germany and the Holocaust in the pink star emblem that had been reanimated by GBLT activists in the AIDS crisis. After some dispute about the fate of Kameny's remains and estate, he was buried near Matlovich on Veterans Day 2015. His headstone is an exact copy of a regulation national cemetery marker and details his military service. On the ground in front of it is another marker, bearing Kameny's most famous slogan from the 1960s, "Gay Is Good!"[86]

As the WIMSA memorial was absorbed into the existing architecture and made barely visible on the Arlington landscape, Army Sgt. Heather Lynn Johnsen became the first woman to walk the mat as a Tomb Guard on March 22, 1996. The path had been opened by orders from Secretary of Defense Les Aspin two years earlier in an effort to increase career opportunities and avenues of advancement for servicewomen. This had been instigated in part by the light thrown on military women's contributions and day-to-day realities during Desert Storm, which had made clear the real battle dangers confronted by all noncombat troops, including women. While ground combat units remained closed to women, new options included engineering, reconnaissance, intelligence, and ceremonial duties, which meant the Army's Old Guard. Ceremonial units in the Navy, Air Force, and Coast Guard already included women, but the elite Army division had few women and none in the premier units. The military face of the capital and Arlington remained decidedly masculine. In order to protect the Old Guard's combat infantry status, a new military police platoon, an area of the service already open to women, was attached. While service as a tomb sentinel might not put women in positions of obvious danger, it would put them on the front lines of public perception and make them embodiments of the Army's most elite representation of military honor. It would tie their living service to the sacrifices of the Unknowns. The Old Guard's commander lauded the change in just these terms, as sending "a signal that is loud and clear to the public that the Army has expanded its roles for women."[87] Many members of his unit openly expressed concerns, however, that standards, including the uniform height requirement, would have to be changed—lowered—in order to incorporate women, that precision and ceremony would suffer, and that honor would be degraded by their physical presence.

When Johnsen, a twenty-three-year-old white woman from California, took her place in the changing of the guard, she necessarily changed the ceremony's meaning. "This is a great day for the Army," proclaimed the unit's commander. Students in a school tour group from Alabama agreed, including ten-year-old Jessica Wallace, who said, "It shows women are tough, too, and can guard just as good as men can." Some in the unit still grumbled, though, including a fellow sentinel who had mustered out the same day. "There's a certain image" to the Tomb Guard that did not include the "henhouse," he said, adding, "You don't expect to see a woman there." Still, he had to admit respect for Johnsen's perfect score on the qualifying exam. "She was good," he conceded. Johnsen's presence among the Tomb Guards was a visible argument for women's honorable military service and valor—for their capacities and necessity as citizen-soldiers.

The superior officer performing Johnsen's first rifle and uniform inspection, a key feature of the guard changing ceremony, was African American. The image accompanying the *Washington Post*'s coverage the next day was a stark representation of the demographics of change and inclusion—and the story of multicultural nationalism—of the All-Volunteer Force.[88] The following year, Sgt. Danyell Elaine Wilson from Montgomery, Alabama, became the second woman and first black woman to serve as a Tomb Guard. She cited her home state's civil rights legacies as her inspiration for seeking the position. Around that same time, the Women in Military Service for America Memorial was dedicated, on October 18, 1997.[89]

The announcement in 1995 of renewed plans to make room for more graves by clearing the section of hardwood forest to the west of Arlington House dating to the days of the Custises not only prompted controversy but also brought fresh attention from the public to space concerns at the cemetery. The same land had been made an issue when John Metzler Sr. announced it would be cleared in 1964, stating the cemetery might otherwise be "full" by 1967. A negotiated agreement between the Department of the Army and the Department of the Interior stopped it and transferred the land to the National Park Service, attaching it to the Arlington House grounds the NPS already managed. Expansion of the cemetery's boundaries and a large columbarium had extended Arlington's availability for the eligible, but ground scarcity was once again a problem, and now Metzler's son was at the center of a similar storm. At issue in part was the persistent tension between maintaining the historical grounds of Arlington House, including preserving the last of the original trees, while dealing with continued pressures to find more space for in-ground burials. Noting that the loss of the historic forest would only provide about ten more years of availability for the cemetery if interment rates remained the same, one Arlington resident took to the pages of the *Washington Post* to urge closing Arlington when its remaining grounds could support no more interments. Under the headline "Let Arlington Cemetery Rest in Peace," Judith Rhodes argued, "responsible and conscientious government officials should recognize that the time has come to gracefully close

Arlington."[90] Officials disagreed, and Congress soon appropriated funds for archaeological work on the parcel in preparation for its transition to cemeterial uses.

The possibility for considering a limit to Arlington's ability to expand, to preparing the military and public for a satisfying closure and its transition to a strictly historic site, became more distant when House Republicans accused the Clinton administration of "selling" Arlington burials to ineligible officials who were also Democratic Party donors. The woodlands expansion controversy had morphed into another congressional investigation of the Clintons in the pitched partisan struggles of 1997 that would soon yield the Monica Lewinsky scandal and Bill Clinton's impeachment in 1998. While the investigation produced little more than accusation and press coverage, it catalyzed fears about the cemetery's space limitations and kept the issue at the forefront of popular and political concerns.

On November 21, 1997, Clinton signed legislation ensuring that Timothy McVeigh, convicted and sentenced to death for bombing the Alfred P. Murrah Federal Building in Oklahoma City in 1995, could not be buried in Arlington. This terrorist act, which had killed 168 people, including 19 children in the building's day-care facility, had been immediately presumed the work of Muslims from the Middle East. It had, in fact, been committed by two white American military veterans: McVeigh and his accomplice, Terry Nichols. Both had served in the Gulf War, and McVeigh had earned a Bronze Star, making him eligible for burial at Arlington. They also both had connections to antigovernment militias that had proliferated on the far right in the 1980s and early 1990s. Some people found in this moment and in these men an opportunity to address the place of both aspects of their histories, the honorable and the horrific, in their actions in Oklahoma City. Writing in the *Nation*, Katha Pollit argued that people seeking answers to McVeigh's actions should "start by acknowledging that the state he now claims to oppose gave him his first lesson in killing."[91] This raised the question of where the line was drawn between odious acts and murder, on the one hand, and justifiable killing in the service of national security, freedom's protection, and honor, on the other.

In 1982, the Army had been forced by the courts to allow an Arlington burial for a qualifying veteran who was killed by police as he threatened to blow up the Washington Monument. Some people pointed to that case in urging the need for action now.[92] Congress and President Clinton moved quickly after McVeigh's sentencing, amending the United States Code "to prohibit interment or memorialization in certain cemeteries of persons committing Federal or State capital crimes." The scholar Edward T. Linenthal notes that after McVeigh's execution in 2001, the measures taken to ensure that his "corpse could not be allowed to contaminate sacred ground" were extended to private spaces as well by cremating his remains and entrusting them to one of his attorneys to be scattered in an undisclosed location.[93]

While many officials worked to keep McVeigh and others like him out of hallowed ground, they simultaneously had to confront the fact that one of the most precious honored dead could no longer be kept in Arlington. Facing enormous public pressure and a desperate family, the Defense Department was compelled to consider disinterring the Vietnam Unknown for DNA testing. Suspicions that the remains in the crypt were those of Michael Blassie had circulated for years but elicited no action from the Pentagon. A series of CBS reports in early 1998 that featured the Blassie family and charged that Reagan's Pentagon had pressured the lab to produce an Unknown proved impossible to ignore. Much of the subsequent coverage quoted Jean Blassie, Michael's mother: "That's all I want, for them to open the tomb. If it's Michael, I want him to be brought home."[94] A Defense Department special committee ruled in favor of opening the tomb, although some people felt it should be preserved intact, that the Unknowns' symbolic importance overwhelmed the possibility of an identification, and that opening the crypt was opening a can of worms. To this argument, *USA Today* editorialized, "As far as the bones beneath the Vietnam slab: they deserve a name now more than an honor guard."[95] DNA identification confirmed the Vietnam Unknown's identity as Air Force First Lieutenant Michael J. Blassie. Today he is buried near his hometown in the Jefferson Barracks National Cemetery in St. Louis, Missouri. Among his decorations and service, Blassie's headstone lists his time as an "Unknown Soldier, May 28, 1984–May 14, 1998." On September 17, 1999, National POW/MIA Recognition Day, the Vietnam crypt empty once more was rededicated to the missing with a new inscription: "honoring and keeping faith with America's missing servicemen."[96]

American Airlines Flight 77 came in low at Arlington's edge before striking the Pentagon's west side at 9:37 a.m. on September 11, 2001. The approach and crash were witnessed by cemetery employees and visitors used to seeing the constant flow of air traffic into nearby Reagan National Airport higher overhead.[97] Two planes had already been flown into the World Trade Center in New York; another was brought down soon after by passengers over Shanksville, Pennsylvania, en route to Washington. The plane and the destruction and intense fire generated by Flight 77's impact tore through the outer three of the five concentric rings that compose the building complex, killing all aboard—fifty-four passengers, five crew members, and five hijackers—and 125 people on the ground.

In the days that followed, many people were drawn to Arlington's solemnity and expressly hallowed ground. Washington-area papers reported spontaneous collections of people in the cemetery in 9/11's immediate aftermath, perhaps seeking to be surrounded by death framed through honor and patriotism as much as to get a clear sight line on the devastation at the Pentagon. The cemetery satisfied deeper emotional and patriotic registers for a stunned and distraught population, hungry for solace, strength, triumph, and even revenge. Arlington National Cemetery "is even a more hallowed ground since September 11," explained the cemetery's historian, Tom Sherlock, less than two months after the attacks. "That is reflected in the mood of the people who visit."[98]

In some ways, Arlington was an obvious place to honor those who died in the Pentagon given its proximity to the building that symbolizes and houses the highest American military authority and the qualifying status of several victims. But controversy had erupted within days of the attack when the families of several civilian Pentagon employees sought to have their loved ones honored with burial in Arlington as well, despite the deceased's lack of uniformed service. They had been integral to the functioning of the military as electronics and communications specialists and budget analysts, among other things, and should be honored as "part of the military community," the family members urged.[99] Arguably, this notion of the Pentagon victims' military status helped facilitate the diminished place of the Pentagon and its victims in popular perceptions of 9/11 over time, overwhelmed by New York's staggering human loss, physical destruction, the televisual record, and event-framing language like "Ground Zero." It was difficult to absorb those who worked and died in the Pentagon into the same narratives of innocence assigned to victims at the World Trade Center and aboard the four doomed flights. The Army ultimately denied the petitions, citing the rules and ongoing space concerns and the fact that it had previously denied waiver requests from the families of civilian Defense Department employees who died in the Oklahoma City bombing of 1995.[100]

The controversy became even more heated when the pilot of Flight 77, Charles F. Burlingame, a twenty-five-year veteran with the Air Force, was denied an Arlington burial because he did not qualify as a reservist who had not reached the age of sixty. Burlingame was fifty-one years old when he died in the Pentagon attack. His family was astounded and outraged and appealed to the secretary of the Army and then the White House. The refusal to grant an exception was affirmed at each of these levels, and the family rejected offers to allow Burlingame to be buried with his father in the same grave or inurned in the columbarium. Public outcry was so significant that the George W. Bush White House reversed itself the next day, and Burlingame was buried in his own grave on December 12.[101]

On September 12, 2002, Defense Secretary Donald H. Rumsfeld presided over the burial with full military honors of a single casket in Arlington National Cemetery containing both unidentified and identified remains representing all 184 victims of the 9/11 attack on the Pentagon, a number that included civilian and military personnel on the ground and the crew and passengers of Flight 77. Military spokespeople had taken great pains to be clear that none of the hijackers' remains could be among those comingled in the coffin. Before the interment, Rumsfeld addressed a crowd of more than 1,000 mourners in Memorial Amphitheater at the Tomb of the Unknown Soldier; it was the first funeral of its kind since services for the Unknown Soldier of the Vietnam War in 1984. With special reference to the five people killed who could never be identified, including a three-year-old girl who had been aboard the hijacked plane, the secretary stood next to the flag-draped coffin and said, "Today, these five join the unknown of past wars even as we pursue the war that is still unfolding."[102] Rhetorically linking the dead of a terrorist incident, many of whom were civilians and some of whom were children, to the lost uniformed soldiers, martial valor, and national honor represented at the Tomb of the Unknown Soldier, Rumsfeld's eulogy suggested the radical reimagining of war and who constitutes a "hero," a "warrior," an "enemy," a "combatant," and an "innocent" that was under way in the formulation of the War on Terror and the Bush Doctrine, one that mirrored the logic and aims of terrorism itself—a war that was, indeed, "still unfolding."[103] Arlington's history and memorial landscape was not simply a backdrop for this linkage but made it possible.

A large procession moved from the Tomb of the Unknown Soldier to Section 64 near the Pentagon for the interment. Mourners followed honor guards from each branch of the service and a horse-drawn caisson carrying the casket. Sixty-four active and retired servicepersons were individually buried in Arlington in the months following the attack, most together in three rows in Section 64. The group burial site was nestled beside them and marked by a four-and-a-half-foot-high, pentagonal monument of solid Vermont granite, a smaller version of an intact, but forever changed, Pentagon. It is inscribed around the top in relief letters: "Victims Of / Terrorist / Attack On / The Pentagon / September 11, 2001." The rest of each of the five sides is covered almost entirely by large aluminum plates that together carry the names of all 184 victims in alphabetical order. A system of symbols defined at the bottom of the last plate designates those whose remains were never identified and the passengers and crew of Flight 77.

The first-anniversary ceremonies at the Pentagon and the next day's group burial at Arlington further solidified the Bush administration's position that the attacks of September 11, 2001, were acts of war demanding—and justifying—an expansive, global military response that would include the invasion of Iraq. While Rumsfeld presided over events in Arlington, President Bush was addressing the United Nations General Assembly in New York outlining his early case against Iraq, capitalizing on the first-year anniversary of 9/11 to lay the groundwork for invasion and make claims that Iraq was a legitimate front in an expansive war against terrorism and al-Qaeda in particular.[104] President Bush and several members of his national security team, most of whom had long records of experience with Republican administrations reaching back to Nixon and long histories with one another, quickly absorbed the events of 9/11 into already-extant military goals. Chief among them was to "finish the job" that George H. W. Bush had left incomplete in the first Gulf War by leaving Saddam Hussein in power and to enact Rumsfeld's vision of a transformed military.[105]

The service and monument dedication at Arlington, as a place with unique purchase on the American imagination, was especially powerful in popularizing these aims. Today the September 11th Memorial, or the Pentagon Group Burial Marker, is linked in both official and unofficial narratives to a set of monuments and graves scattered throughout the cemetery that are related to incidents of terrorism in the post-Vietnam era. These include the Iran Rescue Mission Memorial, dedicated in 1983; the memorial to servicemen killed in the Beirut Marine barracks bombing of the same year, dedicated in 1984; and the Lockerbie Memorial Cairn for the victims of the 1988 bombing of Pan Am Flight 103, dedicated in 1995. Imbued with fresh urgency as markers for casualties from the War on Terror, these monuments are freighted with new historical meanings. They are knit together in official cemetery materials, walking maps, tours, and in popular histories and guidebooks in a pattern that popularizes a longer story of American victimization, Islamic aggression, reluctant empire, and virtuous triumph.[106]

The official category of military unknown was not an easy fit for the unidentified victims of the Pentagon attack. While no remains could be found, all five were known and known to be lost. Only two were members of the armed services, and one of those was retired and working as a civilian employee at the time of his death. One was a child. None had died in a conventionally defined act of war on a clearly established battlefield. But in a clear indication of the historical frames to which the Bush administration appealed through its orchestrations of mourning on September 12, 2002, their memorial service was designed to suggest that they had died in such a conflict and that each was, in fact, a kind of soldier and hero in the new War on Terror. Constituting a near-perfect inversion of the concept of the military unknown, the Pentagon group burial has begotten new ghosts and new national imaginings. If the notion of a "hero" had become slippery in the context of 9/11's losses, burial in Arlington and a service at the Tomb of the Unknown Soldier for all of the Pentagon victims sought to ground them, literally, in earth that defined honorable death and service to the nation. Rather than making hallowed the ground where they were buried, the civilian victims' collective burial in Arlington transformed them into warriors.

As the wars in Afghanistan and Iraq continued, these categories became only more indistinct, still to be worked out in the grounds of the cemetery. The first official casualty of the war in Afghanistan was not a member of the armed forces but a CIA agent. He had been interred in Arlington with special waiver just two days before Charles Burlingame on December 10, 2001.[107] More CIA employees followed in the months and years to come, indicating wider slippage between the military and intelligence communities, made stark in the drone program's initial operational location in the CIA and then in Leon Panetta's move from serving as Barack Obama's Director of the CIA to Secretary of Defense in 2011.[108]

The post-9/11 history of Arlington National Cemetery has been defined by constant war in the context of the wide net of the "War on Terror," the longest war in U.S. history in Afghanistan (2001–2016), and officially the third-longest war in Iraq (2003–2012), although American forces, intelligence officers, and private contractors never fully demobilized there and new deployments were announced in 2016. Military personnel and others with waivers who have perished fighting these wars rest together in Section 60, a large rectangular expanse near the columbarium complex. Distant from primary tourist destinations up the rise and rarely visited by those without friends and loved ones interred there, the section is one of the more active places in Arlington. Marked by fresh graves and fresher grief, it often seems a place apart from the rest of the cemetery. Or, as one reporter described it, "This is not the antiseptic postcard Arlington . . . if a graveyard can be alive, this part of Arlington is, in marked contrast to other sections."[109] Until late 2013, Section 60 was also distinct in the diverse collection of headstone decorations and mementos

left at many of the graves, blending common practices in various cemeteries across the country with a public memorial tradition that emerged
from popular engagements with the Vietnam Veterans Memorial.[110] After
clearing the section of all non-regulation items and discarding most of it
without notice to families, cemetery officials announced that Arlington
would henceforth enforce long-standing restrictions on adornments in
Section 60 as it did in the rest of the cemetery. In response to family complaints and activism, Arlington has since embarked on a "Mementos Pilot Program" for Section 60 alone that seeks to balance individual family
wishes with maintenance and mowing concerns and aesthetic goals.[111]

Under the current program, regulation military headstones must remain free of additional decoration, as in the rest of the cemetery. This
means they can only carry officially engraved identifications, Medal of
Honor insignias, a Union Shield or Confederate Southern Cross from the
Civil War, and one of sixty-one currently possible emblems of belief, including atheism, located in the top center of the headstone. This diverse
set of symbols has grown over time, mostly at the request of military
personnel and families of the deceased. This was not the case for pagan
servicepersons, however. After nine years of petitioning the Department
of Veterans Affairs to no avail for a Wiccan pentacle among the emblems
available for headstones, a group of families and churches sued the VA
on behalf of deceased pagan servicemen and -women, active-duty personnel, and veterans in September 2006. At the time, the list of approved
emblems numbered thirty-eight. The religion was already recognized by
the military at large, available for engraving on dog tags and included in
chaplains' handbooks. By April the following year, the Bush Administration settled the case and added the Wiccan pentacle to the options for
marking belief and faith practice, or its absence, on military-issue gravestones, including at Arlington.[112]

Representing multiculturalism in the military and the diversity of the
nation it serves, the inclusion of a growing range of religious iconography
within Arlington's terrain of honorable service contrasts with the Judeo-
Christian assumptions of most of its history. After the Vietnam War, this
history was simultaneously marked by the merging of Middle Eastern
terror threats with Soviet influence as the greatest dangers to American
security in foreign policy and the popular imagination. The geography

of the Middle East was increasingly defined by religion and radical fundamentalism as the "Islamic World"—as a singular religious culture beyond the pale of the American character and honor.[113] This shaped official and popular responses to the attacks of 9/11 and subsequent military engagements, foreign and domestic policies, and predominant conceptions of Islam as singularly un-American. At the same time, many people have pointed to the graves of Muslim military personnel in Arlington, particularly those from the wars in Iraq and Afghanistan in Section 60, to counter Islamophobic discourses and violence, the visual argument of an iconic regulation military headstone engraved with the crescent and star often standing on its own. The blunt power of the optics relies on surprise, presupposing the viewer's assumption that an American military headstone would not carry an emblem of Islam, while deriving its patriotic effect from the sacrifice of Muslim American soldiers. Like the Japanese American soldiers interred in Arlington shortly after World War II, the clearest demonstration of patriotism and citizenship is death.

Perhaps the most famous instance of this argument came from one of the most famous black soldiers of the late twentieth and twenty-first centuries, General Colin Powell (Ret.). The first African American to serve as Chairman of the Joint Chiefs, Powell emerged from the First Gulf War as one of the most recognized and respected public figures in the country. Encouraged to run for the Republican presidential nomination himself, Powell went on to serve as Secretary of State for George W. Bush. In 2008, he defied his party affiliations and assumptions of shared experience as a Vietnam veteran with John McCain to endorse Barack Obama for the presidency. Responding to claims that Obama was a "secret Muslim," Powell focused on the Islamophobic sentiment undergirding the claim, noting that being a Muslim did not make one less American or unfit for the presidency. As a career serviceman who had expressed his own wishes to be interred in Arlington as he left for his first deployment to Vietnam in 1968, Powell appealed to the national cemetery to make his point now:

> I feel strongly about this particular point because of a picture I saw in a magazine. It was a photo essay about troops who are serving in

Iraq and Afghanistan. And one picture at the tail end of this photo essay was of a mother in Arlington Cemetery, and she had her head on the headstone of her son's grave. And as the picture focused in, you could see the writing on the headstone. And it gave his awards— Purple Heart, Bronze Star—showed that he died in Iraq, gave his date of birth, date of death. He was 20 years old. And then, at the very top of the headstone, it didn't have a Christian cross, it didn't have the Star of David, it had crescent and a star of the Islamic faith. And his name was Kareem Rashad Sultan Khan, and he was an American. He was born in New Jersey. He was 14 years old at the time of 9/11, and he waited until he can go serve his country, and he gave his life.[114]

Describing the iconic national sacrifices of two figures, the soldier dead and his grieving mother, Powell's own history and body gave moral energy to his argument. As a popular embodiment of American progress and military egalitarianism, he simultaneously gestured to the long history of black freedom struggles reaching back to slavery and the Civil War. Arlington's ability to affirm patriotism and national belonging—its power as hallowed ground—relies upon both.

CONCLUSION

Hereafter

[T]he hallowed remains of men and women rest in Arlington
Cemetery, they who believed, fought, and died for their country.
May their spirit infuse our being to work together with respect,
enabling us to continue to build this nation.

—Myrlie Evers-Williams, Invocation, Presidential
Inauguration (2013)

A S THE SECRETARY of the Army neared the end of his prepared remarks, his voice caught, thick with emotion. Sitting before members
of the press on June 10, 2010, flanked by the Army's inspector general and
the newly appointed civilian director of Arlington National Cemetery,
Secretary John H. McHugh said, "On behalf of the United States Army
and on behalf of myself, I deeply apologize to the families of the honored
fallen resting in that hallowed ground who may now question the care afforded to their loved ones. To the men and women of the—who wear the
uniform of the United States; to all citizens of this great nation who believe, as I do, that Arlington National Cemetery is the most sacred place
on this planet, the Army owes better."[1] McHugh's apology came with the
report of an investigation finding gross mismanagement and a dysfunc-
tional institutional culture at the cemetery. Many people were stunned to
discover that beneath Arlington's iconic vistas of uniform white headstones, grand memorials, and ceremonies of mourning and honorable
sacrifice lurked the accumulated effects of years of ineptitude, chaos, and
carelessness. The scandal, which only worsened with continued investigations by Congress, the Government Accountability Office, and the
Army, brought to light a long history of privileging appearances and

big symbolic acts over attention to individual loss and day-to-day maintenance.

The "heart of the republic" was terribly broken, taking with it the trust of active-duty servicepeople, veterans, their families and friends, and a horrified public. Of the many charges investigated—which ranged from accusations of sexual harassment and nepotism in hiring to astounding levels of negligence and budget irregularities—public outrage focused most intently on revelations that no less than 211 and possibly more than 6,600 graves and remains had been mismarked, lost, or discarded, including those of servicepersons killed recently in Iraq and Afghanistan.[2] This news was particularly devastating to the families and friends of those who are buried in Arlington, many of whom flooded its newly established crisis hotline with requests for assurance that their loved ones rest in the right graves. Some sought exhumations and physical proof, as did the parents of Marine Private Heath Warner, killed in Iraq in 2006 at the age of nineteen. When inaccuracies in the paperwork offered as evidence of their son's proper burial only magnified their fears, the Warners traveled to Virginia from their home in Ohio to have their son disinterred and his casket opened for a positive visual identification.[3] They demanded to see beneath the surface.

Aware of the burial discrepancies for some time, Arlington officials had taken measures to fend off exactly the kind of scrutiny and scandal they faced in 2010. When workers began digging a new grave in Section 68 in 2003, they were surprised to discover a casket of remains already in the plot. Those remains stayed there, unmarked and unreported outside Arlington management, for six years. Then, in 2009, facing a wrongful-dismissal case, official inquiries, and questions from the investigative journalist Mark Benjamin, the cemetery installed a headstone at the plot, inscribed simply "Unknown."[4] Joining thousands of other such stones from the nineteenth and early twentieth centuries, this marked the first official burial of unknown service personnel in Arlington since the state funeral of the Unknown Soldier of the Vietnam War on Memorial Day in 1984. The treatment of the remains of these two servicepersons could not have been more different, although they ultimately shared certain outcomes. When the Vietnam Unknown was identified in 1998 as Air Force First Lieutenant Michael J. Blassie, most people assumed then that advances in forensic science and military organization meant that there would never be another unknown.[5] In the context of wide-ranging investigations, Senate hearings, and the creation in 2011 of an Arlington Gravesite Accountability Task Force, a new headstone was quietly placed at Grave 449, Section 68, identifying the man buried there as Air Force Lieutenant Colonel Robert A. Gray, who served in World War II, Korea, and Vietnam and died in December 1988.[6]

The secrecy and rush with which Arlington officials, including John Metzler Jr., placed the "Unknown" headstone over remains, which they had no idea they had lost and might have easily identified, called into question the entire structure of national honor and public feeling embodied in the tomb. It cast doubt on the ability of the state to meet its obligations to active-duty servicepersons, veterans, and their loved ones.[7] These doubts were compounded by subsequent revelations of problems at Dover Air Force Base, responsible for the "dignified transfer" of repatriated remains and site of the largest mortuary facility in the United States military, as well as across the system of Veterans Health Administration.[8] Veterans and those serving at the time who might have envisioned a funeral for themselves in Arlington, who might have longed for their own eternal rest in the nation's hallowed ground, surely now could not help but imagine their remains mishandled, lost, or accidentally discarded in a cemetery landfill. Compelled to ponder their identities and actions erased and transformed, rather than eternally honored, they now had to entertain the possibility of being made unknown and unknowable through the neglect, incompetence, or corruption of the bureaucratic state. It was a betrayal of the highest order to the promise of "hereafter."

The vision of "hereafter" embedded in the early twentieth-century expansion of burial benefits for all service personnel across time exceeds the language of policy and regulation and reaches into something more profound and intimate. It carries the history of Lincoln's description at Gettysburg of the meaning of sacrifice for the nation and the sense that no honors, statue, or memorial act could ever fully recognize the weight and awesome depths of "the last full measure of devotion." As a synonym for the afterlife, or life after death, it also denotes eternal glory in martial valor reaching back at least to the elegies of ancient Greece such as the lines by Simonides for the Spartan dead at Thermopylae:

Having died, they are not dead;
For their valor, by the glory which it brings,
Raises them from above out of the house of Hades.[9]

Sacred conceptions of the hereafter make it difficult to separate these martial and memorial connotations from faith. This shifts the action from
obligation, or the veterans' benefit and the responsibility to provide it, to
the active-duty serviceperson or veteran and her or his belief that the
benefit and honor will be provided, that she or he will, in fact, be raised
"from above."

This faith and set of commitments are literalized in the hallowed
ground of Arlington National Cemetery; it is the earthly terrain of "hereafter." But beyond recent and historic betrayals and corruption, its promises of perpetuity run into the physical limitations of the space. It is believed that current expansion plans will make the cemetery functional
into the 2050s, or for roughly four more decades.[10] Since 1963, the country
has faced dire predictions of reaching Arlington's capacity in the very
near or not so distant future. At every turn, some portion of ground has
been claimed or other measure taken to forestall the inevitable, often in
the form of greater restrictions on eligibility and tiered access placing
primacy on in-ground burials. In 2015, the VA embarked on an expansion of the entire national cemetery system that it celebrated as the largest
such initiative since the Civil War. When completed, more than 96 percent
of veterans and their families will live within 75 miles of a cemetery in
the system, bringing the country closer than ever to the long-standing
wish of many people for a national cemetery in every state and territory
of the United States.[11] Greater official commitments to providing military
burial options close to home may relieve some of the pressure on Arlington. The timing is telling. Unlike the first draconian changes to eligibility requirements for Arlington interments while the country was at war
in 1967, the awful calculus of space concerns in the twenty-first century
has been shaped by the open-endedness of the "war on terrorism" and the
individual conflicts it has begotten. The "hereafter" has been hounded
by perpetual war.

Changes to the transportation infrastructure that moves tens of thousands of people around Northern Virginia and through it to Washington

every day, which forms some of the barriers to cemetery expansion, resulted in a new memorial to Freedman's Village in September 2015. When the crumbling old bridge over Columbia Pike at Washington Boulevard was slated for replacement in 2008, activists with the Black Heritage Museum of Arlington, including its founding president, the late Talmadge T. Williams, worked to have it renamed Freedman's Village Bridge. On the clover exchange near the Pentagon, it abuts land that was once farmed by village residents and more immediately marks the exact location of the former Queen City neighborhood, primarily home to Freedman's Villagers evicted at the end of the nineteenth century—and then evicted again for the Pentagon project. The bridge that was replaced had been built in 1942 as part of the Pentagon Roadway Network. The new Freedman's Village Bridge (the apostrophe removed by the county for construction purposes) was dedicated on September 10, 2015. Several descendants were in attendance, including Ruth Burton, who at ninety-seven years old explained that she was born in Queen City in 1918, at 1011 Columbia Pike— land that is beneath the bridge today. Of the monumental recognition, she said, "It's a long time coming, but finally got here, . . . and it's a beautiful bridge."[12]

While much work remains to be done in historicizing Arlington's deeper histories of slavery and black freedom, the Freedman's Village Bridge offers an important symbol for linking the plantation and the people once enslaved there to the hallowed ground it became as a national cemetery. Bridging history had been on the mind of Myrlie Evers-Williams on January 21, 2013, when she became the first woman and the first non-clergy person to give the invocation at a presidential inauguration for the start of Barack Obama's second term in office. That year also marked the fiftieth anniversary of her first husband's murder. She spoke of the cemetery's power and promise as a place for honoring individual and collective national acts of heroism and sacrifice, and as a place for reckoning with the past and building a better future: "Approximately four miles from where we are assembled, the hallowed remains of men and women rest in Arlington Cemetery, they who believed, fought, and died for their country. May their spirit infuse our being to work with respect, enabling us to continue to build this nation. And in so doing, we send a message to the world that we are strong, fierce in our strength, and ever vigilant in our pursuit of freedom."[13] Where Montgomery Meigs had argued in the early days of the national cemetery that "all care for the dead is for the sake of the living," Myrlie Evers-Williams echoed Lincoln at Gettysburg to argue that the dead call the living to action and vigilance in freedom's pursuit for all—past, present, and future—for "hereafter."

Notes

Acknowledgments

Illustration Credits

Index

NOTES

Abbreviations

ACPL   Arlington Public Library, Central Library, Center for Local History, Arlington, VA

ARHO   Arlington House, The Robert E. Lee Memorial, National Park Service, Arlington, VA

LOC   Library of Congress, Washington, DC

NARA   National Archives and Records Administration, Washington, DC, and College Park, MD

VHS   Virginia Historical Society, Richmond, VA

WIMSA   Women in Military Service for America Memorial Foundation Collection, Arlington, VA

Introduction

1. The first female Tomb Guard, Sgt. Heather Lynn Johnsen, began walking the mat in March 1996. Details of current Tomb Guard training and service, day-to-day ceremony, and "lifestyle" can be found at their website: https://tombguard.org/tomb-of-the-unknown-soldier/the-tomb-guard/.

2. G. Kurt Piehler, *Remembering War the American Way* (Washington, DC: Smithsonian Books, 2004), 122.

3. "The President's Address," *Boston Daily Globe*, November 12, 1921, 8.

4. The foundational text on the relationship of death and mourning to nationalism is Ernest Renan's 1882 address "What Is a Nation?" in Geoff Eley and Ronald Grigor Suny, eds., *Becoming National: A Reader* (New York: Oxford University Press, 1996),

42–55. His work influenced a host of twentieth-century theorists of nationalism, most notably Benedict Anderson, who argued of memorials for unknown warriors, "No more arresting emblems of the modern culture of nationalism exist," as they are verily "saturated with ghostly *national* imaginings." Benedict Anderson, *Imagined Communities: Reflections on the Origin and Spread of Nationalism*, rev. ed. (New York: Verso, 1992), 9. See also Benedict Anderson, "Replica, Aura, and Late Nationalist Imaginings," in *The Spectre of Comparison: Nationalism, Southeast Asia, and the World* (New York: Verso, 1998), 46–57. For critical reconsiderations of Anderson's argument and his conception of the "imagined community," especially in relation to the particularities of race, gender, and sexuality, see: Homi K. Bhabha, "DissemiNation: Time, Narrative, and the Margins of the Modern Nation," in Bhabha, ed., *Nation and Narration* (New York: Routledge, 1990), 291–322; Sharon Patricia Holland, *Raising the Dead: Readings of Death and (Black) Subjectivity* (Durham, NC: Duke University Press, 2000), 22–28; Dana Luciano, *Arranging Grief: Sacred Time and the Body in Nineteenth-Century America* (New York: New York University Press, 2007), 219–227; Christopher Peterson, *Kindred Specters: Death, Mourning, and American Affinity* (Minneapolis: University of Minnesota Press, 2007), 1–36; Mark Redfield, "Imagi-nation: The Imagined Community and the Aesthetics of Mourning," *diacritics* vol. 29, no. 4 (Winter 1999): 58–83; Rebecca Schneider, *Performing Remains: Art and War in Times of Reenactment* (New York: Routledge, 2011), 2–22; and Priscilla Wald, *Constituting Americans: Cultural Anxiety and Narrative Form* (Durham, NC: Duke University Press, 1995), 1–13.

5. On public memorials as sites for educating publics in the feelings of national belonging and citizenship, see Erika Doss, *Memorial Mania: Public Feeling in America* (Chicago: University of Chicago Press, 2010); Kirk Savage, *Monument Wars: Washington, DC, the National Mall, and the Transformation of the Memorial Landscape* (Berkeley: University of California Press, 2009).

6. Committee on Interior and Insular Affairs, House of Representatives, "Committee Print No. 15: Data on National Cemeteries," 87th Cong., 2nd sess. (Washington, DC: US Government Printing Office, 1962), 1.

7. The brochure can be downloaded as a PDF at http://www.arlingtoncemetery.mil /about.

8. Drew Gilpin Faust, *This Republic of Suffering: Death and the American Civil War* (New York: Knopf, 2008), xi. Recent demographic research suggests that this number may have been as high as 750,000. Guy Gugliotta, "New Estimate Raises Civil War Death Toll," *New York Times*, April 3, 2012, p. D1.

9. Julia Wilbur Diary, November 17, 1862, transcribed and annotated by Paula T. Whitacre for the Alexandria (VA) Archaeology Museum, transcription, 28. Whitacre notes that Sunday was actually the sixteenth. Original diaries held in the Julia Wilbur Papers, 1843–1908, Collection No. 1158, Haverford College Library Special Collections, Haverford, PA.

10. Abraham Lincoln, Address at Gettysburg, Pennsylvania, November 19, 1863, *The Gettysburg Address* (New York: Penguin Books, 2009), 115.

11. Linda Kerber, *No Constitutional Right to Be Ladies: Women and the Obligations of Citizenship* (New York: Hill and Wang, 1999), chap. 5.

12. Frederick Douglass, "Should the Negro Enlist in the Union Army?," July 6, 1863, in Nicholas Buccola, ed., *The Essential Douglass: Selected Writings & Speeches* (Indianapolis: Hackett Publishing Company, 2016), 187–190.

13. Robert Pogue Harrison argues that people bury the dead "to humanize the ground on which they build their worlds and found their histories." Harrison, *The Dominion of the Dead* (Chicago: University of Chicago Press, 2003), xi.

14. The brochure can be downloaded as a PDF at http://www.arlingtoncemetery.mil /about.

15. On subjectivity, citizenship, and the politics of death and mourning, see: Vincent Brown, *The Reaper's Garden: Death and Power in the World of Atlantic Slavery* (Cambridge, MA: Harvard University Press, 2008); Judith Butler, *Precarious Life: The Powers of Mourning and Violence* (New York: Verso, 2004); Russ Castronovo, *Necro Citizenship: Death, Eroticism, and the Public Sphere in the Nineteenth-Century United States* (Durham, NC: Duke University Press, 2001); Anne Cheng, *The Melancholy of Race: Psychoanalysis, Assimilation, and Hidden Grief* (Oxford: Oxford University Press, 2000); Douglass Crimp, *Melancholia and Moralism: Essays on AIDS and Queer Politics* (Cambridge, MA: MIT Press, 2004); David Eng and David Kazanjian, eds., *Loss: The Politics of Mourning* (Berkeley: University of California Press, 2002); Gail Holst-Warhaft, *The Cue for Passion: Grief and Its Political Uses* (Cambridge, MA: Harvard University Press, 2000); Joseph Roach, *Cities of the Dead: Circum-Atlantic Performance* (New York: Columbia University Press, 1996); and Katherine Verdery, *The Political Lives of Dead Bodies: Reburial and Postsocialist Change* (New York: Columbia University Press, 1999).

16. Susan Zerbe describes her son, Daniel Lee Zerbe, Air Force Technical Sergeant, killed in Afghanistan, August 6, 2011, in *Arlington National Cemetery*, February 4, 2014, WETA Television, PBS. "Honor the Fallen," *Military Times*, n.d., http://thefallen .militarytimes.com/air-force-tech-sgt-daniel-l-zerbe/6567930 (accessed March 20, 2016).

1. Keeper of the Keys

1. Folder: "Arlington Biography—Gray," Vertical Files, ACPL.

2. On Harry W. Gray's approximate birth year, see U.S. Bureau of the Census, *Ninth Census of the United States, 1870*, Arlington Township, Alexandria County, Va., Roll M593-1632. On the Gray family generally, see Folder: "Arlington Biography—Gray," Vertical Files, ACPL; Box One, Folder: "Army Occupation—Slaves Who Remained during the Civil War" and Folder: "Harry Gray," Slavery Files, ARHO; Box Two, Folder: "Inventories & Will," Folder: "Identities of Slaves," Folder: "Gray Family Papers," Slavery Files, ARHO. Charles Fisher, Chad Randl, and Kaaren Staveteig, *Arlington House, The Robert E. Lee Memorial: South Dependency Historic Structure Report* (Washington, DC: National Park Service, U.S. Department of the Interior, 2009).

3. This calls to mind questions that the historian Tiya Miles has asked of another plantation landscape: "What really took place on these well-worn grounds? What does this house *stand* for?" Miles, *The House on Diamond Hill: A Cherokee Plantation Story* (Chapel Hill: University of North Carolina Press, 2010), xiv.

4. Philip Bigler, *In Honored Glory: Arlington National Cemetery the Final Post,* 4th ed. (St. Petersburg, FL: Vandamere, 2007), 11–13; Jennifer Hanna, *Cultural Landscape Report, 1802–1861 Historic Period Plan, Arlington House, The Robert E. Lee Memorial* (Washington, DC: National Park Service, U.S. Department of the Interior, 2001), 7–10.

5. Bigler, *In Honored Glory,* 4–6; Hanna, *Cultural Landscape Report,* 7–22; James Edward Peters, *Arlington National Cemetery: Shrine to America's Heroes,* 3rd ed. (Bethesda, MD: Woodbine House, 2008), 1–3. G. W. P. Custis was not born at Arlington but at his mother's family's plantation in Maryland.

6. Scott E. Casper, *Sarah Johnson's Mount Vernon: The Forgotten History of an American Shrine* (New York: Hill and Wang, 2008), 5.

7. Hanna, *Cultural Landscape Report,* 22–23. On the history of Washington, DC, generally, see Kirk Savage, *Monument Wars: Washington, DC, the National Mall, and the Transformation of the Memorial Landscape* (Berkeley: University of California Press, 2009).

8. Elizabeth Brown Pryor, *Reading the Man: A Portrait of Robert E. Lee through his Private Letters* (New York: Viking, 2007), 49.

9. Robert E. Lee, quoted in *Arlington House, The Robert E. Lee Memorial* (Washington, DC: National Park Service, U.S. Department of the Interior, 1978).

10. Hanna, *Cultural Landscape Report,* 28, 39. On the popularity of Southern Colonial Revival architecture at the turn of the last century, see Catherine W. Bishir, "Landmarks of Power: Building a Southern Past in Raleigh and Wilmington, North Carolina, 1885–1915," in *Where These Memories Grow: History, Memory, and Southern Identity,* ed. W. Fitzhugh Brundage (Chapel Hill: University of North Carolina Press, 2000), 139–168.

11. Undated memorandum, Box Two, Folder: "Jim Parks," Slavery Files, ARHO.

12. Godfrey T. Vigne, *Six Months in America* (London: Whittaker Treacher, 1832), 147, quoted in Hanna, *Cultural Landscape Report,* 46.

13. Benson Lossing, "Arlington House: The Seat of G. W. P. Custis, Esq.," *Harper's New Monthly Magazine* 7, no. 4 (1853): 436–437.

14. On the range of problems and accusations, see Pryor, *Reading the Man,* 127, 518n11; G. W. P. Custis to William O. Winston, January 28, 1857, quoted in Hanna, *Cultural Landscape Report,* 62.

15. Karl Decker and Angus McSween, *Historic Arlington* (Washington, DC: Decker and McSween, 1892), 37, VHS.

16. Emory M. Thomas, *Robert E. Lee: A Biography* (New York: W. W. Norton, 1995), 61.

17. Peters, *Arlington National Cemetery,* 11.

18. Eric Burin, *Slavery and the Peculiar Solution: A History of the American Colonization Society* (Gainesville: University Press of Florida, 2005); Elizabeth R. Varon, *We Mean to Be Counted: White Women and Politics in Antebellum Virginia* (Chapel Hill: University of North Carolina Press, 1998), chap. 2.

19. Mary Custis Lee, diary, June 9, 1853, Lee Family Papers, 1810–1914, Section 5, VHS.

20. Thavolia Glymph, *Out of the House of Bondage: The Transformation of the Plantation Household* (New York: Cambridge University Press, 2008).

21. Mary Lee Fitzhugh Custis to William Henry Fitzhugh Lee, March 15, 1853, quoted in Pryor, *Reading the Man,* 128.

22. Pryor, *Reading the Man,* 261–262.

23. Robert E. Lee to Martha Custis Williams, March 11 and 15, 1854, quoted in ibid., 54.

24. On Robert E. Lee's attempt to change the will's conditions, see Michael Fellman, *The Making of Robert E. Lee* (Baltimore: Johns Hopkins University Press, 2000), 195–200; Michael Korda, *Clouds of Glory: The Life and Legend of Robert E. Lee* (New York: HarperCollins, 2014), 200–203; Thomas, *Robert E. Lee,* 175–178; Pryor, *Reading the Man,* 261–263, 274–275.

25. Mary Lee to W. G. Webster, February 17, 1858, quoted in Thomas, *Robert E. Lee,* 177.

26. Robert E. Lee to William Henry Fitzhugh Lee, May 30, 1858, and Robert E. Lee to George Washington Custis Lee, January 17, 1858, quoted in ibid., 177.

27. Mary Custis Lee, Diary, May 1 or 10 [slightly illegible], May 11, and August 8, 1858, Lee Family Papers, 1810–1914, Section 5, VHS.

28. There was significant interest in the abolitionist press about the parameters of Custis's will and Lee's failure to free people immediately. See, for instance, *Liberator,* December 18, 1857; *Liberator,* January 8, 1858. For another account of Lee's abuse of enslaved people at Arlington that is anonymous and shares some information with the Sally Norris incident, see "Virginia Chivalry," *Liberator,* May 29, 1863.

29. "Testimony of Wesley Norris," *National Anti-Slavery Standard,* April 14, 1866, reprinted in *Slave Testimony: Two Centuries of Letters, Speeches, Interviews, and Biographies,* ed. John Blassingame (Baton Rouge: Louisiana State University Press, 1977), 467–468.

30. Ibid., 467.

31. *New York Daily Tribune,* June 24, 1859, 6.

32. "The Custis Slaves," *Douglass' Monthly,* August 1859.

33. Many biographers have built from Douglas Southall Freeman's outright and angry rejection of the story as "exaggerated," libelous, and an "extravagance of irresponsible anti-slavery agitators." Freeman, *R. E. Lee: A Biography, Volume I* (New York: Charles Scribner's Sons, 1934), 392–393. See Roy Blount Jr., *Robert E. Lee: A Penguin Life* (New York: Penguin, 2003), 62–63. Others acknowledge the story to an extent but minimize Lee's involvement. See Fellman, *Making of Robert E. Lee,* 66–67; Korda, *Clouds of Glory,* 206–209; Robert M. Poole, *On Hallowed Ground: The Story of Arlington National Cemetery* (New York: Bloomsbury, 2009), 13; Thomas, *Robert E. Lee,* 178.

34. Pryor, *Reading the Man,* 269–273.

35. Robert E. Lee, quoted in Poole, *On Hallowed Ground,* 13.

36. "Testimony of Wesley Norris," in Blassingame, *Slave Testimony,* 468.

37. John Vincent Hinkel, *Arlington: Monument to Heroes,* rev. ed. (New York: Prentice Hall, 1970), 16.

38. See for instance, Korda, *Clouds of Glory,* 198–203.

39. *New York Daily Tribune,* June 24, 1859, 6.

40. On the manumissions and paternity, see Hanna, *Cultural Landscape Report,* 58, 190n124; E. Delores Preston Jr., "William Syphax, a Pioneer in Negro Education in the District of Columbia," *Journal of Negro History* 20, no. 4 (1935): 450; "Senator's Blast Serves to Open Closet Wider," *Baltimore Afro-American,* April 22, 1939, 24; "Riled by Linking Washington Kin to Colored Girl," *Baltimore Afro-American,* April 15, 1939, 1; Box One, Folder: "Syphaxes," Slavery Files, ARHO.

41. Hanna, *Cultural Landscape Report,* 59. On the complexities of slavery, freedom, and mixed families (enslaved and free), see Emily West, *Family or Freedom: People of Color in the Antebellum South* (Lexington: University of Kentucky Press, 2012).

42. Elizabeth Brown Pryor, "'Thou Knowest Not the Time of Thy Visitation': A Newly Discovered Letter Reveals Robert E. Lee's Lonely Struggle with Disunion," *Virginia Magazine of History and Biography* 119, no. 3 (2011): 290, 296n61.

43. "Arrangements for an Attack on the National Capital," *New York Herald,* April 24, 1861, 1, 3; and "By Telegraph for the Boston Daily Advertiser," *Boston Daily Advertiser,* April 24, 1861, 1.

44. See, for example, the letters from Robert E. Lee to Mary Custis Lee reprinted in *The Wartime Papers of Robert E. Lee,* ed. Clifford Dowdey and Louis H. Manarin (Boston: Little, Brown, 1961), 12–13, 18–19, 25–26.

45. Mary Lee, quoted in Robert E. L. deButts Jr., "Mary Custis Lee's 'Reminiscences of the War,'" *Virginia Magazine of History and Biography* 109, no. 3 (2001): 315.

46. Ibid., 316–317.

47. Carol Borchert Cadou, *The George Washington Collection: Fine and Decorative Arts at Mount Vernon* (Manchester, VT: Hudson Hills, 2006), 108–109. On American new national investments in the China trade and luxury goods, see John Kuo Wei Tchen, *New York before Chinatown: Orientalism and the Shaping of American Culture* (Baltimore: Johns Hopkins University Press, 1999).

48. Mary Lee, quoted in deButts, "Mary Custis Lee's 'Reminiscences of the War,'" 315.

49. Mary Lee, quoted in Poole, *On Hallowed Ground,* 23.

50. "Our War Correspondence," *New York Times,* May 26, 1861, 1.

51. "From the New York Eighth Regiment," *New York Times,* June 1, 1861, 1.

52. Hanna, *Cultural Landscape Report,* 66.

53. "From the New York Eighth Regiment," *New York Times,* June 1, 1861, 1. The reprinted letter itself, from an unnamed private, is dated "Arlington Heights, Tuesday, May 28, 1861."

54. "Affairs at the National Capital," *New York Times,* June 13, 1861, 1. The article's dateline is Sunday, June 9, 1861. Another soldier remarked in a letter on the empty frames a year later, "The pictures have nearly all been taken away, and the house much injured." John H. Carter, April 25, 1862, quoted in Robert Goldthwaite Carter, *Four Brothers in Blue; or, Sunshine and Shadows of the War of the Rebellion; a Story of the Great Civil War from Bull Run to Appomattox* (Washington, DC: Gibson Bros., 1913), 150.

55. Theodore Winthrop, *Life in the Open Air, and Other Papers* (Boston: Ticknor and Fields, 1863), 287.

56. Quoted in Helen Nicolay, *Our Capital on the Potomac* (New York: Century, 1924), 375. The ellipses are hers.

57. Ibid.

58. Ibid.

59. Mary Custis Lee to George Sandford, May 30, 1861, quoted in Hanna, *Cultural Landscape Report,* 73.

60. Hanna, *Cultural Landscape Report,* 73; Poole, *On Hallowed Ground,* 28.

61. Hanna, *Cultural Landscape Report,* 74; Poole, *On Hallowed Ground,* 29. This was not the last time Mary Lee tried to reach the overseer and her slaves that summer. In

July, Robert wrote to Mary that he had received a letter intended for them: "The other day a package was sent to me addressed by you to Mr. McGuinn at Arlington, which had been opened. The contents I suppose undisturbed. It contains a letter to Aunt Sally, Marcelena &c. I suppose seeing it directed within the enemy's lines, the postmasters considered it illicit. Why it was sent to me I do not know." Robert E. Lee to Mary Custis Lee, July 2, 1861, reprinted in *Wartime Papers of Robert E. Lee*, 56.

62. Mary Custis Lee to Annie Lee, containing a letter from Markie Williams, July 30, 1861, transcript in Box One, Folder: "Army Occupation—Slaves Who Remained during the Civil War," Slavery Files, ARHO.

63. Leonard and Sally Norris are often suggested to have been born at Arlington, and Selina Gray gets called a "second generation" Arlington slave in some NPS documents; but Leonard was probably around fifteen and Sally ten when G. W. P. Custis started building Arlington. They have also been called "Mt. Vernon slaves," which seems unlikely. They do not appear in George Washington's 1786 or 1799 slave inventories or his will, and at least one postwar census record (1870) identifies Leonard as having been born in Maryland.

64. It is impossible to tell definitively from extant records, but see: Inventory of Custis Slaves, Box Two, Folder: "Jim Parks," Slavery Files, ARHO; U.S. Bureau of the Census, *Ninth Census of the United States, 1870*, Arlington Township, Alexandria County, Va., Roll M593-1632.

65. Fisher, Randl, and Staveteig, *Arlington House*, 5; Emma Gray Syphax and Sarah Gray Wilson testimony, December 6, 1929, transcription, 1, Box Two, Folder: "Gray Family Papers," Slavery Files, ARHO. Emma Gray married Ennis Syphax, son of Maria and Charles Syphax, in 1874. U.S. Bureau of the Census, *Twelfth Census of the United States, 1900*, Jefferson, Alexandria, Va., Roll 1698, 7A.

66. John H. Carter, April 25, 1862, quoted in Carter, *Four Brothers in Blue*, 150.

67. Mary Custis Lee to Annie Lee, containing a letter from Markie Williams, July 30, 1861, transcript in Box One, Folder: "Army Occupation—Slaves Who Remained during the Civil War," Slavery Files, ARHO.

68. Observer, "Our Washington Correspondence: Disaster at Manassas," *New York Times*, July 25, 1861, 1.

69. "Woman Born Lee Estate Slave Observes 100th Birthday," *Washington DC Evening Star*, December 11, 1950, B16.

70. Fisher, Randl, and Staveteig, *Arlington House*, 8, 38.

71. On everyday forms of resistance and enslaved people's alternative geographies and uses of plantation spaces, see Stephanie M. H. Camp, *Closer to Freedom: Enslaved Women and Everyday Resistance in the Plantation South* (Chapel Hill: University of North Carolina Press, 2004); and John Michael Vlatch, *Back of the Big House: The Architecture of Plantation Slavery* (Chapel Hill: University of North Carolina Press, 1993).

72. William Howard Russell, "English Letters from America," *New York Times*, November 18, 1861, 2.

73. Anthony Trollope, *North America, Volume II* (Philadelphia: J. B. Lippincott, 1863), 21, 23.

74. Robert E. Lee to Mary Custis Lee (daughter), December 25, 1861, quoted in Hanna, *Cultural Landscape Report*, 77.

75. Robert E. Lee to Mary Custis Lee (wife), December 25, 1861, quoted in Thomas, *Robert E. Lee*, 215.

76. Robert E. Lee Jr. to Mildred Lee, January 5, 1862, transcript in Murray H. Nelligan Papers, Research Files 1650–1967, Box 7 of 14, Folder: "1862," ARHO.

77. On White House "in ashes and desolation," see Thomas, *Robert E. Lee*, 239.

78. On McDowell and Lyon, see "Relics of the Washington Family," *Lowell Daily Citizen and News*, March 8, 1862, reprint from the *New York Post*, January 1862. My thanks to Kirk Savage for this document. On the *Captured at Arlington* exhibit, see Robert E. Lee Jr., *Recollections and Letters of General Robert E. Lee* (Garden City, NY: Garden City Publishing Co., 1924), 337; and Ruth Preston Rose, "Mrs. General Lee's Attempts to Regain Her Possessions after the Civil War," *Arlington Historical Magazine* 6, no. 2 (1978): 29.

79. Robert E. Lee to Mary Custis Lee, December 21, 1862, reprinted in *Wartime Papers of Robert E. Lee*, 379.

80. Major General George C. Meade to Major General H. W. Halleck, September 6, 1863, Box Two, Folder: "Gray Family Papers," Slavery Files, ARHO.

81. "Arlington Slaves Returned," *Independent*, November 24, 1864, 4. This was reprinted in the *Liberator*, December 9, 1864, 199.

82. "Testimony of Wesley Norris," in Blassingame, *Slave Testimony*, 468.

83. On tax scheme and sale, see Poole, *On Hallowed Ground*, 55.

84. E. Deloris Preston Jr., "William Syphax, a Pioneer in Negro Education in the District of Columbia," *Journal of Negro History* 20, no. 4 (1935): 453–455; Hanna, *Cultural Landscape Report*, 101–102.

85. The historian Annette Gordon-Reed's exploration of the relationships at Monticello, including Thomas Jefferson's sexual relationship with his slave Sally Hemings, is an invaluable guide here. Gordon-Reed, *The Hemings of Monticello: An American Family* (New York: W. W. Norton, 2008).

86. U.S. Bureau of the Census, *Ninth Census of the United States, 1870*, Arlington Township, Alexandria County, Va., Roll M593-1632.

87. Selina Gray to Mary Custis Lee, 1872, Mary Custis Lee, 1835–1918, Papers, 1694–1917, Section 26, VHS.

88. Ibid.

89. Ibid.

90. Ibid.

91. Ibid.

92. U.S. Bureau of the Census, *Ninth Census of the United States, 1870*, Arlington, Alexandria (Independent City), Va., Roll M593-1632, 181B. It is unclear when and where Sally Norris married Mr. Hoffman (whose first name may have been Herman) and why they were not living together in August 1870 when the census taker came around. An 1864 article about her return to Arlington in the *Liberator* says that she was living "near" but not with her parents at that time. "Arlington Slaves Returned," *Liberator*, December 9, 1864, 199.

93. U.S. Bureau of the Census, *Tenth Census of the United States, 1880*, Arlington, Alexandria, Va., Roll T9-1351, 414A; U.S. Bureau of the Census, *Twelfth Census of the United States, 1900*, Jefferson, Alexandria, Va., Roll T623-1698, 2B; U.S. Bureau of

the Census, *Fourteenth Census of the United States, 1920,* Arlington, Alexandria, Va., Roll T625-1879, 47B; Gray Subdivision map in Folder: "Arlington Biography—Gray," Vertical Files, ACPL; Louie Estrada, "Arlington View: A Sense of History," *Washington Post,* June 5, 1993, E1. On Edward C. Hoffman and the Hoffman-Boston School, which was then a secondary school and is today Hoffman-Boston Elementary, see Arlington Historical Society, *Images of America: Arlington* (Portsmouth, NH: Arcadia Publishing, 2005), 58; *Commending Hoffman-Boston Elementary School,* House Joint Resolution No. 810, Virginia General Assembly, Sess. 2015, February 25, 2015.

94. Emma Gray Syphax and Sarah Gray Wilson testimony, December 16, 1929. ARHO.

95. Enoch Aquila Chase, *The History of Arlington: Where America's Sons of Valor Sleep* (Washington, DC: National Art Service, 1929): n.p.

96. Enoch Aquila Chase, "The Restoration of Arlington House," *Records of the Columbia Historical Society, Washington, DC* 33–34 (1932): 251–252, 254.

97. Murray Nelligan, *Curtis-Lee Mansion, The Robert E. Lee Memorial,* Historical Handbook Series 6 (Washington, DC: National Park Service, 1955, rev. 1962), http://www .nps.gov/parkhistory/online_books/hh/6/hh6toc.htm.

98. National Park Service, U.S. Department of the Interior, *Arlington House, The Robert E. Lee Memorial* (brochure 1978), Folder 2 of 2: "Historic Buildings, Arlington House," Vertical Files, ACPL.

99. Karen Byrne, "'We Have a Claim on this Estate': Remembering Slavery at Arlington House," *CRM* 25 No. 4 (2002): 27–29; James Oliver Horton, "Slavery in American History: An Uncomfortable National Dialogue," ed. James Oliver Horton and Lois E. Horton, *Slavery and Public History: The Tough Stuff of American Memory* (Chapel Hill: University of North Carolina Press, 2006), 35–55; Edward T. Linenthal, "Healing and History: The Dilemmas of Interpretation," *Rally on the High Ground: The National Park Service Symposium on the Civil War* (2001) http://www.nps.gov /parkhistory/online_books/rthg/chap3b.htm; Kevin Strait, *Presenting Race and Slavery at Historic Sites: Arlington House, Robert E. Lee Memorial* (National Park Service and Center for the Study of Public Culture and Public History of the George Washington University, revised October 28, 2004); Anne Mitchell Whisnant, Marla R. Miller, Gary B. Nash, and David Thelen, *Imperiled Promise: The State of History in the National Park Service* (Organization of American Historians, 2011); Robin Winks, "Sites of Shame," *National Parks* 68, no. 3/4 (1994): 22–23.

100. See, for instance, Edward C. Smith, "In Defense of General Lee," *Washington Post,* August 21, 1999; and Smith, "Opinion: U.S. Racists Dishonor Lee by Association," *National Geographic News Online,* September 7, 2001. Bruce Levine analyzes Smith's work on black Confederates and its toxic impacts in "In Search of a Usable Past: Neo-Confederates and Black Confederates," in *Slavery and Public History: The Tough Stuff of American Memory,* 187–211.

101. Edward C. Smith, "The Keeper of the Keys," *Civil War* 21 (1989): 17–18.

102. Karen Byrne, "The Remarkable Legacy of Selina Gray," *CRM* 21, no. 4 (1998): 21.

103. Ibid.

104. Ibid., 22.

105. Frederick Douglass, *My Bondage and My Freedom* (New York: Miller, Orton and Mulligan, 1855), 48.

106. Note that Selina Gray is no longer referenced as "second generation" to Arlington, and her parents are called "Mt. Vernon slaves."
107. See the National Park Service's Arlington House webpage: http://home.nps.gov/arho.
108. See Jerry Pinkney's home page: http://www.jerrypinkneystudio.com/frameset.html. My thanks to the late Joyce Schiller for providing information about Pinkney.
109. National Park Service, U.S. Department of the Interior, *Arlington House: The Robert E. Lee Memorial* (brochure, 2013); Liza Mundy, "Neighborhood of Slaves and Presidents," *Washington Post,* February 15, 2010, C1.
110. National Park Service, *Museum Collections: Arlington House, The Robert E. Lee Memorial* (Washington, DC: Eastern National, 2008), 44. See also the National Park Service, Museum Management Program, "Archeology Group," http://www.nps.gov /museum/exhibits/arho/exb/slavery/ARHO111_2_121_2Archelogy-Gr.html (accessed May 25, 2013); and National Park Service, Museum Management Program, "Cincinnatiware Plate (replica) with Excavated Cincinnatiware Sherds," http://www.nps.gov /museum/exhibits/arho/exb/slavery/Lee%20Plate.html (accessed May 25, 2013).
111. National Park Service, Museum Management Program, "Archeology Group."
112. "'Priceless' Civil War–era Photo of Slave Selina Gray Found on Ebay," NBCNews .com, October 10, 2014, http://www.nbcnews.com; "Priceless Civil War–era Photo of Robert E. Lee's Slave—Only Second in Existence—Found on Ebay and Bought from British Junk Collector for Just $700," *Daily Mail* (UK), October 12, 2014, http://www .dailymail.co.uk; "Slave Photo from Robert E. Lee's Home Discovered on Ebay," FoxNews.com, October 12, 2014, http://www.foxnews.com; Mary Beth Griggs, "Rare Photo of Robert E. Lee's Slave Acquired by National Park Service," Smithsonian .com, October 11, 2014, http://www.smithsonianmag.com; John Johnson, "Rare Photo Found of Robert E. Lee's Slave," *USA Today,* October 11, 2014, http://www .usatoday.com; Michael E. Ruane, "Rare Photo Shows Robert E. Lee's Slave, Selina Gray—The Hero of Arlington House," *Washington Post,* October 9, 2014, http://www .washingtonpost.com. The photo was also the subject of at least one television report in the greater DC area on the ABC affiliate WJLA, October 9, 2014. My thanks to Edward L. Bell who first told me about the picture's discovery.
113. WJLA report, October 9, 2014. The NPS employee is Jenny Anzelmo-Sarles.
114. Kim A. O'Connell, "Arlington's Enslaved Savior," *Civil War Times* 54, no. 1 (2015): 34.

2. Freedman's Village

1. "Special Dispatch from Washington," *New York Times,* May 30, 1861, 1.
2. "The Landing at Newport News," *New York Times,* May 30, 1861, 1. On early assessments of the importance of formerly enslaved laborers to the Union military effort, see Heather Cox Richardson, *The Greatest Nation on Earth: Republican Economic Policies During the Civil War* (Cambridge, MA: Harvard University Press, 1997), 215–217.
3. "Entrance of Ohio Troops into Western Virginia," *New York Times,* May 30, 1861, 1.
4. W. E. B. Du Bois, *Black Reconstruction in America, 1860–1880* (1935; repr., New York: Simon and Schuster, 1992), 81.

5. Lt. Col. Elias M. Greene to Major General S. P. Heintzelman, May 5, 1863, RG 92, Records of the Office of the Quartermaster General, Consolidated Correspondence File, 1794–1915, Box 49, Folder: "Arlington, Virginia," NARA. On Freedman's Village generally, see Joseph P. Reidy, " 'Coming from the Shadow of the Past': The Transition from Slavery to Freedom at Freedmen's Village, 1863–1900," *Virginia Magazine of History and Biography* 95, no. 4 (1987): 403–428.

6. Abraham Lincoln, "First Inaugural Address," in *Lincoln: Speeches, Letters and Miscellaneous Writings, Presidential Messages and Proclamations, 1859–1865* (New York: Library of America, 1989), 215–223.

7. James Oliver Horton and Lois E. Horton, *Slavery and the Making of America* (New York: Oxford University Press, 2005), 175. The Fugitive Slave Act was repealed by an act of Congress in July 1864.

8. "Contraband of War," *New York Times,* June 2, 1861, 3.

9. Kate Masur, " 'A Rare Phenomenon of Philological Vegetation': The Word 'Contraband' and the Meanings of Emancipation in the United States," *Journal of American History* 93, no. 4 (2007): 1050–1084. See also Rebecca Scott, *Degrees of Freedom: Louisiana and Cuba after Slavery* (Cambridge, MA: Harvard University Press, 2008).

10. J. K. F. Mansfield to Mr. Justice Dunne, July 4, 1861, in *The Destruction of Slavery,* ser. 1, vol. 1 of *Freedom: A Documentary History of Emancipation, 1861–1867,* ed. Ira Berlin, Barbara J. Fields, Thavolia Glymph, Joseph P. Reidy, Leslie S. Rowland (New York: Cambridge University Press, 1985), 167; *The Wartime Genesis of Free Labor: The Upper South,* ser. 1, vol. 2 of *Freedom: A Documentary History of Emancipation, 1861–1867,* ed. Ira Berlin, Steven F. Miller, Joseph P. Reidy, Leslie S. Rowland (New York: Cambridge University Press, 1993), 245.

11. James M. Goode, *Capital Losses: A Cultural History of Washington's Destroyed Buildings,* 2nd ed. (Washington, DC: Smithsonian Books, 2003), 328–331.

12. Berlin et al., *Wartime Genesis,* 246; Constance McLaughlin Green, *The Secret City: A History of Race Relations in the Nation's Capital* (Princeton, NJ: Princeton University Press, 1967), 61; Margaret Leech, *Reveille in Washington, 1860–1865* (1941; repr., New York: New York Review of Books, 2011), 304.

13. Willie Lee Rose, *Rehearsal for Reconstruction: The Port Royal Experiment* (New York: Oxford University Press, 1964).

14. "What Shall Be Done with the Slaves?," *New York Anglo African,* November 23, 1861, quoted in James McPherson, *The Negro's Civil War: How American Blacks Felt and Acted during the War for the Union* (1965; repr., New York: Vintage, 2003), 297.

15. Eric Foner, *Reconstruction: America's Unfinished Revolution, 1863–1877* (New York: Perennial, 2002), 50–54, 70–71; Julie Saville, "Rites and Power: Reflections of Slavery, Freedom, and Political Ritual," *Slavery & Abolition: A Journal of Slave and Post-Slave Studies* 20, no. 1 (1999): 81–102.

16. "President's Message," *Chicago Tribune,* December 4, 1861, 2. For a broad discussion of Lincoln and his complex commitments to colonization, see Daniel R. Biddle and Murray Dublin, " 'God Is Settling the Account': African American Reactions to Lincoln's Emancipation Proclamation," *Pennsylvania Magazine of History and Biography* 137, no. 1 (2013): 57–78; and Eric Foner, *The Fiery Trial: Abraham Lincoln and American Slavery* (New York: W. W. Norton, 2010), chap. 6.

17. McPherson, *Negro's Civil War*, chap. 6.

18. District of Columbia Emancipation Act, April 16, 1862, digital image and transcript available at http://www.archives.gov/exhibits/featured_documents/dc_emancipation _act/.

19. Bernard Kock to Abraham Lincoln, October 1, 1862; Bernard Kock to Abraham Lincoln, October 4, 1862; Jacob R. S. Van Vleet to Abraham Lincoln, December 11, 1862; and Bernard Kock to Abraham Lincoln, January 17, 1863, all in Series One, General Correspondence, 1833–1916, Abraham Lincoln Papers, LOC. Phillip W. Magness, "The Île à Vache: From Hope to Disaster," *Opinionator* (blog), *New York Times*, April 12, 2013, http://opinionator.blogs.nytimes.com/2013/04/12/the-le-vache-from-hope-to -disaster/?_r=0; McPherson, *Negro's Civil War*, 98–99.

20. Robin D. G. Kelley, *Freedom Dreams: The Black Radical Imagination* (New York: Beacon, 2002), chap. 1. Steven Hahn cautions against scholars' tendencies to analyze black histories and politics in the United States through a "liberal integrationist framework" that privileges the aims of inclusion, assimilation, and national citizenship at the expense of alternatives such as separatism and emigration. Hahn, *A Nation under Our Feet: Black Political Struggles in the Rural South from Slavery to the Great Migration* (Cambridge, MA: Harvard University Press, 2003).

21. Mary Custis Lee, diary, June 9, 1853, Lee Family Papers, 1810–1914, Section 5, VHS.

22. Rosabella Burke to Mary Custis Lee, February 20, 1859, in *Slave Testimony: Two Centuries of Letters, Speeches, Interviews, and Autobiographies,* ed. John W. Blassingame (Baton Rouge: Louisiana State University Press, 1977), 107.

23. William Burke to Ralph Randolph Gurley, September 29, 1863, ibid.

24. James De Long (U.S. Consul to Haiti) to Henry Conrad, June 25, 1863, Series Two, General Correspondence, 1858–1864, Abraham Lincoln Papers, LOC; Willis D. Boyd, "The Île à Vache Colonization Venture, 1862–1864," *Americas* 16, no. 1 (1959): 45–62; Foner, *Fiery Trial*, 259.

25. Harriet Jacobs to Lydia Maria Child, March 26, 1864, quoted in Jean Fagan Yellin, *Harriet Jacobs: A Life* (New York: Basic Books, 2004), 179–180. The letter was published in the *National Anti-Slavery Standard* on April 16, 1864.

26. Ibid.

27. Adjutant General Thomas to Colonel J. P. Taylor, January 2, 1862, transcript in Murray H. Nelligan Papers, Research Files 1650–1967, Box 7 of 14, Folder: "1862," ARHO; Horatio King to Danforth Nichols, November 11, 1863; and Thomas J. Carlile to Danforth Nichols, November 21, [year unclear], D. B. Nichols Scrapbooks—MMC 3859, Folder: D. B. Nichols Scrapbooks, Volume 1, 1863–1864, LOC.

28. Harriet Jacobs (as Linda Brent), letter to the editor, *Liberator*, August 1862, reprinted in *We Are Your Sisters: Black Women in the Nineteenth Century*, ed. Dorothy Sterling (New York: W. W. Norton, 1997), 247.

29. Yellin, *Harriet Jacobs*, 170–171.

30. Patricia C. Click, *Time Full of Trial: The Roanoke Island Freedmen's Colony, 1862– 1867* (Chapel Hill: University of North Carolina Press, 2001), 74–77; Carol Faulkner, *Women's Radical Reconstruction: The Freedmen's Aid Movement* (Philadelphia: University of Pennsylvania Press, 2004); and Robert Harrison, *Washington during Civil*

War and Reconstruction: Race and Radicalism (New York: Cambridge University Press, 2011), 21.

31. Henry M. Turner, quoted in McPherson, *Negro's Civil War,* 138.

32. Click, *Time Full of Trial,* 7; Ernest B. Furgurson, *Freedom Rising: Washington in the Civil War* (New York: Knopf, 2004), 256; Leech, *Reveille in Washington,* 307.

33. A.D.C. John A. Kress to Mr. [Danforth] Nichols, July 2, 1862, in Berlin et al., *Wartime Genesis,* 294.

34. Richard Franklin Bensel, *Yankee Leviathan: The Origins of Central State Authority in America, 1859–1877* (New York: Cambridge University Press, 1990), 169; Max M. Edling, *A Hercules in the Cradle: War, Money, and the American State, 1783–1867* (Chicago: University of Chicago Press, 2014), 204–211; Laura F. Edwards, *A Legal History of the Civil War and Reconstruction: A Nation of Rights* (New York: Cambridge University Press, 2015), 24–32.

35. On riots in Brooklyn and Cincinnati, see James M. McPherson, *Battle Cry of Freedom: The Civil War Era* (New York: Oxford University Press, 1988), 506–507. On conflicts surrounding the presence of contraband workers in southern Illinois, see Allen C. Guelzo, "Defending Emancipation: Abraham Lincoln and the Conkling Letter, 1863," *Civil War History* 48, no. 4 (2002): 317; and Leslie Schwalm, "'Overrun with Free Negroes': Emancipation and Wartime Migration in the Upper Midwest," *Civil War History* 50, no. 2 (2004): 148, 158–161.

36. *Mankato Semi-Weekly Record,* April 23, 1862, quoted in Schwalm, "Overrun with Free Negroes," 161.

37. David Sears, *Contrabands and Vagrants* (Newport, RI, July 23, 1861), 6–7.

38. Michelle Ann Krowl, "Dixie's Other Daughters: African American Women in Virginia, 1861–1868" (Ph.D. diss., University of California–Berkeley, 1998), 30.

39. Louis P. Masur, *Lincoln's Hundred Days: The Emancipation Proclamation and the War for the Union* (Cambridge, MA: Harvard University Press, 2012).

40. Brig. Genl. Jas. S. Wadsworth to the Hon. Secy. of War, September 25, 1862, in Berlin et al., *Wartime Genesis,* 269–270.

41. George E. H. Day to Col. Foster, Head of Bureau for Colored Troops, December 6, 1864, referred to and responded on back of document by Foster and Captain John M. Brown, Superintendent of Freedman's Village, December 7, 1864, RG 92, Records of the Office of the Quartermaster General, Consolidated Correspondence File, 1794–1915, Box 49, Entry 225, NM-81, Folder: "Arlington—Housing for Negroes," NARA. See also George E. H. Day to Edwin M. Stanton, December 8, 1864, referred to and responded on back of document by Montgomery C. Meigs, December 14, 1864, notation: "Capt. Brown informed," December 15, 1864, RG 92, Records of the Office of the Quartermaster General, Consolidated Correspondence File, 1794–1915, Box 49, Folder: "Arlington, Virginia," NARA.

42. General Order No. 46, December 5, 1863, quoted in Krowl, "Dixie's Other Daughters," 116–117.

43. Linda Kerber, *No Constitutional Right to Be Ladies: Women and the Obligations of Citizenship* (New York: Hill and Wang, 1999), chap. 2; Thavolia Glymph, "'This Species of Property': Female Slave Contrabands in the Civil War," in *A Woman's War:*

Southern Women, Civil War, and the Confederate Legacy, ed. Edward D. C. Campbell Jr. and Kim S. Rice (Charlottesville: University of Virginia Press, 1997), 55–70; Leslie Schwalm, "Between Slavery and Freedom: African American Women and the Occupation of the Slave South," in *Occupied Women: Gender, Military Occupation, and the American Civil War*, ed. LeeAnn Whites and Alecia P. Long (Baton Rouge: Louisiana State University Press, 2009), 137–154; Amy Dru Stanley, *From Bondage to Contract: Wage Labor, Marriage and the Market in the Age of Slave Emancipation* (Cambridge: Cambridge University Press, 1998).

44. Captain C. B. Ferguson to Colonel D. H. Rucker, November 26, 1862, and Colonel D. H. Rucker to Brigadier General Montgomery C. Meigs, December 1, 1862, RG 92, Records of the Office of the Quartermaster General, Consolidated Correspondence File, 1794–1915, Box 401, Folder: "Contraband Tax (1862)," NARA. The request was sent by Meigs to Stanton's office. An assistant wrote that Stanton declined to modify the order on December 23, but this was crossed out by Stanton, who wrote below that black Commissary workers would be taxed, as well: "A similar order has been put to the Commissary Department."

45. "Unsigned petitions to Col. Bell," August 3 and August 16, 1863, and "Colord labours of Alexandria va Commissary Dept to Honorable Secretary Stanton," August 31, 1863, in Berlin et al., *Wartime Genesis*, 307.

46. Glymph, "This Species of Property"; Chandra Manning, "Working for Citizenship in Civil War Contraband Camps," *Journal of the Civil War Era* 4, no. 2 (June 2014): 172–204; Schwalm, "Between Slavery and Freedom."

47. On free black resistance to being associated with contrabands, see Berlin et al., *Wartime Genesis*, 251–253. On the gendered parameters of dependency in U.S. history generally as well as Civil War–specific contexts, see Nancy Fraser and Linda Gordon, "A Genealogy of Dependency: Tracing a Keyword of the U.S. Welfare State," *Signs* 18, no. 2 (1994): 309–336; Kerber, *No Constitutional Right to Be Ladies*, chap. 2; Stephanie McCurry, "War, Gender, and Emancipation in the Civil War South," in *Lincoln's Proclamation: Emancipation Reconsidered*, ed. William A. Blair and Karen Fisher (Chapel Hill: University of North Carolina Press, 2009), 120–150; Amy Dru Stanley, "Instead of Waiting for the Thirteenth Amendment: The War Power, Slave Marriage, and Inviolate Human Rights," *American Historical Review* 115, no. 3 (June 2010): 732–765.

48. American Freedmen's Inquiry Commission, *Records of the American Freedmen's Inquiry Commission, Final Report*, Senate Executive Document 53, 38th Cong., 1st sess., Serial 1776, 1864; Foner, *Reconstruction*, 68–69.

49. Testimony of Danforth B. Nichols before the American Freedmen's Inquiry Commission (AFIC), April 1863, and Capt. Chas. H. Tompkins to Colonel D. H. Rucker, May 1, 1863, Berlin et al., *Wartime Genesis*, 288, 296–297; Danforth B. Nichols to AFIC, September 8, 1863, United States American Freedmen's Inquiry Commission Records (MS Am 702), Series I: Letters to the AFIC, Houghton Library, Harvard University.

50. Testimony of Danforth B. Nichols before the American Freedmen's Inquiry Commission (AFIC), April 1863, *Wartime Genesis*, 290, 292.

51. Danforth B. Nichols to AFIC, September 8, 1863, United States American Freedmen's Inquiry Commission Records, Harvard University.

52. General Orders No. 28, Headquarters, Dept. of Washington, May 22, 1863, *Wartime Genesis*, 299.

53. Julia Wilbur Diary, June 25, 1863, transcribed and annotated by Paula T. Whitacre for the Alexandria (VA) Archaeology Museum, transcription, 93. Original diaries held in the Julia Wilbur Papers, 1843–1908, Collection No. 1158, Haverford College Library Special Collections, Haverford, PA.

54. On the relationships among military authorities, civilian federal officials, and philanthropic organizations such as the AMA or ATS in relation to contraband, see Click, *Time Full of Trial*, chap. 4.

55. On the July 4, 1863, events, see Reidy, "Coming from the Shadow of the Past," 411; J. R. Johnson, "Virginia, Arlington Heights, August 5, 1863," *American Missionary*, September 1, 1863, 208.

56. The American Tract Society was quick to correct reports that the government or the military was responsible for the school and hospital. See, for example, H. E. Simmons, Superintendent of Educational Work, American Tract Society, "The Freedman's Village at Arlington Heights," letter to the editor, *Hartford Courant*, September 28, 1864, 2.

57. Julia Wilbur Diary, December 3, 1863, transcription, 127–128.

58. "Dedication at Freedmen's Village, VA," *New York Observer and Chronicle*, December 17, 1863, 1.

59. "The Freedman's Settlement at Arlington," *Liberator*, January 1, 1864, 1. The article was reprinted as "The Freedmen's Village at Arlington," *Friend's Review*, January 2, 1864, 17–18, where it was attributed to Samuel Wilkinson of the *Philadelphia Inquirer*.

60. Clinton B. Fisk, *Plain Counsels for Freedmen: In Sixteen Brief Lectures* (Boston: American Tract Society, 1866), 34. On the obligations of freedom and "fettered individualism" of capitalism in this period generally, including their gendered parameters, see Eric Foner, *Nothing but Freedom: Emancipation and Its Legacies* (Baton Rouge: Louisiana State University Press, 2007); Saidiya Hartman, *Scenes of Subjection: Terror, Slavery, and Self-Making in Nineteenth-Century America* (New York: Oxford University Press, 1997); Heather Cox Richardson, *The Death of Reconstruction: Race, Labor, and Politics in the Post–Civil War North, 1865–1901* (Cambridge, MA: Harvard University Press, 2001); Stanley, *From Bondage to Contract*.

61. McCurry, "War, Gender, and Emancipation."

62. W. A. Benedict to Elias M. Greene, January 22, 1864; H. E. Simmons to Elias M. Greene, January 23, 1864; Captain R. C. Perry to Elias M. Greene, January 23, 1864; and E. A. Holman to Elias M. Greene, January 23, 1864, all in RG 92, Records of the Office of the Quartermaster General, Consolidated Correspondence File, 1794–1915, Box 401, Folder: "Contrabands Tax," NARA.

63. Danforth B. Nichols to Elias M. Greene, January 23, 1864, ibid. The superintendent of Camp Barker, James I. Ferree, testified that 115 moved to Freedman's Village and

said that he had urged waiting until after winter to effect the move, "for humanity's sake." Testimony of James I. Ferree, January 1864, in Berlin et al., *Wartime Genesis,* 328.

64. Testimony of J. B. Holt, January 1864, in Berlin et al., *Wartime Genesis,* 329.

65. Testimony of Lucy Smith, January 1864, and Testimony of Lewis Johnson, January 1864, ibid., 331–332, 295–296. Luisa Jane Barker, the wife of a Union chaplain, testified to Nichols's abuse of a woman named Lucy Ellen Johnson, whose husband believed he had secured a place and rations for her at Freedman's Village while he was away working. Barker described her punishment and torture at the hands of men supervised by Nichols. Testimony of Luisa Jane Barker, January 14, 1864, ibid., 308–311.

66. Testimony of Georgiana Willets, January 1864, ibid., 329–331.

67. Testimony of Lieutenant Charles H. Shepard, First Massachusetts Heavy Artillery, undated, in "Destruction of a Contraband Village settled near the Colord Camp at Arlington," ibid., 312.

68. Testimony of Danforth B. Nichols, undated, ibid., 313.

69. Testimony of Luisa Jane Barker, January 14, 1864, ibid., 312.

70. Testimony of Danforth B. Nichols, and Testimony of Luisa Jane Barker, ibid., 313, 312.

71. Testimony of George W. Simms before the Southern Claims Commission, March 6, 1878, ibid., 274; Robert A. Stanley et al. to Secretary of War Stanton, November 27, 1863, RG 92, Records of the Office of the Quartermaster General, Consolidated Correspondence File, 1794–1915, Box 401, Folder: "Contraband Tax (1)," NARA; and Sergt. Edward Thomas et al. to Honorable Edwin M. Stanton, November 28, 1864, in Berlin et al., *Wartime Genesis,* 353–355.

72. Lt. Col. Elias M. Greene to Col. Chas. Thomas, December 17, 1863, in Berlin et al., *Wartime Genesis,* 315–321. On December 28, this report was forwarded by Thomas with a note saying that the tax is "wise, prudent and just to the colored persons, who have been gathered in and around this City; that it has already accomplished much good, and should it be continued will produce still more." Ibid., 314.

73. Elias M. Greene to Rev. D. B. Nichols, March 18, 1864, and Elias M. Greene to Rev. D. B. Nichols, May 7, 1864, D. B. Nichols Scrapbooks, Volume I, 1863–1864, MMC 3859, LOC. On Secretary of State William Seward's visits with diplomats, see Kate Masur, *An Example for All the Land: Emancipation and the Struggle over Equality in Washington, D.C.* (Chapel Hill: University of North Carolina Press, 2010), 66.

74. "A Few Interesting Facts Respecting Freedmen," *Christian Recorder,* December 17, 1864; Elizabeth Keckley, *Behind the Scenes; or, Thirty Years a Slave, and Four Years in the White House* (New York: G. W. Carleton, 1868), 143.

75. Schwalm, "Overrun with Free Negroes," 158–161.

76. H. A. Holman, Supt. of Govt. Farms, to Danforth B. Nichols, March 29, 1864, and Elias M. Greene to Danforth B. Nichols, April 28, 1864, D. B. Nichols Scrapbooks, Volume I, 1863–1864, MMC 3859, LOC.

77. H. A. Holman to Danforth B. Nichols, September 28, 1864, ibid.

78. Elias M. Greene to Danforth B. Nichols, April 15, 1864, ibid.; Elias M. Greene to John M. Brown, June 24, 1864, ibid.

79. Elias M. Greene to Danforth B. Nichols, April 1, 1864, ibid.; Elias M. Greene to Danforth B. Nichols, March 26, 1864, ibid.

80. D. B. Nichols to Lt. Col. Greene, April 2, 1864, in Berlin et al., *Wartime Genesis, 333*; Elias M. Greene to Danforth B. Nichols, April 4, 1864, D. B. Nichols Scrapbooks, Volume I, 1863–1864, MMC 3859, LOC.

81. *Report to the Executive Committee of New England Yearly Meeting of Friends upon the Condition and Needs of the Freed People of Color in Washington and Virginia* (New Bedford, MA: E. Anthony & Sons, 1864), 5.

82. Julia Wilbur, *Thirteenth Annual Report of the Rochester Ladies' Anti-Slavery Society* (1864), quoted in Yellin, *Harriet Jacobs,* 169.

83. Elias M. Greene to Danforth B. Nichols, March 19, 1864, D. B. Nichols Scrapbooks, Volume I, 1863–1864, MMC 3859, LOC.

84. Chief Clerk Collins to Danforth Nichols, April 8, 1864, ibid.

85. Office of the Chief Quartermaster to Danforth Nichols, September 3, 1864, ibid.

86. Sojourner Truth, quoted in Nell Irvin Painter, *Sojourner Truth: A Life, a Symbol* (New York: W. W. Norton, 1996), 215.

87. Sojourner Truth to Amy Post, October 1, 1865, quoted in ibid., 215; Sojourner Truth, Olive Gilbert, and Frances W. Titus, *Narrative of Sojourner Truth; A Bondswoman of Olden Time, Emancipated by the New York Legislature in the Early Part of the Present Century, with a History of Her Labors and Correspondence, Drawn from Her "Book of Life"* (Boston, 1875), 183.

88. Elias M. Greene Report, RG 92, Records of the Office of the Quartermaster General, Consolidated Correspondence File, 1794–1915, Box 401, Folder: "Contraband Tax," NARA.

89. Warren H. Hurd, Rect. Officer, 23rd Regiment U.S. Colored Troops, to Lt. Col. C. S. Campbell, Commanding, 23rd Regt. USCT, March 24, 1864, D. B. Nichols Scrapbooks, Volume I, 1863–1864, MMC 3859, LOC; D. B. Nichols to Lt. Col. Greene, April 2, 1864, in Berlin et al., *Wartime Genesis, 332–336*; and A. Gladwin to Capt. Rolland C. Gale, October 1, 1864, in Berlin et al., *Wartime Genesis, 347–348*.

90. Special Orders No. 114, Elias M. Greene to Danforth Nichols, May 9, 1864, D. B. Nichols Scrapbooks, Volume I, 1863–1864, MMC 3859, LOC.

91. Unidentified newspaper clipping, August 1864, Murray H. Nelligan Papers, Research Files 1650–1967, 1860–1890, Box 6 of 14, Folder: "1864," ARHO.

92. H. H. Howard, Supt. of Freedman's Village, to Brig. Genl. Charles H. Howard, n.d., and August 14, 1864, Freedman's Village: Letters Sent by the Superintendent, vol. III, *Records of the Field Offices for the District of Columbia, Bureau of Refugees, Freedmen, and Abandoned Lands, 1865–1870* (National Archives Microfilm Publication M1902, roll 20).

93. "Freedman's Village, Arlington, Virginia," *Harper's Weekly,* May 7, 1864, 294.

94. See, for instance, "A Freedmen's Village," *Liberator,* August 5, 1864, 34.

95. Elias M. Greene to J. H. Taylor, January 30, 1864, in Berlin et al., *Wartime Genesis, 323*.

96. Major E. H. Ludington and Major C. E. Compton to Col. James A. Hardie, July 30, 1864, ibid., 342.

3. A National Cemetery

1. Noah Brooks, quoted in Robert Harrison, *Washington during Civil War and Reconstruction: Race and Radicalism* (New York: Cambridge University Press, 2011), 23. See also Jim Downs, *Sick from Freedom: African American Illness and Suffering during the Civil War and Reconstruction* (New York: Oxford University Press, 2012).

2. On James Parks's history and biography generally, see Box 2, Folders: "Jim Parks," and "James Parks," Slavery Files, ARHO; RG 66, Commission of Fine Arts, Project Files, 1910–1952, Box 21, Folder: "ANC-Parks, James," NARA; Luis Aguilar, "Family Honors Ex-Slave Who Made History," *Washington Post*, 1987, clipping, Folder: "Freedman's Village," Black History Files, ACPL; Ken Parks, "James Parks," *Parke Society Newsletter* 45, no. 2 (2009): 17–22.

3. "Volunteer Enlistment Paper of William Christman," March 25, 1864, and "Record of Death and Interment of William Christman," May 11, 1864 (death) and May 13, 1864 (interment), RG 94, Records of the Adjutant General's Office, 1762–1984, Carded Records Showing Military Service of Soldiers Who Fought in Volunteer Organizations During the American Civil War, 1890–1912, File Unit: "William Christman, Civil War Compiled Military Service Record, 67th Pennsylvania Infantry, 1890–1912," NARA.

4. Edwin M. Stanton, order of June 15, 1864, RG 92, Records of the Office of the Quartermaster General, Consolidated Correspondence File, 1794–1915, Box 49, Folder: "Arlington Estate," NARA.

5. On desires to bury Abraham Lincoln in Washington and struggles around the "ownership" of his body and appropriate memorialization, see Michael Burlingame, *Abraham Lincoln: A Life*, vol. 2 (Baltimore: Johns Hopkins University Press, 2008), 827; and Thomas J. Croughwell, *Stealing Lincoln's Body* (Cambridge, MA: Harvard University Press, 2007), 20–28.

6. On Robert Todd Lincoln's burial in Arlington, see Croughwell, *Stealing Lincoln's Body*, 207–208; George W. Dodge, *Images of America: Arlington National Cemetery* (Charleston, SC: Arcadia, 2006), 56. On contemporary tourism at Oak Ridge and Arlington, see Croughwell, *Stealing Lincoln's Body*, 205.

7. On General Orders 75, see "The Soldier's Grave," *New York Times*, September 16, 1861, 4; and "National Cemeteries," *Harper's New Monthly Magazine*, August 1, 1866, 312. General Orders 33 is quoted in Michael Sledge, *Soldier Dead: How We Recover, Identify, Bury, and Honor Our Military Fallen* (New York: Columbia University Press, 2005), 33.

8. National Cemetery Administration, Department of Veterans Affairs, "History and Development of the National Cemetery Administration" (Washington, DC: Communications and Outreach Support Division, January 2009), 1–2; Monro MacCloskey, *Hallowed Ground: Our National Cemeteries* (New York: Richards Rosen Press, 1968), 22–25; John R. Neff, *Honoring the Civil War Dead: Commemoration and the Problem of Reconciliation* (Lawrence, KS: University Press of Kansas, 2005), chap. 3; Sledge, *Soldier Dead*, 32–33; Catherine W. Zipf, "Marking Union Victory in the South: The Construction of the National Cemetery System," ed. Cynthia Mills and Pamela H. Simpson, *Monuments to the Lost Cause: Women, Art, and the Landscapes of Southern Memory* (Knoxville: University of Tennessee Press, 2003), 27–45.

9. On the rural cemetery movement, see James J. Farrell, *Inventing the American Way of Death, 1830–1920* (Philadelphia: Temple University Press, 1980), chap. 4; David Charles Sloane, *The Last Great Necessity: Cemeteries in American History* (Baltimore: Johns Hopkins University Press, 1991), 46–79.

10. The literature on Lincoln's Gettysburg Address is enormous and varied. Especially pertinent to this study are Drew Gilpin Faust, *This Republic of Suffering: Death and the American Civil War* (New York: Knopf, 2008), 99–101; Dana Luciano, *Arranging Grief: Sacred Time and the Body in Nineteenth-Century America* (New York: New York University Press, 2007), 221–224; Robert Pogue Harrison, *The Dominion of the Dead* (Chicago: University of Chicago Press, 2003), 27–29; Franny Nudelman, *John Brown's Body: Slavery, Violence, and the Culture of War* (Chapel Hill: University of North Carolina Press, 2004), 36–39; and Sloane, *Last Great Necessity*, 113–115.

11. "A Great National Cemetery," *Washington Morning Chronicle*, June 17, 1864; "Gen. Lee's Lands Appropriately Consecrated," *Washington Republican*, June 17, 1864, in Murray H. Nelligan Papers, Research Files 1650–1967, 1860–1890, Box 6 of 14, Folder: "1864," ARHO. See also "New Cemetery for Soldiers," *Daily National Intelligencer* (Washington, DC), June 15, 1864, ibid.; "Gen Lee's Lands Appropriately Consecrated," *New York Times*, June 20, 1864, 8; and "Gen Lee's Lands Appropriately Consecrated," *Chicago Tribune*, June 23, 1864, 2.

12. For this and other biographical information on Montgomery C. Meigs, see Guy Gugliotta, *Freedom's Cap: The United States Capitol and the Coming of the Civil War* (New York: Hill and Wang, 2012), chap. 8, 316–317, 376–384; David W. Miller, *Second Only to Grant: Quartermaster General Montgomery C. Meigs* (Shippensburg, PA: White Mane Books, 2000); Simon Schama, *The American Future: A History* (New York: Ecco, 2009), part 1; Russell F. Weigley, *Quartermaster General of the Union Army, a Biography of M. C. Meigs* (New York: Columbia University Press, 1959); "Introduction," ed. Wendy Wolff, *Capitol Builder: The Shorthand Journals of Montgomery C. Meigs, 1853–1959, 1861* (Washington, DC: U.S. Government Printing Office, 2001), xxiii–xxxvii.

13. Meigs shorthand journal, March 3, 1861, *Capitol Builder*, 774.

14. Ibid., April 1, 1861, 777.

15. Ibid., May 1, 1861.

16. Meigs shorthand journal, quoted in Weigley, *Quartermaster General of the Union Army*, 169.

17. On Meigs and the cemetery's origins generally, see William A. Blair, *Cities of the Dead: Contesting the Memory of the Civil War in the South, 1865–1914* (Chapel Hill: University of North Carolina Press, 2004), 175; Laurie Burgess, "Buried in the Rose Garden: Levels of Memory at Arlington National Cemetery and the Robert E. Lee Memorial," ed. Paul A. Shackel, *Myth, Memory, and the Making of the American Landscape* (Gainesville: University Press of Florida, 2001), 161–163; Miller, *Second Only to Grant*, 259–260; Neff, *Honoring the Civil War Dead*, 192–194; Robert M. Poole, *On Hallowed Ground: The Story of Arlington National Cemetery* (New York: Bloomsbury, 2009), 29, 60–66; Weigley, *Quartermaster General of the Union Army*, 296. The site was first suggested as a possibility by two officers in Meigs's command, Major Daniel H. Rucker and Captain James Monroe. Jennifer Hanna, *Cultural*

Landscape Report, 1802–1861 Historic Period Plan, Arlington House, The Robert E. Lee Memorial (Washington, DC: National Park Service, U.S. Department of the Interior, 2001), 84.

18. Montgomery C. Meigs to Edwin M. Stanton, April 12, 1874, quoted in Poole, *On Hallowed Ground*, 62.

19. Sailors were not interred with regularity in Arlington National Cemetery until later; as of 1871, only two sailors were buried there.

20. Montgomery C. Meigs to Edwin M. Stanton, June 15, 1864, and Edwin M. Stanton, orders of June 15, 1864, RG 92, Records of the Office of the Quartermaster General, Consolidated Correspondence File, 1794–1915, Box 49, Folder: "Arlington Estate," NARA.

21. Schama, *American Future*, 103–106; Weigley, *Quartermaster General*, 308–309.

22. See for example this advertisement, "Position as U.S. Sexton at the Contraband Cemetery Arlington, Va. I will pay about $60 and rations," Assistant Quartermaster's Office, February 1, 1865, D. B. Nichols Scrapbooks—MMC 3859, Folder: D. B. Nichols Scrapbooks, Volume 1, 1863–1864, LOC; and Tim Dennee and the Friends of Freedmen's Cemetery, *A District of Columbia Freedmen's Cemetery in Virginia? African-American Civilians Interred in Section 27 of Arlington National Cemetery, 1864–1867* (Tim Dennee and Friend of Freedmen's Cemetery, 2011 and 2015), 13, PDF available: http://www.freedmenscemetery.org/resources/documents/arlington-section27.pdf.

23. Tim Dennee and the Friends of Freedmen's Cemetery, *A District of Columbia Freedmen's Cemetery in Virginia?*, 24. Phillip W. Magness and Sebastian Page, "Mr. Lincoln and Mr. Johnson," *Opinionator* (blog), *New York Times*, February 1, 2012, http://opinionator.blogs.nytimes.com/2012/02/01/mr-lincoln-and-mr-johnson/.

24. Abraham Lincoln to Gideon Welles, March 16, 1861, quoted in Burlingame, *Abraham Lincoln*, 252.

25. Abraham Lincoln to Salmon P. Chase, November 29, 1861, Series 3, General Correspondence, 1837–1897, Abraham Lincoln Papers, LOC.

26. Eric Foner repeats this story in a recent work: "When Johnson died in 1864, Lincoln arranged for him to be buried at Arlington Cemetery, paid for a tombstone with Johnson's name on it, and chose a one-word inscription: 'citizen.'" Foner, *The Fiery Trial: Abraham Lincoln and American Slavery* (New York: W. W. Norton, 2010), 258.

27. H. N. Howard [Superintendent Freedman's Village] to Brev. Brg Gen C. H. Howard, November 16, 1867, requesting that the "graveyard connected to this village" be moved into the national cemetery; and Supt. Freedman's Village to Major S. Eldridge, April 27, 1868, seeking response to correspondence of November 16, 1867, Freedman's Village: Letters Sent by the Superintendent, vol. III, *Records of the Field Offices for the District of Columbia, Bureau of Refugees, Freedmen, and Abandoned Lands, 1865–1870* (National Archives Microfilm Publication M1902, roll 20). The Arlington plantation's cemetery for enslaved people was still intact in 1928, and the Freedman's Village graves—if next to it—might have still been visible then. See also, Tim Dennee and the Friends of Freedmen's Cemetery, *A District of Columbia Freedmen's Cemetery in Virginia?*, 8, 8n14.

28. "Report of the Secretary of War, 1865," *United States Congressional Serial Set, H.R. Ex. Doc. No. 1*, 39th Cong., 1st sess. (1866), 258.

29. Ibid., 265, 263.

30. The reduction in numbers employed at Arlington in August 1865 is noted in Captain James M. Moore to Bvt. Major General D. H. Rucker, September 12, 1865, RG 92, Records of the Office of the Quartermaster General, Consolidated Correspondence File, 1794–1915, Box 49, Folder: "Arlington National Cemetery," NARA.

31. [Indecipherable] to Rucker Moore, December 11, 1865, Murray H. Nelligan Papers, Research Files 1650–1967, 1860–1890, Box 6 of 14, Folder: "1865," ARHO. After detailing Mary Lee's pledge to regain Arlington, the plantation is called "a legitimate conquest of war," in "Letter from Washington," *New Hampshire Sentinel,* July 20, 1865, 2.

32. "Thirty-Ninth Congress, First Session—The Arlington Estate," *New York Times,* March 22, 1866, 1.

33. "XXXIX Congress, First Session," *Hartford Courant,* March 22, 1866, 3. An almost verbatim notice appeared as "Congressional Summary, Thirty-Ninth Congress—First Session," *Maine Farmer,* March 29, 1866, 2. See also "Thirty-Ninth Congress, First Session—The Arlington Estate."

34. National Park Service Office of Legislative and Congressional Affairs, "Appendix I, VI. National Cemeteries," *Proclamations and Orders Relating to the National Park Service,* vol. 2 (December 2004), 595. Available at http://www.nps.gov/legal/.

35. James F. Russling, "National Cemeteries," *Harper's New Monthly Magazine,* August 1, 1866, 314, 319, 321.

36. Ibid., 321–322.

37. National Park Service Office of Legislative and Congressional Affairs, "Appendix I, VI. National Cemeteries," 595.

38. Mary Lee to Emily Mason, April 20, 1866, quoted in Emory M. Thomas, *Robert E. Lee: A Biography* (New York: W. W. Norton, 1995), 383.

39. Mary Lee (daughter) to Mary Lee, December 9, 1865, quoted in Poole, *On Hallowed Ground,* 68–69.

40. "Report of the Secretary of War, 1866," *United States Congressional Serial Set, H.R. Ex. Doc. No. 1,* 39th Cong., 2st sess. (1866), 308.

41. Charles Wunderlich to Captain James M. Moore, September 15, 1866, in *Sketches Showing Graves of Union Soldiers Whose Remains Were Exhumed and Removed to National Cemetery at Arlington, Virginia, under the Direction of Bvt. Lt. Col. E. E. Camp, A.Q.M. U.S.A.,* RG 92, Records of the Office of the Quartermaster General, Consolidated Correspondence File, 1794–1915, Folder: "Arlington Cemetery— 'Graves of Union Soldiers,'" NARA.

42. Faust, *This Republic of Suffering,* 236.

43. Mrs. E. L. Sherwood, "Arlington and Other Sights," *Ladies Repository,* December 1, 1868, 461.

44. Walt Whitman, "The Million Dead, Too, Summ'd Up," in *Specimen Days & Collect* (Philadelphia: Rees Welsh & Co, 1883), 80.

45. "Report of the Secretary of War, 1866," *United States Congressional Serial Set, H.R. Ex. Doc. No. 1,* 39th Cong., 2st sess. (1866), 308.

46. Colonel Ludington, supervisor of the project, reported that 1,791 remains of "Union soldiers" were removed from Bull Run and 320 from elsewhere along the Orange and

Alexandria line. Marshall I. Ludington to Montgomery C. Meigs, September 21, 1866, RG 92, Records of the Office of the Quartermaster General, Consolidated Correspondence File, 1794–1915, Box 49, Folder: "Arlington Cemetery 'Graves of Union Soldiers'" (folder 2), NARA.

47. [Indecipherable, Dana?] to Edward Clark, Architect, Quartermaster Department, September 25, 1866, RG 92, Records of the Office of the Quartermaster General, Consolidated Correspondence File, 1794–1915, Box 50, Folder: "Arlington National Cemetery—'vault,'" NARA.

48. "Epitome of the Week," *Frank Leslie's Weekly Illustrated Paper,* November 10, 1866; "Political and News Summary," *Vincennes (Indiana) Weekly Western Sun,* November 24, 1866, 1. Laurie Burgess argues that Arlington's ground was made "sacred" and like a battlefield in "receiving" the bodies of the Union dead. Burgess, "Buried in the Rose Garden," 166.

49. "The Union Dead on the Battle-Fields of Virginia," *New York Times,* April 8, 1866, 3. On the likelihood of the presence of Confederate remains in the vault beneath the Civil War Unknowns Monument (as it is called today), see Kathryn Allamong Jacob, *Testament to Union: Civil War Monuments in Washington, DC* (Baltimore: Johns Hopkins University Press, 1998), 157.

50. Quoted with no date in Philip Bigler, *In Honored Glory: Arlington National Cemetery the Final Post,* 4th ed. (St. Petersburg, FL: Vandamere, 2007), 20–21.

51. Harriet Hazelton, "Aunt Mehitable's Winter in Washington, Eighth Paper," *Godey's Lady's Book,* December 1873.

52. "A Burial Party. Cold Harbor, Virginia," April 1865, photographed by John Reekie, in Alexander Gardner, *Gardner's Photographic Sketch Book of the War,* vol. 2 (Washington, DC: Philip and Solomons, 1866), plate 94; digitized by Division of Rare and Manuscript Collections, Cornell University Library, Ithaca, NY, http://rmc.library .cornell.edu/7milVol/plate94.html.

53. "Collecting the Remains of Union Soldiers for Re-interment in National Cemeteries," *Harper's Weekly,* November 24, 1866, 740. On "A Burial Party," see Michael Kammen, *Digging Up the Dead: A History of Notable American Reburials* (Chicago: University of Chicago Press, 2010), 97; Mark S. Schantz, *Awaiting the Heavenly Country: The Civil War and America's Culture of Death* (Ithaca, NY: Cornell University Press, 2008), 184–186.

54. See, for example, "Sketch Showing Graves on Land of——Crocker, near R. Craig, Va.—Colored Soldiers," which shows a smaller group of white men's graves, possibly officers, in a single line beside and distinct from the double row of USCT graves, in *Sketches Showing Graves of Union Soldiers.*

55. See, for example, the records collected in RG 92, Records of the Office of the Quartermaster General, Cemeterial-Sexton's Records of Death and Interment and Orders for Burial, 1864–67, Box 9, NARA.

56. John C. Kimball, "Six Weeks in Washington," *Monthly Religious Magazine,* February 1868, 132.

57. Cecilia Elizabeth O'Leary, *To Die For: The Paradox of American Patriotism* (Princeton, NJ: Princeton University Press, 1999), chap. 3.

58. David Blight, "Decoration Days: The Origins of Memorial Day in the North and South," in *The Memory of the Civil War in American Culture*, ed. Alice Fahs and Joan Waugh (Chapel Hill: University of North Carolina Press, 2004), 94–129.

59. "The Union Dead—Decoration of the Graves of Soldiers at the Cemeteries," *New York Herald*, May 31, 1868, 10.

60. "Honor to the Noble Dead," *Boston Daily Journal*, June 1, 1868, 4.

61. "Decoration of Soldiers' Graves," *Harper's Weekly*, June 20, 1868, 388.

62. Kirk Savage has argued compellingly that Benedict Anderson's popular formulation of nationalism as an "imagined community" generated in the circulation of print cannot account for the special power of the public monument, which "speaks to a deep need for attachment that can be met only in a real place, where the imagined community actually materializes and the existence of the nation is confirmed in a simple but powerful way." Arlington National Cemetery—and the Civil War Unknowns Monument in particular—bring these together in an example of the historical potency of circulated print images and textual narratives of place in facilitating and expanding the experience of a "real place." Savage, *Monument Wars: Washington, DC, the National Mall, and the Transformation of the Memorial Landscape* (Berkeley: University of California Press, 2009), 4.

63. "Arlington Heights Cemetery," *Harper's Weekly*, March 27, 1869, 196.

64. Julia Wilbur Large Diary, May 30, 1866, Julia Wilbur Papers, 1843–1908, Collection No. 1158, Haverford College Library Special Collections, Haverford, PA. I am most grateful to Kate Masur for providing me with this source.

65. Ibid. The segregation of USCT dead and inclusion of "rebel soldiers" among the "loyal dead" is noted in "The Freedman's Village on the Lee Estate at Arlington" (reprint from *New York Evening Post*), *Oregonian*, September 28, 1865, 4.

66. Captain [indecipherable] Payne to General C. H. Tompkins, April 3, 1867, RG 92, Records of the Office of the Quartermaster General, Consolidated Correspondence File, 1794–1915, Box 49, Folder: "Arlington Cemetery 'Graves of Union Soldiers'" (folder 2), NARA.

67. Joseph P. Reidy, "'Coming from the Shadow of the Past': The Transition from Slavery to Freedom at Freedmen's Village, 1863–1900," *Virginia Magazine of History and Biography* 95, no. 4 (1987): 417.

68. "Number and description of families that will be compelled to leave the village in accordance with instructions contained in letter dated Head Quarters Bureau R.F. & A.L. Washington DC November 3rd 1866," *Records of the Field Offices for the District of Columbia, Bureau of Refugees, Freedmen, and Abandoned Lands, 1865–1870* (National Archives Microfilm Publication M1902, roll 20).

69. "The Freedman's Bureau! An Agency to Keep the Negro in Idleness at the Expense of the White Man" (1866), Broadside Collection, Rare Books, LOC.

70. John B. Ellis, *The Sights and Secrets of the National Capital* (1869), clipping, Box Two, Folder: "Freedman's Village," Slavery Files, ARHO.

71. Superintendent A. A. Lawrence to Bvt. Brig. General C. H. Howard, November 9, 1866, Freedman's Village: Letters Sent by the Superintendent, vol. III, *Records of the Field Offices for the District of Columbia, Bureau of Refugees, Freedmen, and Abandoned*

Lands, 1865–1870 (National Archives Microfilm Publication M1902, roll 20). Howard's order is recorded on the outside of the request.

72. Reidy, "Coming from the Shadow of the Past," 420.

73. Friends of the Freedmen, *Addresses and Ceremonies at the New Year's Festival to the
Freedmen, on Arlington Heights* (Washington, DC: McGill and Witherow, 1867),
9–11. On the protests and their outcomes generally, see Reidy, "Coming from the
Shadow of the Past," 419–421.

74. Hanna, *Cultural Landscape Report*, 100–102, 111–113; Harrison, *Washington during
Civil War and Reconstruction*, 74; Reidy, "Coming from the Shadow of the Past,"
421.

75. "Decoration Ceremonies at Arlington National Cemetery," *Boston Daily Journal,*
May 31, 1871, 4; "Imposing Ceremonies at Arlington," *New York Tribune,* May 31,
1871, 1; "Washington," *Cincinnati Enquirer,* May 31, 1871, 1. On McCreery's attempt,
see "Congress," *New York Herald,* December 14, 1870, 4.

76. "Committee on Decorations, Grand Army Hall," *Washington Critic-Record,* May 23,
1871, 2; Frederick Douglass, *Life and Times of Frederick Douglass: His Early Life as a
Slave, His Escape from Bondage, and His Complete History to the Present Time* (Hartford, CT: Park, 1881), 421.

77. Frederick Douglass, "Address at the Graves of the Unknown Dead at Arlington, VA,"
May 30, 1871, Frederick Douglass Papers, Manuscript Division, LOC.

78. "Decoration Ceremonies at Arlington National Cemetery," *Boston Daily Journal,*
May 31, 1871, 4.

79. *Washington Daily Morning Chronicle,* May 31, 1871, 4, cited in Neff, *Honoring the
Civil War Dead,* 194. See also, Blair, *Cities of the Dead,* 176–177.

80. *New National Era,* June 23, 1870, 2, quoted ibid., 194–195.

81. Frederick Douglass, "Men of Color, To Arms," March 3, 1863, Frederick Douglass
Papers, Manuscript Division, LOC.

82. Letter to Chief Surgeon, L'Ouverture Hospital, December 27, 1864, transcription at
Friends of Freedmen's Cemetery website, http://www.freedmenscemetery.org/resources
/documents/louverture.shtml.

83. Captain J. G. C. Lee, Assistant Quartermaster, USA, to Major General M. C. Meigs,
Quartermaster General, USA, December 28, 1864, transcription ibid.

84. Quartermaster General Montgomery C. Meigs to Secretary of War William W.
Belknap, August 2, 1871, copy, Box Two, Folder: "Syphaxes," Slavery Files, ARHO.

85. Poole, *On Hallowed Ground,* 79. See also Caroline E. Janney, *Burying the Dead but
Not the Past: Ladies' Memorial Associations and the Lost Cause* (Chapel Hill: University of North Carolina Press, 2008), 122.

86. Robert B. Beath, *History of the Grand Army of the Republic* (New York: Bryan, Taylor,
1889), 176. On the expansion of burial benefits, see National Cemetery Administration, Department of Veterans Affairs, "History and Development of the National
Cemetery Administration," 3–4.

87. Olmstead counseled keeping it "studiously simple; that ambitious efforts of ignorant
or half-bred landscape gardeners should be especially guarded against." Frederick
Law Olmstead to Montgomery C. Meigs, August 5, 1870, quoted in Sloane, *Last
Great Necessity,* 115. On Rhodes, see Hanna, *Cultural Landscape Report,* 106.

88. Theodore O'Hara, "The Bivouac of the Dead," in *Theodore O'Hara: Poet-Soldier of the Old South,* by Nathaniel Cheairs Hughes Jr. and Thomas Clayton Ware (Knoxville: University of Tennessee Press, 1998), 69.

89. *Arlington National Cemetery, Sheridan Gate,* Historic American Buildings Survey (Washington, DC: National Park Service, U.S. Department of the Interior, 1999), 2–3; *Arlington House Historic District,* National Register of Historic Places Registration Form, entered in the National Register, March 17, 2014, National Park Service, U.S. Department of the Interior, 89–90, 121, 131.

90. Joan Waugh, *U.S. Grant: American Hero, American Myth* (Chapel Hill: University of North Carolina Press, 2009), 276–282; "The Country and Its Dead," *New York Times,* August 8, 1888, 2.

91. The 1908 rule stated, "provided that this privilege be extended to only one wife and that it be not granted in any case unless the remains of the husband are first interred in the national cemetery." Captain James S. Parker to Officer in Charge, Quartermaster Depot, Washington, DC, February 27, 1908, RG 92, Records of the Office of the Quartermaster General, Records Relating to Functions: Cemeterial, 1878–1929, Correspondence Relating to the Administration of National Cemeteries, 1907–1929, misc. records, Box 3, NARA.

92. Sloane, *Last Great Necessity,* 104–107; Cynthia Mills, *Beyond Grief: Sculpture and Wonder in the Gilded Age Cemetery* (Washington, DC: Smithsonian Institution Scholarly Press, 2015), chap. 6.

93. Beth Linker, *War's Waste: Rehabilitation in World War I America* (Chicago: University of Chicago Press, 2011), 13–21.

94. Montgomery C. Meigs, quoted in Jacob, *Testament to Union,* 67.

95. On the Pension Building generally, see ibid., 63–68; and De B. Randolph Keim, *Washington and Its Environs: A Descriptive and Historical Hand-Book* (Washington, DC: De B. Randolph Keim, 1888), 143–146; Linda B. Lyons, "The Pension Building: Function and Form," in ed. William C. Dickinson, Dean A. Herrin, and Donald R. Kennon, *Montgomery C. Meigs and the Building of the Nation's Capitol* (Athens: Ohio University Press, 2001), 91–111.

96. Mary Lee, quoted in Hanna, *Cultural Landscape Report,* 111.

97. Poole, *On Hallowed Ground,* 87–93.

98. Mildred Lee, "Recollections," in *Growing Up in the 1850s: The Journal of Agnes Lee,* ed. Mary Custis Lee deButts (Chapel Hill: University of North Carolina Press, 1984), 120.

99. "A Plan for a Great Park," *Washington Post,* October 20, 1886, 5. On crime and Freedman's Village, see, for example, "City News in Brief," *Washington Post,* June 10, 1879, 4. For a series of *Post* reports on the community as overrun with smallpox and residents' public protests to this framing of their community, see "City Brevities," February 26, 1882, 4; "Smallpox," March 16, 1882, 2; "Exaggerated Reports," March 18, 1882; "Dies of Smallpox," March 22, 1882, 3; "Indignation in Freedman's Village," February 12, 1884, 4.

100. "To Arlington," *Harper's Weekly,* May 29, 1886, 347.

101. John B. Syphax to William C. Endicott, Secretary of War, January 18, 1888, in "Report from the Acting Secretary of the Treasury to Congress, June 1888," *United States Congressional Serial Set, H.R. Ex. Doc. No. 360,* 50th Cong., 1st sess. (1889), 4.

102. Inventory, March 27, 1888, ibid., 8, 10. Note the typo: James Parks is listed as "Jane Parks." ARHO files indicate that this refers to James.
103. "Will of Montgomery C. Meigs who died 1892 (Copy)," Montgomery C. Meigs Collection, Family Papers, Reel 16, Container 11, LOC.

4. Bringing Home the Dead

1. *Annual Report of the Quartermaster General of the Army to the Secretary of War for the Fiscal Year Ending June 30, 1893* (Washington, DC: Government Printing Office, 1893), 14.
2. With particular emphasis on the burial of unknowns from the Civil War to Vietnam, this history is detailed today on a panel in the cemetery's Visitors' Center under the heading "Becoming the Nation's Cemetery."
3. Paul C. Rosier, *Serving Their Country: American Indian Politics and Patriotism in the Twentieth Century* (Cambridge, MA: Harvard University Press, 2009), 39.
4. Some were never repatriated but buried in the Philippines. They are now congregated in the Clark Veterans Cemetery north of Manila, to which they were moved from various post locations in 1948. After being privately maintained by volunteers from a local VFW post, the cemetery was designated for administration by the American Battle Monuments Commission in 2013.
5. George L. Mosse, *Fallen Soldiers: Reshaping the Memory of the World Wars* (New York: Oxford University Press, 1990), chap. 5.
6. Inspired by Shakespeare's *Hamlet,* Gail Holst-Warhaft writes compellingly of the "theater of mourning" in her *The Cue for Passion: Grief and Its Political Uses* (Cambridge, MA: Harvard University Press, 2000).
7. On the Senate Park Commission and plans, see Kirk Savage, *Monument Wars: Washington, DC, the National Mall, and the Transformation of the Memorial Landscape* (Berkeley: University of California Press, 2009), chap 4. On L'Enfant's reinterment, see Michael Kammen, *Digging Up the Dead: A History of Notable American Reburials* (Chicago: University of Chicago Press, 2009), 78–81.
8. International Auto Sight-Seeing Transit Company, "Sight-Seeing Automobile for Touring Arlington Cemetery, Fort Myer, and Virginia Suburbs," pamphlet, c. 1912, VHS.
9. Karl Decker and Angus McSween, *Historic Arlington* (Washington, DC: Decker and McSween, 1892), 3.
10. Ibid., 77. Scott E. Casper describes the white tendency to see black workers in historic plantation spaces as embodiments of faithful slavery as a kind of "historical alchemy," noting "white people in motion romanticized black people seemingly fixed in place." Casper, *Sarah Johnson's Mount Vernon: The Forgotten History of an American Shrine* (New York: Hill and Wang, 2009), 142–143.
11. William Bengough, "On Fame's Eternal Camping-Ground Their Silent Tents Are Spread," in *United States National Military Cemetery Arlington* (New York: Blanchard, 1897), n.p. [25]. While the book has no page numbers, the earlier two photographs, "The Sheridan Gate" and "Monuments to Officers," are on pages 13 and 23, respectively.

12. Ibid., n.p. [24].
13. Ibid., n.p. [18].
14. John M. Thurston, quoted in John Pettegrew, "'The Soldier's Faith': Turn-of-the-Century Memory of the Civil War and the Emergence of Modern American Nationalism," *Journal of Contemporary History* 31, no. 1 (1996): 7.
15. On Civil War memory, sectional reconciliation, and white supremacy, generally, see David W. Blight, *Race and Reunion: The Civil War in American Memory* (Cambridge, MA: Harvard University Press, 2001); Caroline E. Janney, *Remembering the Civil War: Reunion and the Limits to Reconciliation* (Chapel Hill: University of North Carolina Press, 2013); Cecilia Elizabeth O'Leary, *To Die For: The Paradox of American Patriotism* (Princeton, NJ: Princeton University Press, 1999), chap. 11; and Nina Silber, *The Romance of Reunion: Northerners and the South, 1865–1900* (Chapel Hill: University of North Carolina Press, 1992). On black military service in the Spanish-American War, see Adriane Lentz-Smith, *Freedom Struggles: African Americans and World War I* (Cambridge, MA: Harvard University Press, 2009), 18–24; and Michele Mitchell, *Righteous Propagation: African Americans and the Politics of Racial Destiny after Reconstruction* (Chapel Hill: University of North Carolina Press, 2004), chap. 2.
16. On McKinley, the Quartermaster Burial Corps, and Spanish-American War repatriation policies as an interpretation of post–Civil War acts, see Lisa M. Budreau, *Bodies of War: World War I and the Politics of Commemoration in America, 1919–1933* (New York: NYU Press, 2009), 24; Monro MacCloskey, *Hallowed Ground: Our National Cemeteries* (New York: Richards Rosen, 1968), 46; and Michael Sledge, *Soldier Dead: How We Recover, Identify, Bury, and Honor Our Military Fallen* (New York: Columbia University Press, 2005), 135.
17. William McKinley, "Speech before the Legislature in Joint Assembly at the State Capitol, Atlanta, Georgia, December 14, 1898," quoted in Michelle A. Krowl, "'In the Spirit of Fraternity': The United States Government and the Burial of Confederate Dead at Arlington National Cemetery, 1864–1914," *Virginia Magazine of History and Biography* 111, no. 2 (2003): 152.
18. Ibid.
19. William Allen Blair, *Cities of the Dead: Contesting the Memory of the Civil War in the South, 1865–1914* (Chapel Hill: University of North Carolina Press), 179–188; John R. Neff, *Honoring the Civil War Dead: Commemoration and the Problem of Reconciliation* (Lawrence: University Press of Kansas, 2005), chap. 6.
20. "Sad Home-Coming—Bodies of War Victims to Be Brought Back," *Chicago Daily Tribune,* January 29, 1899, 35.
21. "686 Dead Heroes Arrive," *New York Times,* March 30, 1899, 3.
22. *Annual Report of the Quartermaster-General of the Army to the Secretary of War for the Fiscal Year Ending June 30, 1899* (Washington, DC: Government Printing Office, 1899), 38–39.
23. Thomas W. Laqueur, "Names, Bodies, and the Anxiety of Erasure," ed. Theodore R. Schatzki and Wolfgang Natter, *The Social and Political Body* (New York: Guilford, 1996), 128; and MacCloskey, *Hallowed Ground,* 47.
24. "Soldier Dead Removed," *New York Times,* March 31, 1899, 14. See also "686 Dead Heroes Arrive."

25. "Soldier Dead Removed," 14.

26. "Soldier Dead at Rest," *New York Times,* April 7, 1899, 5. The editors of John Ball Osborne's *The Story of Arlington* note that 325 were ultimately interred that day. John Ball Osborne, *The Story of Arlington* (Washington, DC: John F. Sheiry, 1899), 70n.

27. "Dead Come Home," *Boston Daily Globe,* December 26, 1899, 10; and "On a Pretty, Grassy Knoll," *Boston Daily Globe,* December 26, 1899, 10.

28. Osborne, *Story of Arlington,* 1.

29. On William Headley Osborne, see ibid., 62. On Edwin Sylvanus Osborne, see the *Luzerne Legal Register* 12, no. 3 (1883): 345–350; "The Old Soldiers Make a Clean Sweep in the County Convention," *Historical Record* 2, no. 4 (1888): 145; "Osborne, Edwin Sylvanus," in *Biographical Directory of the United States Congress,* http://bioguide.congress.gov.

30. Osborne, *Story of Arlington,* 4.

31. Ibid., 72–73.

32. Ibid., 65–66. Osborne lists them as John C. Allen, lieutenant of the Ninth United States Volunteer Infantry; Arthur K. Barnett, lieutenant of the Twenty-Third Kansas Volunteer Infantry; and L. I. Barnett, lieutenant of the Ninth United States Volunteer Infantry.

33. Ibid., 104–106.

34. Charles Broadway Rouss Camp No. 1101, United Confederate Veterans, Washington, DC, *Report of the Reburial of the Confederate Dead in Arlington Cemetery and Attention Called to the Care Required for the Graves of Confederate Soldiers Who Died in Federal Prisons and Military Hospitals Now Buried in Northern States* (Washington, DC: Judd and Detweiler, 1901), 20.

35. Samuel E. Lewis, quoted in Neff, *Honoring the Civil War Dead,* 225.

36. Krowl, "In the Spirit of Fraternity, " 163–164; Neff, *Honoring the Civil War Dead,* chap. 6; Blair, *Cities of the Dead,* chap. 7; Caroline E. Janney, *Burying the Dead but Not the Past: Ladies Memorial Associations and the Lost Cause* (Chapel Hill: University of North Carolina Press, 2008), 182.

37. All of these accusations are stated or implied in "Confederate Dead at the North," *Confederate Veteran* 9, no. 5 (1901): 196–198.

38. Janet H. W. Randolph, quoted in Neff, *Honoring the Civil War Dead,* 226.

39. Hilary A. Herbert, quoted in Blair, *Cities of the Dead,* 190. Herbert recounts the controversy in his *History of the Arlington Confederate Monument* (Washington, DC: United Daughters of the Confederacy, 1914), 7–8.

40. The inscription carries an incorrect date for the Spanish-American War, which was limited to four months in 1898; the inclusion of 1899 is probably a reference to the start of war with the Philippines.

41. National Society of the Colonial Dames of America, *The National Society of the Colonial Dames of America, Its Beginnings, Its Purpose, and a Record of Its Work, 1891–1913* (New York: Gilliss, 1913), 95–96.

42. Ibid., 96.

43. On the late-nineteenth-century proliferation of hereditary organizations, racial formation, and blood, see Michael Kammen, *Mystic Chords of Memory: The Transformation of Tradition in America* (New York: Vintage Books, 1993), 215–223; Shawn

Michelle Smith, *American Archives: Gender, Race, and Class in American Visual Culture* (Princeton, NJ: Princeton University Press, 1999), chap. 5; and Carolyn Strange, "Sisterhood of Blood: The Will to Descend and the Formation of the Daughters of the American Revolution," *Journal of Women's History* 26, no. 3 (2014): 105–128. On "ancestor worship," see Kammen, *Mystic Chords*, 217–223.

44. Gail Bederman, *Manliness and Civilization: A Cultural History of Gender and Race in the United States, 1880–1917* (Chicago: University of Chicago Press, 1995), chap. 5.

45. Quote from the title page of Mrs. Joseph Rucker Lamar, *A History of the National Society of the Colonial Dames of America from 1891 to 1933* (Atlanta: Walter W. Brown, 1934).

46. National Society of the Colonial Dames of America, *National Society of the Colonial Dames of America*, 95.

47. Lamar, *History of the National Society of the Colonial Dames of America*, 45.

48. "Talks of Soldiers' Duty," *Chicago Daily Tribune*, May 22, 1902, 6; "President Roosevelt on Citizens' Duty," *New York Times*, May 22, 1902, 8. On the Philippine-American War, see Paul A. Kramer, *The Blood of Government: Race, Empire, the United States, and the Philippines* (Chapel Hill: University of North Carolina Press, 2006).

49. Omar Dphrepaulezz, "'The Right Sort of White Men': General Leonard Wood and the U.S. Army in the Southern Philippines, 1898–1906" (Ph.D. diss., University of Connecticut, 2013).

50. Edmund Morris, *Theodore Rex* (New York: Random House, 2001), 110.

51. "Union's Saviors Live in Memory," *Los Angeles Times*, May 31, 1902, 1.

52. "Defends Army," *Hartford Courant*, May 31, 1902, 11.

53. "President's Speech Arouses Southerners," *New York Times*, May 31, 1902, 1; "The President's Speech and Its Critics," *Literary Digest* 24, no. 3 (1902): 762. The Roosevelt biographer Edmund Morris notes that the president's reference to lynching as a greater national shame than some military conduct in the Philippines was not in the planned speech but an on-the-spot improvisation. Morris, *Theodore Rex*, 110.

54. "Defends Army."

55. Roosevelt's absence at Arlington was noted in "They Live in Memory," *Los Angeles Times*, May 31, 1903, 4. On his Wyoming speech and western tour, see Rebecca Hein, "President Theodore Roosevelt's 1903 Visit to Wyoming," *Wyoming State Historical Society Online Encyclopedia*, http://www.wyohistory.org/encyclopedia/president -theodore-roosevelts-1903-visit-wyoming (accessed March 29, 2016).

56. "A Day at Arlington," *New York Times*, May 31, 1903, 13.

57. John V. Wright, quoted in Krowl, "In the Spirit of Fraternity," 171–172.

58. Herbert, *History of the Arlington Confederate Monument*, 7.

59. Kirk Savage, "President Obama and the Confederacy," *Washington Post*, May 23, 2009, A19.

60. Sheryl Gay Stolberg, "'They Answered a Call,' Obama Says of Veterans," *New York Times*, May 26, 2009, A11.

61. Julia Ward Howe, *Reminiscences, 1819–1899* (Boston: Houghton, Mifflin and Company, 1899), 379.

62. "Nurses' Monument," *Trained Nurse and Hospital Review* 23, no. 5 (1899): 308.

63. Kimberly Jensen, *Mobilizing Minerva: American Women in the First World War* (Champaign: University of Illinois Press, 2008), 118–119; Mary T. Sarnecky, *A History*

of the U.S. Army Nurse Corps (Philadelphia: University of Pennsylvania Press, 1999), 29–31; Strange, "Sisterhood of Blood," 119–120.

64. On the persistent gendered connotations of nursing, see Kara Dixon Vuic, *Officer, Nurse, Woman: The Army Nurse Corps in the Vietnam War* (Baltimore: Johns Hopkins University Press, 2010), 47–52. On the variety of nurses in the Spanish-American War, see Charles McGraw, "'The Intervention of a Friendly Power': The Transnational Migration of Women's Work and the 1898 Imperial Imagination," *Journal of Women's History* 19, no. 3 (2007): 137–160; and Sarnecky, *History of the U.S. Army Nurse Corps,* 31–32.

65. "Soldier Dead Removed," *New York Times,* March 31, 1899, 14.

66. It is possible that she was Irene S. Toland, from St. Louis, Missouri, the only person listed among the fourteen deceased nurses for whom the Arlington memorial was especially dedicated to die in Santiago.

67. Sarnecky, *History of the U.S. Army Nurse Corps,* 49–51.

68. "Proposed Monuments," *Reporter* 32, no. 11 (1899): 31.

69. "Sad Home-Coming—Bodies of War Victims to Be Brought Back," *Chicago Daily Tribune,* January 29, 1899, 35.

70. Anita Newcomb McGee, "Reports of the Societies—Second Annual Meeting of the Spanish-American War Nurses," *American Journal of Nursing* 2, no. 2 (1901): 123.

71. "Official Reports of the Societies—Spanish-American War Nurses," *American Journal of Nursing* 3, no. 4 (1903): 309.

72. "Official Reports of Societies—Spanish-American War Nurses," *American Journal of Nursing* 4, no. 2 (1903): 131–132. Men of the Army Hospital Corps, established in 1887, were excluded from the beginning because they were enlisted military personnel, not contract nurses.

73. "In the Nursing World—Spanish-American War Nurses," *Trained Nurse and Hospital Review* 34, no. 6 (1905): 398.

74. Ibid. On regrets from the president and secretary of war, see "In the Nursing World—Spanish-American War Nurses," *Trained Nurse and Hospital Review* 35, no. 1 (1905): 34.

75. Quoted in Herbert, *History of the Arlington Confederate Monument,* 36.

76. "The Monument at Arlington," *Confederate Veteran* 22, no. 7 (1914): 294.

77. Mrs. Thomas S. [Annie Holmes Faulkner] Bocock, Director, Virginia Arlington Confederate Monument Association, to "Daughters and Friends" of the United Daughters of the Confederacy, February 10, 1909, Mss 1 G8626 b 67–69 Manuscripts, Gregory Family Papers, 1900–1962, Section 6, VHS.

78. On the Confederate Monument, generally, see Karen L. Cox, "The Confederate Monument at Arlington: A Token of Reconciliation," in *Monuments to the Lost Cause: Women, Art, and the Landscapes of Southern Memory,* ed. Cynthia Mills and Pamela H. Simpson (Knoxville: University of Tennessee Press, 2003), 149–162; Kathryn Allamong Jacob, *Testament to Union: Civil War Monuments in Washington, D.C.* (Baltimore: Johns Hopkins University Press, 1999), 164–171; and Krowl, "In the Spirit of Fraternity," 180–186.

79. Micki McElya, *Clinging to Mammy: The Faithful Slave in Twentieth-Century America* (Cambridge, MA: Harvard University Press, 2007), 128.

80. Quoted in Herbert, *History of the Arlington Confederate Monument,* 19.

81. Quoted in ibid., 23.
82. Quoted in ibid., 47.
83. "Monument at Arlington," 296.

5. Out of Many, One Unknown

1. Michael Sledge, *Soldier Dead: How We Recover, Identify, Bury, and Honor Our Military Fallen* (New York: Columbia University Press, 2005), 36.
2. "To Bring Back Our Dead," *New York Times*, September 5, 1918, 10.
3. On World War I repatriation controversies generally, see Lisa M. Budreau, *Bodies of War: World War I and the Politics of Commemoration in America, 1919–1933* (New York: NYU Press, 2009); Steven Casey, *When Soldiers Fall: How Americans Have Confronted Combat Losses from World War I to Afghanistan* (New York: Oxford University Press, 2014), chap. 1; Sledge, *Soldier Dead*, 135–137.
4. Minnie Kendall Lowther, *Mount Vernon, Arlington, and Woodlawn* (Washington, DC: Charles H. Potter, 1922), 63.
5. Most scholars argue the dissimilarity of these Arlington monuments to military unknowns; see, for example, Mark Meigs, *Optimism at Armageddon: Voices of American Participants in the First World War* (New York: NYU Press, 1997), 147–149.
6. W. E. B. Du Bois, "Close Ranks," July 1918, ed. Manning Marable and Leith Mullings, *Let Nobody Turn Us Around: Voices of Resistance, Reform, and Renewal, An African American Anthology* (New York: Rowman & Littlefield, 2000), 242–243.
7. Addie W. Hunton and Kathryn M. Johnson, *Two Colored Women with the American Expeditionary Forces* (Brooklyn, NY: Brooklyn Eagle, 1920), 234–245. On segregated labor battalions and grave duty, see Budreau, *Bodies of War*, chap. 6; and Meigs, *Optimism at Armageddon*, 178–179. On the long activist histories of Hunton and Johnson, see Adriane Lentz-Smith, *Freedom Struggles: African Americans and World War I* (Cambridge, MA: Harvard University Press, 2009).
8. Michael S. Sherry, *In the Shadow of War: The United States since the 1930s* (New Haven, CT: Yale University Press, 1995), 93; Nese F. DeBruyne and Anne Leland, *American War and Military Operations Casualties: Lists and Statistics* (Washington, DC: Congressional Research Service, January 2, 2015). Sherry notes that among battle death figures, many were caused by accidents.
9. U.S. Quartermaster Corps, *Tell Me about My Boy*, 1946, available online at http://www.qmfound.com/about_my_boy.htm. See also John Bodnar, *The "Good War" in American Memory* (Baltimore: Johns Hopkins University Press, 2010), 98–102.
10. Quartermaster General Montgomery C. Meigs to Secretary of War William W. Belknap, August 5, 1871, copy, Box Two, Folder: "Syphaxes," Slavery Files, ARHO.
11. Philippe Ariès, *The Hour of Our Death* (New York: Knopf, 1981), 547–550; Thomas W. Laqueur, "Names, Bodies, and the Anxiety of Erasure," ed. Theodore R. Schatzki and Wolfgang Natter, *The Social and Political Body* (New York: Guilford, 1996), 123–141; George L. Mosse, *Fallen Soldiers: Reshaping the Memory of the World Wars* (New York: Oxford University Press, 1990), 45–46.
12. Rupert Brooke, "The Soldier," in *Modern British Poetry*, ed. Louis Untermeyer (New York: Harcourt, Brace and Howe, 1920), 200.

13. U.S. War Department, *A Report to the Secretary of War on American Military Dead Overseas* (Washington, DC: U.S. Government Printing Office, 1920), 22.

14. Ibid., 24.

15. On this debate generally and these organizations, see Budreau, *Bodies of War*; and G. Kurt Piehler, *Remembering War the American Way* (Washington, DC: Smithsonian Books, 2004), 94–98.

16. "Tender Hands Care for Graves of A.E.F.," *Stars and Stripes*, October 11, 1918, 6.

17. Edgar Allen Forbes, "Should We Bring Home Our Soldier Dead?," *Frank Leslie's Weekly*, October 25, 1919.

18. Thomas W. Laqueur, *Grounds for Remembering: Monuments, Memorials, Texts* (Occasional Papers of the Doreen B. Townsend Center for the Humanities 3, University of California–Berkeley), 2.

19. B. C. Mossman and M. W. Stark describe an official request from Brigadier General William D. Connor to Army Chief of Staff General Peyton C. March, to consider burial of an American unknown on October 29, 1919, in *The Last Salute: Civil and Military Funerals, 1921–1969* (Washington, DC: Department of the Army, 1971), 3. For casualty statistics, see Laqueur, *Grounds for Remembering*, 1–2 (Britain); and "The Great Unknowns," *New York Times*, May 30, 2010 (United States).

20. "Pleads for Unknown Dead," *New York Times*, May 31, 1920, 3.

21. Ariès, *Hour of Our Death*, 550.

22. This was the general official sentiment (and assurance) circulated in the Army's newspaper: "Identify All but 4 Per Cent of Dead," *Stars and Stripes*, April 25, 1919, 2; and "Few 'Unknown Dead' to Be Left in France," *Stars and Stripes*, June 6, 1919, 3.

23. Hélène Lipstadt, "Ritual as Radical Change: The Burial of the Unknown Soldier and Ways of Using the Space of Washington, DC, 11 November 1921," ed. Dana Arnold and Andrew Ballantyne, *Architecture as Experience: Radical Change in Spatial Practice* (New York: Routledge, 2004), 237; Mossman and Stark, *Last Salute*, 3. On the burials of British and French Unknowns generally, see K. S. Inglis, "Entombing Unknown Soldiers: From London and Paris to Baghdad," *History and Memory* 5, no. 2 (1993): 7–31; Mosse, *Fallen Soldiers*, 94–98; Jay Winter, *Sites of Memory, Sites of Mourning: The Great War in European Cultural History* (New York: Cambridge University Press, 1995), chap. 4; Laura Wittman, *The Tomb of the Unknown Soldier, Modern Mourning, and the Reinvention of the Mystical Body* (Toronto: University of Toronto Press, 2011), chap. 2.

24. On the Victory Hall Association of New York generally, see "World War Memorials and Collections," *Quarterly Journal of the New York State Historical Association* 2, no. 2 (1921): 137; and Victory Hall Association Records, Manuscripts and Archives Division, New York Public Library.

25. "Topics of the Times—A Request Rightly Refused," *New York Times*, November 29, 1920, 14; "The Unknown Soldier," *New York Times*, December 9, 1920, 12.

26. Ivory G. Kimball, quoted in James Edward Peters, *Arlington National Cemetery: Shrine to America's Heroes*, 3rd ed. (Bethesda, MD: Woodbine House, 2008), 254.

27. "World's Finest Monument to Our Soldier Dead at Arlington," *Hartford Courant*, May 9, 1920, 2. See also "Wilson Lays Cornerstone—Starts Memorial Amphitheatre

at Arlington Cemetery," *New York Times,* October 14, 1915, 5; and Peters, *Arlington National Cemetery,* 253–257.

28. "The Unknown Soldier's Tomb," *New York Times,* February 3, 1921, 6.

29. Budreau, *Bodies of War,* 80; American Battle Monuments Commission, "History," https://www.abmc.gov/about-us/history (accessed March 29, 2016).

30. Monro MacCloskey, *Hallowed Ground: Our National Cemeteries* (New York: Richards Rosen, 1968), 49.

31. Charles Moore, Chairman, Commission of Fine Arts, form letter to members of Congress, November 4, 1920, Commission of Fine Arts Papers, RG 66, Project Files, 1910–1952, Box 10, Folder: "Arlington Mansion, No. 2," NARA.

32. Charles Moore to Major General Harry L. Rogers, November 1, 1920, copy of report concerning Arlington included with form letter, ibid.

33. Ibid.

34. Mossman and Stark, *Last Salute,* 4–13, 18; "Solemn Journey of Dead," *New York Times,* November 12, 1921, 1.

35. "Observance of Armistice Day," *Exhibitor's Trade Review,* November 5, 1921, 1575.

36. "Cohen Urges Exhibitors to Participate in Armistice Day," *Exhibitors Herald,* November 5, 1921, 40.

37. "Finds Pilgrim Echo in Honors to Dead," *New York Times,* November 12, 1941, 3; "Solemn Journey of Dead," *New York Times,* November 12, 1921, 1; M. E. Hennessy, "Stage Set to Sign Death Warrant of War at Washington," *Boston Daily Globe,* November 6, 1921, E2; Oswald Garrison Villard, "Mr. Harding and His Conference," *Nation,* January 11, 1922, 37–38.

38. Mossman and Stark, *Last Salute,* 14–15; Arthur Sears Henning, "Capital Bows as Hero Is Laid in Final Couch," *Chicago Daily Tribune,* November 12, 1921, 1.

39. Joseph Roach, *Cities of the Dead: Circum-Atlantic Performance* (New York: Columbia University Press, 1996), 37–39.

40. "Solemn Journey of Dead."

41. "Amplifiers Tested for Armistice Day," *New York Times,* November 10, 1921, 12; "Making Telephone History," film review, *Educational Screen* 2, no. 8 (1923): 406; Gordon S. Mitchell, "Notes on Public-Address Installation and Operation," *Projection Engineering* 3, no. 6 (1931): 7–9; and Lipstadt, "Ritual as Radical Change," 250.

42. R. J. McLauchlin, "What the Detroit 'News' Has Done in Broadcasting," *Radio Broadcast* 1, no. 2 (June 1922): 141; Harold S. Osborne, "Coaxial Cables and Television Transmission," *Journal of the Society of Motion Picture Engineers* 44, no. 6 (June 1945): 403–418.

43. The role of this expansive publicity and technological innovation in expanding the reach of the "imagined community" of the nation is informed by Benedict Anderson, *Imagined Communities: Reflections on the Origin and Spread of Nationalism,* rev. ed. (New York: Verso, 1992).

44. "The President's Address," *Boston Daily Globe,* November 12, 1921, 8.

45. "Solemn Journey of Dead."

46. "Remember Your Mother," *Christian Register,* May 11, 1922, 438. See also Mona Siegel, " 'To the Unknown Mother of the Unknown Soldier': Pacifism, Feminism, and

the Politics of Sexual Difference among French Institutrices between the Wars," *French Historical Studies* 22, no. 3 (1999): 421–451.

47. Public Act No. 301, H.R. 10384, *An Act to Regulate the Immigration of Aliens to, and the Residence of Aliens in, the United States,* February 5, 1917, 64th Cong., 2nd sess. On immigration and World War I military service, see Christopher Capozzola, *Uncle Sam Wants You: World War I and the Making of the Modern American Citizen* (New York: Oxford University Press, 2008), chap. 1; and Richard Slotkin, *Lost Battalions: The Great War and the Crisis in American Nationality* (New York: Holt, 2005).

48. "President's Address."

49. "Solemn Journey of Dead."

50. Paul C. Rosier refers to this as a "hybrid patriotism" in his discussion of Native American military service in World War I and the boarding-school graduates of the Society of American Indians in his *Serving Their Country: American Indian Politics and Patriotism in the Twentieth Century* (Cambridge, MA: Harvard University Press, 2009), 49.

51. "Solemn Journey of Dead."

52. "Pathe News Does Speedy Work," *Motion Picture News,* November 26, 1921, 2833.

53. "Special Provisions Made for Armistice Day," *Motion Picture News,* November 19, 1921, 2674.

54. Charles Gatchell, "By Aeroplane Limited," *Picture Play Magazine,* February 1922, 20–21; *Exhibitor's Trade Review,* December 3, 1921, 3003. Prizma Color Scenics released a color reel of the ceremony titled "The Glorious Dead" in February 1922. "Prizma Color Scenics," *Motion Picture News Booking Guide,* vol. 2 (New York: Motion Picture News, 1922), 97.

55. Gatchell, "By Aeroplane Limited."

56. Brian G. Shellum, *Black Officer in a Buffalo Soldier Regiment* (Lincoln: University of Nebraska Press, 2010), xi–xii, 230, 242–244.

57. Ibid., 252–254, 260, 274–278; "The Old Soldier Who Wouldn't Surrender," *Ebony* 30, no. 1 (1974): 86–94; "Col. Young Recalled to Army Service," *Savannah Tribune,* November 16, 1918, 1; "Col. Charles Young Dies in Nigeria," *New York Times,* January 13, 1922, 13.

58. Ada Young, quoted in David P. Kilroy, *For Race and Country: The Life and Career of Colonel Charles Young* (Westport, CT: Praeger, 2003), 156.

59. "Pay Tribute to Negro Colonel," *Kalamazoo Gazette,* January 31, 1922, 13.

60. "Services for Col. Young," *Washington Post,* March 6, 1922, 2. See also "To Hold Services for Colonel Young at A.M.E. Church," *Albuquerque Morning Journal,* March 12, 1922, 3; "Colored Notes," *Lexington (KY) Herald,* February 20, 1922, 12, and February 28, 1922, 12.

61. "Harding Sends Word for Memorial Meet for Late Col. Young," *Chicago Daily Tribune,* March 10, 1922, 11.

62. Harry B. Critchlow, "The Citizen Veteran," *Morning Oregonian,* April 9, 1922, 24.

63. "Colonel Charles Young—Victorious!," *Savannah Tribune,* March 16, 1922, 3.

64. "Charles Young," *Crisis* 23, no. 4 (1922): 155.

65. "Col. Young's Body Arrives Here," *New York Amsterdam News,* May 23, 1923, 1.

66. Kilroy, *For Race and Country,* 156–157; David Levering Lewis, *W. E. B. Du Bois, 1919–1963: The Fight for Equality and the American Century* (New York: Henry Holt and Company, 2000), 101–102.

67. "Negro Officer Buried," *New York Times,* June 2, 1923, 11. See also the photograph in the *Washington Post,* June 2, 1923, 22; and "Charles Young," *Crisis* 26, no. 3 (July 1923): 104–106.

68. "Charles Young," *Crisis,* 104.

69. "Arlington Monument Will Honor Col. Young," *Washington Post,* September 26, 1926, M14.

70. Shellum, *Black Officer in a Buffalo Soldier Regiment,* 287. See also, Benjamin Oliver Davis Sr., http://www.history.army.mil/html/topics/afam/davis.html (accessed March 16, 2016); General Benjamin Oliver Davis Jr., http://www.af.mil/AboutUs/Biographies /Display/tabid/225/Article/107298/general-benjamin-oliver-davis-jr.aspx (accessed March 16, 2016).

71. Charles Moore, Chairman, Commission of Fine Arts, form letter to members of Congress, November 4, 1920, Commission of Fine Arts Papers, NARA.

72. Frances Parkinson Keyes, "Letters from a Senator's Wife," *Good Housekeeping* 73, no. 2 (1921): 38, 134.

73. Charles Moore, quoted in Karen Byrne Kinzey, "Battling for Arlington House: To Lee or Not to Lee," *Arlington Historical Magazine,* October 2003, 25.

74. Public Resolution No. 74, H.J. Res. 264, *Joint Resolution Authorizing the Restoration of the Lee Mansion in the Arlington National Cemetery, Virginia,* March 4, 1925, 68th Cong., clipping, Commission of Fine Arts Papers, RG 66, Project Files, 1910–1952, Box 10, Folder: "Arlington Mansion, No. 5," NARA.

75. Grand Army of the Republic resolution, August 21, 1925, annotated copy, Commission of Fine Arts Papers, RG 66, Project Files, 1910–1952, Box 10, Folder: "Arlington Mansion, No. 5," NARA.

76. Kinzey, "Battling for Arlington House," 25–28.

77. Representative Peter F. Tague, Massachusetts, *Congressional Record,* April 8, 1924, quoted in Gerstle, *American Crucible: Race and Nation in the Twentieth Century* (Princeton, NJ: Princeton University Press, 2001), 117.

78. "Arlington County Dotted with Tents of Klan Visitors," *Washington Post,* August 8, 1925, 2; "Klansmen Display Huge Fiery Cross in Weird Pageant," *Washington Post,* August 10, 1925, 1.

79. "'Uncle Jim' Parks, Former Slave, to Lie in Arlington," *Washington Post,* August 23, 1929, clipping, Box 2, Folder: "James Parks," Slavery Files, ARHO; "Memorandum," October 16, 1928, RG 66, Commission of Fine Arts, Project Files—1910–1952, Box 21, Folder: "ANC—Parks, James," NARA.

80. Enoch Aquila Chase, "Ancient Custis Slave Remembers," *Washington Evening Star,* November 4, 1928, n.p. typed transcript labeled "Newspaper Article on James Parks, from the Sunday Star, Washington, DC, Part 7," Box 2, Folder: "Jim Parks," Slavery Files, ARHO. The piece includes, "The slave cemetery is a forlorn, neglected and almost forgotten spot today, although the plow of the government farmers seems not to have uprooted it, as far as the casual eye can judge."

81. "Burial Permit in Famous Cemetery Makes Man Happy," *Chicago Defender*, January 12, 1929, A1.

82. "'Uncle Jim' Parks, Former Slave, to Lie in Arlington." All obituaries mention these facts. One article says it was his grandsons who served in World War I, which makes more sense; "'Uncle Jim' Parks Buried in Arlington Cemetery," *New York Amsterdam News*, August 28, 1929, 4.

83. "Former Custis Slave to Sleep in Death in Arlington Estate," *Washington Evening Star*, August 22, 1929, 1; "'Uncle Jim' Parks, Former Slave, to Lie in Arlington."

84. "Monument Honors Custis' Ex-Slave," *Washington Evening Star*, March 2, 1930, n.p., clipping, Box 2, Folder: "James Parks," Slavery Files, ARHO.

85. Enoch Aquila Chase, "Ancient Custis Slave Remembers." See also Enoch Aquila Chase, "The Restoration of Arlington House," *Records of the Columbia Historical Society, Washington, DC* 33–34 (1932): 239–265.

86. Enoch Aquila Chase, Attorney and Counselor at Law, to H. P. Caemmerer, Director of National Park Service, Interior Department, June 28, 1939, Commission of Fine Arts Papers, RG 66, Project Files, 1910–1952, Box 10, Folder: "Arlington Mansion, No. 5," NARA.

87. John Dos Passos, *U.S.A.* (New York: Library of America, 1996), 756, 758, 760. On Dos Passos, see Meigs, *Optimism at Armageddon*, 146, 148–149; Steven Trout, *On the Battlefield of Memory: The First World War and American Remembrance, 1919–1941* (Tuscaloosa: University of Alabama Press, 2012), 146–150.

88. James Weldon Johnson, "Saint Peter Relates an Incident of the Resurrection Day" (1930) in *Saint Peter Relates an Incident: Selected Poems* (New York: Penguin Classics, 1993). See also Rebecca Jo Plant and Frances M. Clark, "'The Crowning Insult': Federal Segregation and the Gold Star Mother and Widow Pilgrimages of the Early 1930s," *Journal of American History* 102, no. 2 (2015): 406; Trout, *On the Battlefield of Memory*, 132–134; Mark Whalan, *The Great War and Culture of the New Negro* (Gainesville: University Press of Florida, 2008), 205–213.

89. May Miller, "Stragglers in the Dust" (1930), in *Black Female Playwrights: An Anthology of Plays before 1950*, ed. Kathy A. Perkins (Bloomington: Indiana University Press, 1989), 146, 147, 148, 150. My thanks to Margaret Higonnet for pointing me to this play.

90. May Miller, "One Blue Star" (1945), quoted in Whalan, *Great War*, 238.

91. Enoch A. Chase, "Fame's Eternal Camping Ground: Beautiful Arlington, Burial Place of America's Illustrious Dead," *National Geographic*, November 1928, 620; G. Kurt Piehler, *Remembering War the American Way* (Washington, DC: Smithsonian Books, 2004), 122; Robert M. Poole, *On Hallowed Ground: The Story of Arlington National Cemetery* (New York: Bloomsbury, 2009), 168–169.

92. Piehler, *Remembering War*, 122.

93. [Indecipherable, Dana?] to Edward Clark, Architect, Quartermaster Department, September 25, 1866, RG 92, Records of the Office of the Quartermaster General, Consolidated Correspondence File, 1794–1915, Box 50, Folder: "Arlington National Cemetery—'vault,'" NARA.

94. Stephen Ortiz, *Beyond the Bonus March and G.I. Bill: How Veteran Politics Shaped the New Deal Era* (New York: NYU Press, 2010), 56–64; Poole, *On Hallowed Ground*, 169–171, 174–175.

95. "Army to Hold Rites for Bonus Marcher," *Washington Post,* August 2, 1932, 2.

96. "Arlington Dedication to Be Today," *Los Angeles Times,* November 11, 1932, 5; "Dedicate Tomb in Arlington to Unknown Dead," *Chicago Daily Tribune,* November 12, 1932, 6; "VFW Will Mark Bonus Battle Today," *Washington Post,* July 28, 1934, 3.

97. "Clearing the Way to Arlington House," *Washington Star,* March 6, 1931, 1.

98. Major Julia C. Stimson, Superintendent, Army Nurse Corps to the Commission of Fine Arts, February 17, 1937. RG 66, Commission of Fine Arts, Project Files 1910–1952, Box 19, Folder: "ANC—Army-Navy Nurses Memorial." NARA. See also, Mary T. Sarnecky, *A History of the U.S. Army Nurse Corps* (Philadelphia: University of Pennsylvania Press, 1999), 165–166.

99. Carol Frink, "Miss Rich Sees Shaft Created by Daughter," *Washington Herald,* November 9, 1938, clipping, RG 66, Commission of Fine Arts, Project Files 1910–1952, Box 19, Folder: "ANC—Army-Navy Nurses Memorial," NARA.

100. "Unveil Monument to Nation's Nurses," *New York Times,* November 9, 1938, 25. See also "Frances Rich Almost Forgets to Sign Nurses' Memorial," *Los Angeles Times,* November 9, 1938, 13; "Frances Rich Forgets to Initial Sculpture," *Boston Globe,* November 9, 1938, 22.

101. "A Nurses' Monument in Arlington: For the Army and Navy Nurse Corps Plot," *American Journal of Nursing* 37, no. 6 (1937): 623.

102. "Arlington Monument Unveiled to Watch over Nurses," *Washington Post,* November 9, 1938, 2.

103. Julia C. Stimson, quoted in Sarnecky, *A History of the U.S. Army Nurse Corps,* 166.

104. Charles Moore to President Franklin Delano Roosevelt, January 25, 1934, and Harold L. Ickes, Secretary of the Interior, to Charles Moore, February 2, 1934, Commission of Fine Arts Papers, RG 66, Project Files, 1910–1952, Box 10, Folder: "Arlington Mansion, No. 3," NARA. Harry H. Woodring, Assistant Secretary of War, to President Franklin Delano Roosevelt, December 27, 1933; Major General L. H. Bash, Quartermaster General, to Assistant Secretary of War, October 24, 1935; Major General A. W. Brown, Judge Advocate General, "Jurisdiction and Control of Lee Mansion, Arlington National Cemetery, Memorandum for the Assistant Secretary of War," November 7, 1934; and Colonel Charles G. Mortimer, U.S. Army, Ret., to Charles Moore, Chairman, Commission of Fine Arts, December 13, 1935, all in Commission of Fine Arts Papers, RG 66, Project Files, 1910–1952, Box 10, Folder: "Arlington Mansion, No. 5," NARA.

105. Harold Ickes, quoted in Poole, *On Hallowed Ground,* 181.

106. Steve Vogel, *The Pentagon, a History: The Untold Story of the Race to Build the Pentagon—and to Restore It Sixty Years Later* (New York: Random House, 2007), 61–65, 108–111. On the history of Queen City, see also "100 Virginia Families, Forced Out by Defense Project, Appeal to First Lady," *Baltimore Afro-American,* February 21, 1942, 12; clippings in Folder: "Neighborhoods & Communities," Vertical Files, ARL—Black History, ACPL. On "Arlington Farms," see Jane Mersky Leder, *Thanks for the Memories: Love, Sex, and World War II* (Westport, CT: Praeger, 2006), 23–26.

107. Sledge, *Soldier Dead,* 138.

108. Office of Public Affairs, Department of Veterans Affairs, "America's Wars Fact Sheet," May 2015; Steven Anders, "With All Due Honors . . . ," *Quartermaster Professional Bulletin,* Autumn–Winter 1994, http://www.qmfound.com/honors.htm.

109. Sledge, *Soldier Dead*, 138–140. Sledge notes that the 70 percent figure was keyed to the general proportion of remains requested after World War I.

110. John W. Dower, *Cultures of War: Pearl Harbor/Hiroshima/9-11/Iraq* (New York: W. W. Norton, 2010), chap. 9.

111. Edward T. Folliard, "Most War Dead to Be Repatriated," *Washington Post,* November 11, 1945, B1. See also John W. Dower, *War without Mercy: Race & Power in the Pacific War* (New York: Pantheon Books, 1986).

112. Anders, "With All Due Honors."

113. "Bill for Burial of Second Unknown Soldier Signed," *Chicago Tribune,* June 25, 1946, 1; "The Unknown Soldier Will Be Joined by Another," *Los Angeles Times,* June 28, 1946, 4A.

114. "Army Day Parade Seen by Truman, 150,000," *Washington Post,* April 7, 1948, 1. See also "1500 to Take Part in Today's Army Parade," *Washington Post,* April 6, 1948, 1.

115. National Association for the Advancement of Colored People, "Declaration of Negro Voters," March 27, 1948, digital copy, Official File, Truman Papers, http://www.trumanlibrary.org.

116. Christine Knauer, *Let Us Fight as Free Men: Black Soldiers and Civil Rights* (Philadelphia: University of Pennsylvania Press, 2014), 112–129; Kimberly Phillips, *War! What Is It Good For? Black Freedom Struggles and the U.S. Military from World War II to Iraq* (Chapel Hill: University of North Carolina Press, 2014), 7–25.

117. "Veterans Will Make Presentation," *Washington Post,* April 1, 1948, 2.

118. "Top Brass Hats Sound Army Day Call to Prepare," *Chicago Daily Tribune,* April 7, 1948, B8. On the history of Army Day, see Department of Defense, "History of Army Day," http://archive.defense.gov/afd/army.aspx (accessed March 29, 2016).

119. Jean Anderegg, chairwoman of the Air Force Arlington Ladies, quoted in Robert M. Poole, *Section 60 Arlington National Cemetery: Where War Comes Home* (New York: Bloomsbury, 2014), 193.

120. *Arlington National Cemetery*, February 4, 2014, WETA Television, PBS. For the history of the Arlington Ladies generally, see Arlington Cemetery, "Arlington Ladies," http://www.arlingtoncemetery.mil/Funeral-Information/About-Funerals/Arlington-Ladies (accessed March 29, 2016); and Poole, *Section 60 Arlington National Cemetery,* 193–195. In the 21st century there have been a few "Arlington Gentlemen," but they are rare and considered a novelty.

121. "Care of the Dead," n.d., RG 92, Records of the Office of the Quartermaster General, Records of the Quartermaster Historian's Office, Historical Reports 1946–1962, Box 2, Folder: "Care of the Dead, original and one carbon copy," NARA. On debates over whether to build another tomb or add to the existing one, see John G. Norris, *Washington Post,* February 12, 1950, M16; Piehler, *Remembering War,* 140–141; and Sledge, *Soldier Dead,* 140.

122. Gail Holst-Warhaft, *The Cue for Passion: Grief and Its Political Uses* (Cambridge, MA: Harvard University Press, 2000), 191; James Mayo, *War Memorials as Political Landscape: The American Experience and Beyond* (Westport, CT: Praeger, 1988), 112, 251.

6. For Us, the Living

1. "Arlington Honor Paid to Two Historic Nisei," *Los Angeles Times,* June 5, 1948, 14.
2. "Two Nisei GI's to Be Buried Friday at Arlington National Cemetery," *Northwest Times,* June 2, 1948, 2. On Japanese American internment, Nisei military service, and the JACL, see Mire Koikari, "'Japanese Eyes, American Heart': Politics of Race, Nation, and Masculinity in Japanese American Veterans' WWII Narratives," *Men and Masculinities* 12, no. 5 (2010): 547–564; Mai Ngai, *Impossible Subjects: Illegal Aliens and the Making of Modern America* (Princeton, NJ: Princeton University Press, 2004), 173–187.
3. "Nisei War Heroes to Be Buried Friday in Arlington; First Time in History," *Washington Post,* May 30, 1948, M2. For other accounts of the burials, see "Nippon-Americans to Be Buried in National Cemetery, *Boston Globe,* May 30, 1948, C11; "Two Nisei GI's to Be Buried Friday at Arlington National Cemetery," *Northwest Times,* June 2, 1948, 2; "Arlington Honor Paid to Two Historic Nisei," *Los Angeles Times,* June 5, 1948, 14; "Two of Nisei Buried in Arlington," *New York Times,* June 5, 1948, 8.
4. On Cold War racial liberalism, see Thomas Borstelmann, *The Cold War and the Color Line: American Race Relations in the Global Arena* (Cambridge, MA: Harvard University Press, 2001); Robert K. Chester, "'Negroes' Number One Hero': Doris Miller, Pearl Harbor, and Retroactive Multiculturalism in World War II Remembrance," *American Quarterly* 65, no. 1 (2013): 31–61; Mary L. Dudziak, *Cold War Civil Rights: Race and the Image of American Democracy* (Princeton, NJ: Princeton University Press, 2000); Jodi Melamed, "The Spirit of Neoliberalism: From Racial Liberalism to Neoliberal Multiculturalism," *Social Text* 89, no. 2 (2006): 4–13; Brenda Gayle Plummer, *Rising Wind: Black Americans and Foreign Affairs, 1935–1960* (Chapel Hill: University of North Carolina Press, 1996); Nikhil Pal Singh, *Black Is a Country: Race and the Unfinished Struggle for Democracy* (Cambridge, MA: Harvard University Press, 2004).
5. Myrlie Evers, with William Peters, *For Us, the Living* (Garden City, NY: Doubleday and Company, 1967).
6. Martin Luther King Jr., "Beyond Vietnam: A Time to Break the Silence," April 4, 1967, Riverside Church, New York City, in ed. Cornel West, *The Radical King* (Boston: Beacon Press, 2014), 204.
7. Edward B. Fiske, "Arlington Vigil Held on Vietnam," *New York Times,* February 7, 1968, 17. See also, Willard Clopton Jr. and William R. MacKaye, "Clerics Stage a Silent Vigil for Peace," *Washington Post,* February 7, 1968, A1.
8. William S. White, "GI of Mexican Origin, Denied Rites in Texas, to Be Buried in Arlington," *New York Times,* January 13, 1949, 1. See also John Bodnar, *The "Good War" in American Memory* (Baltimore: Johns Hopkins University Press, 2010), 183–189; Patrick James Carroll, *Felix Longoria's Wake: Bereavement, Racism, and the Rise of Mexican American Activism* (Austin: University of Texas Press, 2003); Robert A. Caro, *Master of the Senate: The Years of Lyndon Johnson* (New York: Alfred A. Knopf, 2002), chap. 32. On the history of racial segregation in private cemeteries in the United States with an emphasis on African American history, see Angelika Krüger-

Kahloula, "On the Wrong Side of the Fence: Racial Segregation in American Cemeteries," in *History and Memory in African American Culture,* ed. Geneviève Fabre and Robert O'Meally (New York: Oxford University Press, 1994), 130–149.

9. Bodnar, *"Good War,"* 185.

10. "Indian Hero Is Buried in Arlington Ceremony after Being Refused Interment in Sioux City," *New York Times,* September 6, 1951, 3.

11. Richard H. Pratt, "The Advantages of Mingling Indians with Whites," in *Americanizing the American Indians: Writings by "Friends of the Indian," 1880–1900,* ed. Frances P. Prucha (Cambridge, MA: Harvard University Press, 1973), 261.

12. William L. Hewitt, "The Indian Who Never Got Home: The Burial of Sergeant John R. Rice," *Nebraska History* 77 (1996): 12–13.

13. "U.S. to Return G.I. Bodies While Fight Goes On," *Chicago Daily Tribune,* March 9, 1951, 7.

14. Shirley Young, Salem, NJ, to President Harry Truman, January 5, 1951, quoted in *Dear Harry: The Truman Administration through Correspondence with "Everyday Americans,"* ed. D. M. Giangreco and Kathryn Moore (Mechanicsburg, PA: Stackpole Books, 1999), 327.

15. The World War II "Return of the Dead" program ended officially on December 31, 1951. Michael Sledge, *Soldier Dead: How We Recover, Identify, Bury, and Honor Our Military Fallen* (New York: Columbia University Press, 2005), 176.

16. Bradley Lynn Coleman, "Recovering the Korean War Dead, 1950–1958: Graves Registration, Forensic Anthropology, and Wartime Memorialization," *Journal of Military History* 72 (January 2008): 187–195; Judith Keene, "Bodily Matters above and below Ground: The Treatment of American Remains from the Korean War," *Public Historian* 32, no. 1 (2010): 64–66; Sledge, *Soldier Dead,* 140–141.

17. Evelyn Rice, quoted in Hewitt, "Indian Who Never Got Home," 14.

18. "Truman Sets Arlington Interment for Indian Denied 'White' Burial," *New York Times,* August 30, 1951, 1. See also Edward T. Folliard, "Truman Grants Hero's Burial to Indian Barred by Cemetery," *Washington Post,* August 30, 1951, 1; "U.S. Will Honor Indian Denied 'White' Burial," *Los Angeles Times,* August 30, 1951, 1; and Dean J. Kotlowski, "Burying Sergeant Rice: Racial Justice and Native American Rights in the Truman Era," *Journal of American Studies* 38, no. 2 (2004): 211–213. On the wider politics of Native American military service in World War II and the Korean War, see Paul C. Rosier, "'They Are Ancestral Homelands': Race, Place, and Politics in Cold War Native America, 1945–1961," *Journal of American History* 92, no. 4 (2006): 1300–1326.

19. "Discrimination in Death," *Washington Post,* September 2, 1951, B4.

20. Kotlowski, "Burying Sergeant Rice," 213; "Truman's Okay Superficial in Indian Burial," *Chicago Daily Tribune,* September 2, 1951, A10.

21. Mike Masaoka, "Burial Rights," letter to the editor, *Washington Post,* September 1, 1951, 6.

22. "Flag Hero Found Dead," *New York Times,* January 25, 1955, 7; Karal Ann Marling and John Wetenhall, *Iwo Jima: Monuments, Memories, and the American Hero* (Cambridge, MA: Harvard University Press, 1991), 169–170.

23. "Flag Raiser on Iwo Jima Found Dead in Arizona," *Hartford Courant,* January 25, 1955, 4; "Flag Hero Found Dead." See also "Indian in Iwo Jima Flag Raising Found Dead," *Los Angeles Times,* January 25, 1955, 18; Marling and Wetenhall, *Iwo Jima,* 172–174.

24. "Arlington Burial Set," *New York Times,* January 26, 1955, 27.

25. "Ira Hayes, 32, Iwo Jima Hero, Is Found Dead," *Chicago Daily Tribune,* January 25, 1955, 12.

26. "Arlington Burial Set."

27. *Lee Mansion National Memorial: Arlington National Cemetery, Arlington,* brochure (Washington, DC: National Park Service, U.S. Department of the Interior, July 1941), VHS.

28. Public Law 107, "Dedicating the Lee Mansion in Arlington National Cemetery as a Permanent Memorial to Robert E. Lee," June 29, 1955, *United States Statutes at Large* 69, 84th Cong., 1st sess. (Washington, DC: U.S. Government Printing Office, 1955), 190–191. On the Grant Memorial, see Kirk Savage, *Monument Wars: Washington, DC, the National Mall, and the Transformation of the Memorial Landscape* (Berkeley: University of California Press, 2009), 203–228.

29. B. C. Mossman and M. W. Stark, *The Last Salute: Civil and Military Funerals, 1929–1969* (Washington, DC: Department of the Army, 1971), 93–124; Jean White, "Thousands Pay Tribute to Unknowns," *Washington Post,* May 29, 1958, 1.

30. Jack Raymond, "Unknowns of World War II and Korea Are Enshrined," *New York Times,* May 31, 1958, 1. See also "Heat, Emotion Affects Many at Ceremony," *Hartford Courant,* May 31, 1958, 1.

31. The *Globe* also noted, "Mr. Eisenhower stood immobile in the afternoon sun," in "U.S. Proudly Enshrines 2 Unknowns," *Boston Globe,* May 31, 1958, 1.

32. Jean Edward Smith, *Eisenhower in War and Peace* (New York: Random House, 2013), 675–680, 734–735.

33. "U.S. Proudly Enshrines 2 Unknowns."

34. R. L. Duffus, "To Three 'Known but to God,'" *New York Times Magazine,* May 25, 1958, 14.

35. On women, gender, and sexuality in the military in this period, see Margot Canaday, *The Straight State: Sexuality and Citizenship in Twentieth-Century America* (Princeton, NJ: Princeton University Press, 2009), chap. 5; Leisa D. Meyer, *Sexuality and Power in the Women's Army Corps during World War II* (New York: Columbia University Press, 1996); and Ann Elizabeth Pfau, *Miss Yourlovin: GIs, Gender, and Domesticity during World War II* (New York: Columbia University Press, 2008), chap. 2. On "blue discharges" and general military policies concerning homosexuality, see Allan Bérubé, *Coming Out under Fire: The History of Gay Men and Women in World War Two* (New York: Plume, 1991), chaps. 8 and 9; Canaday, *Straight State,* chap. 4; John D'Emilio, *Sexual Politics, Sexual Communities: The Making of a Homosexual Minority in the United States, 1940–1970* (Chicago: University of Chicago Press, 1983), 44–46; and Meyer, *Sexuality and Power,* 171–172.

36. Tom Brokaw, *The Greatest Generation* (New York: Random House, 1997).

37. Senator Joseph McCarthy, speech originally given in Wheeling, West Virginia, February 9, 1950. McCarthy submitted a version of the speech text to the *Congressional Record,* February 20, 1950, 81st Cong. 2nd sess., 1954–1957.

38. David K. Johnson, *The Lavender Scare: The Cold War Persecution of Gays and Lesbians in the Federal Government* (Chicago: University of Chicago Press, 2004), 15–20.

39. "An Open Letter to Senator Dirksen," *Mattachine Review,* January–February 1955, reprinted in *Speaking for Our Lives: Historic Speeches and Rhetoric for Gay and Lesbian Rights, 1892–2000,* ed. Robert B. Ridinger (New York: Routledge, 2012), 42.

40. Some of the details of Moore's experience have become vague or contradictory over time. "Guardians of Nation's Capital: Negroes Serve as President's Escorts, Top Honor Guardsmen in Army's Elite Corps," *Ebony* 16, no. 11 (1961): 67–68, 70, 72; Brian Albrecht, "Fred Moore Recalls Duty as First Black Honor Guard at Tomb of Unknown Soldier," *Cleveland Plain Dealer,* February 25, 2015; Jacqueline M. Hames, "First African American Tomb Guard Recalls 'Walking the Mat,'" *Soldiers Magazine,* http://soldiers.dodlive.mil/2015/02/first-african-american-tomb-guard-recalls-walking-the-mat/ (accessed March 29, 2016).

41. "Guardians of Nation's Capital," 68.

42. Cornelius W. [indecipherable last name], Asst. Regional Director, Conservation, Interpretation, and Use, NPS, to William P. Jones, Park Guide Supervisor, Custis-Lee Mansion, March 27, 1963 [copy], Murray H. Nelligan Papers, Research Files 1650–1967, Box 10, Folder: "Papers, 1963," ARHO; Robert M. Poole, *On Hallowed Ground: The Story of Arlington National Cemetery* (New York: Bloomsbury, 2009), 209–210. This moment is often attributed to Veterans Day ceremonies later, when Kennedy made a similar comment to a congressman. He also expressed appreciation for the site to Secretary of Defense Robert S. McNamara.

43. Ed King, quoted in Michael Vison Williams, *Medgar Evers: Mississippi Martyr* (Fayetteville: University of Arkansas Press, 2011), 282.

44. Myrlie Evers, "He Said He Wouldn't Mind Dying—If . . . ," *Life,* June 28, 1963, reprinted in *The Autobiography of Medgar Evers: A Hero's Life and Legacy Revealed through His Writings, Letters, and Speeches,* ed. Myrlie Evers-Williams and Manning Marable (New York: Basic Books, 2005), 304–308.

45. John Dittmer, *Local People: The Struggle for Civil Rights in Mississippi* (Urbana: University of Illinois Press, 1995); Myrlie Evers with William Peters, *For Us, the Living* (Garden City, NY: Doubleday, 1967), 299–304; Adam Nossiter, *Of Long Memory: Mississippi and the Murder of Medgar Evers* (Boston: Da Capo, 2002); Williams, *Medgar Evers,* 279–284.

46. On the politics of rage, self-preservation, and collective action in black mourning in America over time, and in the particular instance of Evers's memorials, see Shermaine M. Jones, "Presenting Our Bodies, Laying Our Case: The Political Efficacy of Grief and Rage in Alice Walker's *Meridian,*" *Southern Quarterly* 52, no. 1 (2014): 179–195; Suzanne E. Smith, *To Serve the Living: Funeral Directors and the African American Way of Death* (Cambridge, MA: Harvard University Press, 2010), 139.

47. Evers, *For Us, the Living,* 308.

48. On history, community, racial formation, and the repertoire of public mourning, see Joseph Roach, *Cities of the Dead: Circum-Atlantic Performance* (New York: Columbia University Press, 1996).

49. Evers, *For Us, the Living*, 322.

50. "500 Marchers Honor Evers in Washington," *Chicago Tribune*, June 18, 1963, 9.

51. Phil Casey, "Tears Greet Arrival of Evers' Body," *Washington Post*, June 18, 1963, 1. See also "500 March in Capital Behind Evers' Hearse," *Los Angeles Times*, June 18, 1963, 20; "Kennedy Pushes Clergy to Help," *Boston Globe*, June 18, 1963, 20; and "Negroes Mourn Evers in Capital," *New York Times*, June 18, 1963, 23.

52. Evers, *For Us, the Living*, 323.

53. Marjorie Hunter, "Evers Is Interred at Arlington: His Fight for Freedom Extolled," *New York Times*, June 20, 1963, 18; "Negro Leader Buried with Military Honors," *Hartford Courant*, June 20, 1963, 4; Karla F. C. Holloway, *Passed On: African American Mourning Stories* (Durham, NC: Duke University Press, 2002).

54. Medgar Evers, quoted in Williams, *Medgar Evers*, 249.

55. Myrlie Evers, quoted ibid., 325–326.

56. Andrew J. Glass, "Slain Negro Rests with Heroes," *Boston Globe*, June 20, 1963, 8.

57. Evers, *For Us, the Living*, 329; Abraham Lincoln's Gettysburg Address quoted as one of the epigraphs to ibid.

58. Nossiter, *Of Long Memory*, 93, 117, 130–132; "New Autopsy Is Performed for 3d Trial in Evers Slaying," *New York Times*, June 6, 1991, A16; Myrlie Evers-Williams, with Malinda Blau, *Watch Me Fly: What I Learned on Becoming the Woman I Was Meant to Be* (New York: Little Brown and Company, 1999), 208. See also, Renee C. Romano, *Racial Reckoning: Prosecuting America's Civil Rights Murders* (Cambridge, MA: Harvard University Press, 2014), chap. 4. Medgar Evers's body was returned to his Arlington grave on June 5, 1991. No reports were made of the exhumation until the following day.

59. Evers, *For Us, the Living*, 347–350.

60. "Evers Also Buried in Arlington," *New York Amsterdam News*, November 30, 1963, 19.

61. Richard V. Oulahan, "Taft Borne to Arlington, Receives Soldier's Burial as the Nation Pays Homage," *New York Times*, March 12, 1930, 1; "Arlington Burial Urged for Wilson," *New York Times*, February 4, 1924, 2.

62. "Burial Site Chosen in Arlington," *Washington Post*, November 24, 1963, A4; "The Family in Mourning," *Time*, December 6, 1963, 46; Edward T. Folliard, "De Gaulle, Others to Arrive; Burial Will Be in Arlington," *Washington Post*, November 24, 1963, A1; Cal Fussman, "Robert McNamara," *Esquire* 137, no. 1 (2002): 84; Mossman and Stark, *Last Salute*, 188–205.

63. Tom Wicker, "Crowd Is Hushed, Mourners at Capitol File Past Coffin Far into the Night," *New York Times*, November 25, 1963, 1.

64. John Lennon and Malcolm Foley, *Dark Tourism: The Attraction of Death and Disaster* (New York: Continuum, 2000), 79.

65. Jack Gould, "Millions of Viewers See Oswald Killing on 2 TV Networks," *New York Times*, November 25, 1963, 1.

66. Marita Sturken, *Tangled Memories: The Vietnam War, the AIDS Epidemic, and the Politics of Remembering* (Berkeley: University of California Press, 1997), 25–26.

67. Jimmy Breslin, "A Grave Digger Works Extra . . . It's an Honor," *Boston Globe*, November 26, 1963, 42.

68. Jimmy Breslin, "Still They Come to the Hillside: Arlington National Cemetery," *Saturday Evening Post*, November 21, 1964, 22.

69. T. Rees Shapiro and Emily Langer, "Arlington Caretaker Clifton Pollard: It was 'An Honor' to Prepare JFK's Grave," *Washington Post*, November 23, 2013. On Edward C. Hoffman and the Hoffman-Boston School, which was then a secondary school and is today Hoffman-Boston Elementary, see Arlington Historical Society, *Images of America: Arlington* (Portsmouth, NH: Arcadia Publishing, 2005), 58; *Commending Hoffman-Boston Elementary School*, House Joint Resolution No. 810, Virginia General Assembly, Sess. 2015, February 25, 2015.

70. Jack Raymond, "Arlington Assigns Plot of Three Acres to Kennedy Family," *New York Times*, December 6, 1963, 1.

71. John F. Kennedy Jr. ("John John") was killed with his wife and sister-in-law in a plane crash in 1999. Their ashes were scattered at sea off the coast of Martha's Vineyard, Massachusetts.

72. Lyndon B. Johnson, "Address Before a Joint Session of Congress, November 27, 1963," in *Public Papers of the Presidents of the United States, Lyndon B. Johnson, 1963–64, Book I* (Washington, DC: U.S. Government Printing Office, 1965), 11.

73. Poppy Cannon White, "'Two Heroines," *New York Amsterdam News*, December 7, 1963, 13.

74. See, for example, "To Visit 2 Graves," *New York Amsterdam News*, April 18, 1964; "Where Medgar Evers Lay Buried," *New York Amsterdam News*, November 21, 1964.

75. Walter B. Douglas, "Kennedy Burial Raises Arlington Site Queries," *Washington Post*, January 3, 1964, B19.

76. Hugh Mulligan, "Millions Pay Homage to Grave of Kennedy," *Los Angeles Times*, November 22, 1964, 2.

77. Robert G. Kaiser, "Grave Not So Hallowed Now: Tourists Turn Kennedy Shrine into Just Another Capital Sight," *Washington Post*, August 10, 1964, C1.

78. Nan Robertson, "Thousands Expected to Pay Respects at Grave," *New York Times*, November 22, 1964, 74.

79. Folder: "Arlington Biography—Gray," Vertical Files, ACPL.

80. Raymond, "Arlington Assigns Plot."

81. Committee on Interior and Insular Affairs, House of Representatives, *Committee Print No. 15: Data on National Cemeteries*, 87th Cong., 2nd sess. (Washington, DC: U.S. Government Printing Office, 1962). On connections to the popularity of Mitford's book, see Gary Laderman, *Rest in Peace: A Cultural History of Death and the Funeral Home in 20th Century America* (New York: Oxford University Press, 2003), xxxi–xli; Jessica Mitford, *The American Way of Death* (New York: Simon and Schuster, 1963).

82. "Arlington Cemetery to Open Wooded Area to Gravesites," *New York Times*, February 6, 1964, 20; Richard Homan, "Last Wooded Section to Be Cleared for Graves at Arlington Cemetery," *Washington Post*, February 5, 1964, B1.

83. Chester J. Pach Jr., "And That's the Way It Was: The Vietnam War on the Network Nightly News," in *The Sixties: From Memory to History*, ed. David Farber (Chapel Hill: University of North Carolina Press, 1994), 94; Office of Public Affairs, Department of Veterans Affairs, "America's Wars Fact Sheet," May 2015.

84. Andrew J. Huebner, *The Warrior Image: Soldiers in American Culture from the Second World War to Vietnam* (Chapel Hill: University of North Carolina Press, 2008), 209.

85. "Arlington Cemetery Needs More Space," *Hartford Courant*, September 20, 1968, 18; "Pentagon Restricts Burials at Arlington," *New York Times*, February 11, 1967, 1; Charles W. Corddry, "Arlington Burials Restricted," *Boston Globe*, February 11, 1967, 22; Monro MacCloskey, *Hallowed Ground*, 150–151.

86. Sledge, *Soldier Dead*, 141.

87. Michael S. Sherry, *In the Shadow of War: The United States since the 1930s* (New Haven, CT: Yale University Press, 1995), 287–289.

88. Richard Condon, *The Manchurian Candidate* (New York: McGraw-Hill, 1959); *The Manchurian Candidate*, dir. John Frankenheimer, 1962.

89. Sylvia H. Thompson with Milton G. Wolff and Gerald Cook, *The Arlington Case: Robert Thompson—Story of an Unburied Soldier* (New York: Sylvia H. Thompson, 1967), 1–3. On the Smith Act trial and convictions, see Scott Martelle, *The Fear Within: Spies, Commies, and American Democracy on Trial* (New Brunswick, NJ: Rutgers University Press, 2011).

90. Martelle, *Fear Within*, 241–245.

91. Thompson, *Arlington Case*, 6.

92. "Red to Rest in Arlington," *Los Angeles Times*, January 23, 1966, D11; "Burial of US Red, Convicted in 1949, to Be in Arlington," *New York Times*, January 23, 1966, 49. None of the stories gives an indication of how the journalists learned of Thompson's burial plan.

93. Lyndon B. Johnson, Presidential Recordings, January 24, 1966, 9529-Nicholas Katzenbach (WH6601.10), Presidential Recordings Program, Miller Center, University of Virginia, http://millercenter.org/scripps/archive/presidentialrecordings/johnson/1966/01_1966 (accessed March 29, 2016).

94. Thompson, *Arlington Case*, 12.

95. Richard Corrigan, "Pentagon Refers Red's Burial for Justice Department Study," *Washington Post*, January 26, 1966, B10; "Moscow Protests Arlington Delay on Burial of Red," *New York Times*, January 26, 1966, 19; Fred P. Graham, "Communist Denied Burial in Arlington," *New York Times*, January 28, 1966, 1; Thompson, *Arlington Case*, 11.

96. Graham, "Communist Denied Burial in Arlington"; Thompson, *Arlington Case*, 19.

97. "Beyond Death," *Washington Post*, January 30, 1966, E6.

98. "Make Room," *Washington Daily News*, January 28, 1966, quoted in Thompson, *Arlington Case*, 14.

99. Robert F. Kennedy, *Congressional Record*, January 29, 1966, quoted in Thompson, *Arlington Case*, 15.

100. Paul W. Valentine, "Widow Sues US on Burial Ruling," *Washington Post*, March 12, 1966, B1; Fred P. Graham, "Warren Disputes Katzenbach on Burial of Red," *New*

York Times, March 2, 1988, 18; Paul W. Valentine, "Arlington Burial Still Denied Communist," *Washington Post,* November 30, 1966, A3; "A Matter of Honor," *Washington Post,* December 5, 1966, A20.

101. Willard Clopton Jr., "Mothers Visit Tomb, Voice 2 Views on War," *Washington Post,* May 15, 1967, 1.

102. Amy Swerdlow, *Women Strike for Peace: Traditional Motherhood and Radical Politics in the 1960s* (Chicago: University of Chicago Press, 1993).

103. Clopton Jr., "Mothers Visit Tomb, Voice 2 Views on War."

104. Ibid.

105. David Remnick, *King of the World: Muhammad Ali and the Rise of an American Hero* (New York: Random House, 1998), 286–291.

106. Marjorie Hunter, "5000 Women Rally in Capital against War," *New York Times,* January 16, 1968, 3; Swerdlow, *Women Strike for Peace,* 135–138.

107. Shulamith Firestone, "The Jeanette Rankin Brigade: Woman Power?," *Notes from the First Year,* June 1968, 18.

108. Kathie Amantiek, "Funeral Oration for the Burial of Traditional Womanhood," *Notes from the First Year,* June 1968, 21. On this confrontation and the Arlington action, see Alice Echols, *Daring to Be Bad: Radical Feminism in America, 1967–1975* (Minneapolis: University of Minnesota Press, 1989), 54–57; Ruth Rosen, *The World Split Open: How the Modern Women's Movement Changed America* (New York: Viking, 2000), 201–203; Swerdlow, *Women Strike for Peace,* 138–140.

109. "Court Hears Request for Red's Burial," *Washington Post,* October 10, 1967, C8; J. R. Roseberry, "Ban on Burial of Red in Arlington Voided," *Washington Post,* December 14, 1968, A3; "Communist's Ashes Buried in Arlington," *Washington Post,* January 23, 1969, B8.

110. Martin Luther King Jr., CBS News interview by Mike Wallace, September 27, 1966.

111. Nixon-Agnew Campaign Committee, "Vietnam," 1968, Museum of the Moving Image, *The Living Room Candidate: Presidential Campaign Commercials, 1952–2012,* http://www.livingroomcandidate.org/commercials/1968. On Nixon's promise, see Beth Bailey, *America's Army: Making the All-Volunteer Force* (Cambridge, MA: Harvard University Press, 2009), 2.

112. "Unknown Soldier Tomb Guard Wins Delay on Viet Nam Duty," *Sarasota (FL) Journal,* May 15, 1969, 13; Carl Bernstein, "Army Secretary Rules Sergeant Fit, Says He Must Serve in War Zone," *Washington Post,* June 5, 1969, A15.

113. "Honor Guard Raps War," *Dull Brass* 1, no. 2 (May 15, 1969); 5; "Screwed! Model G.I. to Vietnam for Anti-War Views," *We Got the Brass* (Asian edition), no. 1 (Fall 1969): 1, 12. On the alternative military press generally, see Heather Marie Stur, *Beyond Combat: Women and Gender in the Vietnam Era* (New York: Cambridge University Press, 2011), 185.

114. "Sgt Michael Sanders Charges Army Is Sending Him to Vietnam as Punishment for Speaking Out Against War," May 23, 1969, NBC News, clip 5112464982_s01, NBC Universal Archives.

115. On Eisenhower's state funeral, see William M. Blair, "Rites Will Start Today, Burial in Kansas," *New York Times,* March 29, 1969, 1.

116. Associated Press, "Anti-War GI Sent to Viet Highlands," *New SOS News,* July 27, 1969, 7.

117. Michael Kernan, "A Woman's Vigil," *Washington Post,* July 12, 1969, E1; Susan Goodier, "The Price of Pacifism: Rebecca Shelley and Her Struggle for Citizenship," *Michigan Historical Review* 36, no. 1 (2010): 71–101.

118. On the public framings of which war deaths are appropriately mourned, when, and where, see Judith Butler, *Frames of War: When Is Life Grievable* (Brooklyn, NY: Verso, 2009).

119. "March Against Death—A Vietnam Memorial," *GI News Service,* November 27, 1969, 191; *Left Face!* 1, no. 2 (1969): back cover.

120. James Doyle, "Nixon's Viet Policy Backed in Veterans Day Parades, 10,000 in DC," *Boston Globe,* November 12, 1969, 1. See also Sandra Scanlon, *The Pro-War Movement: Domestic Support for the Vietnam War and the Making of Modern Conservatism* (Amherst: University of Massachusetts Press, 2013), 188–195.

121. "Vets in DC," *Up against the Bulkhead* 2, no. 3 (June 1971): 6. On Vietnam Veterans Against the War and the Dewey Canyon III action, see Huebner, *The Warrior Image,* chap. 7; Andrew E. Hunt, *The Turning: A History of Vietnam Veterans Against the War* (New York: New York University Press, 1999), chap. 5; Gerald Nicosia, *Home to War: A History of the Vietnam Veterans' Movement* (New York: Crown Publishers, 2001), chap. 3.

122. Douglas Brinkley, *Tour of Duty: John Kerry and the Vietnam War* (New York: William Morrow, 2004), 81.

123. Ibid., 11.

7. Knowns and Unknowns

1. Public Law No. 90-363, "An Act to Provide for Uniform Annual Observances of Certain Legal Public Holidays on Mondays, and for Other Purposes," June 28, 1968; Office of Public Affairs, Department of Veterans Affairs, "History of Veterans Day," http://www.va.gov/opa/vetsday/vetdayhistory.asp (accessed March 30, 1916).

2. Richard Nixon, "Statement Following the Laying of a Wreath on the Tomb of the Unknowns in Arlington National Cemetery, November 11, 1971," in *Public Papers of the Presidents of the United States, Richard Nixon, 1971* (Washington, DC: U.S. Government Printing Office, 1972), 1096.

3. "The Unknown Soldier, 1971," *1st Casualty* 1, no. 1 (1971): 4.

4. "Veterans Action Group," *1st Casualty* 1, no. 1 (1971): 4. See also, Mark Boulton, *Failing Our Veterans: The GI Bill and the Vietnam Generation* (New York: New York University Press, 2014).

5. *Satiacum v. Laird,* 475 F. 2d 320—U.S. Court of Appeals, District of Columbia Circuit, November 5, 1972.

6. "500 Indians Here Seize Building," *Washington Post,* November 3, 1972, A1.

7. "Court Permits Indian Rite at Arlington," *Washington Post,* November 6, 1972, A1; Paul C. Rosier, *Serving Their Country: American Indian Politics and Patriotism in the Twentieth Century* (Cambridge, MA: Harvard University Press, 2009), 260. On the Trail

of Broken Treaties action, see Vine Deloria Jr., *Behind the Trail of Broken Treaties: An Indian Declaration of Independence* (Austin: University of Texas Press, 1985).

8. Rosier, *Serving Their Country*, 249.

9. Hamilton Fish IV, quoted in Thomas M. Hawley, *The Remains of War: Bodies, Politics, and the Search for American Soldiers Unaccounted For in Southeast Asia* (Durham, NC: Duke University Press, 2005), 190.

10. "No 'Unknowns,' U.S. Dead in Asia All Identified," *Los Angeles Times*, July 6, 1971, 9; "Nixon Plan to Bury Hero Countered by Pentagon," *Boston Globe*, November 12, 1971, 24.

11. Christopher Wallace, "Unknown Soldier: Not in This War," *Boston Globe*, September 24, 1972, 1.

12. Public Law 93-44, National Cemeteries Act, June 19, 1973.

13. *The Report of the President's Commission on an All-Volunteer Armed Force* (Washington, DC: U.S. Government Printing Office, February 1970). See also Beth Bailey, *America's Army: Making the All-Volunteer Force* (Cambridge, MA: Harvard University Press, 2009).

14. Jay Mathews, "3d 'Unknown's' Tomb Eyed," *Washington Post*, July 1, 1972, B1.

15. "Unknown Soldier Tomb to Get Asia War Crypt," *New York Times*, October 25, 1973, 58.

16. "Arlington Cemetery Expansion Set," *Washington Post*, April 29, 1974, A3.

17. Michael J. Allen, "'Sacrilege of a Strange, Contemporary Kind': The Unknown Soldier and the Imagined Community of the Vietnam War," *History & Memory* 23, no. 2 (2011): 96; Hawley, *Remains of War*, 190–191.

18. National League of Families of American Prisoners and Missing in Southeast Asia, press release, September 17, 1974, quoted in Michael J. Allen, *Until the Last Man Comes Home: POWs, MIAs, and the Unending Vietnam War* (Chapel Hill: University of North Carolina Press, 2009), 149. On Ford's 1974 amnesty plan, see Robert D. Schultzinger, *A Time for War: The United States and Vietnam, 1941–1975* (New York: Oxford University Press, 1997), 318.

19. Allen, *Until the Last Man Comes Home*, 149–160.

20. Jimmy Carter, quoted in Francis McDonnell, "Reconstruction in the Wake of Vietnam: The Pardoning of Robert E. Lee and Jefferson Davis," *Civil War History* 40, no. 2 (1994): 129.

21. "McGovern Hits Delay on Unknown Soldier," *Hartford Courant*, April 7, 1978, 3.

22. "To the Unknown—Dead and Living," *Boston Globe*, May 29, 1979, 3.

23. Jan C. Scruggs, "We were young. We have died. Remember us," *Washington Post*, November 11, 1979, B4. See also, Jan C. Scruggs and Joel L. Swerdlow, *To Heal a Nation: The Vietnam Veterans Memorial* (New York: Harper & Row, 1985).

24. Frank Reynolds quoted in Melani McAlister, *Epic Encounters: Culture, Media and U.S. Interests in the Middle East since 1945*, updated ed. (Berkeley: University of California Press, 2005), 213. See also, Allen, *Until the Last Man Comes Home*, 202–206.

25. Jimmy Carter, "Rescue Mission for American Hostages in Iran, April 29, 1980," in *Public Papers of the Presidents of the United States: Jimmy Carter, 1980–81, Book I* (Washington, DC: U.S. Government Printing Office, 1981), 793.

26. William Branigin, "Bodies of U.S. Dead Will Be Sent Home, Iran Says Hostages Have Been Moved," *Washington Post,* April 27, 1980, A1; Don A. Schanche, "Iranian Cleric Exhibits Bodies of Americans," *Los Angeles Times,* April 28, 1980, 1; Harvey Morris, "Iran Puts Yanks' Bodies on Display," *Chicago Tribune,* April 28, 1980, 1; William K. Stevens, "Outrage over Bodies," *New York Times,* April 29, 1980, A1; " 'Valiant Eight' Return Home," *Chicago Tribune,* May 7, 1980, 1.

27. Jimmy Carter, "American Servicemen Killed in Iran: Eulogy at the National Memorial Service, May 9, 1980," in *Public Papers of the Presidents of the United States: Jimmy Carter, 1980–81, Book I,* 864.

28. Ronald Reagan, quoted in Patrick Hagopian, *The Vietnam War in American Memory: Veterans, Memorials, and the Politics of Healing* (Amherst: University of Massachusetts Press, 2009), 37–38.

29. Denis Collins, "Veterans Day Farewell by VA Director," *Washington Post,* November 12, 1980, C1.

30. On refugee policy from 1975–1985, see Robert D. Schultzinger, *A Time for Peace: The Legacy of the Vietnam War* (New York: Oxford University Press, 2006), 111–128. On later imaginings of the relationship of American veterans to Southeast Asian refugees as primarily one of friendship, rescue, and debt, see Yen Le Espiritu, "The 'We-Win-Even-When-We-Lose' Syndrome: U.S. Press Coverage of the Twenty-Fifth Anniversary of the Fall of Saigon," *American Quarterly* 58, no. 2 (2006): 329–352; Mimi Thi Nguyen, *The Gift of Freedom: War, Debt, and Other Refugee Passages* (Durham, NC: Duke University Press, 2012).

31. "Vietnam Vets Launch 'Grey Berets,' " *Stars and Stripes National Tribune,* November 15, 1979, 1, clipping, H. John Heinz III Collection, Carnegie Melon University Libraries.

32. Ibid.

33. U.S. Senate, *Hearing on Small Business Administration's Veterans' Assistance Programs,* June 4, 1980, 96th Cong., 2nd sess., 14.

34. "Grey Berets: Viet Vets Fight SBA Neglect," *Buffalo (NY) Veteran,* 11, clipping, n.d. (ca. 1979), H. John Heinz III Collection, Carnegie Melon University Libraries. See also, Jennifer Mittelstadt, *The Rise of the Military Welfare State* (Cambridge, MA: Harvard University Press, 2015).

35. Ronald Reagan, "Inaugural Address, January 20, 1981," in *Public Papers of the Presidents of the United States, Ronald Reagan, 1981* (Washington, DC: U.S. Government Printing Office, 1982), 3–4.

36. "Speedy Runners North of Ourcq Race with Death," *Stars and Stripes,* August 9, 1918, 3; Liberty Loan Committee, "Pvt. Treptow's Pledge," poster, 1918, in *The War on the Walls: Posters from the George F. Tyler WWI Collection,* Temple University Libraries, http://gamma.library.temple.edu.

37. "Soldier's Pledge Cited in Inaugural," *Milwaukee Sentinel,* January 21, 1981, 18; Richard Halloran, "The Pledge of Private Treptow," *New York Times,* January 21, 1981, B7. One of the speechwriters, Ken Khachigian, reports that the correct location of Treptow's grave was discovered while the address was still being drafted but that Reagan chose to keep the language implying his interment in Arlington. Robert

Schlesinger, *White House Ghosts: Presidents and Their Speechwriters* (New York: Simon and Schuster, 2008), 314.

38. Ronald Reagan, "Statement on the Death of World Heavyweight Boxing Champion Joe Louis, April 13, 1981," in *Public Papers of the Presidents of the United States, Ronald Reagan, 1981*, 351; "Reagan Orders Hero Burial," *Jet*, May 7, 1981, 56.

39. Kimberly L. Phillips, *War! What Is It Good For? Black Freedom Struggles and the U.S. Military from World War II to Iraq* (Chapel Hill: University of North Carolina Press, 2012), 27–38; Lauren Rebecca Sklaroff, "Constructing G.I. Joe Louis: Cultural Solutions to the 'Negro Problem' during World War II," *Journal of American History* 89, no. 3 (2002): 958–983. See also, Robert K. Chester, " 'Negroes' Number One Hero': Doris Miller, Pearl Harbor, and Retroactive Multiculturalism in World War II Remembrance," *American Quarterly* 65, no. 1 (2013): 31–61.

40. Dave Anderson, "A Corporal for Arlington," *New York Times*, April 20, 1981, C4.

41. John Hope Franklin, *The Color Line: Legacy for the Twenty-First Century* (Columbia: University of Missouri Press, 1994), 14–16; Ronald Reagan, "Nomination of Clarence Thomas to Be an Assistant Secretary of Education, May 1, 1981," in *Public Papers of the Presidents of the United States, Ronald Reagan, 1981*, 400.

42. David Stout, "At Tomb of Unknown, Policy versus the Heart," *New York Times*, February 15, 1998, A14; Steven Lee Myers, "Remains of Unknown Soldier Are Ordered Exhumed from Tomb of Unknowns," *New York Times*, May 8, 1998, A20; Michael J. Allen, " 'Sacrilege of a Strange, Contemporary Kind,' " 109–110; Michael Sledge, *Soldier Dead: How We Recover, Identify, Bury, and Honor Our Military Fallen* (New York: Columbia University Press, 2005), 127–130.

43. "Unknown Soldier Is Selected," *New York Times*, April 15, 1984, 36.

44. William M. Hammond, *The Unknown Serviceman of the Vietnam Era* (Washington, DC: U.S. Government Printing Office, 1985), 7–11.

45. Ibid., 11.

46. Ronald Reagan, *The Reagan Diaries*, ed. Douglas Brinkley (New York: HarperCollins, 2007), 243.

47. Robert D. Hershey Jr., "One of 58,012 Vietnam Dead Join Unknowns," *New York Times*, May 29, 1984, A1.

48. Hammond, *Unknown Serviceman*, 23. On the Vietnam Veterans Memorial generally, see Kristin Ann Hass, *Carried to the Wall: Memory and the Vietnam Veterans Memorial* (Berkeley: University of California Press, 1998); Kirk Savage, *Monument Wars: Washington, D.C., the National Mall, and the Transformation of the Memorial Landscape* (Berkeley: University of California Press, 2009), 270–279; Marita Sturken, *Tangled Memories: The Vietnam War, the AIDS Epidemic, and the Politics of Remembering* (Berkeley: University of California Press, 1997), 44–84.

49. Hammond, *Unknown Serviceman*, 33–38.

50. Gene Grabowski, "Uninvited Vets Join in Procession," *Times-News* (Twin Falls, ID), May 29, 1984, 1.

51. Hammond, *Unknown Serviceman*, 12.

52. Ronald Reagan, "Remarks at Memorial Day Ceremonies Honoring an Unknown Serviceman of the Vietnam Conflict, May 28, 1984," in *Public Papers of the Presidents of*

the United States, Ronald Reagan, 1984 Book I (Washington, DC: U.S. Government Printing Office, 1986), 748–750.

53. Hammond, *Unknown Serviceman*, 14.

54. George H. W. Bush quoted in Steven Casey, *When Soldiers Fall: How Americans Have Confronted Combat Losses from World War I to Afghanistan* (New York: Oxford University Press, 2014), 207–208. On "Vietnam Syndrome," see Christian G. Appy, *American Reckoning: The Vietnam War and Our National Identity* (New York: Viking, 2015), xvii–xviii; Hagopian, *The Vietnam War in American Memory*, chap. 1.

55. George H. W. Bush, "Remarks at the Tomb of the Unknown Soldier, November 11, 1991," in *Public Papers of the Presidents of the United States, George Bush, 1991 Book II* (Washington, DC: U.S. Government Printing Office, 1992), 1435.

56. Bailey, *America's Army*, 133; Michael Sherry, *In the Shadow of War: The United States since the 1930s* (New Haven, CT: Yale University Press, 1995), 367.

57. Public Law 99-610, Joint Resolution, *Congressional Record*, vol. 131 (November 6, 1986): 4.

58. Judith Lawrence Bellafaire, "Women in Military Service for America Memorial Foundation, Inc. (WIMSA)," in *Gender Camouflage: Women and the U.S. Military*, ed. Francine D'Amico and Laurie Weinstein (New York: NYU Press, 1999), 176–177; Kristin Ann Hass, *Sacrificing Soldiers on the National Mall* (Berkeley: University of California Press, 2013), 102–104.

59. Women in Military Service for America Memorial Foundation, *Site Selection Report for the Women in Military Service Memorial,* June 10, 1988, 5, WIMSA History, Folder: "Site Selection Report 1988," WIMSA. See also, Laurie Burgess, "Buried in the Rose Garden: Levels of Meaning at Arlington National Cemetery," in ed. Paul A. Shackel, *Myth, Memory, and the Making of the American Landscape* (Gainesville: University Press of Florida, 2001), 170–171; Loren E. Miller, "Women in Military Service for America Memorial, exhibition review," *Journal of American History* 102, no. 1 (2015): 193–198.

60. Women in Military Service for America Memorial Foundation, *Site Selection Report for the Women in Military Service Memorial,* 11–12.

61. Women in Military Service for America Memorial Foundation, *Site Selection Report for the Women in Military Service Memorial,* 11.

62. On women and gender in war memorials produced in the 1980s and 1990s, see Hagopian, *The Vietnam War in American Memory*, chap. 9.

63. Women in Military Service for America Memorial Foundation, "The Memorial Story . . . Ten Points of Light for Service to the Nation," *Register,* Spring 1990, 5, WIMSA History, Folder: "Newsletter, The Register Spring 1990," WIMSA.

64. Karrie Jacobs, "A Woman's Place," *George* 1, no. 1 (1995): 72.

65. Hass, *Sacrificing Soldiers on the National Mall*, 109–114.

66. Kristin Ann Hass calls the resulting monument the "Unseen Memorial," ibid., 115–116.

67. Brig. Gen. Wilma L. Vaught, USAF (Ret.), President Emeritus, WIMSA, "A Message from the President," e-mail to "Charter Members, Members, and Supporters,"

January 4, 2016. As of January 1, 2016, the new WIMSA president is Army Major General Dee Ann McWilliams (Ret.).

68. Evelyn Hsu, "Redoing a Cemetery's Welcome Mat," *Washington Post,* April 27, 1988, B3. See also, Jonathan Higuera, "$18.6 Million Visitors Center Opens at Arlington National Cemetery," *Washington Times,* January 17, 1989, B3, clipping, WIMSA History—National Design Competition—Early Design Competition Files, 1988–1990, Folder: "Arlington National Cemetery Visitors Center," WIMSA.

69. Stephanie Griffith, "Arlington Welcomes Native Son," *Washington Post,* February 17, 1991, B3. For example, in minutes for a July 24, 1991, meeting, WIMSA adviser Carla Corbin noted "(new director of cem: these people are not going to park in <u>my</u> [underlined in original] garage) Gen. V. to work on top down," WIMSA History—National Design Competition—Women's Memorial Professional Advisers' Files (Carla Corbin and John Carr), Folder: "Communications, NCMC," WIMSA.

70. "Commemorative Services, Memorialization of the African Americans of the Civil War, Freedman's Village—Section 27, Arlington National Cemetery," October 11, 1991 (program), Folder 3 of 5: "Freedman's Village," ARL—Vertical Files, ACPL.

71. *Hearings before a Subcommittee of the Committee on Appropriations,* Departments of Veterans Affairs and Housing and Urban Development, and Independent Agencies Appropriations for 1993, February 4, 1992, House of Representatives, 102nd Cong. 2nd sess. (Washington, DC: U.S. Government Printing Office, 1992), 51–53; "Cemeterial Expenses, Army," *Congressional Record—House,* September 24, 1992, 27384.

72. *Hearings before a Subcommittee of the Committee on Appropriations,* Departments of Veterans Affairs and Housing and Urban Development, and Independent Agencies Appropriations for 1994, March 31, 1993, House of Representatives, 103rd Cong. 1st sess. (Washington, DC: U.S. Government Printing Office, 1993), 158–173; *Hearings before a Subcommittee of the Committee on Appropriations,* Departments of Veterans Affairs and Housing and Urban Development, and Independent Agencies Appropriations for 1995, February 4, 1994, House of Representatives, 103rd Cong. 2nd sess. (Washington, DC: U.S. Government Printing Office, 1994), 63–64. In his investigative work on the problems at Arlington in 2009, journalist Mark Benjamin showed that the careless treatment revealed in that scandal had characterized these efforts in Section 27 from 1992 to 1994. Many of the replacement stones carried incorrect information and a number of graves appear to have been left unmarked. Mark Benjamin, "Vanishing History at Arlington National Cemetery," *Salon.com,* April 7, 2010, http://www.salon.com/2010/04/07/arlington_cemetery_graves_disappear/.

73. Arlington National Cemetery brochure and walking map, 1993 orig. (Washington, DC: U.S. Government Printing Office, 2006).

74. Cemetery Superintendent John C. Metzler Jr. confirmed this February 4, 1992, in his response to the question of whether there are Freedman's Village graves in Arlington. Having already explained that Freedman's Village had been in a different part of the cemetery, on the opposite side from Section 27, Metzler answered, "Well, it is hard to define the actual boundaries of Freedman's Village any more. I would have to say yes, because the other part of the cemetery has been incorporated into that area itself," in *Hearings before a Subcommittee of the Committee on Appropriations,* Departments of

Veterans Affairs and Housing and Urban Development, and Independent Agencies Appropriations for 1993, February 4, 1992, 51. For the current official description of Section 27, see http://www.arlingtoncemetery.mil/Explore/Notable-Graves/Section -27 (accessed March 30, 2016).

75. The marker is at the intersection of Southgate Drive and Oak Street in Arlington, VA. Katherine B. McGuire, Arlington County Historical Affairs and Landmark Review Board Chairman, "Freedman's Village Historical Marker Dedication Ceremony," letter of invitation for October 21, 1995, Folder 1 of 5: "Freedman's Village," ARL— Vertical Files, ACPL. See also, Lan Nguyen, "Refuge for Former Slaves Makes Its Mark on History," *Washington Post*, no date (clipping), and Nita Rao, "Freedman's Village Marker Placed," *Northern Virginia Sun*, November 2, 1995, n.p. (clipping) in Folder 2 of 5: "Freedman's Village," ARL—Vertical Files, ACPL. The Black Heritage Museum of Arlington, which describes itself as a "museum without walls," was promised a land grant near the original Freedman's Village site as part of a future expansion plan, and continues to fundraise, http://arlingtonblackheritage.org/ (accessed March 30, 2016).

76. James Edwards Peters, *Arlington National Cemetery: Shrine to America's Heroes* ed. 3 (Bethesda, MD: Woodbine House, 2008), 243, 269.

77. Chia Youyee Vang, *Hmong America: Reconstructing Community in Diaspora* (Chicago: University of Illinois Press, 2010), 127.

78. "Rep. Costa Reacts to Denial of Arlington Burial Waiver for Hmong General Vang Pao," press release, February 28, 2011, https://costa.house.gov/media-center/press -releases/rep-costa-reacts-denial-arlington-burial-waiver-hmong-general-vang-pao. See also, Mark Arax, "For a Hmong Hero, a Lavish Farewell," *New York Times*, February 7, 2011, A11.

79. On the "gift" of freedom and debts it implies, see Nguyen, *The Gift of Freedom*. See also, Yen Le Espiritu, *Body Counts: The Vietnam War and Militarized Refugees* (Berkeley: University of California Press, 2014); Viet Thanh Nguyen, *Nothing Ever Dies: Vietnam and the Memory of War* (Cambridge, MA: Harvard University Press, 2016), 44; Nguyen-Vo Thu-Huong, "Forking Paths: How Shall We Mourn the Dead?" *Amerasia Journal* 31, no. 2 (2005): 157–175.

80. Sherry, *In the Shadow of War*, 368–370.

81. Department of Defense quoted in Bailey, *America's Army*, 220.

82. Douglass Crimp, "Mourning and Militancy," *October* 51 (Winter 1989): 3–18. See also, Steve Estes, *Ask and Tell: Gay and Lesbian Veterans Speak Out* (Chapel Hill: University of North Carolina Press, 2009); Randy Shilts, *Conduct Unbecoming: Gays and Lesbians in the U.S. Military* (New York: Ballantine Books, 1994). For historical and contemporary resistance to the harnessing of GBLTQ rights and citizenship to military service, see, for example, the essays collected in *Against Equality: Queer Revolution, Not Mere Inclusion*, ed. Ryan Conrad (Chico, CA: AK Press, 2014); Justin David Suran, "Coming Out Against the War: Antimilitarism and the Politicization of Homosexuality in the Era of Vietnam," *American Quarterly* 53, no. 3 (2001): 452–488.

83. Bailey, *America's Army*, 221–224; Chandan Reddy, *Freedom with Violence: Race, Sexuality, and the U.S. State* (Durham, NC: Duke University Press, 2011), 219–233.

84. John D'Emilio, *Sexual Politics, Sexual Communities: The Making of a Homosexual Minority in the United States, 1940–1970* (Chicago: University of Chicago Press, 1983), chap. 9; Michael Sherry, *In the Shadow of War*, 487–492.

85. "In Memoriam," *This Week*, episode 62, ABC News, October 16, 2011.

86. Will Kohler, "The Bizarre Story Behind Gay Rights Hero Frank Kameny's Headstone and Heir Timothy Lamont Clark," *Back2Stonewall.com*, November 12, 2015, http://www.back2stonewall.com/2015/11/bizarre-story-gay-rights-hero-frank-kamenys-headstone-heir-timothy-lamont-clark.html.

87. Charles W. Hall, "The Timeless, They Are a-Changing," *Washington Post*, February 16, 1994, B1.

88. Marylou Tousignant, "A New Era for the Old Guard," *Washington Post*, March 23, 1996, C1.

89. "First Black Woman Guards Tomb," *Washington Post*, January 23, 1997, B4.

90. Judith M. Rhodes, "Let Arlington Cemetery Rest in Peace," *Washington Post*, July 14, 1996, C8. See also, Ellen Nakashima, "Environmentalists Fear Effects of Expanded Arlington Cemetery," *Washington Post*, July 6, 1995, B3; Ellen Nakashima, "Plan to Expand Cemetery Angers Preservationists," *Washington Post*, June 22, 1996.

91. Katha Pollit, "Subject to Debate," *The Nation*, June 5, 1995, 784, quoted in Edward T. Linenthal, *The Unfinished Bombing: Oklahoma City in American Memory* (New York: Oxford University Press, 2001), 23.

92. Blaine Harden and Joe Pichirallo, "Despite Army, Terrorist's Ashes Go to Arlington," *Washington Post*, December 18, 1982, A1.

93. Public Law 105-116, "An Act to Amend Title 38, United States Code, to Prohibit Interment or Memorialization in Certain Cemeteries of Persons Committing Federal or State Capital Crimes," November 21, 1997, 105th Cong.; Linenthal, *Unfinished Bombing*, 20, 240.

94. David Stout, "At Tomb of the Unknown, Policy Versus the Heart," *New York Times*, February 15, 1998, A14. See also, Steven Lee Myers, "Remains of the Vietnam Soldier Are Ordered Exhumed from the Tomb of the Unknowns," *New York Times*, May 8, 1998, A20.

95. "Nameless No Longer," *USA Today*, April 29, 1998, 12A.

96. Allen, " 'Sacrilege of a Strange, Contemporary Kind,' " 115–122; Hawley, *Remains of War*, 194; Hagopian, *The Vietnam War in American Memory*, 181–183.

97. Robert M. Poole, *On Hallowed Ground: The Story of Arlington National Cemetery* (New York: Bloomsbury, 2009), 251–254; Steve Vogel, *The Pentagon, a History: The Untold Story of the Wartime Race to Build the Pentagon—and to Restore It Sixty Years Later* (New York: Random House, 2007), 423–427; Arlington National Cemetery Tourmobile guide narrative, author's notes, April 25, 2010.

98. Karen Goldberg Goff, "Field of Honor; Veterans Receive Final Tribute at Arlington National Cemetery," *Washington Times*, November 4, 2001, D4. On gatherings in the cemetery after 9/11, see also Laura Bly, "Tourism Suffers in Wary Washington," *USA Today*, September 21, 2001, D3; David Cho and Jamie Stockwell, "Pentagon Wreckage Lures Thousands," *Washington Post*, September 16, 2001, C2; Stephan Dinan and Margie Hyslop, "Hush Prevails as Citizens Remember, Grieve," *Washington Times*, September 15, 2001, C1.

99. Raymond Hernandez, "Pentagon Deaths—Pleas to Bury Civilian Victims at Arlington Spark Debate," *New York Times,* September 21, 2001, B6.

100. "No Arlington Burial for Civilian Victims," *New York Times,* November 2, 2001, B5; Steve Vogel, "Remains Unidentified for 5 Pentagon Victims; Bodies Were Too Badly Burned, Officials Say," *Washington Post,* November 21, 2001, B1.

101. "Arlington's Burial Regulations Anger Family of Hijacked Pilot," *New York Times,* December 5, 2001, B7; "White House Backs Burial Decision," *New York Times,* December 6, 2001, B8; "In a Reversal, Army Permits Pilot's Burial," *New York Times,* December 8, 2001, B7; "Pilot of Hijacked Plane Buried with Honors in Arlington," *New York Times,* December 13, 2001, B7.

102. Donald H. Rumsfeld, "Arlington National Cemetery Funeral Service for the Unidentified Victims of the Attack on the Pentagon," remarks, September 12, 2002, U.S. Department of Defense. On the Pentagon attack generally, see Alfred Goldberg, Sarandis Papadopoulos, Diane Putney, Nancy Berlage, and Rebecca Welch, *Pentagon 9/11* (Washington, DC: Department of Defense, 2007); Vogel, *Pentagon.* On the memorial events of September 12, 2002, at Arlington National Cemetery, see Frank J. Murray, "Pageantry to Mark Pentagon Goodbyes," *Washington Times,* September 4, 2002, 1; Mary Otto, "A Single Coffin, but Many Tales of Lives Lost; Service to Honor the Pentagon Dead," *Washington Post,* September 12, 2002, T1; Alan Pusey, "Final Service Honors Victims of Pentagon Attack," *Dallas Morning News,* September 13, 2002, 26A; and Steve Vogel, "Lost, and Sometimes, Never Found; Pentagon Families Bury Their Dead Together and Mourn Five Not Identified," *Washington Post,* September 13, 2002, B1.

103. Many scholars have analyzed the emergence and cultural work of 9/11's particular idiom; see Judith Butler, *Precarious Life: The Powers of Mourning and Violence* (New York: Verso, 2004); Marc Redfield, "Virtual Trauma: The Idiom of 9/11," *diacritics* 35, no. 1 (2007): 55–80; and David Simpson, *9/11: The Culture of Commemoration* (Chicago: University of Chicago Press, 2006).

104. Mary L. Dudziak, *War Time: An Idea, Its History, Its Consequences* (New York: Oxford University Press, 2012), chap. 4.

105. For a detailed accounting of these histories, interconnections, and aims, see Lloyd C. Gardner, "Mr. Rumsfeld's War," in *Iraq and the Lessons of Vietnam, or, How Not to Learn from the Past,* ed. Lloyd C. Gardner and Marilyn B. Young (New York: New Press, 2007), 174–200; and James Mann, *The Rise of the Vulcans: The History of Bush's War Cabinet* (New York: Viking Penguin, 2004).

106. Arlington National Cemetery brochure and walking map, 2009. David Simpson argues, "With the passage of time it may come to appear that 9/11 did not blow away our past in an eruption of the unimaginable but that it refigured that past into patterns being made into new and often dangerous forms of sense." Simpson, *9/11,* 13.

107. Diana Jean Schemo, "Agent Praised as Patriot in Graveside Ceremony," *New York Times,* December 11, 2001, B5; Poole, *On Hallowed Ground,* 256–257.

108. Mark Mazzetti, *The Way of the Knife: The CIA, the Secret Army, and a War at the Ends of the Earth* (New York: Penguin Press, 2013); Leon Panetta with Jim Newton, *Worthy Fights: A Memoir of Leadership in War and Peace* (New York: Penguin Press, 2014), 268.

109. Neil Genzlinger, "The Things Their Families Carried," *New York Times,* October 11, 2008, C1.
110. Kristin Ann Hass, *Carried to the Wall.* See also, Marita Sturken, *Tourists of History: Memory, Kitsch, and Consumerism* (Durham, NC: Duke University Press, 2007).
111. Greg Jaffe, "Cleanup in Arlington National Cemetery's Section 60 Upsets Families of War Dead," *Washington Post,* October 1, 2013; "Arlington National Cemetery's Pilot Program Section 60 Mementos," n.d., PDF available at: http://www.arlingtoncemetery .mil/Portals/0/Docs/Section_60_Mementos_Program.pdf (accessed March 30, 2016).
112. Alan Cooperman, "Administration Yields on Wiccan Symbol," *Washington Post,* April 24, 2007; Laurie Goodstein, "Pagans Sue for Emblems on Graves," *New York Times,* September 30, 2006, A8; Poole, *Section 60 Arlington National Cemetery,* 185–186.
113. McAlister, *Epic Encounters,* chap. 5.
114. *Meet the Press,* October 19, 2008; Karen DeYoung, *Soldier: The Life of Colin Powell* (New York: Vintage, 2007), 74. On Powell's popularity as an icon of American racial progress and military multicultural egalitarianism, see McAlister, *Epic Encounters,* 253–255.

Conclusion

1. U.S. Army, *Special Defense Department Briefing on the Army Inspector General's Review of Management and Operations at Arlington National Cemetery,* June 10, 2010. The investigations were sparked by a public affairs officer who turned whistleblower and the investigative journalism of Mark Benjamin for *Salon.*
2. U.S. Senate Subcommittee on Contracting Oversight, "Opening Statement of Subcommittee Chairman Claire McCaskill," 4, *Hearing on Mismanagement of Contracts at Arlington National Cemetery,* July 29, 2010, http://mccaskill.senate.gov/index.cfm ?p=soco_documents.
3. Allison Keyes, "Iraq Veteran's Body Is Exhumed at Arlington," *Morning Edition,* National Public Radio, September 16, 2010, http://www.npr.org/templates/story/story .php?storyId=129890675.
4. Mark Benjamin, "Arlington National Cemetery Unveils a New Unknown Soldier," *Salon,* October 7, 2009, http://www.salon.com/news/feature/2009/10/07/arlington _cemetery/index.html.
5. Steven Lee Myers, "'Unknown' Vietnam Soldier Now Has a Name," *New York Times,* June 30, 1998, A1. Michael J. Allen argues that official recourse to the availability of DNA testing in 1998 as the condition of possibility for Blassie's identification belies the fact that evidence was available in 1984 and largely served to avoid acknowledging culpability. Allen, "'Sacrilege of a Strange, Contemporary Kind': The Unknown Soldier and the Imagined Community of the Vietnam War," *History & Memory* 23, no. 2 (2011): 92–93.
6. The case of Grave 449, Section 68, is all over congressional investigation documents yet does not appear as a "success" of the Accountability Task Force or others in recent reports on its work and investigations outcomes. Arlington National Cemetery

Gravesite Accountability Task Force, *Report to Congress on Gravesite Accountability Study Findings* (Washington, DC: Department of Defense, December 22, 2011); and *Report to Congress on Implementation of Army Directive on Army National Cemeteries Program* (Washington, DC: Department of Defense, December 17, 2012).

7. Superintendent John C. Metzler Jr. was allowed to retire. The Army ultimately retained its jurisdiction over Arlington and the Old Soldiers' and Airmen's National Cemeteries.

8. U.S. Department of Defense, "DoD Works with Congress on Dover Review," November 29, 2011 (press release), http://archive.defense.gov/news/newsarticle.aspx?id =66278; Department of Veterans Affairs Office of Inspector General, *Veterans Health Administration Interim Report: Review of Patient Waiting Times, Scheduling Practices, and Alleged Patient Deaths at the Phoenix Health Care System* (Washington, DC: VA Office of Inspector General, May 28, 2014).

9. Simonides quoted in Anthony D. Smith, *Chosen Peoples: Sacred Sources of National Identity* (New York: Oxford University Press, 2003), 219.

10. David Vergun, "Over 27,000 Burial Sites to Open at Arlington Next Year," Army News Service, March 19, 2015.

11. Chris Erbe, "VA Oversees Largest Expansion of National Cemeteries since the Civil War," U.S. Department of Veterans Affairs, August 4, 2015.

12. "Arlington Slave Descendants Celebrate Freedman's Village Bridge Dedication," September 10, 2015, WJLA Channel 7, Washington, DC ABC-affiliate.

13. Myrlie Evers-Williams, Invocation, Presidential Inaugural, January 21, 2013, https://www.whitehouse.gov/photos-and-video/video/2013/01/21/2013-inauguration -ceremony.

ACKNOWLEDGMENTS

Writing about the different forms honor and recognition can take—and the power of these acts or their absence—made me more mindful of the many debts to family, friends, colleagues, students, archivists, and librarians incurred while working on this book and represented in these pages. I am honored and not a little humbled by their love, support, guidance, work, and generosity.

The seed of this project was planted in the first graduate seminar I ever taught in the American Studies Department at the University of Alabama. The subject was slavery, the Civil War, and Reconstruction in American memory, and the students were fantastic—and generous with a new assistant professor. We marveled together at the long history of Freedman's Village and the fact that none of us had known of it before. That shared discovery became a book project shortly after I arrived in my current position with the History Department at the University of Connecticut. I am so appreciative of all my wonderful colleagues, students, and friends at UConn, with special thanks to Fakhreddin Azimi, Peter Baldwin, Dan Caner, Jason Chang, Chris Clark, Jelani Cobb, Nina Dayton, Fe Delos-Santos, Kelly Dennis, Manisha Desai, Anna Mae Duane, Alexis Dudden, Clare Eby, Kristin Eshelman, Emma Gilligan, Jean Givens, Dee Gosline, Ken Gouwens, Robin Greeley, Bob Gross, Mark Healey, Brendan Kane, Charles Lansing, Michael Lynch, Margo Machida, Matt McKenzie, Glenn Mitoma, Jessica Muirhead, Shayla Nunnally, Kathy O'Dea, Jeff Ogbar,

Sherri Olson, Michael Orwicz, Mark Overmyer-Velazquez, Heather Parker, Janet Pritchard, Shirley Roe, Cathy Schlund-Vials, Nancy Shoemaker, Blanca Silvestrini, Evelyn Simien, Jennifer Terni, Judith Thorpe, Chris Vials, Janet Watson, Walt Woodward, and Victor Zatsepine. It is my great fortune that coming to UConn meant joining a dear friend from graduate school in the History Department, Melina Pappademos. Since the days of our dissertation group, her brilliance as a scholar and writer and her warm friendship have meant so much to me. Finally, my thanks to the late Nancy Comarella, with whom I talked a lot about this project, history, and memory; her sudden loss was a tragedy for all who knew her and had their lives as students and teachers of history at UConn made far better for her presence in our department.

   I am grateful for the guidance, insights, and work of several archivists and librarians, including at the National Archives and Records Administration in Washington, DC, and College Park, Maryland, the Virginia Historical Society, the Center for Local History at the Arlington Public Library, the office of Document Delivery & Interlibrary Loan at the University of Connecticut, and the Cambridge (MA) Public Library, especially my local branch in Central Square. Special thanks are due to Maria Cappozi and Kim Robinson at Arlington House, The Robert E. Lee Memorial, which, in addition to being located inside the cemetery, is part of the National Park Service's George Washington Memorial Parkway. Britta K. Granrud, Curator of Collections at the Women in Military Service for America Memorial Foundation Archives, was incredibly generous with her time and knowledge. A University of Connecticut Research Advisory Council Faculty Large Grant supported some of the research at these places, as did an External Faculty Fellowship with the Susan and Donald Newhouse Center for the Humanities at Wellesley College. Special thanks to then-director Carol Dougherty, Jane Jackson, and the entire community of fellows and visiting scholars in the 2010–2011 Newhouse Center cohort.

   Many colleagues and friends provided good advice and sources or read drafts along the way, for which I am most thankful. These include Edward Bell, James Blakey, David Blight, Kate Masur, Kirk Savage, the late Joyce Schiller, and fellow panelists, commenters, and audiences at meetings of the American Historical Association, Organization of American Historians, and Southern Association for Women Historians, as well as at the New-York Historical Society, the Princeton University Modern America Workshop, Rutgers University, the University of Connecticut Humanities Institute, the University of Tennessee College of Law, and Wellesley College. A brief portion of Chapter 7 first appeared in my article "Remembering 9/11's Pentagon Victims and Reframing History in Arlington National Cemetery," in "Historicizing 9/11," special issue, *Radical History Review* 111 (Fall 2011): 51–63, and is reprinted courtesy of the publisher, Duke University Press. My thanks to editors Jim O'Brien and Andor Skotnes and the anonymous reviewer for that piece. I am additionally grateful to Kirk Savage and to the anonymous reader for their reviews of the manuscript for Harvard University Press.

I owe an enormous debt of gratitude to my editor at Harvard, Joyce Seltzer, for her support, excellent counsel, and seemingly bottomless reserves of patience. While any mistakes and limitations to the book are mine alone, it was made immeasurably better for her influence. My thanks to everyone at the press with whom I worked, including Brian Distelberg, Kathi Drummy, Louise Robbins, and Stephanie Vyce, and to Deborah Grahame-Smith and her team at Westchester Publishing Services, including Andrew Katz.

None of this would be possible without the support of friends and family, who experienced the highs and lows of writing this book with me. They made the highs more fun and the lows endurable. My thanks to Viola Augustin, John Bagwell, Brian Bishop, Kim Gilmore, Bill Harris, Merrily Harris, Kate Haulman, Jessica Lacher-Feldman, Tom Little, Tom Lutte, Donna McNally, Chris Molenski, Kevin Murphy, Guy Nelson, Ashley Oates, Leslie Starritt, and Edvin Yegir. I give my love and deepest gratitude to my parents, Mike and Cindy McElya, my brother and his wife, Jim and Kara McElya, and to my entire family—who always asked, "How's the book?" and invariably exclaimed over its wonderfulness, no matter what my answer was. I wish my Papaw, Billy Joe Page, could have seen the finished book, but his love and pride in his grandchildren are always with me. Love and many thanks to my in-laws as well: Llyena Boylan and Donald Spieth, Jim and Jo Ann Boylan, Nicko Boylan, and Gabriel Boylan and Christine Smallwood. Much is owed to Ruby, who enriched our lives in all ways and often helped me work out writing problems over walks and snacks. Finally, I am unendingly thankful for Alexis Boylan, for her love, knowledge, endless rounds of edits, gentle critical voice, and support. I am honored every day to be Alexis's partner; this book is dedicated to her.

ILLUSTRATION CREDITS

Page

115   Collecting remains of Union soldiers. Engraving by S. Fox, photographed by A.
       Gardner, published in *Harper's Weekly*, November 24, 1866, 740. Library of
       Congress Prints and Photographs Division (LC-USZ62-98262).

118   Decorating soldiers' graves. Sketch by C. M. Thomas, published in *Harper's
       Weekly*, June 20, 1868, 388. Courtesy of Archives and Special Collections,
       University of Connecticut Libraries.

119   Soldiers' cemetery at Arlington. Published in *Harper's Weekly*, March 27, 1869,
       196. Library of Congress Prints and Photographs Division (LC-USZ62-100151).

135   Map of the Arlington Estate. Published by U.S. Congress, Washington, DC, 1888.
       Courtesy of Virginia Historical Society.

142   Unidentified black man in Arlington National Cemetery. From William Bengough,
       United States National Military Cemetery Arlington (1897). Courtesy of Virginia
       Historical Society.

168   Arlington Confederate Memorial. Harris & Ewing Collection, Library of Congress
       Prints and Photographs Division (LC-H25-602).

179   Aerial view of Arlington National Cemetery. Harris & Ewing Collection, Library
       of Congress Prints and Photographs Division (LC-H261-30595).

186   Crowd at burial ceremony of Unknown Soldier, 1921. National Photo Company
       Collection, Library of Congress Prints and Photographs Division (LC-USZ6-1754).

203   Black men constructing Tomb of the Unknown Soldier, ca. 1921. Harris & Ewing
       Collection, Library of Congress Prints and Photographs Division (LC-H27- A-3450).

205   First permanent Tomb guard, March 25, 1926. Gift of Herbert A. French (1947),
       National Photo Company Collection, Library of Congress Prints and Photographs
       Division (LC-F81-39542).

208   Aerial view showing Lincoln Memorial and bridge to Arlington National Cem-
       etery, 1935. Harris & Ewing Collection, Library of Congress Prints and Photo-
       graphs Division (LC-H2-B-6823).

209   Memorial to Army and Navy Nurses. Harris & Ewing Collection, Library of
       Congress Prints and Photographs Division (LC-H22-D-4907).

232   Sailor and girl at the Tomb of the Unknown Soldier, 1943. Photograph by John
       Collier. Farm Security Administration, U.S. Office of War Information Collection,
       Library of Congress Prints and Photographs Division (LC-USW36-730).

281   Guard at the Tomb of the Unknown Soldier, ca. 1980–2006. Photograph by
       Carol M. Highsmith. Carol M. Highsmith Archive, Library of Congress Prints and
       Photographs Division (LC-HS503-6476).

286   Aerial view of Arlington National Cemetery, ca. 1997–2006. Photograph by
       Carol M. Highsmith. Carol M. Highsmith Archive, Library of Congress Prints and
       Photographs Division (LC-HS503-5141).

INDEX